Explore secret gardens and hidden gems

Scottish Gardens
open for charity

Sponsored by

❄ RATHBONES

Contents

Welcome	2	Aberdeenshire	32
With thanks to our Patron	3	Angus, Dundee & Kincardineshire South	44
Our people	4		
Our impact	6	Argyll & Lochaber	66
Volunteer	8	Ayrshire & Arran	84
Diana Macnab Award	10	Berwickshire & Roxburghshire	94
Find us online	12	Caithness, Sutherland, Orkney & Shetland	104
Use our website to plan your garden visits	14		
		Dumfriesshire	114
Open your garden for charity	16	Dunbartonshire	122
Visit a garden by arrangement	18	East Lothian	128
Leave a gift in will	20	Edinburgh, Midlothian & West Lothian	140
Cattanach training bursary	21		
Snowdrops & winter walks	22	Fife	156
Groups & villages	24	Glasgow & District	176
Plant sales & special events	26	Inverness, Ross, Cromarty & Skye	184
Gardening in the community	27	Kirkcudbrightshire	198
New gardens for 2025	28	Lanarkshire	210
New gardens by district	29	Moray & Nairn	216
Tips & key to symbols	30	Peeblesshire & Tweeddale	224
Our Districts map	31	Perth & Kinross	234
		Renfrewshire	254
		Stirlingshire	260
		Wigtownshire	268
		Gardens open on a specific date	283

Scotland's GARDENS Scheme

Welcome from our Chair

Dougal Philip

Whatever the weather, Scotland's garden visitors always turn out! In 2024, the weather was really challenging and miserable. Following a dull March and April all gardeners kept hoping for summer to arrive and as the weeks slipped by there was a general acceptance that even an Indian summer would not appear. However we have enjoyed some wonderful autumn colours and the sweet peas, late to start flowering, have continued to offer blooms even into November.

Gardeners always manage to find a silver lining to every disappointment, albeit they'll tell visitors that you should have come last week! Despite the poor weather garden openings and visitor numbers have held up well and the money raised for our many charities has continued to do well, thanks to the dedication of our garden owners and volunteers.

My wife, Lesley Watson, and I have visited many garden openings in the last year from Argyll to East Lothian and from Angus to Dunbartonshire, gardens of many sizes and varying styles, but everywhere we've been there is a common feeling: the proudness of the garden owners, the enthusiasm of all the volunteers and the happy and friendly faces of the visitors. There is a real family feeling at each of these openings, much banter as some folk learn about new plants and gardening tricks, while others take pleasure and strength in being in a safe, calm and beautiful place.

Garden visiting is so good for everyone, and especially the many charities who benefit from your donations at the garden gate.

Dougal Philip

Front cover image: Carolside, Earlston
© Delia Ridley-Thomas

Back cover image: Learmonth Place Garden
© Libby Webb

Artwork: Matt Armstrong – Serious Artworker, Jessica Taylor

Maps: Alan Palfreyman Graphics

FSC
MIX
Paper from responsible sources
www.fsc.org FSC® C015185

Scotland's Gardens Scheme Head Office
2nd Floor, 23 Castle Street, Edinburgh EH2 3DN

T: 0131 226 3714 E: info@scotlandsgardens.org
W: scotlandsgardens.org

Charity no: SC049866

Contains OS Data © Crown Copyright and Database 2024

Printed by Belmont Press

ISBN13: 9780901549419

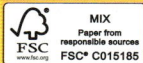

With thanks to Her Majesty The Queen, Patron of Scotland's Gardens Scheme

In 2024, we were delighted to be informed that Her Majesty The Queen retained the Presidency of Scotland's Gardens Scheme. Her Majesty was formerly our President as HRH The Duchess of Rothesay, since 2006. We are so grateful for Her Majesty's continued support.

© Chris Jackson

Our people

Scotland's Gardens Scheme is powered by hundreds of garden owners and volunteers all around Scotland, who work incredibly hard to organise and support garden openings. We are so grateful to everyone involved – the life and soul of our charity!

We have a small Head Office team to support our volunteers, who are in turn supported by our Board of Trustees, all of whom bring their specialist skills and interests to support the charity.

Read more about our staff & trustees here: **scotlandsgardens.org/about-us/**

Meet our Head Office team

Liz Stewart
Chief Executive

Jessica Taylor
Communications
Manager

Hazel Reid
Office Manager

Kate Allan
Volunteer Support
Officer

Meet our Trustees

Dougal Philip
Chair & Garden
Centre Owner

Stephen McCallum
Vice Chair,
Horticulturist &
Garden Opener

Peter Yellowlees
Honorary Treasurer,
Accountant (retired)

David Buchanan-Cook
Board Secretary,
District Organiser West
Fife & Garden Owner

Charlotte Halliday
Marketing Specialist

Colin Crosbie
Horticulturist
& Garden Owner

Helen McMeekin
Charity Specialist
& Horticulturist

Jonathan Cobb
Investment Specialist
& Author

Eric Wright
Garden Owner

Alex Lindsay
Area Organiser,
Perth & Kinross

James Byatt
District Organiser,
Moray & Nairn

Charlotte Hunt
Honorary Vice
President

Where the money goes

In addition to raising funds for our core charities, Maggie's, Perennial and QNIS, Scotland's Gardens Scheme gives our Garden Owners the opportunity to select the charity or local cause to benefit from up to 60% of funds raised at their garden opening. At the time of writing these pages (end of November 2024) over **£213,000** had been donated to **223** charities & causes selected by our garden owners in 2024.

The following charities and causes received over £2k in 2024:

Maggie's (£21,285) *'NB Maggie's donation does not include SGS's core charity donation for 2024 garden income*

Highland Hospice (£11,670)

Marie Curie (£8,263)

Scotland's Charity Air Ambulance (£5,328)

Chest Heart & Stroke Scotland (£4,841)

Alzheimer Scotland – Action On Dementia (£4,448)

British Limbless Ex-Service Men's Association (£3,651)

Leuchie (£3,604)

Parkinson's Disease Society Of The United Kingdom (£3,414)

Rio Centre Organisation (£3,005)

RNLI (£2,961)

St Columbus Hospice Care (£2,949)

The Silver Circle SCIO (£2,819)

Medecins Sans Frontieres (£2,729)

Trees for Life (£2,702)

Fostering Compassion SCIO (£2,568)

Little Sparta Trust (£2,430)

Mary's Meals (£2,356)

Amisfield Preservation Trust (£2,323)

Corsock & Kirkpatrick Durham Church Of Scotland (£2,309)

Loch Arthur Camphill Community Limited (£2,298)

Gateside And District Community Association (£2,280)

Cancer Research UK (£2,276)

Macmillan Cancer Support (£2,102)

Blood Bikes Scotland (£2,095)

Gifford Village Hall (£2,076)

St Salvadors Scottish Episcopal Church: Edinburgh (£2,051)

The following causes were chosen by our garden owners, demonstrating the causes closest to our garden owners' hearts:

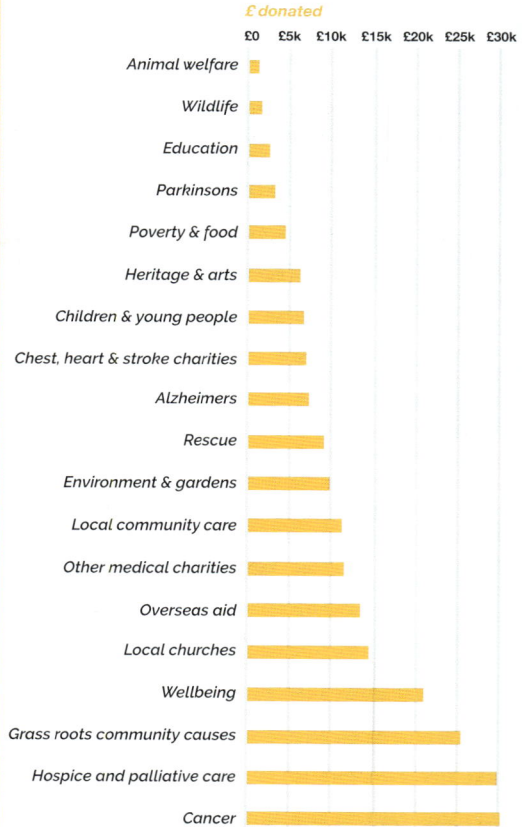

£ donated (bar chart, x-axis: £0, £5k, £10k, £15k, £20k, £25k, £30k)

- Animal welfare
- Wildlife
- Education
- Parkinsons
- Poverty & food
- Heritage & arts
- Children & young people
- Chest, heart & stroke charities
- Alzheimers
- Rescue
- Environment & gardens
- Local community care
- Other medical charities
- Overseas aid
- Local churches
- Wellbeing
- Grass roots community causes
- Hospice and palliative care
- Cancer

Our impact – charity stories

Thank you to all of our garden owners and volunteers who so generously give their time and dedication to raise funds for charities through garden opening. Each cup of tea, each garden gate ticket and each plant sold, it all makes a difference. With over **220** charities supported in **2024**, there are many stories to tell, but let us tell you just this one.

Kincardine & Deeside Befriending works in rural southern Aberdeenshire with vulnerable, isolated and lonely older people, facilitating befriending visits for around 80-85 older people every month. They shared Merle and Jayne's story with us.

Merle, now 84, was referred to us by her GP in early 2021. Merle lives alone, has a cognitive impairment, a visual impairment and suffers from low mood and anxiety. She was very lonely and felt isolated. While Merle's memory can be very poor, she really enjoys lively conversation and is able to reminisce clearly. Merle was delighted to be matched with Jayne. Sometimes they just stay in and chat when Merle doesn't feel like going out. Other times, they are able to go for a trip in the car and stop for tea and cake.

Merle says of Jayne, *"I get excited knowing Jayne is coming. She's lovely. I can really talk to her and we have good conversations."* **Jayne says**, *"It is obvious to me that Merle gets a great deal from our meeting. She often says, 'you have made my day', and how much she is enjoying being out. I think the mental stimulation of talking about the past and taking a drive and having a coffee out is hugely beneficial. For me, I have always enjoyed being a befriender, it is very rewarding to know you have brightened up their day and made them feel better. I love hearing stories about the past, what it was like to live in a different generation and the lives they have led."*

With thanks to the owners of Glensaugh garden, Kincardine & Deeside, who raised just over **£500** to support their chosen charity

Read more charity stories on our website: **scotlandsgardens.org/our-impact**

Come and volunteer with us!

If you enjoy visiting gardens, why not consider getting involved with Scotland's Gardens Scheme by volunteering with us? We have lots of roles for everyone, whether you are an avid gardener or more of a viewing enthusiast, there is an opportunity for everyone.

Volunteers are the heart and soul of Scotland's Gardens Scheme – we are proud to be **98%** volunteer led! If you would like to join in, here are some of the skills you can use across our different roles:

- Garden knowledge for visiting potential new gardens and advising their owners about opening with us.

- Administrative skills for registering garden openings for the next season, within your local district.

- Financial skills for taking on a District Treasurer role, keeping fundraising accounts up to date and paying recipient charities.

- Organisational skills as a District Organiser or Area Organiser, encouraging local garden owners to open their garden and keeping an overall responsibility for a small part of Scotland.

- Baking skills for making homemade tasty treats for a specific open day or two.

- Roll-your-sleeves-up skills for helping at open days, putting up signs, staffing the entry gate, directing and chatting with visitors.

- Social media and PR skills for promoting open days in your local area.

Interested? We would love to hear from you! Find out more:

W: **scotlandsgardens.org /our-volunteers/**

E: **info@scotlandsgardens.org**

T: **0131 226 3714**

You will make some great new friends, garden lovers and gardeners, you will visit beautiful, generally unseen gardens and you will be helping to make a difference by raising funds for charity.

QNIS
THE QUEEN'S
NURSING
INSTITUTE
SCOTLAND

Registered Scottish Charitable Incorporated Organisation SCO05751

Scotland's Gardens Scheme was founded in 1931 to raise money for the Queen's Nursing Institute Scotland.

The Institute has been generously supported by garden owners and visitors in Scotland's communities since.

Today, funding from Scotland's Gardens Scheme goes directly to supporting Scotland's community nurses so they can improve the long-term health of the people and communities they serve.

Together we can drive positive action to make Scotland's communities healthier, kinder, fairer and greener.

Get in touch

Email: office@qnis.org.uk
Website: qnis.org.uk
Telephone: +44 (0) 131 229 2333

Registered Scottish Charitable Incorporated Organisation SCO05751

Diana Macnab Award for outstanding service

Visit our news page on **scotlandsgardens.org** to discover our full list of 2024 nominees!

Sarah Landale
District Organiser, former Trustee, Garden Owner

Minette Struthers
District Organiser, former Trustee, Garden Owner

Every year we ask our community of garden owners and volunteers to nominate somebody who they feel has gone the extra mile to volunteer for Scotland's Gardens Scheme, and deserves to be recognised for their efforts. This year we celebrate two volunteers who have served the Scheme valiantly over many years in so many capacities, Sarah Landale from Dumfriesshire and Minette Struthers from Argyll and Lochaber.

Sarah Landale has been opening her garden in Dumfriesshire for many years, each year involving the local community and various local crafters with stalls and attractions throughout the day. Additionally, she has masterminded the opening of Portrack, the Garden of Cosmic Speculation, every time it has opened in the last 20 years, a huge operation which has raised over £186,000 in the past ten years alone.

Sarah has been the District Organiser for Dumfriesshire for the last 21 years, finding and supporting gardens new and old. Finally, as if all of that is not enough, she has been on the Board of Scotland's Gardens Scheme as a Trustee for the last 17 years, the last five of which as Vice Chair, contributing wisely and with candour to the strategic direction of the charity, retiring at the 2024 AGM.

Sarah is a tireless supporter and advocate for Scotland's Gardens Scheme and continues to share her time and energies with us all in the most humble and gracious way, always with a smile and a very kind and willing heart.

Minette Struthers has been a staunch supporter of Scotland's Gardens Scheme for many years, most notably as the District Organiser for Argyll and Lochaber. She has covered hundreds of miles travelling across her geographically challenging district visiting garden owners and encouraging new gardens to open.

As a Board member and Trustee from 2000 to 2019, Minette sat on many committees and was very much part of the decision-making body of Scotland's Gardens Scheme throughout that time. She also opens her own garden at Ardmaddy Castle under SGS and is a consummate plantswoman and dendrologist in her own right.

Minette has been a truly reliable and tireless member of the Scotland's Gardens Scheme family through a number of decades. She is energetic, calm, full of wisdom and always so encouraging of those around her.

We commend both Sarah and Minette as extremely worthy recipients of the Diana Macnab award for 2025.

For a different kind of cancer care

Just come in to Maggie's

At Maggie's we offer free psychological and practical support to everyone with cancer and the people who love them.

Built in the grounds of NHS hospitals, our centres are warm and welcoming places, with expert staff on hand to offer the support you need to find your way through cancer.

Our centres are open Monday to Friday, 9am to 5pm, and you don't need an appointment, just come in.

You can find your local centre at maggies.org

Maggie's centres across Scotland receive vital funds from every garden opening. Our heartfelt thanks go to everyone who supports Scotland's Gardens Scheme by opening their garden, volunteering or visiting a garden.

Scotland's
GARDENS
Scheme
OPEN FOR CHARITY

MAGGIE's

Maggie Keswick Jencks Cancer Caring Centres Trust (Maggie's) is a registered charity, no. SC024414

Keep up to date with our latest charity news and garden openings online.

1. Visit our website:
scotlandsgardens.org

2. Follow us on social media and tag us using *#lovescotlandsgardens* **with your garden visits:**

(f) *@scotlandsgardens*

(X) *@scotgardens*

(Instagram) *@scotlandgardenscheme*

(YouTube) *@ScotlandsGardensScheme*

(LinkedIn) **Scotland's Gardens Scheme**

(TikTok) *@scotlandsgardens*

3. Sign up to our e-newsletter:
Scan the QR code or visit:
scotlandsgardens.org/newsletter-sign-up/

Spread the word

Perennial is the UK's only horticultural charity dedicated to helping everyone working with plants, trees, flowers or grass through our free, confidential helpline and support services.

"Life without gardens and green spaces is unimaginable. These cherished havens wouldn't exist without the dedicated people who support them, and sometimes, those people need support too."

Carole Baxter, BBC Scotland Beechgrove Garden, presenter.

Find out more or donate at
perennial.org.uk

Helping people
in horticulture
Perennial

Use our website to plan your garden visits!

Did you know that you can use our website to search for exactly where and when you would like to visit a garden? Perfect for planning a trip away or for a garden group or U3A trip. Visit **scotlandsgardens.org** today and try our *Advanced Search function*!

Click here to start your search!

☑ SIMPLE SEARCH   🔍 ADVANCED SEARCH

Garden Name   **Or Garden Location**

[   ] ✕   [Start typing then choose from the list ...] ✕

Dates   *Are you looking for a district ?*
                                         Distance (miles)
[All dates] [Today] [This weekend] [Next weekend]   [5] [10] [25] [50] [100]

[Next 30 days]   **VIEW: 72**

click here!

Choose your garden location:

Districts
[Aberdeenshire] [Angus, Dundee & The Mearns] [Argyll & Lochaber] [Ayrshire & Arran] [Berwickshire] [Berwickshire & Roxburghshire]
[Caithness, Sutherland, Orkney & Shetland] [Dumfriesshire] [Dunbartonshire] [East Lothian] [Edinburgh, Midlothian & West Lothian]
[Fife] [Glasgow & District] [Inverness, Ross, Cromarty & Skye] [Kirkcudbrightshire] [Lanarkshire] [Moray & Nairn]
[Peeblesshire & Tweeddale] [Perth & Kinross] [Renfrewshire] [Stirlingshire] [Wigtownshire]

or here!

Garden Location
[Perth, UK] ✕

Distance (miles)
[5] [10] [25] [50] [100]

You can also search by opening type:

Opening Types
[Specific Date] [Open Regularly] [Open by Arrangement]

or here!

Select your date:

Dates
[All dates] [Today] [Tomorrow] [This weekend]
[Next weekend] [Next 14 days] [Next 30 days] [Jan] [Feb]
[Mar] [Apr] [May] [Jun] [Jul] [Aug] [Sep] [Oct]
[Nov] [Dec]

or search between specific dates:

Between Specific Dates
[Monday, 1 July 2024] ✕   [Friday, 26 July 2024] ✕

click here!

Select specific opening features:

Icons

Search for special features such as teas, disabled access or dog friendly gardens and more... (hover for full icon description)

Your bespoke search is then generated!

[25 miles from Perth, UK ✕] [From 1 July to 26 July ✕] [Clear Filters]   [Print List]

14 GARDEN OPENINGS FOUND. CLICK HERE TO SEE THE LIST.

Running events just became a walk in the garden!

Discover how you can benefit from our simple online event ticketing and booking solution for any type of event.

Our award winning customer service team are on hand to support you, every step of the way.

Delighted to support Scotland's Gardens Scheme.

Always **free** for **free** events.
Discover more here!

trybooking.com

Open your garden for charity with Scotland's Gardens Scheme

We're always on the lookout for new gardens to open for charity – why not come and join us?

What we look for:

☀ Gardens of all shapes, sizes and styles with horticultural interest. We have everything from tiny courtyard gardens to castle gardens this year, all special in their own right.

☀ Gardens that tell a story - this could be collections of plants, art in the garden, wildlife-friendly gardens or even the gardeners behind the garden.

☀ Groups and villages – if you have a tiny garden or don't feel you'd like to 'go it alone', why not open as part of a group or village? Our group openings include a wonderful mix of garden styles, sizes and interest – something for everyone!

☀ We welcome allotments, community and school gardens, helping to share your cause with a wider audience and raise awareness.

As one of our volunteers once said,

'Opening your garden is the nicest way to raise funds for charity!'

What we offer:

☀ Advice and support from our lovely volunteers on how best to go about opening your garden.

☀ Insurance for your opening.

☀ Posters and publicity materials.

☀ Resources and information on how to make a success of your garden opening.

☀ Inclusion in our guidebook, on our website, our national leaflet and in our social media.

☀ Support from our friendly office team.

☀ Over 90 years experience of opening gardens to raise funds for charity!

Still not convinced? Drop us a line or phone call and we'll be happy to have a chat to tell you more. Or visit our website *scotlandsgardens.org/ open-your-garden/*

At Queen Victoria Park one's visitors always get a royal welcome.

Queen Victoria Park is an exclusive residential neighbourhood for the over 55s within a 100-acre garden paradise at Inchmarlo Retirement Village near Banchory in Aberdeenshire on Royal Deeside.

Queen Victoria Park is next to Inchmarlo Golf Centre and the River Dee, and comprises an active community of like-minded people with round-the-clock security and support services.

- 1 bed apartments with balconies from £55,000
- 2 bed apartments with balconies from £75,000

To find out more or to arrange viewings:
please call Fenella Scott on 01330 824981 or
email fenella.scott@inchmarlo-retirement.co.uk

INCHMARLO
RETIREMENT VILLAGE

Where Gracious Living
Comes Naturally

inchmarlo-retirement.co.uk

Discover how Queen Victoria Park might be just your type of place.

Visit a garden open by arrangement

As well as gardens that open on a specific day or days, we have hundreds of gardens that invite visitors to arrange a private visit with the owners. Our garden owners are very welcoming and we find that many groups as well as individuals enjoy their visits.

Gardens open by arrangement are great for:

☀ Organised groups – we have gardening clubs, U3A groups, ramblers and even cycling groups planning days out around garden visits. Why not add us to your list?

☀ A couple or small group of garden-loving friends looking for a special day out.

☀ People with additional support needs and their carers, who may find that a garden open by arrangement can provide a safe and peaceful space for a quiet visit; for example, our garden owners tell us that they have welcomed visits from people with dementia and autism and their carers.

We would highly recommend a visit by arrangement for anyone as it's a really lovely experience and some of our garden owners even provide tea and cake on request!

How to book your visit:

· Browse the guidebook or website and look for gardens open *'by arrangement'* – you can search for this feature on the website.

· Contact the garden owner to arrange your visit – contact details or booking links will be in the book and on the website.

And please remember to tell the garden owner that you heard about their garden through Scotland's Gardens Scheme.

Photo © Malcolm Ross

If our garden owners specify a particular size of group, you will see it on their garden profile in the guidebook or website.

Think *property.* *Think* **Rettie.**

All the property services
you need, all in one place.

RETTIE

0131 220 4160 | mail@rettie.co.uk | **rettie.co.uk**
SALES • LETTINGS • FINANCIAL SERVICES • DEVELOPMENT • CONSULTANCY

Pass on your love of gardening with a gift in your will

Did you know that Scotland's Gardens Scheme now supports horticultural careers through a legacy-funded bursary programme?

Leaving a gift in your will to Scotland's Gardens Scheme will help us to develop our support for Scottish horticulturists through the Cattanach Fund, now in its third year. Read more about our progress so far on the opposite page.

Legacies can also help our wider work in supporting our volunteers to open gardens, raising funds throughout Scotland for hundreds of charities each year, enabling us to continue sharing the joy of open gardens into the future.

*If you would like to find out more about leaving a gift in your will to Scotland's Gardens Scheme, please email **info@scotlandsgardens.org** or visit **scotlandsgardens.org/gift-in-will/***

Supporting horticultural careers in Scotland through legacies

Scotland's Gardens Cattanach Fund is a small grant scheme aimed at people working or training in horticulture in Scotland, supporting personal and professional development relating to gardening careers.

This fund has been made possible thanks to a generous bequest a number of years ago by Mr Albert Cattanach, a regular visitor to SGS open gardens, and has recently been boosted by an additional contribution, with thanks to The Cross Trust for passing on the John Fife Award.

The fund is now entering its third year and to date has helped 24 individuals develop their careers in horticulture, supporting gardens and gardening in Scotland.

"All is going fantastic with my course, I've been loving it. It's so fascinating and has definitely opened my eyes to a whole new perspective. We've been creating a lot of different herbal products, learning so much each weekend."

Anna-Mairead Ferguson – Herbology

Do you or anyone you know need support to develop your horticultural career? Our bursary fund will be opening again early in 2025. Find out more and apply at **scotlandsgardens.org/bursaries/**

Our alumni have benefitted from a range of different courses including:

Course:

Chainsaw Training

RHS Level 2 Theory

Sprayer Training

Herbology

Planting Design

Arboriculture

General Horticulture

Garden Design

Social & Therapeutic Horticulture

Permaculture

= 1 participant (24 total)

Snowdrops & Winter Walks

In the depths of winter there is nothing more uplifting than the sight of snowdrops peeping through the winter leaves. Details of gardens open for snowdrops can be found on each relevant garden listing in this guidebook. You can also discover carpets of snowdrops or curated collections of the rare and unusual, on our website: *scotlandsgardens.org* and look for our snowdrop symbol.

Find a full list at: *scotlandsgardens.org/snowdrops-and-winter-walks/* or scan the QR code:

Find more places to visit at *discoverscottishgardens.org* for gardens taking part in the Scottish Snowdrop Festival, **25 January – 11 March 2025**.

Groups & Villages

Visiting a group of gardens in a city, town, village or even in the countryside is very popular with our garden visitors. It gives the visitor the chance to see small but perfectly-formed gardens in a range of styles and interests and there is always something to suit every taste. Make sure a few of these are on your 'to visit' list in 2025 as there is sure to be something to inspire you. And if you enjoy these, perhaps you might consider joining in with your friends and neighbours to create your own garden trail! We'd love to hear from you so please do get in touch via email **info@scotlandsgardens.org** or **0131 226 3714.**

Aberdeenshire
Two Gardens in Banchory Devenick
Saturday 14 & Sunday 15 June, 2-5pm

Angus, Dundee & Kincardineshire South
Edzell Village Gardens
Sunday 15 June, 1 – 5pm

Brechin Gardens in June
Sunday 22 June, 12 – 5pm

St Bedes and Ashludie Wildflower Garden, Monifieth (NEW)
Saturday 5 & Sunday 6 July, 11am – 4pm

Argyll & Lochaber
Ardverikie with Aberarder, Kinloch Laggan
Sunday 1 June, 2 – 5.30pm

Ayrshire & Arran
Beith Community Gardens (NEW)
Saturday 19 July, 1 – 5pm

Berwickshire & Roxburghshire
Morebattle Mains (NEW)
Saturday 28 & Sunday 29 June, 1 – 5pm

Duns Open Gardens
Sunday 20 July, 12 – 5pm

Dunbartonshire
18 Duchess Park with Westburn, Helensburgh
Sunday 11 May, 2 – 5pm

East Lothian
Tyninghame House and The Walled Garden
Sunday 11 May, 1 – 5pm

Belhaven House with Belhaven Hill School
Sunday 8 June, 2 – 5pm

Gifford Village with Gifford Bank & Broadwoodside
Sunday 22 June, 11 – 5pm

Edinburgh, Midlothian & West Lothian
Temple Village Gardens, Midlothian
Sunday 18 May, 2 – 5pm

Moray Place and Bank Gardens, Edinburgh
Sunday 18 May, 2 – 4.30pm

Stockbridge Open Gardens, Edinburgh
Sunday 22 June, 12 – 4.30pm

Silverburn Village
Sunday 2 August, 2 - 5pm

Fife
Newburgh Hidden Gardens
Sunday 29 June, 12 – 5pm

Crail: Gardens in the Burgh
Saturday 5 & Sunday 6 July, 2 – 5pm

Inverness, Ross, Cromarty & Skye
Kiltarlity Gardens
Sunday 13 July, 2 – 5pm

Lanarkshire
Lanark Town Gardens (NEW)
Sunday 13 July, 1 – 5pm

Peeblesshire & Tweeddale
West Linton Village Gardens
Sunday 27 July, 1 – 5pm

Perth & Kinross
Muckhart Open Gardens
Saturday 31 May & Sunday 1 June, 1 – 5pm

Renfrewshire
Lochwinnoch Road Gardens, Kilmacolm (NEW)
Sunday 20 July, 2 – 5pm

Stirlingshire
Gartmore Village
Sunday 15 June, 1 - 5pm

The perfect
gift for those
who love
all things
Scottish

SCOTTISH FIELD

SCOTLAND'S QUALITY LIFESTYLE MAGAZINE

3 ISSUES FOR ONLY £1

When you subscribe by direct debit*
Call 01778 392014 and quote **GDN2** or
visit **scottishfield.co.uk/subscriptions**

* Terms and conditions apply. For over-18s and UK-based subscribers
only. Direct debit only. Minimum one year subscription to Scottish Field.

Country news   Interiors   Field sports   Heritage   Gardens   Wildlife   Interviews   Whisky

WWW.SCOTTISHFIELD.CO.UK

Plant Sales & Special Events 🌷

Plant sales are always very popular as everyone loves a bargain and it's a great place to pick up a bit of gardening know-how as well as locally-grown plants!

We've also highlighted some special events that offer something a bit different and we will provide updates about these on our website, social media and in our e-news through the season.

Angus, Dundee & Kincardineshire South

Angus Plant Sale, Pitmuies Garden
Saturday 24 May

Argyll & Lochaber

Ardchattan Priory Garden Fete
Sunday 8 June

Caithness, Sutherland, Orkney & Shetland

16 Mulla, Voe, Plant Sales
Saturday 10 and Sunday 11 May
Saturday 26 and Sunday 27 July

Dunbartonshire

Glenarn Plant Sale
Sunday 17 August

Dumfriesshire

Dalswinton Mill – Garden opening includes mini plant fair, talks and demonstrations
Sunday 10 August

Fife

Fife Plant Sale
Sunday 28 September

Teasses Candlelit Snowdrop Walk
Friday 21 February

Teasses Summer Solstice Walk
Wednesday 18 June

Helensbank Summer Concert
Date to be confirmed

Fife Carol Concert
Date to be confirmed

Inverness, Ross, Cromarty & Skye

Glenkyllachy Special Open Day with plant sales, teas, stalls & music
Sunday 15 June

Kirkcudbrightshire

Threave Open Day including plant talks, nurseries, craft fair and children's activities
Monday 5 May

Perth & Kinross

Drummond Castle Gardens – activities and events for a great family day out
Sunday 3 August

Renfrewshire

Kilmacolm Plant Sales
Saturdays 19 April and 12 July

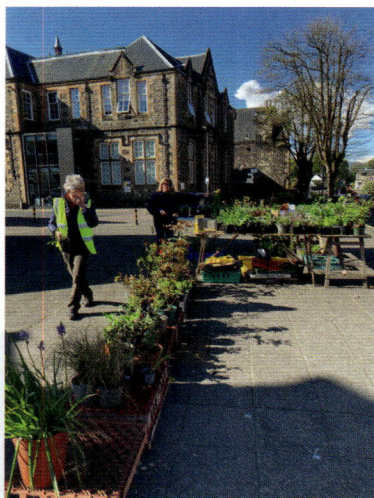

Kilmacolm Plant Sales

Gardening in the Community

We're not just about private gardens! We are always happy to celebrate other kinds of gardens that provide community and wellbeing benefit and are not always open to the wider public. These gardens are often fascinating sources of unusual plants, environmental practices, education and edible gardening as well as doing fantastic work to benefit many people – so please do visit to support their work and be inspired!

Aberdeenshire
Tarland Community Garden

Angus, Dundee & Kincardineshire South
Brechin Cathedral Allotments (Brechin Gardens in June)
Hospitalfield Gardens

Ayrshire & Arran
Barrmill Community Garden
Beith Community Gardens
River Garden, Auchincruive

Beith Community Gardens

East Lothian
Amisfield Walled Garden
Archerfield Walled Garden

Edinburgh, Midlothian & West Lothian
Bridgend Farmhouse Community Allotments
Craigentinny Telferton Allotment
Oatridge College Campus, SRUC
Whitehouse & Grange Bowling Club

Fife
The Gardens of Monimail Tower

Glasgow & District
King's Park Walled Garden
SWG3 Community Garden
Milton of Campsie Community Garden

The Milton of Campsie Community Garden

Kirkcudbrightshire
Dalbeattie Community Allotments Association

Moray & Nairn
Earth House Apothecary Garden
The Biblical Garden

Perth & Kinross
The Bield at Blackruthven

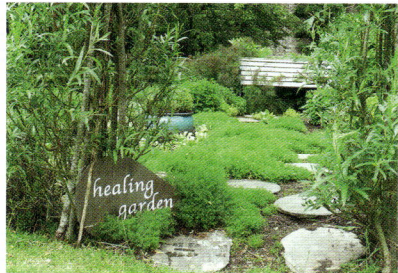

The Bield at Blackruthven

Stirlingshire
Braehead Community Garden

New gardens for 2025

It's always a delight to welcome new and returning gardens to the Scotland's Gardens Scheme family and it's always a thrill to see what's coming on board for the year ahead. This year is no exception. We have tiny and beautiful urban spaces, a roof terrace and community gardens. We also have new groups and villages, wildflower and eco gardens, gardens with spectacular views and lots more. Do enjoy browsing through the book to see what new gardens we have in store – and please do come along and support our new garden openings and help to make their first experience of Scotland's Gardens Scheme special.

Angus, Dundee & Kincardine South:
Orchard Cottage

Berwickshire & Roxburghshire:
Old Melrose

East Lothian:
Belhaven Hill School

Inverness, Ross, Cromarty & Skye:
2 Strathview

Moray & Nairn:
Earth House Apothecary Gardens

Stirlingshire:
Gartmore Village

New gardens by district NEW

Aberdeenshire
Elvanrock
Glenkindie House[1]

Angus, Dundee & Kincardineshire South
15 Fairfield Road
Airlie Castle Gardens
Craigellie House Gardens
Dorward House
Gallery Garden[1]
Kinnordy Walled Garden
Milton of Finavon[1]
Orchard Cottage
St Bedes & Ashludie Wildflower Gardens
The Manse
Westwater House

Argyll & Lochaber
4 Port Ann
Ardchattan Manse
Cruachan Lodge
Ilha de Deus
Kilchoan Gardens

Ayrshire & Arran
Beith Gardens
Caprington Castle[2]
River Garden Auchincruive[1]

Berwickshire & Roxburghshire
Mellerstain[1] [2]
Morebattle Mains
Old Melrose
The Walled Garden at the Hugo Burge Foundation

Caithness, Sutherland, Orkney & Shetland
Laura's Wood
Mill House
Waulkmill Garden

Dumfriesshire
Byreburnfoot House
Gledenholm House

East Lothian
Belhaven Hill School

Edinburgh, Midlothian & West Lothian
Belgrave Crescent Gardens
Bridgend Farmhouse Community Allotments
Eglinton and Glencairn Gardens
Learmonth Place Garden
Oatridge College Campus – SRUC
Quinn Garden
Rosemount

Fife
Wester Craigfoodie

Glasgow & District
Grow Cook Inspire
Elsewhere Garden

Inverness, Ross, Cromarty & Skye
2 Strathview
Buchollie House, Kiltarlity Gardens

Lanarkshire
Lanark Town Gardens
New Lanark Roof Garden[2]

Moray & Nairn
Earth House Apothecary Gardens
Naturally Useful, Marcassie Farm[1]

Peeblesshire & Tweeddale
Bank House
Diadan

Perth & Kinross
17 Strathallan Bank
An Caorann
Overdale
Tarmangie
Tigh-na-Beithe
Torwood House

Renfrewshire
Gardens House
Lochwinnoch Road Gardens, Kilmacolm
The Croft

Stirlingshire
Gartmore Village
Mollan[1]

[1] opened in 2024 as pop-up so was not listed in the 2024 guidebook

[2] returning after a break of more than 5 years

Tips & key to symbols

By Arrangement

This is a great way to see a garden when it's quiet and garden owners will be delighted to hear from you to book a visit. Many gardens welcome visits from larger groups or clubs such as horticultural societies, as well as individuals or couples. Do get in touch.

Photography

Most of our gardens are privately owned so any photographs taken must be for private use only. The garden owner's permission must be sought if images are to be included in publications. Our Volunteer Photographers may take photos on the open day. Please notify them if you don't wish to appear in our promotional materials.

Gardening Advice

Our garden openers love to chat about their gardens. If there's a bit of advice you're after, please do ask!

Extra Assistance

Carers are offered free entry to our gardens and Assistance Dogs are always welcome.

Children & Families

Children are welcome with an accompanying adult, unless otherwise stated, but must be supervised at all times. Some openings offer children's activities – look for the children's activities symbol.

Group Visits

Many of our gardens are pleased to have groups visiting. Get in touch with the garden or contact the local District Organiser for more information.

Toilets

Private gardens do not normally have outside toilets. For security reasons, our Openers have been advised not to admit visitors into their homes.

Cancellations & additional openings

All cancellations and new dates will be posted on our website, scotlandsgardens.org, under the garden listing.

Please bring cash

While some gardens have card readers, please help our garden owners by bringing cash.

Key to symbols

Always check our website before setting out for any cancellations, last-minute changes to opening details or booking arrangements.

Gardens open for the first time, or after a long break

Dogs on short leads welcome

Full or partial wheelchair accessibility

Locally-grown plants for sale

Children's activities

Snowdrops & Winter Walks

Accessible by public transport

Champion Trees, from the UK Tree Register

National Plant Collection®, from Plant Heritage

Gardens & Designed Landscapes by Historic Environment Scotland

Basic teas

Cream teas

Homemade teas

Refreshments

Accommodation available at the garden

Our districts

	Page
Aberdeenshire	32
Angus, Dundee & Kincardineshire South	44
Argyll & Lochaber	66
Ayrshire & Arran	84
Berwickshire & Roxburghshire	94
Caithness & Sutherland, Orkney & Shetland	104
Dumfriesshire	114
Dunbartonshire	122
East Lothian	128
Edinburgh, Midlothian & West Lothian	140
Fife	156
Glasgow & District	176

Inverness, Ross, Cromarty & Skye	184
Kirkcudbrightshire	198
Lanarkshire	210
Moray & Nairn	216
Peeblesshire & Tweeddale	224
Perth & Kinross	234
Renfrewshire	254
Stirlingshire	260
Wigtownshire	268

North of Scotland & Islands

East of Scotland

South East Scotland

West & Central Scotland

South West Scotland

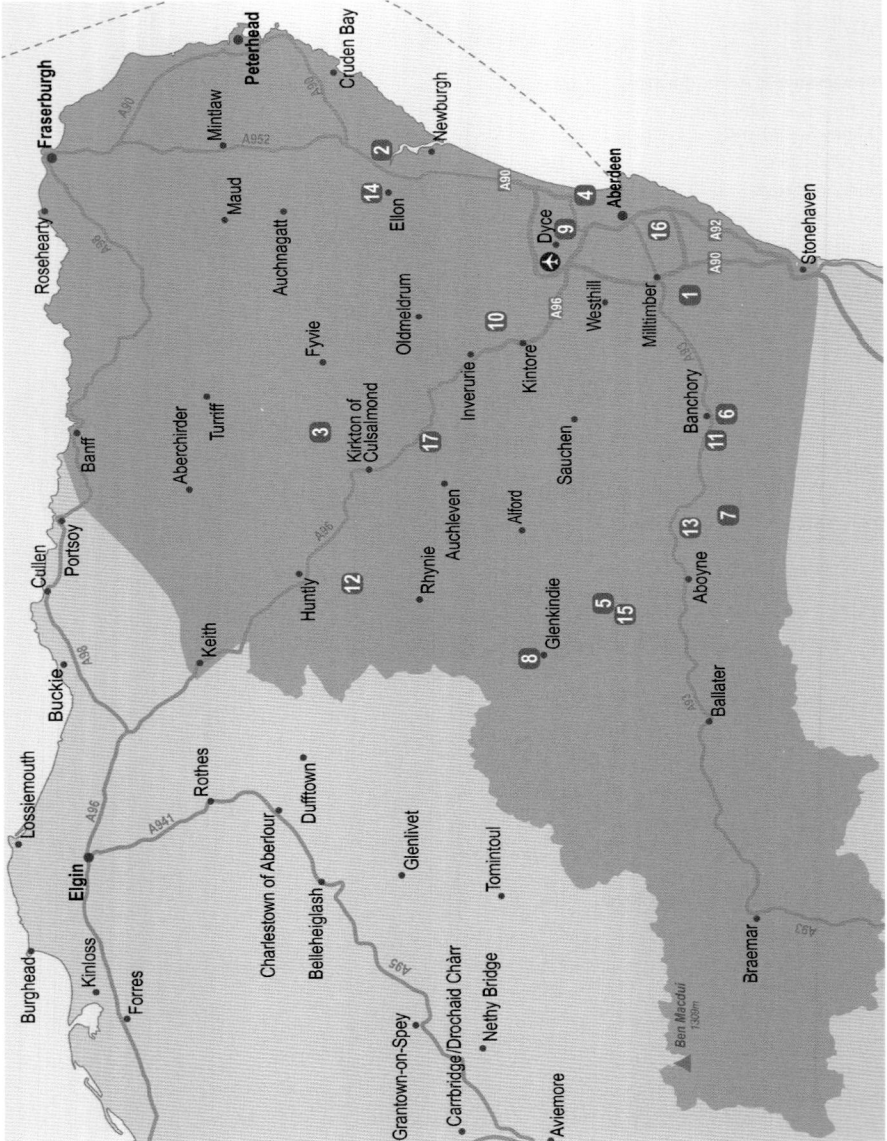

Aberdeenshire

Sponsored by

RATHBONES

Fraserburgh
Peterhead
Cruden Bay
Mintlaw
Newburgh
Rosehearty
Maud
Ellon
2
14
Aberdeen
Dyce
4
Auchnagatt
Oldmeldrum
9
Stonehaven
Westhill
16
Fyvie
10
Milltimber
1
Aberchirder
Turriff
Kirkton of Culsalmond
Inverurie
Kintore
Banchory
Banff
3
17
Sauchen
11
6
Portsoy
Cullen
Auchleven
Alford
13
7
Rhynie
Aboyne
Buckie
Huntly
12
Glenkindie
5
15
Keith
8
Ballater
Rothes
Lossiemouth
Dufftown
Elgin
Charlestown of Aberlour
Glenlivet
Burghead
Belleheiglash
Tomintoul
Kinloss
Braemar
Forres
Grantown-on-Spey
Carrbridge/Drochaid Chàrr
Nethy Bridge
Ben Macdui 130m
Aviemore

Aberdeenshire

OUR VOLUNTEER ORGANISERS

District Organiser:	Verity Walters	Tillychetly, Alford AB33 8HQ
Area Organisers:	Gill Cook	Old Semeil, Strathdon AB36 8XJ
	Anne Fettes	17 Parkhill Circle, Dyce, Aberdeen, AB21 7FN
	Madeleine Fraser	Lavender House, Banchory AB31 4FE
	Jennie Gibson	6 The Chanonry, Old Aberdeen, Aberdeen AB24 1RP
	Tina Hammond	Sunnybank, 7 Watson Street, Banchory AB31 5UB
	Liz Inglesfield	2 Earlspark Circle, Bieldside, Aberdeen AB15 9BW
	Denise Jones	Smiddy House, Glenkindie, Alford AB33 8SS
	Julie Nicol	Cedarwood Lodge, Rhu-Na-Haven Road, Aboyne AB34 5JB
	Helen Rushton	Bruckhills Croft, Rothienorman, Inverurie AB51 8YB
	David Younie	Bealltainn, Ballogie, Aboyne AB34 5DL
District Photographer:	Andy Leonard	Parkvilla, 47 Schoolhill, Ellon AB41 9AJ
Treasurer:	Catherine Nichols	Westerton Steading, Dess, Aboyne AB34 5AY

Follow our District on Facebook: @sgsaberdeenshire and Instagram: @scotgardensaberdeenshire

GARDENS OPEN ON A SPECIFIC DATE

Auchmacoy, Ellon	Sunday, 6 April
Westhall Castle, Oyne, Inverurie	Sunday, 20 April
Inchmarlo Retirement Village Garden, Inchmarlo, Banchory	Sunday, 18 May
Glenkindie House, Glenkindie, Alford	Friday, 23 May
Elvanrock, Watson Street, Banchory	Saturday/Sunday, 31 May/ 1 June
Norton House, 1 North Deeside Road, Kincardine O'Neil, Aboyne	Sunday, 8 June
Two Gardens in Banchory Devenick, Banchory Devenick	Saturday/Sunday, 14/15 June
Altries, Maryculter, Aberdeenshire	Sunday, 22 June
Finzean House, Finzean, Banchory	Sunday, 29 June
Bruckhills Croft, Rothienorman, Inverurie	Sunday, 6 July
Parkvilla, 47 Schoolhill, Ellon	Saturday, 12 July
Douneside House, Tarland	Sunday, 13 July
Tarland Community Garden, Tarland, Aboyne	Sunday, 20 July
Heatherwick Farm, Kintore, Inverurie	Sunday, 10 August
Glenkindie House, Glenkindie, Alford	Friday, 29 August

Aberdeenshire

GARDENS OPEN BY ARRANGEMENT

Laundry Cottage, Culdrain, Gartly, Huntly	1 January - 31 December
Bruckhills Croft, Rothienorman, Inverurie	9 February - 9 March
Chaplains' Court, 20 The Chanonry, Old Aberdeen, Aberdeen	1 March - 30 September
Elvanrock, Watson Street, Banchory	1 April - 30 September
Grandhome, Danestone, Aberdeen	1 April - 31 October
Two Gardens in Banchory Devenick, Banchory Devenick	1 June - 31 August

Elvanrock

Aberdeenshire

1 ALTRIES
Maryculter, Aberdeenshire AB12 5GD
Mr and Mrs Melfort Campbell

The Altries garden has been redesigned to give a feeling of space and to let in the light. The house itself is surrounded by a terraced area, borders and lawns. There is an exceptional view looking west up the River Dee, a woodland walk, a slate sphere sculpture using the original slates of the house following the refurbishment, a striking ten-foot wall making use of the down-takings of the house, a small new greenhouse with rose arbour path and further use of granite, and the original walled garden which has vegetables, fruit, and a picking garden. Each area of the garden has its own feeling of being a separate destination. Beautiful mature beech trees surround the area, giving a great sense of privacy.

Open: Sunday 22 June, 2pm - 5pm, admission £10.00, children free. Disabled parking at the house. £10 entry price includes teas.

Directions: From Bridge of Dee, follow the South Deeside road, B9077. Half a mile after Maryculter House Hotel, turn left at yellow *SGS* sign, and follow signs to car park. For SatNav follow AB12 5GJ.

Opening for: River Dee Trust

2 AUCHMACOY
Ellon AB41 8RB
Mr and Mrs Charles Buchan

Auchmacoy House is set in south-facing grounds with mature trees and rhododendrons. Meadow walk, walled garden with ponds and orchard. We do not use chemicals and during the summer months, the garden grows naturally to encourage wild birds, insects and mammals. In the spring, Auchmacoy House's attractive policies feature spectacular displays of thousands of daffodils.

Open: Sunday 6 April, 1pm - 4pm, admission £5.00, children free. Please, NO dogs. Homemade refreshments at additional charge. Music from the Buchan Pipe Band.

Directions: A90 from Aberdeen. Turn right to Auchmacoy/Collieston.

Opening for: RNLI

Aberdeenshire

3 BRUCKHILLS CROFT

Rothienorman, Inverurie AB51 8YB
Paul and Helen Rushton
T: 01651 821596 E: helenrushton1@aol.com

An informal country cottage garden extending to three-quarters of an acre with a further acre as wildflower meadow and pond. There are several distinct areas which include a white border, a butterfly alley, kitchen garden with Polycrub, greenhouse and fruit cage, an orchard, and a blue and yellow border. Relax on one of the many seats in the garden and soak up the atmosphere. Awarded National Collection status for *Galanthus* (snowdrops) in 2021. National Plant Collection: *Galanthus*.

Open: by arrangement 9 February - 9 March for Snowdrops and Winter Walks. Also open Sunday 6 July, noon - 5pm. Admission £6.00, children free.

Directions: From Rothienorman take the B9001 north for two-and-a-half miles. On the S-bend turn left. When you reach the Bruckhills Farm roadend, signs will direct you to our new access road.

Opening for: SMG: Scotia Medical Group

4 CHAPLAINS' COURT

20 The Chanonry, Old Aberdeen, Aberdeen AB24 1RQ
Irene Wischik
T: 01224 491675 E: irene@wischik.com

This historic walled garden has a long, well-stocked herbaceous border offering a succession of vivid colour from early spring to winter. It is divided by an ornamental pergola, a perfect place to sit and enjoy the garden. Large trees of ash, beech, horse chestnut, oak and sycamore give this garden a mature feel. A specimen Camperdown elm sits in the centre of the lawn, which in spring is covered in a carpet of crocuses, snowdrops and *Scilla*. Vegetables and herbs produce plentiful crops, together with newly-planted espalier and fan-trained apple and pear trees.

Open: by arrangement 1 March - 30 September, admission £6.00, children free.

Directions: Bus 1 or 2 from Aberdeen city centre to St Machar Drive, and head towards St Machar Cathedral. Or drive down St Machar Drive, turn into The Chanonry and drive down until the junction with Don Street.

Opening for: SSAFA Forces Help

Aberdeenshire

5 **DOUNESIDE HOUSE**
Tarland AB34 4UD
The MacRobert Trust
W: www.dounesidehouse.co.uk

Douneside is the former home of Lady MacRobert, who developed these magnificent gardens in the early to mid-1900s. Ornamental borders, an Arts and Crafts themed terraced garden and water gardens surround a spectacular infinity lawn overlooking the Deeside hills. The walled garden houses a large ornamental greenhouse and supplies organic fruit, vegetables, herbs and cut flowers to Douneside House which is a multi-award winning hotel. All areas of the garden will be open and there will be a pipe band, teas and plants for sale.

Open: Sunday 13 July, 2pm - 5pm, admission £6.00, children free.

Directions: On the B9119 towards Aberdeen. Tarland one mile.

Opening for: Perennial

6 **ELVANROCK**
Watson Street, Banchory AB31 5TR
Margaret Owen
E: margaret.owen@gmail.com

A town garden on a south-facing slope, redesigned over five years to manage the slopes. Planned for year round colour and ease of care. The garden offers five peaceful seating areas to enjoy the cottage garden borders, surrounded by a selection of rhododendron, *Cornus kousa* and flowering cherries with views across the Dee Valley.

Open: Saturday 31 May & Sunday 1 June, 2pm - 5pm. Also open by arrangement 1 April - 30 September. Admission £5.00, children free. Access is via Ramsay Road.

Directions: By bus, alight at either Banchory Primary school (3 minute walk along Ramsay Road) or at Banchory High Street (10 minute walk uphill via Arbeadie Terrace and Elms Rise). On street parking is available.

Opening for: Blood Cancer UK

7 **FINZEAN HOUSE**
Finzean, Banchory AB31 6NZ
Mr and Mrs Donald Farquharson

Finzean House was the family home of Joseph Farquharson, the Victorian landscape painter, and the garden was the backdrop for several of his paintings. The garden has lovely views, over the historic holly hedge to the front, of Clachnaben. There is a spring woodland garden, extensive lawns with herbaceous and shrub borders and a working cut-flower garden for late summer, alongside a recently restored pond area. A new vegetable garden was created in 2020.

Open: Sunday 29 June, 2pm - 5pm, admission £5.00, children free.

Directions: On the B976, South Deeside Road, between Banchory and Aboyne.

Opening for: The Forget-Me-Not Club

Aberdeenshire

8 GLENKINDIE HOUSE
Glenkindie, Alford AB33 8ST
Christopher and Camille Bently

Glenkindie House is a 16th-century castle remodelled in the 1900s. The walled gardens are laid out in the Victorian Arts & Crafts style with herbaceous borders, a magnificent rhododendron shrubbery, specimen trees and rose beds. There is a fine collection of 19th-century yew topiary depicting teddy bears, chess pieces and characters from *Alice in Wonderland*. Visitors can also enjoy a stroll around the pond to view the 17th-century dovecot.

Open: Friday 23 May, 10am - 2pm. Also open Friday 29 August, 10am - 2pm. Admission £10.00, children free. Admission £10 including refreshments, children free, no dogs except service dogs. Toilet and disabled toilet facilities available. Christopher Bently will be showcasing an array of bonsai specimens from his collection at Kildrummy Gardens. There will also be a raffle, refreshments marquee, and plant sales.

Directions: On the A97 Alford/Strathdon road, 12 miles west of Alford. Entrance to Glenkindie House is through the main gates, free parking available near the gardens.

Opening for: Scotland's Charity Air Ambulance

Glenkindie House

Aberdeenshire

9 GRANDHOME
Danestone, Aberdeen AB22 8AR
Mrs WJB Paton
T: 01224 722202 E: admin@grandhome.co.uk

Eighteenth-century walled garden incorporating a rose garden and policies with daffodils, tulips, rhododendrons, azaleas, mature trees and shrubs.

Open: by arrangement 1 April - 31 October, admission £5.00, children free. Please, no dogs. We would prefer three working days' notice of your visit when booking.

Directions: From the north end of North Anderson Drive, continue on the A92 over Persley Bridge, turning left at the Tesco roundabout. After 1¾ miles, turn left through the pillars on a left-hand bend.

Opening for: All proceeds to SGS Beneficiaries

10 HEATHERWICK FARM
Kintore, Inverurie AB51 0UQ
Lucy and Joe Narducci

Our garden is mainly open and spacious but with distinct zones created over the last decade to serve different purposes. By summer 2025 we hope to have finished a dedicated herb garden with ambitions of Mediterranean vibes. Densely-packed perennial borders dominate in the front, while an evergreen shrubbery occupies the back. Our busy, rustic vegetable garden is designed to be pretty as well as productive and the apple orchard and wild paddock are meant for wandering. With its open nature and many seats, the garden is accessible to all.

Open: Sunday 10 August, 1pm - 5pm, admission £6.00, children free.

Directions: Please use postcode AB51 0RQ for SatNav and the location as per the map on Scotland's Gardens Scheme's webpage. From Inverurie centre, take the B9001 southwards. At the corner of St Mary's Place and St James's Place follow signs for *Keithhall*. Then follow signs for *Balbithan*. Heatherwick is signposted and on the left after Hogholm Stables. It is three miles from the centre of Inverurie.

Opening for: Myeloma UK

Heatherwick Farm

Aberdeenshire

11 INCHMARLO RETIREMENT VILLAGE GARDEN
Inchmarlo, Banchory AB31 4AL
Skene Enterprises (Aberdeen) Ltd
T: 01330 826242 E: info@inchmarlo-retirement.co.uk
W: www.inchmarlo-retirement.co.uk

Beautiful five-acre woodland garden filled with azaleas and rhododendrons beneath ancient Scots pines, Douglas firs and silver firs (some over 140 feet tall). Also beeches, rare and unusual trees including pindrow firs, Pere David's maple, Erman's birch and a mountain snowdrop tree. The Oriental Garden features a Karesansui, a dry slate stream designed by Peter Roger, *RHS Chelsea* gold medal winner. The keyhole-shaped garden houses a purple *Prunus cerasifera* hedge and a herbaceous border, and has been designed by Billy Carruthers of Binny Plants, an eight-times gold medal winner at Gardening Scotland and a regular at the RHS Chelsea Flower Show.

Open: Sunday 18 May, 1:30pm - 4:30pm, admission £5.00, children free.

Directions: From Aberdeen via North Deeside Road on the A93, one mile west of Banchory turn right at the main gate to the Inchmarlo Estate.

Opening for: Alzheimer Scotland & The Forget-Me-Not Club

12 LAUNDRY COTTAGE
Culdrain, Gartly, Huntly AB54 4PY
Judith McPhun
T: 01466 720768 E: judithmcphun@icloud.com

An informal cottage-style garden of about one-and-a-half acres by the River Bogie. Two contrasting steep slopes make up the wilder parts. The more intensively-gardened area around the cottage includes a wide variety of herbaceous plants, shrubs and trees, an orchard area and fruit and vegetable plots, making a garden of year-round interest.

Open: by arrangement 1 January - 31 December, admission £5.00, children free. Snowdrops during February and March. Groups of up to 12 welcome.

Directions: Four miles south of Huntly on the A97.

Opening for: Amnesty International UK Section Charitable Trust

Aberdeenshire

13 **NORTON HOUSE**
1 North Deeside Road, Kincardine O'Neil, Aboyne, Aberdeenshire AB34 5AA
Andrew and Nicola Bradford

Norton House, on the edge of the historic village of Kincardine O'Neil, dates from 1840. In the main this is a mature garden with large trees, shrubs, herbaceous borders, rockeries and a small orchard. An area that was neglected for decades has seen much tree-felling and work is in progress to make a woodland garden. Following last year's hugely successful first SGS opening you are invited to return to see progress and enjoy a scrummy tea and a social event.

Open: Sunday 8 June, 2pm - 5pm, admission £10.00, children free. £10 entry includes price of tea. Children's free entry to include juice and biscuits, homemade tea available for children by donation. The Open Day will include a well-stocked plant stall with lots of super plants and knowledgeable helpers.

Directions: Situated on the A93 at the eastern end of Kincardine O'Neil. Accessible by bus, the Stagecoach 201 service.

Opening for: Children 1st

Norton House

Aberdeenshire

14 **PARKVILLA**
47 Schoolhill, Ellon AB41 9AJ
Andy and Kim Leonard
T: 07786 748296 E: andy.leonard@btinternet.com

A south-facing Victorian walled garden, lovingly developed from a design started in 1990 to give colour and interest all year. Enjoy densely planted herbaceous borders, pause under the pergola clothed in clematis, honeysuckle and rambling roses, continue on to the bottom of the garden where three ponds and wildflower beds reflect a strong focus on wildlife. This is a hidden gem of a garden that has won awards including *Ellon Best Garden* and with plants rarely seen in north-east Scotland. Parkvilla was featured as Garden of the Week in *Garden News* in 2024.

Open: Saturday 12 July, 2pm - 5pm, admission £5.00, children free. Please, NO dogs, except guide and assistance dogs by prior arrangement.

Directions: From centre of Ellon head north towards Auchnagatt. Schoolhill is third left. From Auchnagatt head into Ellon along Golf Road, Schoolhill is first right after the golf course. Limited on-street parking, car parks in Ellon (five minutes walk) and Caroline's Well Wood. Public toilets in Ellon town centre.

Opening for: St Mary On The Rock Episcopal Church Ellon, Alzheimer Scotland & Ellon Men's Shed

15 **TARLAND COMMUNITY GARDEN**
Tarland, Aboyne AB34 4ZQ
The Gardeners of Tarland

Tarland Community Garden opened in 2013 and is a Tarland Development Group project. It provides an inclusive and accessible community growing space for local residents. It has indoor (polytunnel) and outdoor raised beds for members based on availability, plus communal planting areas including a soft fruit cage, fruit trees and a herb garden. It is a place for members to grow produce, learn, share and have fun.

Open: Sunday 20 July, noon - 4pm, admission £4.00, children free. Teas and coffees included in entry price.

Directions: Take the B9094 from Aboyne or the A96 and B9119 from Aberdeen. Arriving at the village square the gardens will be clearly signposted.

Opening for: Tarland Development Group

Aberdeenshire

16 **TWO GARDENS IN BANCHORY DEVENICK**
Banchory Devenick AB12 5XT
Angela and Derek Townsley and Jane and Terry O'Kelly
T: text 07712 528450 E: janeokelly868@gmail.com

Pinetrees Cottage Banchory Devenick AB12 5XR (Angela and Derek Townsley): A mature garden set in three-quarters of an acre, filled with a wide range of hardy plants including rhododendrons, azaleas, acers, topiary and roses, with two ponds. An alpine house is fronted by stone troughs filled with rock plants. Set in a backdrop of mature pine trees to the north and open fields to the south.

Whin Cottage Ardoe, Aberdeen AB12 5XT (Jane and Terry O'Kelly): A cottage garden of just under half an acre surrounded by farmland. It features a border of rhododendrons and azaleas, several mixed borders, two formal rose beds, a wildlife pond and four raised beds growing a variety of vegetables and flowers for the house. The garden reflects a love of colour and structure and an interest in wildlife.

Open: Saturday/Sunday, 14/15 June, 2pm - 5pm. Also open by arrangement 1 June - 31 August. Admission £6.00, children free. Plants for sale at Pinetrees Cottage. Teas available at Whin Cottage.

Directions: Pinetrees Cottage: Banchory Devenick is four miles from Bridge of Dee. Turn off B9077 at Banchory Devenick church. Follow to T-junction, turn right. Next right is Butterywells Steading. Turn into opening and follow track, go around the back of farmhouse (Lochend) and continue on track to Pinetrees.

Whin Cottage: Take the B9077 out of Aberdeen. After approximately two miles turn left immediately after Banchory Devenick Church, signposted Banchory Devenick. (There is parking available along the verge on the left.) Turn right after 100 metres. Whin Cottage is on the right immediately after you have turned. There is limited parking outside the cottage.

Opening for: Fighting For Sight Aberdeen

17 **WESTHALL CASTLE**
Oyne, Inverurie AB52 6RW
Mr Gavin Farquhar
T: 01224 214301 E: enquiries@ecclesgreig.com

Set in an ancient landscape in the foothills of the impressive and foreboding hill of Bennachie, is a circular walk through glorious daffodils with outstanding views. This interesting garden is in the early stages of restoration, with large groupings of rhododendrons and specimen trees. Westhall Castle is a 16th-century tower house, incorporating a 13th-century building of the bishops of Aberdeen. There were additions in the 17th, 18th and 19th centuries. The castle is semi-derelict, but stabilised from total dereliction. A fascinating house encompassing 600 years of alteration and additions.

Open: Sunday 20 April, 1pm - 4pm, admission £5.00, children free.

Directions: Marked from the A96 at Old Rayne and from Oyne Village.

Opening for: 1st Insch Scout Group

Angus, Dundee &
Kincardineshire South

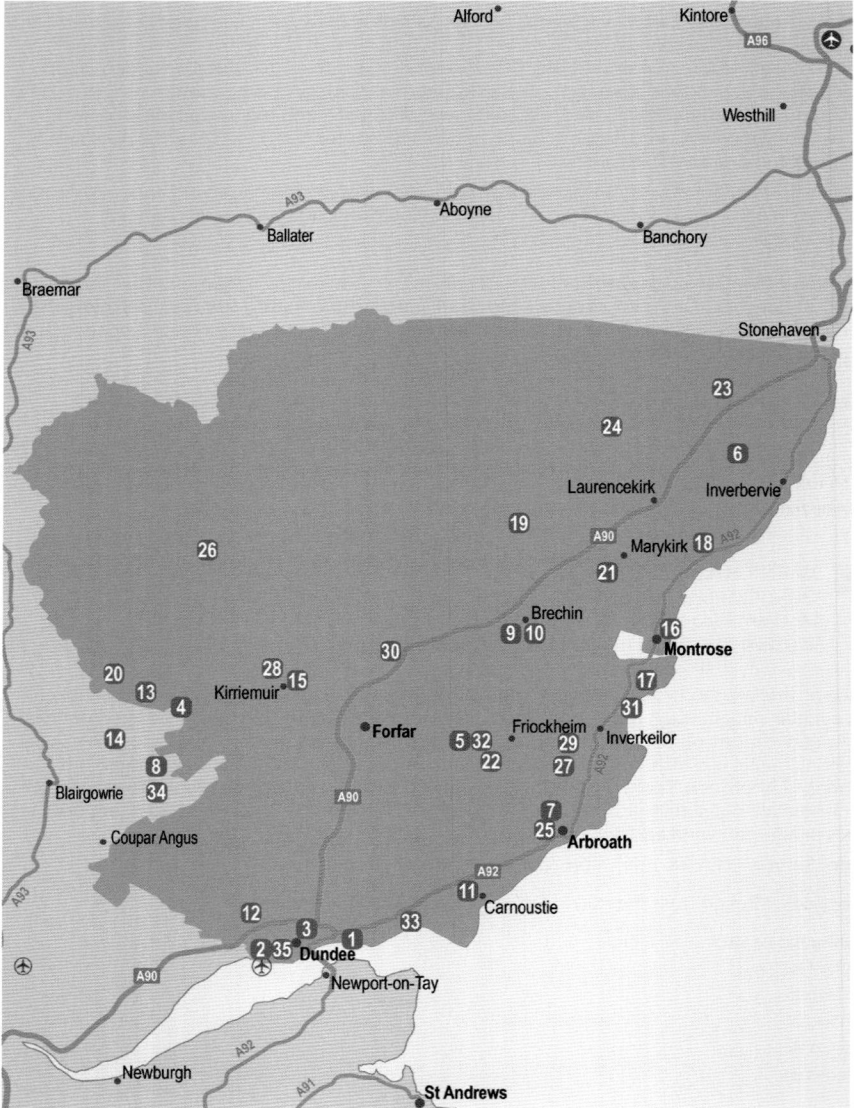

Alford

Kintore

A96

Westhill

A93

Aboyne

Ballater

Banchory

Braemar

A93

Stonehaven

23

24

6

Laurencekirk

Inverbervie

19

A90

Marykirk 18

A92

26

21

Brechin

9 10

30

16

Montrose

20

28 15

13

Kirriemuir

17

4

31

14

Forfar

5 32

Friockheim

29

Inverkeilor

8

22

27

Blairgowrie

34

A90

7

Coupar Angus

25

Arbroath

A92

12

11

Carnoustie

3

33

2 35

Dundee

1

A90

Newport-on-Tay

Newburgh

A92

A91

St Andrews

Angus, Dundee & Kincardineshire South

We are delighted to welcome the beautiful gardens of Kincardineshire South into our District, including this year the gardens at Arbuthnott House, Ecclesgreig, Glenbervie and Glensaugh.

OUR VOLUNTEER ORGANISERS

District Organisers:	Debbie Butler	Top Croft, Arniefoul, Angus DD8 1UD
	Frances Dent	Westgate, 12 Glamis Drive, Dundee DD2 1QL
		sgsangusdundee@gmail.com
Area Organisers:	Pippa Clegg	Easter Derry, Kilry, Blairgowrie PH11 8JA
	Catherine Cowie	Allardyce Castle, Inverbervie, Montrose DD10 0ST
	Jan Crow	Lower Duncraig, 2 Castle Street, Brechin DD9 6JN
	Terrill Dobson	Logie House, Kirriemuir DD8 5PN
	Claire Shepherd	Windyridge, 10 Glamis Drive, Dundee DD2 1QL
	Claire Tinsley	Ethie Mains, Inverkeilor DD11 5SN
	Colin Wilson	28 Prosen Bank, Carnoustie DD7 6GS
Treasurer:	James Welsh	Dalfruin, Kirktonhill Road, Kirriemuir DD8 4HU

Follow our District on Facebook: @sgsangusdundeethemearns

GARDENS OPEN ON A SPECIFIC DATE

Kinblethmont House, by Arbroath, Angus	Saturday/Sunday, 22/23 February
Ecclesgreig Castle, St Cyrus	Sunday, 2 March
Lawton House, Inverkeilor, by Arbroath	Thursday - Sunday, 6-9 March
17a Menzieshill Road, Dundee	Saturday/Sunday, 19/20 April
Inchmill Cottage, Glenprosen, near Kirriemuir	Monday, 21 April
17a Menzieshill Road, Dundee	Saturday/Sunday, 3/4 May
2 Panmure Terrace, Dundee	Saturday, 3 May
Inchmill Cottage, Glenprosen, near Kirriemuir	Thursday, 8 May
Dalfruin, Kirktonhill Road, Kirriemuir	Sunday, 11 May
Balhary Walled Garden, Balhary, Alyth, Blairgowrie	Saturday, 17 May
Milton of Finavon House, Forfar	Saturday, 17 May
Brechin Castle, Brechin	Sunday, 18 May
Inchmill Cottage, Glenprosen, near Kirriemuir	Thursday, 22 May
Angus Plant Sale, Pitmuies Gardens, Guthrie, by Forfar	Saturday, 24 May
Craigellie House Gardens, Alyth	Sunday, 25 May
Hospitalfield Gardens, Hospitalfield House, Westway, Arbroath	Saturday, 31 May
Westgate, 12 Glamis Drive, Dundee	Saturday/Sunday, 31 May - 1 June
Arbuthnott House Gardens, Arbuthnott House, Laurencekirk	Sunday, 8 June
Inchmill Cottage, Glenprosen, near Kirriemuir	Thursday, 12 June
Edzell Village Gardens, Edzell	Sunday, 15 June
Gardyne Castle, by Forfar	Saturday, 21 June
Brechin Gardens in June, Locations across Brechin	Sunday, 22 June
Estir Bogside, Alyth	Sunday, 22 June
The Doocot, Kinloch, Meigle, Blairgowrie	Sunday, 29 June
Dorward House, 24 Dorward Road, Montrose	Sunday, 29 June
St Bedes and Ashludie Wildflower Garden, Monifieth	Saturday/Sunday, 5/6 July

Angus, Dundee & Kincardineshire South

GARDENS OPEN ON A SPECIFIC DATE – CONTINUED

Ashbrook Nursery and Garden Centre, Forfar Road, Arbroath	Saturday, 5 July
Inchmill Cottage, Glenprosen, near Kirriemuir	Thursday, 10 July
Balhary Walled Garden, Balhary, Alyth, Blairgowrie	Saturday, 12 July
Gallery, Montrose	Sunday, 13 July
Kinnordy Walled Garden, Kinnordy House, Kirriemuir, Angus	Saturday, 19 July
Airlie Castle Gardens, Airlie Castle, Airlie, By Kirriemuir, Angus	Sunday, 20 July
Milton of Finavon House, Forfar	Saturday, 26 July
15 Fairfield Road, Broughty Ferry, Dundee	Sunday, 27 July
Glenbervie House, Drumlithie, Stonehaven	Sunday, 3 August
Cotton of Craig, Kilry, Blairgowrie	Saturday/Sunday, 9/10 August
Inchmill Cottage, Glenprosen, near Kirriemuir	Thursday, 14 August
Glensaugh, Glensaugh Lodge, Fettercairn, Laurencekirk	Sunday, 17 August
Balhary Walled Garden, Balhary, Alyth, Blairgowrie	Saturday, 23 August
Carnoustie's Tropical Garden, 28 Prosen Bank, Carnoustie	Saturday, 30 August
Inchmill Cottage, Glenprosen, near Kirriemuir	Thursday, 4 September
Westgate, 12 Glamis Drive, Dundee	Saturday/Sunday, 11/12 October

GARDENS OPEN REGULARLY

Pitmuies Gardens, House of Pitmuies, Guthrie, by Forfar	1 April - 30 September
Dunninald Castle, Montrose	1 May - 31 August (Monday, Tuesday & Sunday)

GARDENS OPEN BY ARRANGEMENT

Charleston Forest Garden, 43 Gourdie Terrace, Dundee	1 January - 31 December
Orchard Cottage, Lunan Bay, Inverkeilor, Arbroath	1 May - 30 September
15 Fairfield Road, Broughty Ferry, Dundee	1 June - 30 September

Angus, Dundee & Kincardineshire South

1 ## 15 FAIRFIELD ROAD
Broughty Ferry, Dundee DD5 1NX
Aileen Scoular
E: aileen.scoular@me.com

This sunny, contemporary garden contains many mature trees and shrubs, plus lots of recently planted beds and borders. A shady courtyard contains Japanese acers and spring-flowering bulbs, while colourful perennial planting near the house attracts pollinating insects. A new productive area, with raised beds and a greenhouse, is used to grow fruit and veg, plus dahlias and annual cut flowers. The garden is being developed in a sustainable way, where possible – no herbicides or pesticides are used; rainwater is harvested; and the stone used in the landscaping was found in the garden and re-purposed. The garden has a prolific bird and insect population, despite being in an urban location.

Open: Sunday 27 July, noon - 5pm. Also open by arrangement 1 June - 30 September. Admission £5.00, children free.

Directions: Fairfield Road is easily reached by car, via Dundee Road (A930) or Arbroath Road (A92); by bus – services 73 and 5 both stop on Strathern Road, a two-minute walk away; and by train – Broughty Ferry train station is a 15-20 minute walk. On street parking available.

Opening for: RNLI

2 ## 17A MENZIESHILL ROAD
Dundee DD2 1PS
Mr and Mrs John Stoa
W: www.johnstoa.com

This Dundee garden is on a fairly steep slope with steps and paths. It features a riot of colour in April/May with thousands of tulip bulbs followed by azaleas and rhododendrons. There is a large fig tree and a grapevine 'Brant' growing on south-facing walls. In the greenhouse, John grows tomatoes and has four grapevines, *Phoenix, Seigerrebe, Muller Thurgau* and *Solaris*, used for his Muscat flavoured wines (samples available). He has recently planted three seedless grapes (Himrod, Glenora and Suffolk Red) outdoors on a south facing fence as a trial. John is a horticulturist, as seen by unusual fruit varieties such as Saskatoon, and an artist. His gallery will be open.

Open: Saturday/Sunday, 19/20 April & Saturday/Sunday, 3/4 May, 11am - 3pm, admission £5.00, children free. Another Dundee garden is open and could be visited on the same day, see entry for 2 Panmure Terrace. (The cafe at the University Botanic Garden is nearby.)

Directions: Turn off the A85/Riverside Ave at the roundabout towards Dundee Botanic Gardens. Pass the Botanics, road bears left and becomes Perth Rd. Right onto Invergowrie Drive and first left on Menzieshill Road. 17A has a prominent white stemmed birch tree. Bus 5A to the foot of Glamis Rd and walk west to Invergowrie Drive.

Opening for: Cancer Research UK

Angus, Dundee & Kincardineshire South

3   2 PANMURE TERRACE
Dundee DD3 6HP
Janet Ireland
E: lunan@me.com

2 Panmure Terrace is situated on the south side of Dundee Law. The front garden is densely planted with silver birch trees, some shrubs, grasses and herbaceous perennials.The back garden has trees, a collection of tree ferns and shade-loving plants. There are several seating areas for quiet contemplation.

Open: Saturday 3 May, 2pm - 5pm, admission £5.00, children free. Another Dundee garden is open and could be visited on the same day, see entry for 17A Menzieshill Road. (The cafe at the University Botanic Garden is near Menzieshill Road.)

Directions: The garden is situated behind Dudhope Park. The best approach from the centre of town is up Barrack Road.

Opening for: Alzheimer Scotland

4   AIRLIE CASTLE GARDENS
Airlie Castle, Airlie, By Kirriemuir, Angus DD8 5NG
David and Tarka Airlie
T: 01575 530387 E: office@airlieestates.com
W: www.airlieestates.com

Airlie was built in the 15th century as a fortified castle. It sits on a promontory high above the Rivers Melgum and Isla. The gorge below is a Site of Special Scientific Interest because it contains rare lichen and wildflowers. The 18th-century walled garden grows fruit, flowers and vegetables and it is intersected by mature yew and box topiary. Within the Castle walls itself, there are two herbaceous borders and a large Kiftsgate rose and climbing wisteria. In large areas of the policies the grass has been left to grow long, and as a consequence of this many varieties of native wild orchid have reappeared. A woodland walk leads down from the Castle and gardens to the River Isla.

Open: Sunday 20 July, 2pm - 6pm, admission £6.00, children free.

Directions: Take the B951 from Kirriemuir signposted Glen Isla. Pass Kinnordy Loch and then turn left signposted Airlie and Alyth. Keep on for three-and-a half-miles, pass Mains of Airlie farm on left. Entrance to Castle is just beyond on the right.

Opening for: MBA: Mountain Bothies Association

Angus, Dundee & Kincardineshire South

5 ANGUS PLANT SALE

Pitmuies Gardens, Guthrie, by Forfar DD8 2SN
The Organisers of SGS Angus, Dundee & Kincardineshire South
E: sgsangusdundee@gmail.com

By kind permission of Ruaraidh and Jeanette Ogilvie, our popular Annual Plant Sale will once again be held at Pitmuies Gardens (see separate entry for description of gardens). As always, there will be a good selection of plants sourced from private gardens and some local nurseries. Please bring boxes and trays if you can. Donations of plants will be welcome, either in advance (use above email address to arrange delivery) or on the day. If you are potting up plants, please use sterile potting compost; we cannot accept plants in garden soil.

Open: Saturday 24 May, 10am - 1pm, admission £6.00, children free. Admission price covers entry to the sale and the gardens.

Directions: From Forfar take the A932 east for seven miles and gardens are signposted on the right. From Brechin take the A933 south to Friockheim and turn right onto the A932. The gardens are signposted on the left after 1½ miles.

Opening for: All proceeds to SGS Beneficiaries

6 ARBUTHNOTT HOUSE GARDENS

Arbuthnott House, Laurencekirk AB30 1PA
Chris and Emily Arbuthnott
E: arbuthnotthouse@gmail.com
W: www.arbuthnott.co.uk

Arbuthnott House is the seat of the Viscount of Arbuthnott, whose family has lived here since 1190. The five-acre garden was laid out in the 17th century and comprises a walled garden with some 1920s Arts and Crafts planting. Thought to be one of the oldest gardens in Scotland, it runs down a steep, south-facing slope that is divided by three main broadwalks which run horizontally and are intercepted with diagonal pathways. The vegetables and soft fruit are contained within beds which are bound by topiary, herbaceous borders, rose beds and long beds for cut flowers.

Open: Sunday 8 June, 2pm - 5pm, admission £5.00, children free. Garden only. Please note that due to the steep layout of the gardens, they are unfortunately not wheelchair accessible. The nearby Grassic Gibbon Centre and Cafe will be open for teas and has toilet facilities (which are not available at the gardens)

Directions: Located at the heart of Arbuthnott Estate, just off the B967 Inverbervie to Fordoun. Three miles off the A90.

Opening for: UNICEF UK: Lebanon Appeal

Angus, Dundee & Kincardineshire South

7 ASHBROOK NURSERY AND GARDEN CENTRE
Forfar Road, Arbroath DD11 3RB
Anne Webster
T: 01241 873408 E: anne@ashbrook.co.uk
W: www.ashbrook.co.uk

This family-run garden centre grows the majority of its plants, including over 2,000 varieties of bedding and patio plants, alpines, herbaceous perennials, ferns and grasses. There are also comprehensive A-Z displays of trees, conifers, shrubs, alpines and perennials.

The garden at Cabrach House – which is between the garden centre and the nursery – will also be open. This has colourful borders and patio, a wee orchard and fruit and vegetable areas.

Open: Saturday 5 July, noon - 5pm, admission £6.00, children free. NURSERY TOURS: Come and see commercial plant production from seed sowing to the final plants and sustainable cut flowers. Tours at 12 noon, 2pm and 4pm. Numbers limited, advance booking advisable (see the SGS website for details). Admission price includes the gardens and a tour. There is a cafe at the nursery.

Directions: Located on the outskirts of Arbroath, on the west side of the A933 opposite Condor Royal Marine Base.

Opening for: All proceeds to SGS Beneficiaries

8 BALHARY WALLED GARDEN
Balhary, Alyth, Blairgowrie PH11 8LT
Teri and Paul Hodge-Neale
W: www.facebook.com/balharywalledgarden/

TWO GARDENS FOR THE PRICE OF ONE!
This two-acre, organic, working walled garden is being lovingly restored by Paul, who is bringing it back to full production with the development and experimentation of the 'no dig' method to grow many heritage and new varieties of vegetables. He works single-handed with help once a week from a volunteer and visitors should be aware that they are visiting a space which is continually in progress, where they will have the opportunity to see the season unfold and discuss with Paul the benefits and learning processes of gardening the way he does. Aside from the vegetables, the herbaceous borders are currently being redeveloped to give added colour and interest. Paul and Teri will also open their own private therapy garden, which is a beautiful and contemplative space with serene water features, statuary, stonework and unusual plants.

Open: Saturday 17 May, Saturday 12 July & Saturday 23 August, 1pm - 5pm, admission £6.00, children free. Please approach the gardens at low speed due to resident wildlife. Access is via a track which can become muddy in wet weather. Please no dogs.

Directions: Situated between Alyth and Meigle on the B954 opposite the sign to *Jordanstone*.

Opening for: Perennial

Angus, Dundee & Kincardineshire South

9

BRECHIN CASTLE

Brechin DD9 6SG
The Earl and Countess of Dalhousie
T: 01356 624566 E: mandyhendry@dalhousieestates.co.uk
W: www.dalhousieestates.co.uk

The uniquely-curving walls are just one of many delightful surprises in store as you wander around Brechin Castle's renowned walled garden. Find charm and splendour in the wide, gravelled walks, secluded smaller paths and hidden corners, whilst you take in the stunning blend of ancient and modern plantings. May sees the rhododendrons and azaleas hit the peak of their flowering to wonderful effect throughout the month, with complementary underplanting and a framework of beautiful trees to further heighten your experience. This is a lovely garden to visit at any time of year, but it is really something to behold in the spring.

Open: Sunday 18 May, 2pm - 5pm, admission £6.00, children free. Please note that the walled garden has limited access for those with wheelchairs or mobility issues.

Directions: A90 southernmost exit to Brechin, one mile past Brechin Castle Centre, castle gates are on the right.

Opening for: The Dalhousie Centre Day Care For The Elderly & The Attic SCIO

Airlie Castle Gardens © Tarka Airlie

Angus, Dundee & Kincardineshire South

10 BRECHIN GARDENS IN JUNE
Locations across Brechin DD9 6JL
The Gardeners of Brechin

9 Pearse Street Brechin DD9 6JR (James Mackie): Opening in memory of its creator Irene Mackie, the well-known plantswoman whose love of plants is reflected in every inch of this beautiful, tranquil garden. There's a secluded and rural feel to this town garden. A huge collection of ferns is a unique feature of the garden, unusually planted to mingle with other interestingly-planted colourful herbaceous plants.

Bishops Walk 11A Argyll St, Brechin DD9 6JL (Steff and Mike Eyres): A collection of acers grown successfully for years in large pots greets you as you access the unexpected door after viewing several different planting areas. You will find a hidden, walled garden planted with scented climbing and shrub roses, lavenders, perennials and evergreen shrubs and conifers including an established Wollemi, the prehistoric tree recently discovered.

Brechin Cathedral Allotments Chanonry Wynd, Brechin DD9 6EU (Will Macfarlane): Eleven varied plots reflect the interests and personalities of each plot holder and include fruit, vegetables and herbs. A unique feature is the historical 'College Well' used by medieval monks.

Kirkton Cottage Aberlemno DD8 3PE (George Henry and Susan Norris): Nestled in a dip beside a stream, this country cottage garden is packed with plants. Mown grass paths meander among mature trees, shrubs and perennials in borders, island beds and rockeries. Rustic steps lead to raised vegetable beds, greenhouse and a prolific nursery area.

Latchlea 17A North Latch Road, Brechin DD9 6LE (Pamela Stevens): A new garden begun as a way of coping with bereavement. Inspired by Queen Elizabeth II saying that 'everyone should plant as many trees as possible', 100 trees are newly planted along The Old Lady Walk. Features include some fine stonework, shrubs, herbaceous plants and bulbs and also a courtyard garden.

Lower Duncraig 2 Castle Street, Brechin DD9 6JN (Jan and Andrew Crow): A densely planted, small town garden including rambling roses a small wildlife pond and a chamomile lawn.

Rosehill West 15C North Latch Road, Brechin DD9 6LF (Robert and Jenny Martin): An acre of newly-planted garden, formerly a field, featuring mature original trees, herbaceous areas, fruit trees (quince and crab apple), and a path through recently planted trees. A work in progress!

The Manse (NEW) 14 Chanonry Wynd, Brechin DD9 6JS (Martyn and Vincent De Winter): A cottage-style garden in the making. It features attractive combinations of shrubs, trees and perennials.

Open: Sunday 22 June, noon - 5pm, admission £8.00, children free. Tickets and teas available at St Andrew's Church hall, 66 St Andrew St, Brechin, DD9 6JB

Directions: Most gardens are located around the town of Brechin. Look for SGS yellow signs. A map with directions will be provided with tickets. A single admission ticket gives access to all gardens.

Opening for: St Andrews Scottish Episcopal Church & The Attic

Angus, Dundee & Kincardineshire South

11 **CARNOUSTIE'S TROPICAL GARDEN**
28 Prosen Bank, Carnoustie DD7 6GX
Colin Wilson

A small tropical garden hidden in Carnoustie. You'll find a small collection of palms, including the spectacular *Brahea armata*, 'Mexican Blue Palm', *Chamaerops humilis cerifera*, *Trachycarpus fortunei, Trachycarpus wagerianus* and *Chamaerops vulcano*. You'll also be met by a stunning circular wall with a Brazilian slate seat to keep you cosy under the tree ferns, *Musa basjoo, Tetrapanax papyrifer* Rex and bamboos. The garden has elegant curves at every turn creating a botanical wonderland. A jungle curved path is surrounded by the tree ferns, *Fatsia japonica* and Zebra grasses. At the journey's end you'll find a beautiful *Betula jacquemontii, Schefflera taiwaniana*, tree ferns, *Colocasia* Pink China in a hidden sun trap patio, accessed through the enchanting moon gate.

Open: Saturday 30 August, 1pm - 5pm, admission £5.00, children free. No dogs, please.

Directions: Buses 73 & 73C from Dundee/Arbroath. Prosen Bank is found by a path via Newton Road. No parking in Prosen Bank. Parking at football pitches on Newton Road or in adjacent streets.

Opening for: Alzheimer Scotland

12 **CHARLESTON FOREST GARDEN**
43 Gourdie Terrace, Dundee DD2 4QT
L Wakefield
E: charlestonforestgarden@gmail.com

A young forest garden in Dundee, practising permaculture principles. Perennial vegetables are scattered throughout the garden, along with medicinal herbs, fruit trees, edible hedges and ornamental edible plants. A small flock of chickens contribute to a composting system and there is also a 'chop and drop' approach being used. This garden is home to some Scottish heirloom vegetable varieties, with the intention to save seeds to share. There is a small patch of alpines and a number of roses throughout, along with some purely ornamental herbaceous perennials, mostly grown with pollinators and wildlife in mind.

Open: by arrangement 1 January - 31 December, admission £5.00, children free. Visits are possible throughout the year. Please email, using above address, to arrange a time.

Directions: In the centre of Charleston, Dundee, with some parking on Gourdie Terrace and Balgarthno Road. The number 28 bus stops around the corner at the community centre.

Opening for: Dementia UK

Angus, Dundee & Kincardineshire South

13 COTTON OF CRAIG
Kilry, Blairgowrie PH11 8HW
Nick Joy and Nici Rymer

An old walled garden, partially under redesign, with fruit house containing espaliered peach, apricot and cherry trees, herbaceous borders, vegetable garden, greenhouse and specimen trees and shrubs. A robot mower keeps the grass in order. There is also a waterfall walk to explore.

Open: Saturday/Sunday, 9/10 August, 2pm - 5pm, admission £5.00, children free.

Directions: From Perth take the A94 to Coupar Angus and just before Meigle take the B954 and follow signs to *Glen Isla* for approximately four miles until you see the *Garden Open* signs on the right, where there is a left turn signposted *Kilry*. From Dundee take the A923 to Muirhead then the B954 to Meigle, turn right up B954 and follow signs as above. Limited parking on the road and up the drive.

Opening for: RNLI

14 CRAIGELLIE HOUSE GARDENS
Alyth PH11 8LA
Liz and Charles Bushby
W: www.craigellie.co.uk

Situated on a south-facing , two-acre plot, Craigellie House dates back to around 1918. When Liz and Charles moved there in 2018 the garden, once open with a grass tennis court but later formalised, had been badly neglected and was overshadowed by enormous conifers. Working with a professional gardener, they have crafted a garden that beautifully complements this historic home. Though still a work in progress, visitors can enjoy vibrant successional planting in the newly-formed herbaceous beds, a small woodland area and a recently-created kitchen garden.

Open: Sunday 25 May, 1pm - 4pm, admission £5.00, children free. There are several cafes nearby in Alyth which, in itself, is an interesting and historic small town.

Directions: Take the Bamff Road from Alyth, passing the church and entrance to the Den of Alyth. Continue for about ½ mile and turn right through the white gate opposite the Tullyfergus & St Fink junction. Stagecoach bus 57 or 57A to Alyth & 25 minute walk.

Opening for: All proceeds to SGS Beneficiaries

Angus, Dundee & Kincardineshire South

15 DALFRUIN
Kirktonhill Road, Kirriemuir DD8 4HU
Mr and Mrs James A Welsh

A well-stocked, connoisseur's garden of about a third of an acre situated at the end of a short cul-de-sac. There are many less common plants like varieties of trilliums, meconopsis (blue poppies), tree peonies (descendants of ones collected by George Sherriff and grown at Ascreavie), dactylorhiza and codonopsis. There is a scree garden and collection of ferns. The vigorous climbing rose, Paul's Himalayan Musk, grows over a pergola. Interconnected ponds encourage wildlife. **This 25th year of opening will be our final year.**

Open: Sunday 11 May, 2pm - 5pm, admission £5.00, children free. Monkey puzzle seedlings for sale. Sorry, no dogs.

Directions: From the centre of Kirriemuir turn left up Roods. Kirktonhill Road is on the left near the top of the hill. Park on Roods or at St Mary's Episcopal Church. Disabled parking only in Kirktonhill Road. Bus 20 (from Dundee) getting off at either stop on the Roods.

Opening for: Kirriemuir Day Care Ltd

16 DORWARD HOUSE
24 Dorward Road, Montrose DD10 8SB
The Trustees of Dorward House

The original house was built in 1839 and became a care home for the elderly in 1950. There have been many changes over the years including the addition of the garden pavilion. The gardens are maintained by the gardener/handyman with assistance from a private contractor and a few keen volunteers. Their hard work and dedication has certainly paid off with stunning herbaceous borders and colourful annuals. There is also a 'sensory garden' to the rear which is dedicated mainly for the vulnerable dementia residents. We hope you enjoy your visit.

Open: Sunday 29 June, 2pm - 5pm, admission £5.00, children free.

Directions: Dorward House is on the corner of Dorward Rd and Warrack Terrace, and is adjacent to the Midlinks park and tennis courts.

Opening for: Dorward House, Montrose

Craigellie House Gardens

Angus, Dundee & Kincardineshire South

17 DUNNINALD CASTLE
Montrose DD10 9TD
The Stansfeld family
T: 01674 672031 E: estateoffice@dunninald.com
W: www.dunninald.com

We welcome our visitors to explore our 100 acres of woods, wild garden, policies and a walled garden. From January to May, the main interest is the wild garden and policies where snowdrops in January are followed by daffodils and finally bluebells in May. In June, the emphasis turns to the walled garden, rich in interest and colour throughout the summer. Situated at the bottom of the beech avenue, the walled garden is planted with rose borders, traditional mixed borders, vegetables, herbs, soft fruits and fruit trees and there is a greenhouse.

Open: 1 May - 31 August (Monday, Tuesday & Sunday), 1pm - 5pm, admission £6.00, children free. See website for Castle Tours.

Directions: Three miles south of Montrose, ten miles north of Arbroath, signposted from the A92.

Opening for: Donation to SGS Beneficiaries

18 ECCLESGREIG CASTLE
St Cyrus DD10 0DP
Mr Gavin Farquhar
T: 01224 214301 E: enquiries@ecclesgreig.com
W: www.ecclesgreig.com

Ecclesgreig Castle, Victorian gothick on a 16th-century core, is undergoing restoration. The castle is thought to be an inspiration for Bram Stoker's *Dracula*. The snowdrop walk, with a variety of snowdrops, starts at the castle, meanders around the estate, along woodland paths and the pond, ending at the garden. In the Italian balustraded gardens, there is a 140-foot-long herbaceous border, classical statues and stunning shaped topiary with views across St Cyrus to the sea. Started from a derelict site, development continues. Also to be found in the grounds is the ancient well of St Cyrus.

Open: Sunday 2 March, 1pm - 4pm for Snowdrops and Winter Walks, admission £5.00, children free.

Directions: *Ecclesgreig* will be signposted from the A92 Coast Road and from the A937 Montrose/Laurencekirk Road.

Opening for: Girlguiding Montrose District

Angus, Dundee & Kincardineshire South

19 **EDZELL VILLAGE GARDENS**
Edzell DD9 7TQ
The Gardeners of Edzell

Union Street, Edzell DD9 7TD (Christy Bing): A walled garden with roses and ancient apple trees.
North Lodge 36 Church Street, Edzell DD9 7TQ (Robin and Paul McIntosh): North Lodge was designed by James Salmon in the Arts and Crafts style and built as a summer home in 1906. The garden is full of mature trees and shrubs, climbers and herbaceous perennials, with numerous flowering azaleas, rhododendrons and spring bulbs.
Tillytoghills Steading, Fettercairn AB30 1YJ (Veronica and Steve Engel): A large country garden with established herbaceous borders, new shubbery borders, native trees and a large pond, as well as productive vegetable and fruit garden with free-range chickens roaming close by.
Westwater House (NEW), Edzell DD9 7TZ (Charles and Rosie Elphinstone): Formerly home to the Dalhousie Estates factor, the garden includes a walled garden, ponds, stone dykes and hedging, with flowering azaleas, rhododendrons and magnolia in a woodland setting. Fruit trees blossom in the orchard and abundant old-fashioned roses and herbaceous beds in the walled garden bloom.

Open: Sunday 15 June, 1 - 5pm, ticket price to be confirmed. Teas at the Cottage, Dalhousie Street. There will also be a plant sale. Other gardens may be added. See website for details.

Directions: Maps and tickets will be available. Check the website for details

Opening for: Edzell Village Improvement Society: Garden Group

20 **ESTIR BOGSIDE**
Alyth PH11 8HU
Morag and Andrew Buist

The garden was started in 1995. There are herbaceous borders, a cottage garden created three years ago with traditional plants including lupins, daylilies and foxgloves, a small rose garden and potager. In 2010 the garden was extended to adjacent land to allow planting of native trees, wildflowers, mown paths, two ponds and a glasshouse.

Open: Sunday 22 June, 1pm - 5pm, admission £5.00, children free.

Directions: From Perth take the A94 to Coupar Angus and just before Meigle take the B954 and follow signs to *Glen Isla* for approximately 3 miles till you see *Garden Open* signs on the left, by the road. From Dundee take the A923 to Muirhead and then the B954 to Meigle, turn right up B954 towards Glen Isla and follow signs as above.

Opening for: MND Scotland

Angus, Dundee & Kincardineshire South

21 GALLERY
Gallery House, Montrose DD10 9LA
Caroline and Alan Macdonald

A mid-18th century walled garden in the grounds of an A-listed Laird's House. The garden retains historic features, such as the paths intersecting at the listed 1786 sundial at the centre, and a fine stone carving of a recumbent retriever over the gate. Gallery's garden was redesigned and replanted in 1999 with a formal layout consisting of 'rooms', including a white garden, rose garden, gold garden and summer lawn. The colourful herbaceous borders, clipped hedges and closely-mown lawns contribute to a peaceful, relaxing atmosphere. Gallery's grounds include a new orchard of crab apple and prunus, laid out in a grid, with paths mown through a meadow of spring bulbs and wildflowers.

Open: Sunday 13 July, 1pm - 5pm, admission £6.00, children free.

Directions: Take the *Hillside* turn off the A90. Turn left towards *Gallery*. The entrance to the parking area is through the third gate on your left (marked *Gallery Home Farm*, it will be signposted). Alternatively, if you are coming from Montrose, turn off the A937 just before Marykirk.

Opening for: Scotland's Charity Air Ambulance & APOPO

22 GARDYNE CASTLE
by Forfar DD8 2SQ
William and Camilla Gray Muir

Gardyne Castle, dating from the 16th century, is one of the most attractive small castles in Angus. After a turbulent history of battles with the neighbouring Guthries, the fortified house now sits in the centre of an enchanting garden created by its current owners over the past 21 years. To the east, the walled garden runs down to the Denton Burn. The castle's extraordinary stone-capped turrets overlook a long, romantic double border, with herbaceous planting in front of the fruit trees trained up the wall facing a mature rose border on the other side of the gravel path. The castle's southern front, which was extended in the 17th, 18th and early 20th centuries, is enhanced by a wisteria and overlooks a large enclosed knot garden of box, bay and yew mixed with white roses, peonies and lavender. Beyond is an immaculate formal lawn surrounded by yew topiaries and specimen trees, leading to a developing perennial wildflower meadow with a gentle path leading down through an orchard. To the north, an upper garden created since 2018, centred on a pepper pot doocot, provides an area for quiet contemplation with further yew topiary, an extended lavender border, white planting, a fishpond and the family's collection of chickens. Beyond the formal gardens the grounds merge into mature woods with romantic walks along the Denton Burn, a range of specimen trees and some lovely naturalistic planting.

Open: Saturday 21 June, 2pm - 5pm, admission £6.00, children free. The castle, which is a private home, is not open to the public and the garden is only open on the advertised date. No dogs, please.

Directions: Turn off A932 at signpost to *Pitmuies Garden*. Go over two stone bridges and follow road uphill past small hamlet. Take first road on left. At sharp right-hand bend take private drive straight ahead (beside cream lodge).

Opening for: Guthrie Heritage SCIO

Angus, Dundee & Kincardineshire South

23 GLENBERVIE HOUSE
Drumlithie, Stonehaven AB39 3YA
Mr and Mrs A Macphie

The nucleus of the large garden at Glenbervie is the traditional Victorian walled garden. It slopes south east for 1½ acres, divided essentially into four sections, including vegetables punctuated by annuals, roses and lawn, surrounded by fruit and perennials. At the top of the garden is an extensive heated greenhouse, well worth exploring. A lovely woodland garden can be found in other parts of the garden, also around the house, lawns with herbaceous and shrub borders.

Open: Sunday 3 August, 2pm - 5pm, admission £6.00, children free. Teas, plant and bakery stalls. Please note some steep pathways and tree roots can make walking difficult in places. Gravel pathways are not accessible for electric wheelchairs. Please no dogs.

Directions: Drumlithie one mile. Garden is 1½ miles off the A90.

Opening for: Scotland's Charity Air Ambulance

Gardyne Castle

Angus, Dundee & Kincardineshire South

24 GLENSAUGH
Glensaugh Lodge, Fettercairn, Laurencekirk AB30 1HB
Donald and Sue Barrie

The twenty-year development of the hillside garden at Glensaugh, with its fine outlook over the Howe of the Mearns, continues as lawn evolves into wildflower meadow and borders are replanted. Trees, species rhododendrons and other shrubs provide year-round interest while herbaceous planting extends colour into the autumn. Yew hedges and well-placed natural stone give structure in the lower garden where a productive kitchen garden and polytunnel exist alongside informal borders and a sunken pond.

Open: Sunday 17 August, 1:30pm - 4:30pm, admission £6.00, children free. No teas, but you are welcome to bring a picnic. The main parking area is 500yds from the garden but those less able to walk can park in the field beside the garden.

Directions: Three miles north of Fettercairn on the B974, turn right at the Clatterin Brig and follow minor road signed *Glensaugh* for ½ mile, then turn right into the Glensaugh farm steading (parking) and follow beech avenue from the steading to Glensaugh Lodge.

Opening for: *Kincardine And Deeside Befriending*

25 HOSPITALFIELD GARDENS
Hospitalfield House, Westway, Arbroath DD11 2NH
Hospitalfield Trust
E: info@hospitalfield.org.uk
W: www.hospitalfield.org.uk

In 2021 the walled garden at Hospitalfield was comprehensively redeveloped to a design by celebrated garden designer and plantsman, Nigel Dunnett. The new garden tells the 800-year horticultural story of this extraordinary site from its monastic origins in the 13th century through to the Victorian passion for ferns. You will be able to explore the garden in its first few years after planting as it continues to grow into its inspirational design; full of diverse textures and striking colours. The house that overlooks the garden was remodelled in the 19th century by Elizabeth Allan-Fraser and her husband, the artist Patrick Allan-Fraser, who designed their home in the Arts and Crafts style. Their fernery, which sits within the walled garden, has been restored and re-planted with ferns from all over the world and will also be open for visitors. Hospitalfield celebrated the opening of its Physic Garden in June of 2023, a project which introduced over 30 new medicinal plants to the garden along with an illustrated guided walk exploring Hospitalfield's herbal history and the garden's themes. For more information about Hospitalfield and its international cultural programme rooted in contemporary visual arts, please visit the website.

Open: Saturday 31 May, 11am - 4pm, admission £6.00, children free. Admission is for the walled garden and fernery and Angus residents will receive an annual pass with their admission. The new glasshouse café offers excellent refreshments.

Directions: Comprehensive directions can be found on the website at hospitalfield.org.uk/visit/location/.

Opening for: *Donation to SGS Beneficiaries*

Angus, Dundee & Kincardineshire South

26 INCHMILL COTTAGE
Glenprosen, near Kirriemuir DD8 4SA
Iain Nelson
T: 01575 540452

This is a long, sloping and terraced garden at over 800 feet in the Braes of Angus, developed to be a garden for all seasons. Half is dominated by bulbs, rhododendrons, azaleas, primulas, meconopsis and clematis. The other half is mainly later summer bulbs, herbaceous plants and roses. There is also a rockery/scree.

Open: Monday 21 April, Thursday 8 May, Thursday 22 May, Thursday 12 June, Thursday 10 July, Thursday 14 August & Thursday 4 September, 2pm - 5pm, admission £5.00, children free.

Directions: Please DO NOT use SatNav. From Kirriemuir take the B955 (signposted *The Glens*) to Dykehead (about five miles). From there follow the *Prosen* sign for about five miles. Inchmill is the white-fronted cottage beside the phone box in the village. There is car parking beside the church (50 yards away) and by the village hall opposite.

Opening for: The Archie Foundation

27 KINBLETHMONT HOUSE
by Arbroath, Angus DD11 4RW
The Ramsay family
E: info@kinblethmont.com
W: www.kinblethmont.com, www.facebook.com/kinblethmont

Kinblethmont is an historic estate which, with its advantageous elevated position, has been settled since Pictish times. In the centre is the Victorian mansion house surrounded by beautiful policy woodlands where specimen trees and snowdrops abound. Paths take you through the woods past the old pet cemetery and to the walled garden with children's play area. A longer walk will take you up around the solar park with spectacular views over to the Angus hills and the North Sea.

Open: Saturday/Sunday, 22/23 February, 10am - 4pm for Snowdrops and Winter Walks, admission £6.00, children free. The estate has some lovely holiday cottages for anyone wanting to make a weekend of it. House tours will also be available, please see website or Facebook for details.

Directions: From Forfar/Brechin, take the A933 towards Arbroath, turn left to Friockheim. Drive through Friockheim and continue along the road, past the crematorium, until you reach a T-junction. Turn right and continue along this road, past a crossroads, until you enter Kinblethmont estate on your left.

Opening for: Friockhub

Angus, Dundee & Kincardineshire South

28   KINNORDY WALLED GARDEN
Kinnordy House, Kirriemuir, Angus DD8 5ER
Mary Gifford
W: Kinnordy.com

Kinnordy Walled Garden is an oblique shape of about two acres with a listed observatory and potting shed. It has been developed in the last ten years from a site for rearing pheasants to an attractive garden including one of the Scottish tea gardens, a wild area where a pair of oyster catchers lay eggs each year, and a vegetable area.

The opening includes a visit to The Sustainable Kirriemuir Field which is a short walk away. This project, started in 2024, is developing an area to grow food for the community. Sustainable Kirriemuir is an environmental charity with a vision for Kirriemuir to be a sustainable, net-zero community where people and nature flourish.

Open: Saturday 19 July, 2pm - 5pm, admission £5.00, children free.

Directions: At the Kirriemuir north west junction of the B995 and the B956 take the turn away from Kirriemuir towards Cortachy, then take the first left onto the estate, and continue to the Estate Office.

Opening for: Sustainable Kirriemuir

Kinnordy Walled Garden

29   LAWTON HOUSE
Inverkeilor, by Arbroath DD11 4RU
Cate and Simon Dessain

Woodland garden of beech trees, carpeted with snowdrops, aconites and crocuses in spring, set around a 1755 house. There is also a walled garden planted with fruit trees and vegetables. The property was owned for many years by Elizabeth and Patrick Allan-Fraser who remodelled Hospitalfield House in Arbroath.

Open: from Thursday to Sunday, 6 - 9 March, 10am - 5pm for Snowdrops and Winter Walks, admission £5.00, children free.

Directions: Take the B965 between Inverkeilor and Friockheim, turn right at the sign for *Angus Chain Saws*. Drive approximately 200 metres, then take the first right.

Opening for: HopeFull (SCIO)

Angus, Dundee & Kincardineshire South

30 MILTON OF FINAVON HOUSE
Forfar DD8 3PY
E: enquiries@miltonoffinavonhouse.co.uk
W: miltonoffinavonhouse.co.uk

Milton of Finavon House is a Grade C listed property in 1.8 acres of gardens. In parts, the house dates from circa 1500. The gardens are currently being restored and replanted. There is a small meadow orchard with fruit trees and mown walkways, a formal semi-walled garden with more restoration and new planting, with further woodland walks and a kitchen garden with new and old restoration planting. We hope that you will enjoy seeing the garden evolve over the coming years.

Open: Saturday 17 May, 2pm - 5pm. Also open Saturday 26 July, 2pm - 5pm. Admission £5.00, children free. There will be a garden search for children.

Directions: 2 minutes off the A90, north of Forfar and south of Brechin. Take the sharp turn off the A90 and then again into Milton Lane and then about 1 mile into the village. Park up and then on foot follow the signs. Parking is free in the village and is a two minute walk to the gardens. Blue Badge holders may park in the courtyard, you will be directed on arrival, so please follow the road and turn right at the T junction. A public WC is available in the courtyard. Water bowls for dogs will be available.

Opening for: All proceeds to SGS Beneficiaries

31 ORCHARD COTTAGE
Lunan Bay, Inverkeilor, Arbroath DD11 5SS
Carol Evans
T: 07485 609506

This is a cottage garden 20 years in the making. Lots of art is incorporated and plenty of seating to catch the precious sun. The garden is divided into four main areas: lawned with wall and borders; a pond area with abundant planting and greenhouse; a productive area with raised beds, fruit cage and a converted aviary; and finally a shaded garden spot to look to Red Castle. The garden is about abundance and cultivated plants sit side-by-side with wild flowers, giving colour and interest for as much of the year as possible.

Open: by arrangement 1 May - 30 September, admission £5.00, children free. Visits can be arranged for Tuesdays and Sundays between 10am and 6pm, or Thursdays 2-6 pm. Please phone 07485 609506 in advance.

Directions: From Inverkeilor on the A92 north of Arbroath, take the turn off for Lunan Bay. After 1½ miles, you come to a T junction. Ignore the farm track opposite. Take the left turn and after 200 yards approx you start to go downhill. There is a house on the left called the Bears Den. Take the first right turn as you start to go downhill. It's an unmade track with four houses listed. Orchard Cottage is the first on the left with wooden gates.

Opening for: LBCP: Lunan Bay Communities Partnership

Angus, Dundee & Kincardineshire South

32 **PITMUIES GARDENS**
House of Pitmuies, Guthrie, by Forfar DD8 2SN
Jeanette and Ruaraidh Ogilvie
T: 01241 828245 E: ogilvie@pitmuies.com
W: www.pitmuies.com

Two renowned, semi-formal walled gardens adjoin an 18th-century house and steading, sheltering long borders of herbaceous perennials, superb old-fashioned delphiniums and roses, together with pavings rich with violas and dianthus. An extensive and diverse collection of plants, interesting kitchen garden, spacious lawns, and river, lochside and woodland walks beneath fine trees. A wide variety of shrubs with good autumn colour and a picturesque turreted doocot and a 'Gothick' wash house. Myriad spring bulbs include carpets of crocus following massed snowdrops and daffodils.

Open: 1 April - 30 September, 10am - 5pm, admission £5.00, children free.

Directions: From Forfar take the A932 east for seven miles and gardens are signposted on the right. From Brechin take the A933 south to Friockheim and turn right onto the A932. The gardens are signposted on the left after 1½ miles.

Opening for: Donation to SGS Beneficiaries

33 **ST BEDES AND ASHLUDIE WILDFLOWER GARDEN**
Monifieth DD5 4RD
Neil Burford (M: 07791851845/E: neil.burford@newcastle.ac.uk) and Scott & Barbara Lindsay (M: 07874058963/E: wl011b2275@btinternet.com)

Ashludie Wildflower Garden (NEW) 10 Margaret Lindsay Place, Monifieth DD5 4RD (Scott and Barbara Lindsay): Striking, small garden consisting predominantly of native wildflowers. Dedicated to attracting wildlife and helping to replace our lost meadows. A homemade bee hotel, a small pond and about 40 types of wildflower aim to attract bees, butterflies, birds and other creatures. Nectar and pollen-rich 'classic' wildflowers include greater knapweed, viper's bugloss, Valerian and musk mallow. The small front garden has plants to provide pollen for our earlier emerging pollinators. Plant stall includes garden-collected seed.
St Bedes Garden (NEW) 6 Ferry Road, Monifieth DD5 4NT (Neil Burford): St Bedes is a small urban plant lovers' garden on a steep slope, enclosed by stone walls. Its design reflects the distant monastic history of the site and it integrates an ecology of native and non-native drought-tolerant trees, grasses and perennials suited to the dry sandy soil of its coastal location. Over the last 17 years, the current owners have extensively landscaped the site with a series of terraces and rooms connected by a winding central path and stairs. Inspired by prairie style planting and using a matrix ecology, the garden has year-round colour, texture and formal interest, with many unusual and rare bulbs, herbaceous perennials and trees. An *Arbutus menzeii* is a central focus of the main space.

Open: Saturday/Sunday, 5/6 July, 11am - 4pm, admission £8.00, children free. Both gardens are easily accessible from the centre of Monifieth where there is adequate public parking and a railway station. National Cycle Route 1 passes through Monifieth between Dundee and Arbroath. The gardens are a 15 minute walk between each other. Ticket price includes entry to both gardens.

Angus, Dundee & Kincardineshire South

Directions: Ashludie Wildlife Garden: Bus 73 from Arbroath or Dundee to Monifieth Tesco. Walk up North Union Street and then Victoria Street to garden – about 15 minutes. Or bus 73A to Ashludie Hospital – about 2 minutes walk to garden. Or buses X7 and 39 to Dobbies – about 15 minutes walk to garden. **St Bedes Garden:** Coming from Dundee, the house is 50 yards before the pedestrian crossing at the junction of Albert Street, 500 yards west of Monifieth centre on the north side of Ferry Road. Buses 73, 73A from Dundee and Carnoustie stop near the house.

Opening for: Chest Heart & Stroke Scotland & Scottish Mountain Rescue

34 THE DOOCOT
Kinloch, Meigle, Blairgowrie PH12 8QX
Liz and George McLaren

The house and garden sit in a two-acre site with views to the Sidlaws and Grampians. The house is a converted 18th century steading with a large doo'cot tower, completed in 2009. Garden development began in 2013 with several flowering cherries and two small herbaceous beds, and expanded in 2014 with the creation of a parterre rose garden, and the addition of shrub, herbaceous beds and areas of heather and hard planting including rhododendrons, azaleas and a variety of trees. In 2019 the garden was further developed to create seated areas and themed beds. A wildlife pond was added in 2022 and a vegetable garden is being gradually developed.

Open: Sunday 29 June, 1pm - 5pm, admission £6.00, children free.

Directions: Approximately two miles west of Meigle on the A94 (towards Coupar Angus). Just before the hamlet of Longleys there is a turning to the right with a small lodge with red eaves on the roadside. Turn up that tarmac road and The Doocot is 400 metres on the right.

Opening for: Strathmore Parish Church of Scotland: Glamis Church Guild

35 WESTGATE
12 Glamis Drive, Dundee DD2 1QL
John and Frances Dent

This established garden, with many mature trees, occupies a south-facing site overlooking the River Tay and Fife hills. The tennis court lawn is surrounded by herbaceous plants and shrubs. A short woodland walk reveals a miniature knot garden, a bower and other surprise features. There are also rose beds and two oriental-themed water gardens. At the summer opening there will be a chance to relax with tea, cake and music . In October, all the areas will be displaying their autumn colours and, as darkness falls, they will be further enlivened by a variety of lighting techniques (torches recommended).

Open: Saturday 31 May & Sunday 1 June, 2pm - 5pm, admission £6.00, children free. Also open Saturday/Sunday, 11/12 October, 3pm - 7:30pm, admission by donation. Children's activities. No dogs, please.

Directions: Buses 5, 22 or 73 from Dundee city centre. Please note there is no roadside parking on Glamis Drive. Limited disabled parking is available at the house.

Opening for: Maggie Keswick Jencks Cancer Caring Centres Trust (Dundee) (Saturday 31 May & Sunday 1 June) & Dr Graham's Homes Kalimpong (UK) (Saturday/Sunday, 11/12 October)

Argyll & Lochaber

Sponsored by

⬡ RATHBONES

Invermoriston
Loch Cluanie
Loch Ness
Fort Augustus
Soay
Canna
Ardvasar
Sound of Canna
A87
A887
A87
A82
Invergarry
Rùm
Sound of Sleat
A87
Loch Lochy
Kinloch Laggan
Mallaig
Loch Quoich
11
Sound of Rùm
Arisaig
Loch Morar
Loch Arkaig
A86
Muck
Eigg
Sound of Arisaig
A830
Glenfinnan
Spean Bridge
Loch Eil
Loch Treig
Loch Ericht
INNER
HEBRIDES
Acharacle
Loch Shiel
Fort William/
An Gearasdan
Ben Nevis
1344m
Kinloch Laggan
Coll
Loch Sunart
Loch Leven
Kinlochleven
Arinagour
Tobermory
Sound of Mull
Loch Linnhe
Ballachulish
A82
Loch Rannoch
Tiree
Scarinish
Loch Tuath
10
Lochaline
16 27
Loch Etive
L Lyon
Treshnish
Isles
Ulva
Salen
29
Lismore
A828
Killin
ISLE OF
MULL
Loch na Keal
Craignure
18
2 6 5
Taynuilt
Tyndrum
A85
Killin
21
Kerrera
Oban
19
4
Dalmally
A85
Iona
L Scridain
Lochbuie
Firth of Lorn
Kilninver
20 14
Loch Awe
Crianlarich
Lochearnhead
Fionnphort
Ross of Mull
3
Seil
8
25
Melfort
22
9 7
Loch Katrine
Garvellachs
Luing
24
Inveraray
Tarbet
Aberfoyle
Scarba
Baluachraig
Furnace
Strachur
Loch Lomond
Colonsay
Scalasaig
17
Lochgilphead
28
Drymen
Oronsay
Ardlussa
JURA
1
15
Helensburgh
A811
23
Dunoon
Greenock
A82
Milngavie
Port
Askaig
Tighnabruaich
Collintraive
Port Glasgow
A8
M8
Glasgow
Bowmore
Tarbert
13
Rothesay
12
Largs
A78
A737
Paisley
ISLAY
Kennacraig
Isle
of Bute
M77
Portnahaven
Laggan Bay
Port
Ellen
Claonaig
Lochranza
Dalry
Port
Ellen
Isle of Gigha
A83
Kilbrannan Sound
ISLE
OF
ARRAN
Brodick
Irvine
A71
Galston
Kilmarnock
Mull of
Oa
A78 A77
Mauchline
Troon
A76
Kintyre
Campbeltown
Whiting
Bay
Ayr
A70
Cumnock
26
Dunure
Mull of
Kintyre
Sanda
Maybole
A77
Dalmellington
Ailsa
Craig
Girvan
Carsphairn

Argyll & Lochaber

OUR VOLUNTEER ORGANISERS

District Organiser:	Minette Struthers	Camasmaddy, Ardmaddy, by Oban PA34 4QY info@scotlandsgardens.org
Area Organisers:	Grace Bergius	Craignish House, Ardfern, by Lochgilphead PA31 8QN
	Shian Carlow	Balliemore, Loch Striven, Dunoon PA23 8RH
	Mary Lindsay	Dal an Eas, Kilmore, Oban PA34 4XU
	Frances Hardie	Rudha Loisgte, Pier Road, Tarbert, PA29 6UG
	Claire Davies	Tigh na Claddach, Cullipool, Oban PA34 4TX
Media Volunteer:	Victoria Winters	Victoria@barr-minard.com
District Photographer:	Maurice Wilkins	Dunrobian, Laurel Road, Oban PA34 5EA
Treasurer:	Shelagh Cannon	Kames Bay, Kilmelford, By Oban PA34 4XA

GARDENS OPEN ON A SPECIFIC DATE

Ardchattan Manse, Ardchattan, Oban, Argyll	Sunday, 9 February
Kames Bay, Kilmelford	Saturday/Sunday, 3/4 May
4 Port Ann, Lochgilphead, Argyll	Saturday/Sunday/Monday, 3/4/5 May
Baravalla Garden, by West Loch Tarbert, Argyll	Thursday, 8 May
Cruachan Lodge, North Connel, Oban	Saturday/Sunday, 17/18 May
Kilchoan Gardens, Kilmelford	Saturday/Sunday, 17/18 May
Inveryne Woodland Garden, Kilfinan, Tighnabruaich	Saturday/Sunday, 24/25 May
4 Port Ann, Lochgilphead, Argyll	Monday/Tuesday, 26/27 May
Ardverikie with Aberarder, Kinloch Laggan, Newtonmore	Sunday, 1 June
Ilha de Deus, Tiroran, Isle of Mull	Sunday, 8 June
Ardchattan Priory, North Connel	Sunday 8 June
Ilha de Deus, Tiroran, Isle of Mull	Sunday, 6 July
Kilchoan Gardens, Kilmelford	Saturday/Sunday, 12/13 July
4 Port Ann, Lochgilphead, Argyll	Saturday/Sunday/Monday, 2/3/4 August
Ilha de Deus, Tiroran, Isle of Mull	Sunday, 3 August
Cruachan Lodge, North Connel, Oban	Saturday/Sunday, 20/21 September
Benmore Botanic Garden, Benmore, Dunoon	Sunday, 28 September

GARDENS OPEN REGULARLY

Angus's Garden, Barguillean, Taynuilt	1 January - 31 December
Ardmaddy Castle, by Oban	1 January - 31 December
Ardkinglas Woodland Garden, Cairndow	1 January - 31 December
Ardtornish, by Lochaline, Morvern	1 January - 31 December
Achnacloich, Connel, Oban	1 January - 31 December (Saturdays only)
Kinlochlaich Walled Garden, Appin	3 March - 31 October

Argyll & Lochaber

GARDENS OPEN REGULARLY – CONTINUED

Knock Newhouse, Lochgair	20 March - 30 September
Inveraray Castle Gardens, Inveraray	27 March - 29 September & 2 October - 27 October
Crinan Hotel Garden, Crinan	29 March - 31 October
An Cala, Ellenabeich, Isle of Seil	1 April - 31 October
Ardchattan Priory, North Connel	2 April - 29 October (Wednesdays only)
Ascog Hall Garden and Fernery, Ascog, Isle of Bute	1 May - 31 July (Fridays, Saturdays, Sundays only)
The Secret Garden Lismore	1 May 1 September (Wednesdays and Saturdays)

GARDENS OPEN BY ARRANGEMENT

Kilchoan Gardens, Kilmelford	1 January - 31 December
Ardchattan Manse, Ardchattan, Oban, Argyll	9 February (pre-booking requested)
Berandhu, Appin, Argyll	1 April - 31 October
Barochreal, Kilninver, Oban, Argyll	1 May - 30 September
Dal an Eas, Kilmore, Oban	1 May - 30 September
The Secret Garden, Isle of Lismore, Oban, Argyll	1 May - 1 September
Kildalloig, Campbeltown	1 May - 31 October
Ardno, Cairndow	1 May - 30 September
Eas Mhor, Cnoc-a-Challtuinn, Clachan Seil, Oban	1 May - 31 October
Ilha de Deus, Tiroran, Isle of Mull	1 June - 31 August
Baravalla Garden, by West Loch Tarbert, Argyll	(Groups of 15 or more by arrangement)
Kinlochlaich Walled Garden, Appin	Winter by arrangement
4 Port Ann, Lochgilphead, Argyll	Small groups welcome

Angus's Garden, Barguillean

Argyll & Lochaber

1 4 PORT ANN
Lochgilphead, Argyll PA31 8SE
Chris and Anne Buckland
E: chrisbuckland3@hotmail.com

This half-acre tiered garden is situated in the former forestry village of Port Ann, enjoying a sheltered position between Loch Fyne and a pine forest. It is a fine example of what can be achieved in a relatively small space. Created over the last 15 years by Anne and Chris. Since Chris has become a wheelchair user part of the top level of the garden has been made accessible with a viewing platform to the garden and loch beyond. The garden has a water feature, a pond teeming with newts and dragonflies, a labyrinth designed by artist Margaret Ker, many neuks and crannies creatively filled with plants and small trees, including rhododendrons, azaleas, hawthorn, fig, maple and acers, and ends in a walk through a wilder area of hazels on the burn side where the ground is smothered in bluebells in May.

Open: Saturday/Sunday/Monday, 3/4/5 May, Monday/Tuesday, 26/27 May & Saturday/Sunday/Monday, 2/3/4 August, 2pm - 5pm, admission £4.00, children free. There is a bus to Port Ann, stop at entrance to village. Small groups are welcome by appointment. Please note refreshments will be available.

Directions: Heading north on A83 from Inveraray, before you reach Lochgilphead, Port Ann is signposted on the right. Please park in central square. Only the top garden deck is accessible by wheelchair.

Opening for: MND Scotland

2 ACHNACLOICH
Connel, Oban PA37 1PR
Mr T M Nelson
T: 01631 710223 or Gardener David Field 07929 336217
E: davefield6@hotmail.co.uk and cassandhu@gmail.com

The 20-acre woodland garden overlooking Loch Etive has been planted over the last century with a wide range of trees and shrubs from Asia, China, Japan, North America, Chile and New Zealand. Many have grown to considerable size. The light woodland canopy consists of native oaks and a number of magnificent 150-year-old Scots pines and European larch. Amongst these are open glades, carpeted with bluebells and numerous other bulbs. Two ponds and streams are planted with primulas, iris species, lysichitum and astilbes. The woodland contains innumerable species of rhododendron and azalea, of which the triflorums and yunnanense are outstanding. Amongst these are species of *acer, betula, camellia, cercidiphyllum, cornus, crinodendron, drimys, embothrium, enkianthus, eucryphia, hoheria, magnolia, malus, nothofagus, pieris, sorbus, stewartia, telopea* and *viburnum*. Beside the house is a giant Douglas fir from Douglas' original introduction. One of the first Dawyck beeches stands beside the drive. Fine autumn colours.

Open: 1 January - 31 December (Saturday only), 10am - 4pm, admission £6.00, children free.

Directions: On the A85 two miles east of Connel. The car park is at the bottom of the drive.

Opening for: Macmillan Cancer Support

Argyll & Lochaber

3 **AN CALA**
Ellenabeich, Isle of Seil PA34 4RF
Mrs Sheila Downie
W: www.gardens-of-argyll.co.uk/view-details.php?id=447

A wonderful example of a 1930s designed garden, An Cala sits snugly in its horseshoe shelter of surrounding cliffs. A spectacular and very pretty garden with streams, waterfall, ponds, many herbaceous plants as well as azaleas, rhododendrons and cherry trees in spring. Archive material of Thomas Mawson's design was found recently and is available to visitors.

Open: 1 April - 31 October, 10am - 6pm, admission £6.00, children free.

Directions: Proceed south from Oban on Campbeltown Road for eight miles, turn right at the *Easdale* sign, a further eight miles on the B844; the garden is between the school and the village. Bus Oban – Easdale.

Opening for: *Cancer Research UK & Scotland's Charity Air Ambulance*

An Cala

Argyll & Lochaber

4 ANGUS'S GARDEN, BARGUILLEAN
Taynuilt PA35 1HY
The Josephine Marshall Trust
T: 01866 822333 E: info@barguillean.co.uk
W: www.barguillean.co.uk

Created in 1957 as a memorial garden by Betty Macdonald of Barguillean for her son Angus, this picturesque nine-acre woodland garden is set around the tranquil shores of Loch Angus in historic Glen Lonan. Whilst famous for its extensive collection of hybrid rhododendrons and azaleas, this glorious garden cleverly retains the natural atmosphere of the landscape. Visitors can enjoy an informal network of paths, lined with spring flowering shrubs and bulbs, through native woodland and by shoreland whilst surrounded by the magnificent views of Ben Cruachan and the mountains of Glen Etive. This unspoilt natural setting attracts a wide range of wildlife, and the eleven-acre loch is home to swans and ducks. On the north-west side of the garden overlooking the loch stands Betty's bell paying tribute to her 40 years of work creating this magical garden. The garden reaches its full glory between April and the end of June but is a place of special tranquillity and charm at all times of the year. Three marked, circular walks from the car park taking between 30 minutes and 1.5 hours. Not suitable for wheelchairs.

Open: 1 January - 31 December, 9am - dusk, admission £5.00, children under 16 free. Coach tours welcome by appointment.

Directions: Off A85 Crianlarich/Oban road at Taynuilt, road marked *Glen Lonan*, three miles up a single track road, turn right at the sign opposite Barguillean Farm.

Opening for: SSAFA Forces Help

5 ARDCHATTAN MANSE
Ardchattan, Oban, PA37 1RG
Mr and Mrs Colin Campbell-Preston
T: 07745 345680 E: r.campbellpreston@btinternet.com
W: Instagram:@ardchattan_manse

Ardchattan Manse is situated on the south facing shores of Loch Etive and has a mild climate compared to many plant collections further inland. Snowdrops open early here, often in the first week of February. The snowdrop collection has been established over several years and has been moved to the garden at Ardchattan Manse relatively recently where it is now building up numbers. There is information on different species and cultivars and the owners will accompany the groups round the collection.

Open: Open by arrangement on Sunday 9 February, 11am - dusk. Please book – ring 07745 345680. Admission £5.00, children free.

Directions: From Connel, follow the signs to Ardchattan Priory on the B845. Ardchattan Manse is the next house on the right after Ardchattan Priory.
What3words address: www.w3w.co/sponge.rotations.diet

Opening for: TAC: (a community centre nearby)

Argyll & Lochaber

6 ARDCHATTAN PRIORY

North Connel PA37 1RQ
Mrs Sarah Troughton
E: admin@ardchattan.co.uk
W: www.ardchattan.co.uk

Overlooking Loch Etive, Ardchattan Priory Garden has a mature rockery and extensive herbaceous and rose borders to the front of the house. On either side of the drive, shrub borders, numerous roses and ornamental trees, together with bulbs, give colour throughout the season. The Priory, founded in 1230, is now a private house. The ruins of the chapel and graveyard are in the care of *Historic Environment Scotland* and open with the garden.

Open: Open 1 April – 31 October (Wednesdays only) 9.30am - 5.30pm. Garden Fete Sunday 8th June 12 – 4pm (Teas available on 8th June only). Admission £6 each day. Children under 16 free.

Directions: Oban 10 miles. From north, turn left off the A828 at Barcaldine onto the B845 for six miles. From east or from Oban on the A85, cross Connel Bridge and turn first right, proceed east on Bonawe Road.

Opening for: *Donation to SGS Beneficiaries*

7 ARDKINGLAS WOODLAND GARDEN

Cairndow PA26 8BG
Ardkinglas Estate
T: 01499 600261
W: www.ardkinglas.com

In a peaceful setting overlooking Loch Fyne, the garden contains one of the finest collections of rhododendrons and conifers in Britain. This includes the mightiest conifer in Europe – a silver fir – as well as many other Champion Trees. There is a gazebo with a unique scriptorium based around a collection of literary quotes. For younger visitors, the garden features a Fairy Trail, Gruffalo Trail and Snakey Slide. It is a *VisitScotland* 3-star garden.
Champion Trees: The mightiest conifer in Europe and others..

Open: 1 January - 31 December, dawn – dusk, admission £5.00. Children over three, £2.50. Tickets available online at www.ardkinglas.com or pay on arrival. All admission fees go to helping maintain and preserve the garden, as well as a donation to SGS charities.

Directions: Entrance through Cairndow village off the A83 Loch Lomond/Inveraray road.

Opening for: *Donation to SGS Beneficiaries*

Argyll & Lochaber

8 **ARDMADDY CASTLE**
by Oban PA34 4QY
Mr and Mrs Archie Struthers
T: 01852 300353 E: minette@ardmaddy.com
W: www.ardmaddy.com

The gardens lie in a truly spectacular setting in the centre of a horseshoe bay, sheltered by mixed mature wooded hills and the castle atop a volcanic mound. The 18th-century walled garden has been much restored and improved over the last 50 years, hence its well-earned reputation as a plantsman's garden for all seasons. In addition to the magnificent rhododendron collection, it is now also home to many rare and unusual shrubs and plants. These all sit alongside productive fruit and vegetable beds, all given formal structure by dwarf box hedges. The walled garden is flanked by shrub lined avenues bordering the burn, leading to woodland walks and a water garden. Don't miss the 60 foot *Hydrangea petiolaris* on Lady Murray's Walk and the towering stand of gunnera next to the ponds. The latest additions in an always-evolving garden are new medicinal herb beds and the beginnings of a new arboretum in the old orchard area.

Open: 1 January - 31 December, 9am - 6pm, admission £6.00, children free. Holiday cottages available sleeping 4 - 12. Find out more at www.ardmaddy.com

Directions: Take the A816 south of Oban for eight miles. Turn right onto the B844 to Seil Island/Easdale. Four miles on, turn left to Ardmaddy (signposted) and follow for a further two miles.

Opening for: Donation to SGS Beneficiaries

Ardmaddy Castle

Argyll & Lochaber

9   **ARDNO**
Cairndow PA26 8BE
Denzil How
T: Rob Backhouse, Gardener 01499 302304 E: denzil.how@btconnect.com

From the rich, varied landscape, a romantic garden has been created from scratch over the past 25 years. Visitors can stroll in the walled garden near the house, or explore the old oak wood planted with many interesting shrubs. These are growing up fast, adding shape and colour. Across the burn is the gorge and a wonderful waterfall. The woodland garden ends in the meadow, planted with irises and a collection of unusual trees, which continues down to the beach and a magnificent huge rock. My garden is a place to be peaceful in. Come and enjoy, but be prepared as some of the paths are steep with lots of steps and are unfortunately not suitable for wheelchairs.

Open: by arrangement 1 May - 30 September, admission £6.00, children free. Small groups of up to six people by application to the Gardener, Robert Backhouse, Ardno Cottage T: 01499 302304 from May – September. The Rediweld Foundation supports charities in London and the west coast of Scotland that are primarily but not exclusively involved with children's educational activities.

Directions: Situated at the top end of Loch Fyne between Cairndow and St Catherines, off the A815.

Opening for: Rediweld Foundation

10   **ARDTORNISH**
by Lochaline, Morvern PA80 5UZ
Mrs John Raven
W: www.ardtornish.co.uk

Ardtornish Estate spreads out around Loch Aline, a huge, wooded, U-shaped bay, a natural haven. Wonderful gardens of interesting mature conifers, rhododendrons, deciduous trees, shrubs and herbaceous plantings, set amid magnificent scenery. Much of the garden is covered by native birch, alongside extensive planting of exotic species, under mature groups of larch, firs and pine, whose strong form and colour complement the pink sandstone towers and gables of Ardtornish House.

Open: 1 January - 31 December, 10am - 6pm, admission £5.00, children free. Groups must be pre-booked.

Directions: Three miles from Lochaline along the A884.

Opening for: Donation to SGS Beneficiaries

Argyll & Lochaber

11 ARDVERIKIE WITH ABERARDER

Kinloch Laggan, Newtonmore PH20 1BX
The Fielden family, Mrs P Laing and Mrs E T Smyth-Osbourne
T: 01528 544300 E: amanda@ardverikie.com

Ardverikie

Kinloch Laggan, Newtonmore, PH20 1BX (Mrs P Laing and Mrs E T Smyth-Osbourne):
Lovely setting on Loch Laggan with magnificent trees. Walled garden with large collection of acers, shrubs and herbaceous plants. Architecturally interesting house (not open) featured in *Monarch of the Glen* and *The Crown*.

Aberarder

Kinloch Laggan, Newtonmore, PH20 1BX (The Fielden Family):
The garden has been laid out over the last 20 years to create a mixture of spring and autumn plants and trees, including rhododendrons, azaleas and acers. The elevated view down Loch Laggan from the garden is exceptional.

Open: Sunday 1 June, 2pm - 5:30pm. Admission price £8.00 for both gardens, children free.

Directions: On the A86 between Newtonmore and Spean Bridge. **Ardverikie House** entrance is at the east end of Loch Laggan via the bridge by Gatelodge.
Aberarder Lodge entrance is about 200 metres west of the Ardverikie entrance, next to the small cottage.

Opening for: Laggan Parish Church & Highland Hospice

12 ASCOG HALL GARDEN AND FERNERY

Ascog, Isle of Bute PA20 9EU
Josceline and Jane Wheatley
T: 01700 503461 (house) 07824 393009 (Josceline)
E: janejoswheatley@gmail.com

The unique feature of this three-acre garden is its Victorian Fernery with its elaborate glazed roof, springs and ponds providing a haven for many exotic fern species, including Britain's oldest, a 1000-year-old King Fern. Surrounding the Fernery are newly-planted garden rooms featuring Australasian, Asian and South American species set within its original landscaping. While in many ways a young garden set in mature surroundings, with renovation works still underway, the well-labelled, exotic plantings carry on the curiosity of its founders in the tremendous diversity of plants.

Open: 1 May - 31 July, 10am - 5pm (Fridays, Saturdays, Sundays only), admission £5.00, children free. Restricted mobility parking at the top of the drive (close to the house).

Directions: Three miles south of Rothesay on the A844. Close to the picturesque Ascog Bay. There is a bus every half hour Rothesay – Kilchattan.

Opening for: All proceeds to SGS Beneficiaries

Argyll & Lochaber

13 BARAVALLA GARDEN
by West Loch Tarbert, Argyll PA29 6YE
Baravalla Garden Partnership – Matt Heasman, Director
T: 07793604609 E: mtheasman@outlook.com
W: rscg.org.uk

This wild garden of 26 acres is carved out of typical Argyll woodland, with mature oak, beech, hazel and alder that run down to the shores of the West Loch some seven miles from Tarbert. The 'Two Peters', Sir Peter Hutchison Bt. CBE FRSE and Peter Cox MBE, both botanical travellers, were looking for an area to plant the more tender plants from their colder east coast gardens. They found the site here with the help of the Mackie Campbell Family and some 50 years ago started to create a garden with collections of plants from all over the world, rhododendrons, magnolias, azaleas, camellias, tender shrubs and so much more. The garden now is mature, managed and maintained by the Rhododendron Species Conservation Group. This garden is very rarely open. This is a truly wild garden and stout footwear and clothing for protection against the Argyll weather are recommended.

Open: Thursday 8 May, 10am - 7pm, admission £6.00, children free. Teas on site and picnic tables available if you want to bring a picnic lunch. Groups of 15 or more by arrangement. Plant stall with plants from the garden.

Directions: From Tarbert Village, through the village take the B8024 past the golf course, turn left on the Kilberry road for about seven miles. SGS signs will direct you to a car park just through the gate on the right-hand side. Please do not attempt to come down the forest track but follow the signs and walk down the track to the garden. We will provide guided tours at regular intervals.

Opening for: Rhododendron Species Conservation Group

14 BAROCHREAL
Kilninver, Oban, Argyll PA34 4UT
Nigel and Antoinette Mitchell
T: 01852 316151 E: antoinettemitchell1946@gmail.com
W: www.barochreal.co.uk

The garden was started in 2006. Fencing and stone walling define it from the rest of Barochreal land. Every year an area has been added, resulting in the gardens you will see today. There are rhododendron banks, a water feature, waterfalls and burns, a pond, a walled rose garden, active beehives (now housed in a purpose-built bee shelter built in 2021), tiered areas, a greenhouse and wild garden across the burn. Maintained walking tracks in the fields lead to viewpoints. Biodiversity studies revealed that rare butterflies inhabit the small glen by the waterfall. There are forty different species of moths including rare micro moths and over seventy species of wildflowers in the fields, including three types of wild orchid. There is an abundance of wildlife including red squirrels, pine martens and a wide range of birds can be seen. This garden is a haven of tranquillity, as seen in episode 9 of 2022 *Beechgrove Garden*.

Open: by arrangement 1 May - 30 September, admission £5.00, children free. Visiting by arrangement allows the owners to personally show visitors around if they wish, and explain the history around Barochreal, a village in the 1700s before Oban existed.

Directions: Fifteen minutes south of Oban. On the main A816 Oban to Lochgilphead road just to the south of the village of Kilninver on the left-hand side of the road. Bus Oban – Lochgilpead stops at Kilninver School, short walk after. Please disregard SatNav and use What3words address instead www.w3w.co/albums.forest.tinned

Opening for: Scottish SPCA

Argyll & Lochaber

15 BENMORE BOTANIC GARDEN

Benmore, Dunoon PA23 8QU
A Regional Garden of the Royal Botanic Garden Edinburgh
T: 01369 706261 E: benmore@rbge.org.uk
W: www.rbge.org.uk

Benmore's magnificent mountainside setting is a joy to behold. Its 120 acres boast a world-famous collection of plants from the Himalayas, China and Japan to North and South America, as well as an impressive avenue of giant redwoods, one of the finest entrances to any botanic garden. Established in 1863, these majestic giants stand over 150 feet high. Seven miles of trails throughout lead to a restored Victorian Fernery and a dramatic viewpoint at 420 feet looking out to surrounding mountains and Holy Loch. There are also traditional Bhutanese and Chilean pavilions and the magnificent Golden Gates. Keep an eye out for red squirrels and other wildlife as you explore the garden.
National Plant Collection: Abies, South American Temperate Conifers, Picea.
Champion Trees: Many rare trees and giant conifers.

Open: Sunday 28 September, 10am - 5pm, admission by donation. Admission details can be found on the garden's website.
Also see website for details of regular opening times – www.rbge.org.uk

Directions: Seven miles north of Dunoon or 22 miles south from Glen Kinglass below Rest and Be Thankful pass. On the A815. Bus service is limited.

Opening for: Donation to SGS Beneficiaries

Berandhu

16 BERANDHU

Appin, Argyll PA38 4DD
John and Fiona Landale
T: 01631 730585 M: 07900 377414 E: johnllandale@gmail.com

A sheltered one-and-a-half acre coastal garden in a scenic setting offering fabulous views over Loch Laich to Loch Linnhe, Castle Stalker and the Morvern hills beyond. Craggy limestone abounds on the undulating site, some of which forms natural rockeries. Native trees mix with introduced firs and conifers. A variety of rhododendrons and azaleas provide spring and early summer colour. A mix of limestone overlaid with peat gives an unusual mix of wild flowers. This well-tended garden also has lovely wild areas of bog garden and woodland.

Open: by arrangement 1 April - 31 October, admission £5.00, children free.

Directions: In Appin turn off the A828 Connel to Ballachulish road at Gunn's Garage signposted for *Port Appin*. After one mile when the road turns uphill, it's the first entrance on the right, half way up the hill.

Opening for: The Appin Village Hall & Alzheimer Scotland

Argyll & Lochaber

17 **CRINAN HOTEL GARDEN**
Crinan PA31 8SR
Mrs N Ryan
T: 01546 830261 E: macdonaldart.crinan@gmail.com
W: www.crinanhotel.com

A small, mature garden behind the Crinan Hotel which has been open with SGS for over 25 years. It is 100 years old and was originally the walled vegetable garden for the Hotel. In 1980 it was cleared and reinstated with azaleas, rhododendrons and herbaceous beds. Approached from a patio under ancient *griselinia* boughs, the garden catches the afternoon sun and is a peaceful escape! Also enjoy the gallery on the rooftop of the hotel and a wonderful scone by baker Paul in the coffee shop by the canal basin.

Open: 29 March - 31 October, dawn – dusk, admission by donation. Raffle of signed, limited edition fine art print by Frances Macdonald. Tickets available at the coffee shop, art gallery and hotel. Cream teas are available at the coffee shop by the canal basin at a very special garden rate. Anyone can visit any time, no need to arrange.

Directions: Take the A83 to Lochgilphead, then the A816 to Oban, then the A841 Cairnbaan to Crinan. Daily bus.

Opening for: *Alzheimer Scotland & Guide Dogs*

18 **CRUACHAN LODGE**
North Connel, Oban PA37 1RE
Mrs Karen Brown
E: healthylifebykaren1@gmail.com

A lovely garden full of exciting all year round colour and interest on the shores of Loch Etive. Many unusual plants and shrubs attracting a diversity of insects and birds. My poly tunnel keeps us supplied with organic fruit and vegetables. Red squirrels are regular visitors.

Open: Saturday/Sunday, 17/18 May & Saturday/Sunday, 20/21 September, 10am - 4pm, admission £5.00, children free. Groups welcome by appointment.

Directions: From the A85 head north over the Connel Bridge turning first right heading for Bonawe on the B845. Cruachan Lodge is 2.5 miles on the left-hand side of the road. Parking is limited so please car share where possible.

Opening for: *Alzheimer Scotland & Macmillan Cancer Support*

19 **DAL AN EAS**
Kilmore, Oban PA34 4XU
Mary Lindsay
T: 01631 770246 E: marylindsayargyll@googlemail.com

An informal organic country garden with the aim of increasing the biodiversity of native plants and insects while adding interest and colour with introduced trees, shrubs and naturalised perennials. There is a structured garden round the house and beyond there are extensive flower-filled 'meadows' with five different species of native orchid. Grass paths lead to waterfalls, vegetable plot, woodland garden, views and ancient archaeological sites.

Open: by arrangement 1 May - 30 September, admission £5.00, children free. Teas on request

Directions: From Oban take the A816 to Kilmore three-and-a-half miles south of Oban. Turn left on the road to Barran and Musdale. Keep left at the junction for Connel. Dal an Eas is approximately one mile on the left before the big hedges.

Opening for: *All proceeds to SGS Beneficiaries*

Argyll & Lochaber

20 EAS MHOR

Cnoc-a-Challtuinn, Clachan Seil, Oban PA34 4TR
Mrs Kimbra Lesley Barrett
T: 01852 300469 E: kimbra1745@gmail.com

All the usual joys of a west coast garden plus some delightful surprises! A small contemporary garden on a sloping site – the emphasis being on scent and exotic plant material. Unusual and rare blue Borinda bamboos (only recently discovered in China) and bananas. The garden is at its best in mid to late summer when shrub roses and sweet peas fill the air with scent. The delightful, sunny deck overlooks stylish white-walled ponds with cascading water blades. Recent additions include a 20-foot citrus house, Chinese pergola walk and peony border.

Open: by arrangement 1 May - 31 October, admission £6.00, children free.

Directions: After arranging a visit and agreeing a time, you will be met at the Tigh An Truish car park by the Atlantic Bridge, Isle of Seil. Or if travelling by bus, you will be met off the bus and taken to Eas Mhor. Please inform Mrs Barrett the time of your arrival. The bus stops at the bottom of Cnoc-a-Challtuinn Road.

Opening for: ABWA: Argyll & Bute Woman's Aid – support for domestic abuse – Oban Branch

21 ILHA DE DEUS

Tiroran, Isle of Mull PA69 6ET
John Innes
T: 01681705022 E: johninnes2009@hotmail.com

Half-acre garden with stunning views of Loch Scridain, the Ross of Mull, and surrounded by mountains and community forest. The current owner has been developing the garden over the last four years with a collection of rhododendrons, camellias, fruit trees, roses, ferns, peonies, lilies and a few exotics from the southern hemisphere, together with three small ponds. Dogs welcome on leads. Small selection of plants for sale. Kindly walk on gravel paths and grassy areas only.

Open: Sunday 8 June, Sunday 6 July & Sunday 3 August, noon - 5pm. Also open by arrangement 1 June - 31 August. Admission £5.00, children free. Tea and coffee available

Directions: From A849 (Craignure to Fionnphort) turn right at Kinloch junction onto B8035 'Scenic route to Salen'. The Garden is on the left after 4.5 miles immediately opposite Balevulin. The Saltire is flying when the wind is below 30mph.

Opening for: Open Doors with Brother Andrew

Argyll & Lochaber

22 **INVERARAY CASTLE GARDENS**
Inveraray PA32 8XF
The Duke and Duchess of Argyll
T: 01499 302203 E: manager@inveraray-castle.com
W: www.inveraray-castle.com

With Inveraray Castle as an imposing backdrop, the 16-acre garden has formal, meadow, park and woodland areas and is one of the most important designed landscapes in Scotland. The formal gardens consist of vivid green manicured lawn; the Flag Borders, historically laid out in the shape of the St Andrew's cross; a spectacular rose garden and herbaceous borders. A number of significant trees, including notable specimens of *Magnolia acuminata* and *Oxydendrum arboreum*, provide structure and form in this section of the garden. Colour is abundant from April until well into the autumn. The wildflower meadow is managed with native flora and fauna in mind and links the formal and informal parts of the garden. The carpet of fragrant bluebells is a feast for the senses throughout the spring, following straight on from thousands of narcissi. With views over Loch Fyne and the majesty of the West Highlands, the garden holds numerous rhododendrons, hydrangeas and other plants known to flourish in the Argyll climate.

Open: 27 March - 29 September 10am - 5pm & 2 October - 27 October 10am - 4pm, admission £10.00 (garden only), children under five free. Tearoom and shop on site. Free parking with castle and garden entrance. Pre-booking via website recommended. Tours with the Head Gardener can be arranged in advance. Only assistance dogs within the castle and garden. **Please check the website** for opening days (currently shut Tuesdays and Wednesdays) and times, further information and accessibility. www.inveraray-castle.com

Directions: Inveraray is 60 miles north of Glasgow and 45 miles from Oban. Regular bus services from Glasgow, Oban and Campbeltown. SatNav PA32 8XF.

Opening for: Donation to SGS Beneficiaries

23 **INVERYNE WOODLAND GARDEN**
Kilfinan, Tighnabruaich PA21 2ER
Mrs Jane Ferguson

In ten acres of a 100-year-old amenity wood at Inveryne Farm, on a sloping site, somewhat sheltered from Loch Fyne, the garden was begun in 1994. Scrub birches were gradually cleared, bridges installed and amongst rocky outcrops were planted rhododendrons, azaleas, dogwoods, Japanese maples, sorbuses, eucryphias, hydrangeas and more. Gunnera, primulas and rodgersias cling to the banks of the burn and ferns provide the backdrop for our growing shrubs. Storms have varied its character and created features, and it is still a work in progress. Spring and autumn colour and an interest in varied vistas and textures of bark and leaf inspire us.

Open: Saturday (1pm - 5pm)/Sunday (10am - 1pm), 24/25 May, admission £6.00, children free. Please park at the red-roofed barn. Teas on Saturday only – no teas on Sunday.

Directions: Approximately six miles north of Tighnabruaich towards Kilfinan on the B8000. After turning right at the crossroads at Millhouse, follow the road past the turning to Ardmarnock, over the little bridge at the bottom of the hill. The next track on the left is unpaved and leads to Inveryne.

Opening for: Cowal Elderly Befrienders SCIO

Argyll & Lochaber

24 KAMES BAY
Kilmelford PA34 4XA
Stuart Cannon
T: 07770 817877 E: kamesbay@talk21.com

Kames Bay garden has evolved from two acres of scrub and bracken on an exposed lochside hill into a natural, almost wild garden spread over 13 acres, which blends into the contours of the coastal landscape. A garden where visitors can wander at peace on the woodland walk, or the hillside walk edged with wild primroses and violets, or around the pond edged with hydrangeas. Relax on hidden benches to enjoy the magnificent views over Loch Melfort and the islands to the west. An enchanting garden full of vibrant colours, especially in the spring, with more than 100 varieties of azaleas and rhododendrons.

Open: Saturday/Sunday, 3/4 May, 2pm - 6pm, admission £5.00, children free. We would prefer visitors to email us.

Directions: On the A816 Oban to Lochgilphead road. Opposite Kames Bay and the fish farm. Two-and-a-half miles south of Kilmelford and two-and-a-half miles north of Arduaine.

Opening for: Netherlorn (Church of Scotland): Kilmelford Church New Annexe

25 KILCHOAN GARDENS
Kilmelford PA34 4XD
Kilchoan Estate/Luke Senior – Head Gardener
T: 07425 054 743 or 01852 200 500 E: luke@kilchoanestate.co.uk

An eclectic private garden, open on specific dates and year round by appointment. Since 2016, when Kilchoan Estate was taken into new ownership, the grounds have been developed and expanded; areas that had fallen into ruin and garden spaces reclaimed by nature have been uncovered; surviving plantings and mature trees have been enhanced; the footprint of further expansive garden and policies laid out. A cosmopolitan collection of plants and artwork are displayed throughout the grounds, featuring a Himalayan garden, walled garden, arboretum with International Conifer Conservation Program collection, formal planting within native woodlands. Planting has been designed with conservation, diversity and beauty in mind, providing year-round interest. There is plenty to see and many places to sit, rest and reflect. The chapel will be open. Teas available on SGS specific dates.

Open: Saturday/Sunday, 17/18 May & Saturday/Sunday, 12/13 July, 10am - 5pm, admission £6.00, children free. Also open by arrangement 1 January - 31 December.

Directions: 4.5 miles along the road from the A816 turn off south of Kilmelford signed Degnish. Turn left after 1.5 miles at the bridge and Melfort Holiday Village. Follow this for 3 miles and look out for signage.

Opening for: Netherlorn (Church of Scotland): Kilmelford Church New Annexe & The Kilchoan Melfort Trust

Argyll & Lochaber

26   KILDALLOIG
Campbeltown PA28 6RE
Mr and Mrs Joe Turner
T: 07979 855930 E: kildalloig@gmail.com

Coastal garden with some interesting and unusual shrubs including Australasian shrubs and trees, climbing roses, and herbaceous perennials. There is a woodland walk and a pond garden with aquatic and bog plants.

Open: by arrangement 1 May - 31 October, admission £5.00, children free. Group visits must be pre-booked.

Directions: Take the A83 to Campbeltown, then three miles south-east of the town past Davaar Island.

Opening for: Marie Curie & Macmillan Cancer Support

27   KINLOCHLAICH WALLED GARDEN
Appin PA38 4BD
Miss F M M Hutchison
T: 07881 525754 E: fionakinlochlaich@gmail.com
W: www.kinlochlaichgardencentre.co.uk

Octagonal walled garden incorporating a large Nursery Garden Centre with a huge variety of plants growing and for sale. Bluebell woodland walk and spring garden. Many rhododendrons, azaleas, trees, shrubs and herbaceous plants, including many unusual ones such as *embothrium, davidia, stewartia, magnolia, eucryphia* and *tropaeolum*. A quarter of the interior of the walled garden is borders packed with many unusual and interesting plants, espaliered fruit trees, and with an ancient yew in the centre, and another quarter is vegetable growing.

Open: 3 March - 31 October, 10am - 4pm, admission by donation. Winter by appointment – we are generally about. Accommodation also available, please see www.kinlochlaichgardenselfcatering.co.uk/

Directions: On the A828 in Appin between Oban, 18 miles to the south, and Fort William, 27 miles to the north. The entrance is next to the police station. Infrequent bus Oban to Fort William – request stop.

Opening for: The Appin Village Hall & Down's Syndrome Scotland: West of Scotland Branch

Knock Newhouse

Argyll & Lochaber

28 KNOCK NEWHOUSE

Lochgair PA31 8RZ
Mrs Hew Service
T: 01546 886628 E: corranmorhouse@aol.com

Like all good gardens, it has evolved over time. The garden is centred on a 250-foot lochan, a small waterfall and lily pond. The first trees and rhododendrons were planted in the 1960s, with major additions in the 1990s. A variety of cut leaf and flowering trees were added after the storms of 2011/12. As a result, the garden now has a wide range of specimen trees, *camellias, hoheria, eucryphia, stewartia* to name a few in addition to the azaleas and rhododendrons. January flowering is followed by spring flowers and bluebells and then into the autumn by spectacular colours. I am delighted to welcome visitors at any time.

Open: 20 March - 30 September, 10am - 4pm, admission £6.00, children free. Plants for sale. Please pre-book group visits and teas.

Directions: On the A83. The house is not visible from the road. From Lochgilphead, a ½ mile south of Lochgair Hotel and on the left-hand side of the road, and from Inveraray on the right-hand side of the road a ½ mile after the Lochgair Hotel; the drive opening is marked and enters the woods. Bus Route – Inveraray to Lochgilphead

Opening for: Cancer Research UK & The Lochgair Association (SCIO): Village Hall Fund

29 THE SECRET GARDEN

Isle of Lismore, Oban, Argyll PA34 5UL
Eva Tombs
T: 07786 374931 E: eva.tombs@gmail.com

A unique garden at the centre of a biodynamic farm on the Island of Lismore in the Inner Hebrides. The garden created from a field has a strong geometric layout that reflects the ecclesiastical history of the island. It has a vegetable garden, a tree nursery, a physic garden, an orchard and a polytunnel. The garden is a haven for wildflowers, birds, bees and butterflies. Standing stones, meadows, new woodlands, mountains and the sea encompass the whole. There is also a herd of rare breed Shetland cattle, chickens, ducks and friendly cats.

Open: 1 May - 1 September (Wednesday & Saturday), 10am - 5pm. Also open by arrangement 1 May - 1 September. Admission £6.00, children free. Plants, seeds, fruit and vegetables, flowers, meat and eggs for sale. No dogs please, there are lots of animals around. Refreshments by arrangement.

Directions: Please telephone for directions. Approximately two miles from Port Appin ferry.

Opening for: Oban Gaelic Choir & Scotland's Charity Air Ambulance

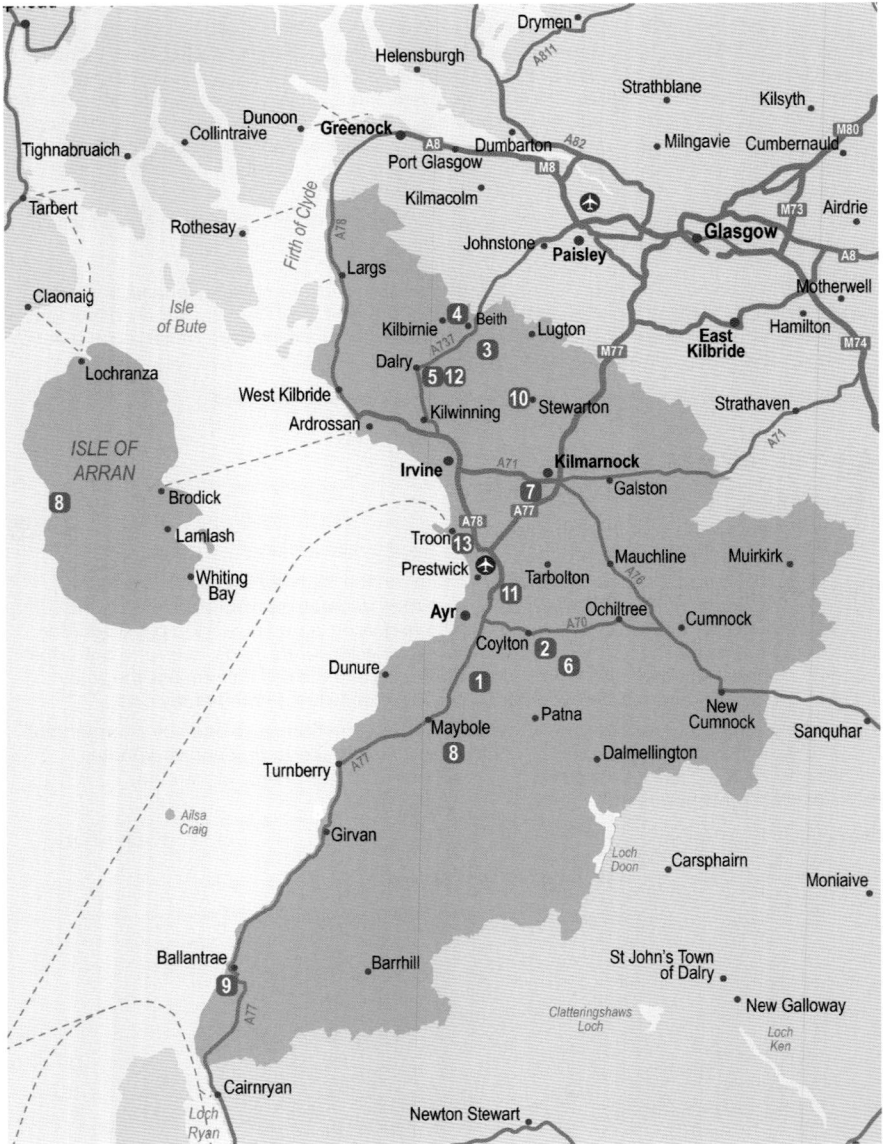

Ayrshire & Arran

Sponsored by

❀ RATHBONES

Drymen
A811
Helensburgh
Strathblane
Kilsyth
Dunoon
Collintraive
Greenock
Milngavie
Cumbernauld
M80
Tighnabruaich
A8
Dumbarton
A82
Port Glasgow
M8
Tarbert
Kilmacolm
M73
Airdrie
Rothesay
Johnstone
Glasgow
Largs
Paisley
A8
Claonaig
Isle
of Bute
Motherwell
Kilbirnie
Beith
Lugton
Hamilton
East
Kilbride
M74
Lochranza
Dalry
West Kilbride
Kilwinning
Stewarton
Strathaven
Ardrossan
ISLE OF
ARRAN
Irvine
A71
Kilmarnock
A71
Brodick
Galston
Lamlash
Troon
A78
A77
Prestwick
Mauchline
Muirkirk
Whiting
Bay
Ayr
Tarbolton
Ochiltree
Cumnock
Coylton
Dunure
Patna
New
Cumnock
Sanquhar
Maybole
Dalmellington
Turnberry
A71
Ailsa
Craig
Girvan
Loch
Doon
Carsphairn
Moniaive
Ballantrae
Barrhill
St John's Town
of Dalry
New Galloway
Clatteringshaws
Loch
Loch
Ken
A77
Cairnryan
Loch
Ryan
Newton Stewart

Ayrshire & Arran

OUR VOLUNTEER ORGANISERS

District Organisers:	Rose-Ann Cuninghame	45 Towerhill Avenue, Kilmaurs KA3 2TS E: ayrshire@scotlandsgardens.org T: 07748 280036
	Lavinia Gibbs	Dougarie, Isle of Arran KA27 8EB
District Administrator:	Jacqueline Young	
Area Organisers:	Sarah Hay Pattie Kewney Lauren MacFadyen Kirsten McClelland-Brooks Marjorie Quinn Wendy Sandiford Jane Tait Sue Veitch	
District Photographer:	David Blatchford	
Treasurers:	Lizzie Adam Carol Freireich	

GARDENS OPEN ON A SPECIFIC DATE

Caprington Castle, Kilmarnock	Saturday/Sunday, 5/6 April
Blair Castle & Estate, Dalry, Ayrshire	Sunday, 4 May
River Garden, The Restoration of Auchincruive, The Bothy Office	Saturday/Sunday 31 May/1 June
River Garden, The Restoration of Auchincruive, The Bothy Office	Saturday/Sunday, 7/8 June
Barrmill Community Garden, Barrmill Park and Gardens	Saturday, 14 June
Dougarie, Isle of Arran	Tuesday, 1 July
Beith Community Gardens, Beith Community Centre, Kings Road	Saturday, 19 July
The Pines, Southwood Road, Troon	Saturday/Sunday, 26/27 July

GARDENS OPEN REGULARLY

Glenapp Castle, Ballantrae, Girvan	1 January - 31 December

GARDENS OPEN BY ARRANGEMENT

Dougarie, Isle of Arran	1 January - 31 December
The Carriage House, Blair Estate, Dalry	29 March - 26 October
Burnside, Littlemill Road, Drongan	1 April - 30 September
Kirkmuir Cottage, Kllwinning Road, Stewarton	1 April - 31 August
Auldbyres Farm Garden, Coylton	12 April - 31 August
1 Burnton Road, Dalrymple	1 June - 31 August

Ayrshire & Arran

1 1 BURNTON ROAD
Dalrymple KA6 6DY
David and Margaret Blatchford
T: 01292 561988 E: d.blatchford273@btinternet.com

A tiny slice of jungle nestled within a small triangular plot. To the front of the house are two beds planted with nectar-secreting plants and seasonal colour. To the rear, an anonymous door leads to a small patio, home to some bonsai, a collection of potted terrestrial ferns and stone troughs hold tender and hardy succulents. A serpentine path meanders through dense planting of palms, brugmansia, bananas and tree ferns. Of note is the use of hardy and tender bromeliads and a collection of aroids such as *Arisaemia, Alocasia, Colocasia* and giant *Zantedeschia*. Flower highlights are provided by lilies (species and cultivars) and later in the season, cannas, and hardy gingers such as *Hedychium, Cautleya* and *Roscoea*. Nestling amongst the foliage is the giant leafed *Tetrapanax* together with the rare, giant terrestrial fern *Lophosoria*.

Open: by arrangement 1 June - 31 August, admission £5.00, children free.

Directions: From the north take the A77 Ayr to Stranraer. At the roundabout, turn left onto the A713 and follow the road past the hospital to the junction with B742, turn right into the village. The garden is on the corner of Burnton and Barbieston Roads. From the south take the A77 towards Ayr, turn right onto the B7034. Follow into the village, at Kirkton Inn junction turn left onto Barbieston Road. Bus 52 from Ayr. The 52 leaves Ayr bus station at 20 minutes to the hour and will drop you at the White Horse Pub in the centre of the village.

Opening for: Dalrymple, Skeldon and Hollybush Project

1 Burnton Road

Ayrshire & Arran

2 **AULDBYRES FARM GARDEN**
Coylton KA6 6HG
Marshall and Sue Veitch
E: su.pavet@btinternet.com

Surrounded by a working farm, this compact, established garden has mature shrubs, wildlife pond, bog garden and stream, borrowing stunning countryside views towards Ayr and Arran. Well-behaved spring borders give way to a riot of summer perennial favourites. Many 'found objects' of agricultural interest. Extensive containers brighten the farmyard with seasonal displays.

Open: by arrangement 12 April - 31 August, admission £5.00, children free. Personal tour on request. Ideal for couples and small groups. Extend your visit by walking the adjacent community nature trail.

Directions: In Coylton take the road signposted *B742*, past Coylton Arms Pub in Low Coylton, *Auldbyres* is signposted on the left after ½ mile.

Opening for: Beatson West of Scotland Cancer Centre

3 **BARRMILL COMMUNITY GARDEN**
Barrmill Park and Gardens KA15 1HW
The Barrmill Conservation Group
E: jean42gilbert@gmail.com
W: www.facebook.com/BarrmillCG

This large woodland garden is carved from a 19th-century whinstone quarry and situated within an 1890s parkland, once known for the quoiting green provided for the village thread mill and ironstone pit workers of that time. Enhancement of the gardens began in 2010 by volunteers, with assistance from *Beechgrove* in 2012. Features include enchanted woodland walks, a fairy trail, a nature trail, the Vale Burn, views of the Dusk Water, a restored 19th-century cholera pit aka 'The Deid Man's Plantin', a new Celtic tree circle and guided walks. The woodland backdrop is complemented by an understorey of natural planting throughout. There is also an established allotment growing area and 'Threads of Time' mural to visit at the rear of the community centre.

Open: Saturday 14 June, 2pm - 5pm, admission £6.00, children free.

Directions: From Stewarton take the A735 to Dunlop, go left down Main Street B706 to Burnhouse, over at crossroads to Barrmill B706. From Lugton south on the A736, take the right at Burnhouse, B706 to Barrmill. From Glasgow on the M8 take J28A signposted *Irvine*, on Beith bypass take the left at B706 to Barrmill.

Opening for: Barrmill and District Community Association

Ayrshire & Arran

4 ## BEITH COMMUNITY GARDENS
Beith Community Centre, Kings Road KA15 2BQ
The Gardeners of Beith Community
W: www.beithca.org.uk. All of the gardens can be found on Facebook.

Beith Community Food Garden (NEW): An allotment growing edible and useful plants, together with those beneficial to pollinators. We are into our third year of the project, are funded by Arran CVS, and have built a beautiful oasis of colour, mindfulness space and creative hub. The garden was awarded a *Keep Scotland Beautiful* Level 4 this year.
Beith Orr Park Neighbourhood Watch Community Garden (NEW): A *Keep Scotland Beautiful* Level 5 – Outstanding community garden built on a derelict gap site at the junction of Main Street with Wilson Street. Created over ten years ago and well established with many unique features.
The Wee Potager at the Cross (NEW): This is a free food and flower garden in curved feature beds in front of Beith Auld Kirk. We grow most of our produce using organic and no dig methods. Inspired by Hidden Gardens and Incredible Edible Network.

Open: Saturday 19 July, 1pm - 5pm, admission £6.00, children free.

Directions: Come to Beith and park in or near Beith community centre car park on Kings Road where Beith Community Food Garden is located. The other two gardens are within easy walking distance.

Opening for: Neighbourhood Watch Scotland SCIO: Beith Orr Park Neighbourhood Watch 20% to The Wee Potager at the Cross & Beith Community Association SCIO: Beith Community Food Garden

5 ## BLAIR CASTLE & ESTATE
Dalry, Ayrshire KA24 4ER
Siobhan Nanson, Castle Manager
T: 01294 833100 E: Siobhan@blairestate.co.uk

Blair Castle's private gardens will be open for visitors – allowing them to walk around the beautiful, landscaped gardens which include a collection of trees dating back to the 18th century. The gardens are continually evolving with a wonderful collection of rhododendrons, magnolias and azaleas. May is the perfect time to see the bluebells on the estate.

Open: Sunday 4 May, 12:30pm - 4:30pm, admission £6.00, children free. Refreshments available. Plants for sale. Cash only. No dogs allowed.

Directions: Exit the A737 at the Highfield roundabout. Take the first exit towards Stewarton on the B707. Follow this road for 0.8 mile and then turn right onto Blair Road. Turn left to enter the estate at the north gates – KA24 4EL for your SatNav. We will be operating a one-way system on the day for visitors.

Opening for: Hessilhead Wildlife Rescue

Ayrshire & Arran

6 BURNSIDE
Littlemill Road, Drongan KA6 7EN
Sue Simpson and George Watt
T: 01292 592445 E: suesimpson33@btinternet.com

This maturing and constantly changing six-and-a-half acre garden began in 2006. There is a wide range of plants from trees to alpines, giving colour and variability all year. Next to the road flows the Drumbowie Burn, parallel to which is a woodland border with snowdrops, erythroniums, hellebores, trilliums, rhododendrons and acers. Near the house are a raised bed and large collection of troughs, with an interesting range of alpines. The garden boasts herbaceous beds, ericaceous garden, screes, three alpine glasshouses with award-winning plants, an extensive streptocarpus collection, polytunnel, pond and arboretum – underplanted with daffodils, camassia, fritillaries and crocus. With a view towards matrimonial harmony, there are two sheds which may be of interest. The garden is only 15 minutes from Dumfries House.

Open: by arrangement 1 April - 30 September, admission £6.00, children free. Sue and George are happy to receive single visitors and groups, large or small. If we don't answer, simply send an email – we check regularly. Hot drinks and biscuits available on request for £4.00. Visit Scotland's Gardens Scheme website for additional openings.

Directions: From the A77 Ayr bypass take the A70 Cumnock for 5¼ miles, at Coalhall, turn onto the B730 Drongan (south) for 2½ miles. Burnside entrance is immediately adjacent to a black/white parapeted bridge. Ordnance survey grid ref: NS455162.

Opening for: Alzheimer's Research UK

7 CAPRINGTON CASTLE
Kilmarnock KA2 9AA
Mr William Cuninghame
T: 01563 524012

Open for daffodils and woodland walks and the extensive walled garden will also be open. There is a range of fruit trees and some shrubs against the very high walls with a layout of lawn, hedges of yew and the large box divide flower borders, fruit bushes and vegetable plots including rhubarb of historical provenance. The original Head Gardener's cottage lies outside, close to the circular pond leading to the woodland walks, with early daffodils, possibly primroses, bluebells and white anemones as the season goes on.

Open: Saturday/Sunday, 5/6 April, 1:30pm - 4pm, admission £6.00, children free. Stout footwear is recommended. Dogs on short leads welcome. Locally grown plants.

Directions: From the M77 take the A71 to Irvine and exit at the first roundabout to *Gatehead, Dundonald, Troon.* In Gatehead go over the railway line and river bridge. Take the first left at Old Rome Farmhouse. The twin lodges are about ½ a mile on. Follow the yellow signposts from Ayr-Kilmarnock road after Bogend Toll.

Opening for: IFDAS

Ayrshire & Arran

8 DOUGARIE
Isle of Arran KA27 8EB
Mrs S C Gibbs
E: laviniawgibbs@gmail.com

Most interesting terraced garden in a castellated folly built in 1905 to celebrate the marriage of the 12th Duke of Hamilton's only child to the Duke of Montrose. Good selection of tender and rare shrubs and herbaceous border. Small woodland area with trees including *azara, abutilon, eucryphia, hoheria* and *nothofagus.*

Open: Tuesday 1 July, 2pm - 5pm. Also open by arrangement. Admission £5.00, children free. Cream teas will be served in the 19th century boat house. Cash payments only. There is free parking.

Directions: Five miles from Blackwaterfoot. Regular ferry sailing from Ardrossan and Claonaig (Argyll). Information from Caledonian MacBrayne, Gourock, T: 01475 650100. Parking is free.

Opening for: Pirnmill Village Association

9 GLENAPP CASTLE
Ballantrae, Girvan KA26 0NZ
Mr Paul Szkiler
T: 01465 831212 E: info@glenappcastle.com
W: www.glenappcastle.com

The 36-acre grounds at Glenapp Castle are secluded and private. Many rare and unusual plants and shrubs can be found, including magnificent specimen rhododendrons. Paths meander round the azalea pond, through established woodland leading to the wonderful walled garden with a 150-foot Victorian glasshouse. Fresh herbs and fruit from the garden are used every day in the castle kitchen. Much of the gardens were designed by Gertrude Jekyll (1843-1932), the world-famous garden designer, applying the principles of the Arts and Crafts Movement, who worked in collaboration with Edwin Lutyens. A new walk has been created opening up the Glen, where Glenapp's Champion Trees will be found.
Champion Trees: *Abies cilicica, Cercidiphyllum japonicum* and *Picea likiangensis.*

Open: 1 January - 31 December, dawn - dusk, admission by donation.

Directions: From the north take the A77 south. Pass through Ballantrae, crossing the River Stinchar as you leave. Take the first turning on the right, 100 yards beyond the river (not signposted). From the south take the A77 north, turn left 100 yards before the bridge over Stinchar at Ballantrae. The castle gates are one mile along this road.

Opening for: Donation to SGS Beneficiaries

Ayrshire & Arran

10 **KIRKMUIR COTTAGE**
Kilwinning Road, Stewarton KA3 3DZ
Mr and Mrs Brian Macpherson
E: dhmmacp@gmail.com

This garden was created in 1997 from a small field and includes a large pond which was originally a small quarry. It covers approximately one-and-a-half-acres of mature garden and, using hedging and shrubbery the garden is split into garden 'rooms' including woodland, formal borders, laburnum arch, herbaceous borders, rhododendrons and azaleas. Large lawn area and wildlife pond. The garden also features many interesting and unusual artefacts and sculptures.

Open: by arrangement 1 April - 31 August, admission £6.00, children free. All garden visitors, societies and walking groups are welcome. Dogs on leads please.

Directions: From the M77 take the B778 to Stewarton. At the traffic lights, turn left and continue to the mini-roundabout. Turn right towards the B778 Kilwinning. Continue for 100 yards under the railway bridge, take an immediate left at the war memorial and continue along Kilwinning Road until you reach the countryside. Kirkmuir is the first farm road on the right hand side. The cottage and garden is on the left at the end of the farm road. Please follow these directions not SatNav.

Opening for: Capability Scotland

11 **RIVER GARDEN, THE RESTORATION OF AUCHINCRUIVE**
The Bothy Office, Auchincruive KA6 5AE
Head Gardener
E: enquiries@ifdas.net

The gardens date back to the 1900s. Auchincruive is steeped in horticultural history as the site used to be the West of Scotland Agricultural College. The gardens are going through major redevelopment to bring them back to their former glory, including restoring the secret garden, walled garden, herbaceous borders and ponds that are within the gardens. Our main focus is to produce vegetables for the Bothy Cafe. We have two large vegetable growing areas; one plot is no-dig and the other is dig. We also have an arboretum that contains rare and endangered trees, including *Sorbus arranensis, Sequoia sempervirens, Sequoiadendron giganteum* and *Cryptomeria japonica.* The gardens also contain fruit, orchids and greenhouses and the grounds have a total of 48 acres that consist of woodlands, cafe and gardens. Our gardens are used therapeutically to help residents overcome addiction and improve their mental well being.

Open: Saturday/Sunday 31 May & 1 June & Saturday/Sunday, 7/8 June 12:30pm - 3:30pm, admission £6.00, children free.

Directions: River Garden is located two minutes by car from the main Whitletts roundabout at the junction of the A77/B743. At the roundabout, take the B743 turn signposted *Mossblown.* At the bend in the road turn right into the Nellie's Gate entrance at bus stop KA65.

Opening for: IFDAS

Ayrshire & Arran

12 THE CARRIAGE HOUSE
Blair Estate, Dalry KA24 4ER
Mr and Mrs Luke Borwick
T: 07831 301294 E: lina@blairtrust.co.uk

Set within the historic Blair policies dating back to the 1500s, at the Carriage House the Borwicks have planted a beautiful arboretum. Built on the vision of generations of Blairs of creating a sanctuary of rare species trees, over the past four years a collection of over 160 trees and shrubs has transformed a 10-acre field into a peaceful refuge with year-round variety and colour. Mown pathways offer different vistas and points of interest including mermaids rescuing a girl, carved by a local artist from a Portuguese Laurel stump. View the 24-year old Wellingtonia *(Sequoiadendron giganteum)* grown from Blair seed, an avenue of eight different lime trees which earned a *Queen's Green Canopy Award*, a *Metasequoia glyptostroboides* 'Golden Dawn', and other rare trees. From a bench created from our own wood, enjoy the arboretum's energy – a special experience. New since 2024 is a beautiful Cumbrian green slate commemorative stone, with superb engraving by the Cordozo Kindersley Workshop: it frames Blair Castle perfectly and honours the three related families who have nurtured this special place since 1105. The Blair crest heads the inscription with the motto 'Amo Probos', and the Royal Scots Greys badge 'second to none' recognises the generations of family members serving our country in Scotland's only cavalry regiment. Wander the Carriage House garden, created from a field since 2002 and planted with many varieties of roses and mature shrubs.

Open: by arrangement 29 March - 26 October, admission £6.00, children free. Email us or text 07831 301294 using 'Garden Visit' as the subject. Please leave your contact name and number. Dogs very strictly on short leads due to sheep in the field. We welcome garden societies and walking groups – bring a picnic!

Directions: A737 from Beith. At the roundabout before Dalry take the first left signposted *Stewarton*. Then go straight on, signposted *Bike Route Irvine*. Keep going for approximately two miles and keep the estate wall on the right until you come to South Lodge (white building). Turn right down the drive for Blair Estate – The Carriage House is on the right. Public transport to Dalry. Follow SatNav KA24 4ER and enter Blair Estate through the South Lodge.

Opening for: The National Trust for Scotland

The Carriage House

Ayrshire & Arran

13 THE PINES

Southwood Road, Troon KA10 7EL
Cheryll and Alasdair Cameron
E: pinesopengarden@gmail.com

In nine years our one-acre plot has been transformed from a barren children's playground with only mature pine trees and rhododendrons, to a colourful seaside garden. Our exposed coastal situation causes windburn in many supposedly hardy plants, so we have formed a windbreak for the borders with mixed shrubs including griselinia, hawthorn and photinia. Billowing grasses sit alongside perennials including helenium, euphorbia and agapanthus, all interspersed with tulips, lilies and alliums. The coastal theme is accentuated by cordyline, phormium, *Fatsia japonica* and eucalyptus. We have bark woodland paths, and our garden is a haven for birds, bees and butterflies.

Open: Saturday/Sunday, 26/27 July, 2pm - 5pm, admission £6.00, children free.

Directions: From the A77 at Dutch House Roundabout, follow the A78 and then the A79, then immediately right to Troon on the B749. Southwood Road is first left and The Pines is the last property. Stagecoach X14 passes the property.

Opening for: The Ayrshire Hospice

The Pines

Berwickshire & Roxburghshire

Sponsored by

❀ RATHBONES

Berwickshire & Roxburghshire

OUR VOLUNTEER ORGANISERS

District Organiser:	Victoria Tweedie	The House of Narrow Gates, St.Boswells, Roxburghshire TD6 0AX berwickshire@scotlandsgardens.org
Treasurer:	Alastair Harris	

GARDENS OPEN ON A SPECIFIC DATE

Mellerstain House and Gardens, Gordon	Saturday, 22 February
Harlaw Farmhouse, Eccles near Kelso, Berwickshire	Sunday, 13 April
Mellerstain House and Gardens, Gordon	Saturday, 31 May
West Leas, near Bonchester Bridge, Roxburghshire	Sunday, 1 June
Morebattle Mains, Morebattle, Kelso	Saturday 28 and Sunday 29 June
Duns Open Gardens, Duns, Berwickshire	Sunday, 20 July
West Leas, near Bonchester Bridge, Roxburghshire	Sunday, 3 August
Larch House, Clerklands, near Lilliesleaf	Wednesdays, 6/13/20/27 August
Old Melrose, Melrose	Sunday, 24 August
Corbet Tower, Morebattle, near Kelso	Saturday, 6 September
Mellerstain House and Gardens, Gordon	Saturday, 25 October

GARDENS OPEN REGULARLY

Mellerstain, Gordon	1 January - 31 December
Monteviot, Jedburgh	1 April - 31 October
Bughtrig, near Leitholm, Coldstream	1 May - 30 September
Floors Castle, Kelso	1 May - 30 September
The Walled Garden at The Hugo Burge Foundation, Marchmont, Duns	4 July - 29 August (Fridays only)

GARDENS OPEN BY ARRANGEMENT

Ruthven House, Coldstream	1 January - 12 September
Broomhill Villa, 4 Edinburgh Road, Greenlaw	1 April - 30 June
Thirlestane, Yetholm, near Kelso	1 April - 31 October
West Leas, near Bonchester Bridge, Roxburghshire	1 May - 31 October
Lennel Bank, Coldstream	1 May - 31 October
Netherbyres, Eyemouth	1 May - 31 August
Larch House, Clerklands, Near Lilliesleaf	1 July - 31 August

Berwickshire & Roxburghshire

1 BROOMHILL VILLA
4 Edinburgh Road, Greenlaw TD10 6XF
Tatyana Aplin
T: 07957 288557 E: aplin848@btinternet.com

The garden at Broomhill is on the northern side of Greenlaw, comprising half-an-acre of spring colour nestled between village and farmland. The garden is maintained by a passionate plant collector featuring narcissi, tulips, meconopses and hundreds of other flowers. The collection has been developed along informal lines with treats at every turn. A radiant display of blooms that changes through the year is intended not only for the visual pleasure of the garden but also for the house with cut flower arrangements as well as produce for the table and larder.

Open: by arrangement 1 April - 30 June, admission £5.00, children free. Small groups are welcome.

Directions: On the A697 at the northern end of Greenlaw.

Opening for: Cancer Research UK

2 BUGHTRIG
near Leitholm, Coldstream TD12 4JP
Mr and Mrs William Ramsay
E: ramsay@bughtrig.co.uk

A traditional, hedged, Scottish family garden with an interesting combination of sculpture, herbaceous plants, shrubs, annuals and fruit. It is surrounded by fine specimen trees, which provide remarkable shelter. In the grounds of Bughtrig Gardens is the recently opened Admiral Ramsay Museum, which has been created in memory of all who served at D-Day, Dunkirk and during World War II.

Open: 1 May - 30 September, 9am - 4:30pm, admission £5.00, children free.

Directions: ¼ mile east of Leitholm on the B6461.

Opening for: Donation to SGS Beneficiaries

3 CORBET TOWER
Morebattle, near Kelso TD5 8AQ
Bridget Fraser
E: bridgetafraser@yahoo.co.uk

Charming Scottish Victorian garden set in parklands in the foothills of the Cheviots. This well-established garden includes a traditional walled kitchen garden, well stocked with fruit, vegetables and cutting flowers, including dahlias, gladioli and annuals. There is also a formal box parterre rose garden with old-fashioned early roses, long borders and terraced lawns around the Victorian house and medieval peel tower. The gardens are approached via an attractive woodland walk with lime avenue.

Open: Saturday 6 September, 2pm - 5pm, admission £5.00, children free.

Directions: Off the A698 from Kelso and the A68 north of Jedburgh. At Kalemouth follow the B6401 to Morebattle, then the road marked Hownam to Corbet Tower.

Opening for: Cheviot Churches: Church of Scotland

Berwickshire & Roxburghshire

4 **DUNS OPEN GARDENS**
Volunteer Hall, Langtongate, Duns TD11 3AF
The Gardeners of Duns

The former county town of Duns retains a thriving market square and is home to an award-winning museum dedicated to Formula 1 Champion, Jim Clark OBE. There are extensive green areas in and around the town offering delightful walks all year round. After three hugely successful years of opening our gardens we had a break in 2024 but have decided to open again in a different month, July, to show the huge variety of our gardens. They are lovingly tended by keen gardeners, happy to share them with fellow enthusiasts. They offer a wonderful variety of size, layout and planting, ensuring that there is something for everyone, from small courtyards to extensive shrub areas, vegetable gardens, pond areas and magnificent lawns. Come and enjoy spending the day in Duns, visiting the beautiful gardens and exchanging ideas.

Open: Sunday 20 July, noon - 5pm, admission £6.00, children free. Tickets available to purchase at the Volunteer Hall on Langtongate TD11 3AF, along with route maps, our very own showcased 'Duns Flowerbed Trail' leaflets, teas and coffees. For visitors wishing a more substantial lunch or treat, our Market Square cafes offer a variety of hot and cold food with seating inside and out. Car parking is available on Newtown Street, TD11 3AU and also throughout the town close to all open gardens.

Directions: Situated on the crossroads of the A6112 and A6105, about 14 miles west of Berwick upon Tweed, easily accessible from the A1 onto the A6112 or from the A68/A697 onto the A6105.

Opening for: AHFD

5 **FLOORS CASTLE**
Kelso TD5 7SF
The Duke of Roxburghe
T: 01573 223333
W: www.floorscastle.com

The gardens are situated within the grounds of Floors Castle. Meander through to the formal Millennium Parterre and soak up the spectacular visions of colour, texture and the most delicious scents around the four herbaceous borders in one of the finest Victorian kitchen gardens in Scotland. Features include perennial gardens, fruit cage, Tapestry Garden and glasshouse access as well as the Terrace Cafe, Apple Shed Gift Shop and Deli and children's play area. Explore the grounds, which offer woodland and riverside walks from May to the end of September.

Open: 1 May - 30 September, 10am - 5pm, admission details can be found on the garden's website. The Walled Garden, Terrace Cafe and Apple Shed are also open all year round and access to those during the winter months is via the B6397 only, NOT via the main entrance to the Castle on Roxburgh Street.

Directions: Floors Castle can be reached by following the A6089 from Edinburgh; the B6397 from Earlston; or the A698 from Coldstream. Go through Kelso, up Roxburgh Street to the Golden Gates.

Opening for: Donation to SGS Beneficiaries

Berwickshire & Roxburghshire

6 HARLAW FARMHOUSE
Eccles near Kelso, Berwickshire TD5 7RA
Jean Wood
T: 07883 422519 E: jean.greenfingers@gmail.com

Harlaw is set in a one-acre garden surrounding a typical Berwickshire farmhouse, in a truly rural setting with lovely Border views. The owner has spent many years building up a collection of over 65 varieties of named daffodils and narcissus, naturalised throughout the garden. It has a mature nuttery with several highly productive walnut and hazel trees as well as *Gingko biloba*, and an orchard with apple, pear and plum trees. In the summer there is a large cutting garden and vegetable patch. There are two greenhouses with a large cactus collection. The garden owner is a keen plantswoman, propagating most of her own stock.

Open: Sunday 13 April, 2pm - 5pm, admission £5.00, children free.

Directions: From the east drive through Eccles village then take the first turning on the right signposted *Loan Knowe.* Continue to the *cycle route* sign, turn left and the house is one mile on the left. From Ednam, go through the village, take the left turn to Hume, go to the T-junction, turn right and continue to the white cottage, take the right fork *cycle route* and Harlaw is ½ mile on the right. There is parking by the house.

Opening for: Border Womens Aid

7 LARCH HOUSE
Clerklands, Near Lilliesleaf TD6 9JR
David and Julia King
T: 01835 870888 E: northcorner14@btinternet.com

The garden at Larch House is constantly evolving. Extending to over three acres and building on a layout, design and planting by the previous owners, further landscaping and renovation is ongoing. It includes a terraced area of vegetables and cut flowers edged by fruit trees, several mixed borders surrounding a lawn, a large natural wildlife pond and a newly-planted bog garden. The garden leads into a mixed wood planted about six years ago where meandering paths, sometimes steep, lead to extensive views of the Cheviots. Many of the paths are gravel and may prove difficult for wheelchairs.

Open: 6 - 27 August (Wednesdays only) 11am - 4pm. Pre-booking is required on these days due to limited parking. Also open by arrangement 1 July - 31 August. Admission £5.00, children free. Self service refreshments will be available on open garden days, and on request for the 'by arrangement' visits – donations would be welcomed. There may be plants for sale. Please note the limited parking may affect the maximum group size for 'by arrangement' visits.

Directions: Clerklands is a small hamlet approximately two miles from Lilliesleaf. On the A7 from Selkirk, turn left and follow signs to Clerklands. After approximately three miles the house will be clearly signed. On the A7 from Hawick, turn right and follow signs towards Lilliesleaf and the house will be clearly signed. Car parking is on site.

Opening for: All proceeds to SGS Beneficiaries

Berwickshire & Roxburghshire

8 LENNEL BANK

Coldstream TD12 4EX
Mrs Honor Brown
T: 01890 882297 E: honor.b.brown@gmail.com

Lennel Bank is a terraced garden overlooking the River Tweed, consisting of wide borders packed with shrubs and perennial planting, some unusual. The water garden, built in 2008, is surrounded by a rockery and utilises the slope, ending in a pond. There is a small kitchen garden with raised beds in unusual shapes. Different growing conditions throughout the garden from dry, wet, shady and sunny, lend themselves to a variety of plants and enhance interest in the garden.

Open: by arrangement 1 May - 31 October, admission £5.00, children free. Refreshments can be provided for visiting groups, with advance notice

Directions: On the A6112 Coldstream to Duns road, one mile from Coldstream.

Opening for: British Heart Foundation

9 MELLERSTAIN

Mellerstain House and Gardens, Gordon TD3 6LG
Gill Harrop, Administrator
T: 01573 410225 E: enquiries@mellerstain.com
W: www.mellerstain.com

Mellerstain will be hosting three special open days to celebrate the garden and grounds at their finest. In February carpets of snowdrops spread throughout the grounds, followed by the glorious colour of rhododendrons and azaleas at the end of May, and finishing with stunning autumn colours in late October. 100 acres of mature parkland, formal gardens and lakeside walks set off this Robert Adam masterpiece. The formal gardens to the south of the house were designed in 1910 by Sir Reginald Blomfield in an Italianate style sympathetic to the earlier 18th century layout. These beautiful terraces with herbaceous borders and yew trees lead to lower terraces via a *cryptoporticus*, and then a sweeping expanse of lawn descends to the lake. Among the sturdy oaks and majestic beeches in the north parkland, you'll find an enchanting tiny thatched cottage discreetly tucked away with its own parterre garden. A map is available of the woodland and lakeside walks, picnic spots are available and the cafe is open during the summer season. Look out for the Highland cattle and Hebridean sheep too!

Open: Saturday 22 February for Snowdrops and Winter Walks, Saturday 31 May for Rhododendrons, Saturday 25 October for Autumn Colour, all 11am-5pm, admission £6, children free, light refreshments available outwith cafè opening.
The garden is also open all year round, 1 January - 31 December, 11am-5pm, and the House Tours and Courtyard Cafe are available from Good Friday, April 18 - September 29. Further details can be found on the garden's website.

Directions: The house is signposted on the A6089 Kelso-Gordon road. The approach from the A68 Jedburgh-Edinburgh road is through Earlston on the A6105, then via the B6397 towards Smailholm.

Opening for: Mellerstain Trust (Saturday 22 February, Saturday 31 May & Saturday 25 October) & Donation to SGS Beneficiaries (1 January - 31 December)

Berwickshire & Roxburghshire

10 MONTEVIOT
Jedburgh TD8 6UQ
The Marchioness of Lothian
T: 01835 830380
W: www.monteviot.com

A series of differing gardens displaying rose and herbaceous plants surrounded by foliage plants. A water feature linked by bridges and falls passes through the Dene Garden and Water Garden. The Garden of Persistent Imagination is planted with rose and clematis beside paths which meander across a bridge and under the Moonstone Gate, past the Dali-style clock.

Open: 1 April - 31 October, noon - 5pm, admission £6.00, children free. Card payment only.

Directions: Turn off the A68, three miles north of Jedburgh on to the B6400. After one mile turn right.

Opening for: Donation to SGS Beneficiaries

11 MOREBATTLE MAINS
Morebattle, Kelso TD5 8QU
Catherine Henderson and Helen Kemp & Paul Grime
T: 01573440378 (Catherine)
E: helen.kemp@mac.com; cath.henderson1957@gmail.com

The Granary (Catherine Henderson): An acre in size, laid out over last few years and now beginning to mature, with an outstanding view of the Borders hills and countryside. Differing heights of stone terraces give structure. There are many trees, shrubs and diverse range of perennial herbaceous plants plus various collections of non flowering plants, including grasses, *pinus, cornus and picea,* giving an extensive range of colour, textures and foliage.
The Steading (Helen Kemp & Paul Grime): A wildlife friendly garden, run with permaculture principals, with distinct areas featuring herbaceous borders, ponds, meadow and wildflowers, vegetable garden and orchard, glasshouses and polytunnel. We started here in 2015, with only six mature trees in place.

Open: Saturday/Sunday, 28/29 June, 1pm - 5pm, admission £5.00, children free. Teas will be served at The Granary

Directions: The Steading is half a mile from Morebattle Village centre. Take the road opposite the community shop (Mainsfield Avenue). We are the first house on the right hand side. Morebattle can be reached by the number 81 bus from Kelso (not Sundays).

Opening for: Médecins Sans Frontières

12 NETHERBYRES
Eyemouth TD14 5SE
Col S J Furness
T: 01890 750337

An unusual, elliptical walled garden, dating from 1740, with a mixture of flowers, fruit and vegetables. A very old pear tree, possibly dating from the 18th century, and the largest rose in Berwickshire, *Rosa filipes* 'Kiftsgate'. A wide variety of roses and herbaceous borders.

Open: by arrangement 1 May - 31 August, admission £5.00, children free.

Directions: ½ mile south of Eyemouth on the A1107 to Berwick.

Opening for: All proceeds to SGS Beneficiaries

Berwickshire & Roxburghshire

13 **OLD MELROSE**
near Melrose TD6 9DF
William and Frankie Younger
T: 07811 389551 E: frankie.younger@btinternet.com
W: www.oldmelrose.co.uk

The charm of Old Melrose lies in its idyllic setting – a woodland peninsula surrounded on three sides by the River Tweed, the site that St Aidan chose to build a monastery in 640AD. With a wonderful array of plants, trees and wildlife, come and explore this conservation focused estate and connect with nature in its beautiful surroundings. A one-mile signed walk will be laid out through the private grounds taking in stunning viewpoints, wonderful mature specimen trees, riverside trails and a view of the 19th century summer house standing high above the river. Stop to contemplate on the spot where a chapel once stood dedicated to St Cuthbert. Finish in the Victorian walled garden where teas will be available. The garden features three distinct areas: a small orchard with bee hives, perennial wildflower planting and fruit, vegetable and flower beds. Be sure to say hello to the friendly Boer goats, the rare breed pigs and the free roaming chickens.

Open: Sunday 24 August, 2pm - 5pm, admission £5.00, children free. Estate tearooms open (Tues-Sat 10-4, Sun 11-4) for a light lunch, starting point for the Monks Trail, a 45-minute circular walk that follows the route taken by the Monks who lived here 1,300 years ago when they moved between Old Melrose and Dryburgh Abbey.

Directions: On the A68 between Melrose and St Boswells

Opening for: Royal Highland Education Trust

The Granary, Morebattle Mains

Berwickshire & Roxburghshire

14 ## RUTHVEN HOUSE
near Coldstream TD12 4JU
Keith and Karen Fountain
T: 01890 840680 E: ruthvenhouse@btconnect.com

The three acres of Ruthven's garden have lovely views towards the Cheviots. The garden's central feature is two ponds joined by a winding stream. The garden is composed of various differing areas – herbaceous borders, woodland areas, a gravel garden, a knot garden, rockeries, an orchard laid to meadow, a kitchen garden, a highland garden, a nuttery, a small lavender field, a shade bed to the back of the house and, adjacent to the house, a formal rose garden. A small fold of Highland cattle in the adjacent field complete the scene. The garden is constantly evolving but this year we will not be having an open garden day to allow for a sustained period of development and renewal. Visitors by arrangement, as ever, will be very welcome.

Open: by arrangement 1 January - 12 September, admission £6.00, children free. Groups and individuals are welcome.

Directions: Four miles north of Coldstream, and one mile south of Swinton Mill, on the old Duns road.

Opening for: *Scottish Action for Mental Health*

15 ## THE WALLED GARDEN AT THE HUGO BURGE FOUNDATION
Marchmont Estate, Duns, Berwickshire TD10 6YL
The Hugo Burge Foundation
E: enquiries@hugoburgefoundation.org
W: www.hugoburgefoundation.org

A recently-redeveloped walled garden in the grounds of the Marchmont Estate. Run as a space to inspire creativity as part of the Hugo Burge Foundation, a newly-formed arts charity based in the Scottish Borders. The garden contains herbaceous borders, a kitchen garden, a colonnade, wildflower meadows, cut flower borders, a sculpture collection and newly restored Mackenzie and Moncur glasshouses.

Open: every Friday from 4 July to 29 August, noon - 4pm, admission £7.00, children free. Pre-booking of tickets is essential, please see www.hugoburgefoundation.org to book

Directions: From the A6105 (Duns to Greenlaw), take the Polwarth road for 1.5 miles. From the B6460, take the Fogo turning and continue for 1.5 miles.

Opening for: *The Hugo Burge Foundation*

Berwickshire & Roxburghshire

16 THIRLESTANE
Kelso TD5 8PD
Catherine Ross and John Wylie
T: 01573 420487 E: catherineaross37@gmail.com

Thirlestane is a large informal garden. There is a walled garden with colour-themed borders and an orchard with many old varieties of fruit trees. In front of the house prairie planting is surrounded by high beech hedges. The young nine-acre wood has trees and shrubs selected for autumn colour and for decorative bark and fruit. These include Persian Ironwood, Golden Rain Tree, Scarlet Oak, Monarch Birch, Himalayan Birch, Tibetan Cherry, Chinese Hawthorn and various maples.

Open: by arrangement 1 April - 31 October, admission £5.00, children free. Please feel free to bring a picnic to enjoy in the garden. Dogs welcome.

Directions: Thirlestane is near Yetholm, not to be confused with Thirlestane Castle, Lauder. Do not follow SatNav, it will try to take you to Lochside. From Kelso, take the B6352 towards Yetholm for about six miles. Continue past a cottage on the edge of the road. Thirlestane is next on the left, opposite the road to Lochside. From Yetholm, take the road to Kelso for about two miles. After a very sharp corner, Thirlestane is on the right.

Opening for: Alzheimer Scotland

17 WEST LEAS
near Bonchester Bridge TD9 8TD
Mr and Mrs Robert Laidlaw
T: 01450 860711 E: ann@johnlaidlawandson.co.uk

The visitor to West Leas can share in an exciting and dramatic project on a grand scale, one that is constantly growing and evolving. A feat of liquid engineering, with a cascading stream contrasting with slow water pools. At its core is a passion for plants, allied to a love and understanding of the land in which they are set. Collections of perennials and shrubs lighten up the landscape to magical effect. The lily pond and woodland planting was added in 2019 and a courtyard garden links to the humidity controlled garden rooms housing a collection of exotics.

Open: Sunday 1 June & Sunday 3 August, 2pm - 5pm. Also open by arrangement 1 May - 31 October. Admission £5.00, children free. Teas in Bedrule Village Hall (Sunday 1 June & Sunday 3 August).

Directions: Signposted off the Jedburgh/Bonchester Bridge Road.

Opening for: Macmillan Cancer Support: Borders Appeal

Mellerstain

Caithness & Sutherland

PENTLAND FIRTH

Dunnet Head

Cape Wrath

Strathy Point

Scrabster • **Thurso** • Mey • John o' Groats ⑭

Durness

Melvich

Dounreay

Sinclair's Bay

Kinlochbervie

Bettyhill

Tongue

Loch Eriboll

Loch Hope

Loch Loyal

Mybster

Wick

Handa Island

Loch Naver

Forsinard

Eddrachillis Bay

Scourie

Altnaharra

Kinbrace

Latheron • Lybster

Dunbeath

Enard Bay

Lochinver

Inchnadamph

⑦ • Berriedale

Ledmore

Helmsdale

Loch Assynt

Oykel Bridge

Lairg

Brora

Ullapool

Bonar Bridge

Golspie

⑬

② Dornoch

Dornoch Firth

MORAY FIRTH

Fionn Loch

Tain

Lossiemouth

Orkney

Mull Head

North Ronaldsay

Papa Westray

Westray

The North Sound

Start Point

Sanday

Rousay

Sanday Sound

Brough Head

Eday

Stronsay

Twatt

③

MAINLAND

Kirkwall ⑫

Shapinsay

Stromness

⑯

Deerness

Hoy

⑮

Scapa Flow

Rora Head

HOY

Graemsay

Burray

Lyness

⑰ St Margaret's Hope

S Walls

South Ronaldsay

Dunnet Head

PENTLAND FIRTH

Scrabster

Duncansby Head

John o' Groats

Thurso

Shetland

Herma Ness

Unst

Haroldswick

Gutcher

Uyeasound

Tabister

Mid Yell

Fetlar

YELL

Esha Ness

Hillswick

Toft

Uista

Bruray

St Magnus Bay

Papa Stour

Brae

Hillside

Muckle Roe

Whalsay

Sandness

Tresta

Walls

Foula

Linwick

Scalloway

Bressay

West Burra

Cunningsburgh

Sandwick

Sumburgh

Sumburgh Head

Caithness, Sutherland, Orkney & Shetland

OUR VOLUNTEER ORGANISERS

District Organisers:	Fay Wilkinson Lisa Croft (Orkney) To be advised (Shetland)	42 Astle, Dornoch, IV25 3NH Quoyostrey, Rousay, Orkney KW17 2PS
Area Organiser:	Sara Shaw	Amat, Ardgay, Sutherland IV24 3BS
District Photographer:	Colin Gregory	Iona, Reay, Caithness, KW14 7RG
Treasurer:	Amanda Hoare	

GARDENS OPEN ON A SPECIFIC DATE

16 Mulla, Voe, Shetland	Saturday/Sunday, 10/11 May
Westlea, Cromarty Square, St. Margaret's Hope, Orkney	Sunday, 8 June
Laura's Wood, Hools, St. Margaret's Hope, Orkney	Sunday, 8 June
Waulkmill Garden, Sandygill, Waulkmill, Orkney	Saturday, 21 June
Mill House, Lyness, Hoy, Orkney	Saturday, 28 June
Round House, Berstane Road, Kirkwall, Orkney	Saturday, 5 July
Kierfiold House, Kierfiold House, Sandwick, Orkney	Sunday, 6 July
Hattamoa, Rendall, Orkney	Sunday, 6 July
Amat, Amat Lodge, Ardgay	Saturday/Sunday, 12/13 July
Kierfiold House, Kierfiold House, Sandwick, Orkney	Sunday, 20 July
16 Mulla, Voe, Shetland	Saturday/Sunday, 26/27 July
Skelbo House, Skelbo, Dornoch	Saturday/Sunday, 26/27 July
Langwell, Berriedale	Sunday, 27 July
The Quoy of Houton, Orphir, Orkney	Sunday, 27 July
Hattamoa, Rendall, Orkney	Sunday, 3 August

GARDENS OPEN REGULARLY

Norby, Burnside, Sandness, Shetland	1 April - 31 December
The Castle and Gardens of Mey, Mey	1 May - 30 May
Nonavaar, Levenwick, Shetland	1 June - 30 September

GARDENS OPEN BY ARRANGEMENT

16 Mulla, Voe, Shetland	1 April - 30 September
Amat, Amat Lodge, Ardgay	1 May - 31 July
Highlands Garden, East Voe, Scalloway, Shetland	1 May - 31 October (Mon, Wed, & Fri)
Keldaberg, Cunningsburgh, Shetland	1 June - 30 September

Caithness, Sutherland, Orkney & Shetland

1 16 MULLA
Voe, Shetland ZE2 9XQ
Linda Richardson
T: 07765 037516 E: linda@lindarichardson.co.uk

A garden on the Clubb of Mulla, a hillside overlooking Olnafirth with views of the sea and Lower Voe. Started in October 2016, the steep overgrown plot looked like a continuation of the moor at the back of the house. This garden shows what can be achieved in a very windy and exposed situation, battling against the extremes of the Shetland weather. Gardening with wildlife in mind, trees were planted in the spring of 2017, now providing shelter for birds. There are herbaceous borders, rockery, vegetable bed, 3.6 x 2.4 metre greenhouse, mini wildflower meadow strips and a natural water feature which is a long drainage ditch planted up with willows and water-loving plants. Always a work in progress, more trees have been planted to increase wildlife habitat. The owner is an artist-printmaker with an open studio that folk are welcome to look around too.

Open: Two plant sale weekends with tea and cake on Saturday/Sunday, 10/11 May and Saturday/Sunday, 26/27 July, 10:30am - 4:30pm. Also open by arrangement 1 April - 30 September. Admission by donation. Look for the open sign for 16 Mulla on the main road. If the sign is out, the garden and studio are open or you can telephone us to arrange a visit.

Directions: Eighteen miles north of Lerwick on the A970 is Voe. Pass the *North Isles junction* and *Tagon Stores* on your right. Turn right into Mulla and number 16 is up the hill on your left. Bus no. 21 (Hillswick) and 23 (Toft) stop on the main road at the bottom of Mulla.

Opening for: RSPB: for projects in Shetland

2 AMAT
Amat Lodge, Ardgay IV24 3BS
Jonny and Sara Shaw
T: 07712 266500 E: sara.amat@aol.co.uk

Over the last few years there have been big changes in the garden and there is now much more interest during the summer months. There is a new mini stumpery and many changes to the original borders. The river Carron flows around the edge of the garden and the old Amat Caledonian Forest is close by. Large specimen trees surround the house, plus many new ones planted in the policies in the last few years. There are several herbaceous borders, rhododendrons, trees and shrubs, all set in a large lawn. It is possible to go on a short woodland and river walk and you may see red squirrels which were reintroduced some years ago and are often in and around the garden.
Champion Trees: Abies Procera, Noble Fir.

Open: Saturday/Sunday, 12/13 July, 2pm - 5pm. Also open by arrangement 1 May - 31 July. Admission £5.00, children free.

Directions: Take the road from Ardgay to Croick, nine miles. Turn left at the red phone box and the garden is 500 yards on the left.

Opening for: Alzheimer Scotland & Marie Curie

Caithness, Sutherland, Orkney & Shetland

3 HATTAMOA
Rendall, Orkney KW17 2HF
Caroline Macleod

Set in an acre of land, we have been breaking through the weeds for around three years. Our garden has a mixture of flowers, vegetables, raised beds, wildlife and a pond. There are also a few mature shrubs, windbreak boundaries of willow and dog rose, two polytunnels, one of which houses fruit trees. There is a new hornbeam hedge and a gabion basket windbreaker wall. The garden is very much a work in progress.

Open: Sunday 6 July, noon - 5pm. Also open Sunday 3 August, noon - 5pm. Admission by donation.

Directions: Follow the A966 through Norsman Village, past Lyron and around the bend at Layburn and the first *Hackland* sign. Drive up the gentle rise until you come to the second *Hackland Kirk* sign pointing to the right. Directly opposite this take the left turn up a track and we are the first property, on the left. The tunnels are a sign you are in the right place.

Opening for: The Clan Strachan Charitable Trust

4 HIGHLANDS GARDEN
East Voe, Scalloway, Shetland ZE1 0UR
Sarah Kay
T: 01595 880526/ 07818 845385 E: info@easterhoull.co.uk
W: www.selfcatering-shetland.co.uk/the-garden/

The garden is in two parts. The upper garden is mostly a rockery, with a large selection of plants, shallow pond, seating area, polycrub and greenhouse with fruit and vegetables. The lower garden is on a steep slope with a spectacular sea view over the village of Scalloway. There is a path to lead visitors around and the garden features a large collection of plants, vegetable patch, deep pond and pergola. It was awarded a *Shetland Environmental Award* in 2014 for its strong theme of recycling. The owner also has an art studio which you are most welcome to visit when you view the garden.

Open: by arrangement 1 May - 31 October (Monday, Wednesday & Friday), admission £4.00, children free. Enjoy a self guided wander around the garden. Dogs are not allowed.

Directions: Follow the A970 main road towards the village of Scalloway. Near the top of the hill heading towards Scalloway take a sharp turn to the left, signposted *Easterhoull Chalets*. Follow the road to chalets (painted blue with red roofs) and you will see the yellow *SGS* sign for the garden. Bus 4 from Lerwick/Scalloway.

Opening for: Macmillan Cancer Support

Caithness, Sutherland, Orkney & Shetland

5 KELDABERG
Cunningsburgh, Shetland ZE2 9HG
Mrs L Johnston
T: 01950 477331/07774539693 E: linda@cunningsburghhall.com

A 'secret garden' divided into four areas. A beach garden of grasses, flowers and driftwood. The main area is a sloping perennial border leading down to a greenhouse and vegetable plot and up to a decked area with containers and exotic plants including agaves, pineapple lilies, cannas and gunneras. There is a small pond with a waterfall and goldfish. The area to the back of the house has retaining walls in which rockery plants can be found and, nestled among trees, an arbour in which to rest. In the newer part of the garden there is a wildlife pond with aquatic plants including water lilies, a gunnera and a few frogs! This is situated below the polycrub, in which I grow vegetables, passion flower and fruit trees such as a peach, pear and plum as well as a grapevine. My other vegetables plots are east of the polycrub.

Open: by arrangement 1 June - 30 September, admission £5.00, children free.

Directions: On the A970 south of Lerwick is Cunningsburgh, take the Gord junction on the left after passing the village hall. Continue along the road to the second house past the *Kenwood* sign.

Opening for: Chest Heart & Stroke Scotland

6 KIERFIOLD HOUSE
Kierfiold House, Sandwick, Orkney KW16 3JE
Fiona and Euan Smith

A 150-year-old walled garden in Orkney's West Mainland, which provides a unique micro climate against the windy, coastal conditions. The 'gardens within gardens' layout provides sheltered growing for hostas, irises, grasses and a collection of more than 120 species and hybrids of perennial geraniums. Organically gardened, the space is alive with birds, bees and butterflies. The garden has featured in the *Scottish Field, Scotland on Sunday* and *Beechgrove*. It is included in the books *Island Gardens* by Jackie Bennet, and *Scotland for Gardeners* by Ken Cox.

Open: Sunday 6 July & Sunday 20 July, 11am - 4:30pm, admission £5.00, children free.

Directions: Located on the B9057, a quarter of a mile north of Skaill Loch.

Opening for: Orkney Foodbank

7 LANGWELL
Berriedale KW7 6HD
Welbeck Estates
T: 01593 751278 / 751237 E: caithness@welbeck.co.uk

A beautiful and spectacular old walled garden with outstanding borders situated in the secluded Langwell Strath. Charming wooded access drive with a chance to see deer.

Open: Sunday 27 July, noon - 4pm, admission £5.00, children free.

Directions: Turn off the A9 at Berriedale Braes, up the private (tarred) drive signposted *Private – Langwell House*. It is about 1¼ miles from the A9.

Opening for: RNLI

Caithness, Sutherland, Orkney & Shetland

8 LAURA'S WOOD

Hools, St. Margaret's Hope, Orkney KW17 2RH
Arthur and Laura Cromarty
E: acrom265@aol.com
W: www.westshaird.co.uk

Tree planting began in March 2010. 1,500 varied species were planted into a half acre of rough ground. Several varieties of willow were planted around the perimeter to provide a wind break for other less hardy trees. There was once a house on this site which is long gone but some of the ground around it remains very stony which has hampered planting in those areas. We used a pick to assist planting here; not everything survived so we have planted annually to fill in any gaps. Half an acre adjacent to the trees is annually sown with bird seed mix. Seeds included kale, mustard, crimson clover, phacelia, rape, buckwheat, borage, corn marigolds, oats and barley to feed the wild birds. We have added various bulbs such as daffodils, crocuses and bluebells. We also planted pampas, New Zealand Flax, gunnera and ferns.

Open: Sunday 8 June, 11am - 4pm, admission £5.00, children free. Self catering: www.westshaird.co.uk

Directions: Follow the A961 past the village of St Margaret's Hope then take the first signed road for *Herston* (B9042). Follow this road past Kirkhouse Mill and Farm then turn right over the brig. Follow this road until you come to a forked junction. Take the left hand branch up the hill (not the Herston turn off) and Hools is second left on this road (signposted at the end of *Farm Road*). Parking will be available in the field below the house.

Opening for: Parkinsons UK

9 MILL HOUSE

Lyness, Hoy, Orkney KW16 3NU
Helen Hiscoke

Mill House gardens are a seaside sanctuary of quiet contemplative rooms on many levels, with amazing views. The many secluded seated areas are accessed by steps, tree lined paths and walled garden routes leading around the sprawling grounds, with an array of trees, shrubs, flowers for seasonal colour and interest with formal and natural ponds attracting abundant wildlife. There is a seafront rockery overlooked by a glazed deck from where you can view Scapa Flow. The fruit and vegetable garden is home to a self-built recycled green house, a sheltered potting area, cold frames, raised beds for growing the family's produce including a dappled shaded herb garden behind the house, all giving hours of peace and health benefits working with the steady processes of gardening.

Open: Saturday 28 June, 11am - 4pm, admission £5.00, children free. Cream teas, coffee and cake available at Emily's Tea Room, adjacent to Mill House Gardens. Booking ahead suggested.

Directions: From Lyness ferry terminal, follow signs for *Emily's Tea Room* for two miles, passing over a river. Mill House is on the right past Emily's.

Opening for: Headway – The Brain Injury Association

Caithness, Sutherland, Orkney & Shetland

10 NONAVAAR
Levenwick, Shetland ZE2 9HX
James B Thomason
T: 01950 422447

This is a delightful country garden, sloping within drystone walls and overlooking magnificent coastal views. It contains ponds, terraces, trees, bushes, varied perennials, annuals, vegetable garden and greenhouse.

Open: 1 June - 30 September, 2pm - 5pm, admission £5.00, children free.

Directions: Head south from Lerwick. Turn left at the *Levenwick* sign soon after the Bigton turn-off. Follow the road to the third house on the left after the Midway stores. Park where there is a *Garden Open* sign. Bus 6 from Lerwick – Sumburgh.

Opening for: Cancer Research UK

11 NORBY
Burnside, Sandness, Shetland ZE2 9PL
Mrs Gundel Grolimund
T: 01595 870246 E: gundel.g5@btinternet.com

A small but perfectly-formed garden and a prime example of what can be achieved in a very exposed situation. Blue painted wooden pallets provide internal wind breaks and form a background for shrubs, climbers and herbaceous plants, while willows provide a perfect wildlife habitat. There are treasured plants such as *Chionochloa rubra*, pieris, Chinese tree peonies, a selection of old-fashioned shrub roses, lilies, hellebores and grasses from New Zealand. There is also a lovely selection of interesting art and textiles in the house.

Open: 1 April - 31 December, dawn - dusk, admission £4.00, children free.

Directions: Head north on the A970 from Lerwick then west on the A971 at Tingwall. At Sandness, follow the road to Norby, turn right at the Methodist Church, Burnside is at the end of the road. Bus 10 Sandness – Walls.

Opening for: Survival International

12 ROUND HOUSE
Berstane Road, Kirkwall, Orkney KW15 1SZ
David and Gill Newstead

Half-an-acre site (including the house) with a view towards North Isles. Established windbreak surround of mixed shrubs and trees, seven raised beds for vegetables and flowers, bog garden with huge gunnera and water-loving plants. A very large rockery, non alpine, with a path over the top. There are two small wooded areas, one with bluebells and areas of grass made over to a wildflower meadow.

Open: Saturday 5 July, 11am - 4pm, admission £5.00, children free.

Directions: There is no parking up our lane. Vehicles can be left on the verge at the top of Berstane Road and it's a 100 metre walk from there. The town bus no 9 stops at Berstane Loan at the top of our lane.

Opening for: Orkney Foodbank

Caithness, Sutherland, Orkney & Shetland

13 **SKELBO HOUSE**
Skelbo, Dornoch IV25 3QG
Alison Bartlett
E: SkelboHouseGarden@gmail.com

Extensive woodland garden with spectacular views over Loch Fleet. Mixed herbaceous borders, rose garden and shrubberies surround the house. Lawns slope down to a small lochan and river walkway. Mature trees throughout. Large kitchen garden.

Open: Saturday/Sunday, 26/27 July, 11am - 4pm, admission £7.00, children free.

Directions: from the south, on the A9 take the small turning opposite the Trentham Hotel (just past the Dornoch turn-offs). At the side of Loch Fleet turn left, then at the ruined castle take the second farm road which is fairly rough, and follow round to your right. If coming from the north take the Loch Fleet road signposted to *Embo* from the A9.

Opening for: Mary's Meals

Skelbo House

Caithness, Sutherland, Orkney & Shetland

14 THE CASTLE AND GARDENS OF MEY
Mey KW14 8XH
The Queen Elizabeth Castle of Mey Trust
T: 01847 851473 E: enquiries@castleofmey.org.uk
W: www.castleofmey.org.uk

Her Majesty Queen Elizabeth the late Queen Mother, bought what was then Barrogill Castle in 1952 before renovating and restoring the z-plan castle and creating the beautiful gardens you see today, renaming it The Castle and Gardens of Mey. This romantic and unique garden is a reminder that, however daunting the weather, it is often possible with a little vision and energy to create and maintain a garden in the most unlikely of locations. The castle now includes an animal centre, gift shop and tearoom serving delicious locally sourced food and drinks, often using produce from the castle's very own gardens.

Open: 1 May - 30 May, 10:30am - 4pm, admission details can be found on the garden's website. Card and contactless payments only. The gardens are closed in late July and early August, please check the website for specific dates.

Directions: On the A836 between Thurso and John O'Groats.

Opening for: Donation to SGS Beneficiaries

15 THE QUOY OF HOUTON
Orphir, Orkney KW17 2RD
Dr Colleen Batey

An unusual, historic, walled panoramic garden with 60-foot rill which leads the eye to the spectacular coastal views of Scapa Flow. Carefully planted to withstand winds in excess of 60 mph, with floral interest from March to September. Winner of *Gardeners' World* Britain's best challenging garden 2017 and listed in the top ten *UK coastal gardens*. Featured on *Beechgrove* and in the book *Island Gardens.*

Open: Sunday 27 July, 2pm - 5pm, admission £5.00, children free. Refreshments at the Quoy. Sorry, no dogs.

Directions: From Orphir take the turning to Houton Ferry at the first junction signed *Quoy of Houton*, turn right by the car park. Park here and walk 10 minutes along the coastal road around the bay to the gardens. The gardens are a 10-minute walk from the bus stop. There is limited parking at the garden, available on a first come first serve basis.

Opening for: The Peedie Retreat [SCIO]

Langwell

Caithness, Sutherland, Orkney & Shetland

16 ## WAULKMILL GARDEN
Sandygill, Waulkmill, Orkney KW17 2RA
Tracey Jackson

Waulkmill is a three-acre garden overlooking the sands of Waulkmill Bay. Created over the last 15 years amidst bog and heathland, the garden sits alongside Hobbister Bird reserve. The native, wild, naturalistic-style planting includes hardy plants for the windy plot and Orkney native shrubs and trees. A dipping pond, long borders and perennial planting are designed to take in the spectacular views over Scapa Flow. The St Magnus Way cuts through the land and a sculpture garden is currently under development.

Open: Saturday 21 June, 11am - 5pm, admission £5.00, children free.

Directions: From the A964 follow the signs to *Waulkmill Bay.* Follow the road all the way to the end and the garden is at the end of the road.

Opening for: Orkney Amateur Swimming Club

17 ## WESTLEA
Cromarty Square, St. Margaret's Hope, Orkney KW17 2SN
Shaun Hourston-Wells

This relatively sheltered garden (by Orkney standards!), centrally placed within the village of St. Margaret's Hope, has a wonderful, established tree backdrop. The garden demonstrates that a relatively small space can be transformed into a plant-packed paradise! Plants that are usually difficult to grow in Orkney thrive here and the lush green paths give wonderful access to a rich range of plants.

Open: Sunday 8 June, 11am - 4pm, admission by donation.

Directions: Westlea is at the top of Cromarty Square, furthest from the sea, and sits adjacent to the Cromarty Hall, in St. Margaret's Hope (known locally as "The Hup"). Parking is available in Cromarty Square. The X1 bus (Stromness and Kirkwall, to St. Margaret's Hope) stops right outside Westlea.

Opening for: All proceeds to SGS Beneficiaries

Laura's Wood

Kierfiold House

Dumfriesshire

Sponsored by

✿ RATHBONES

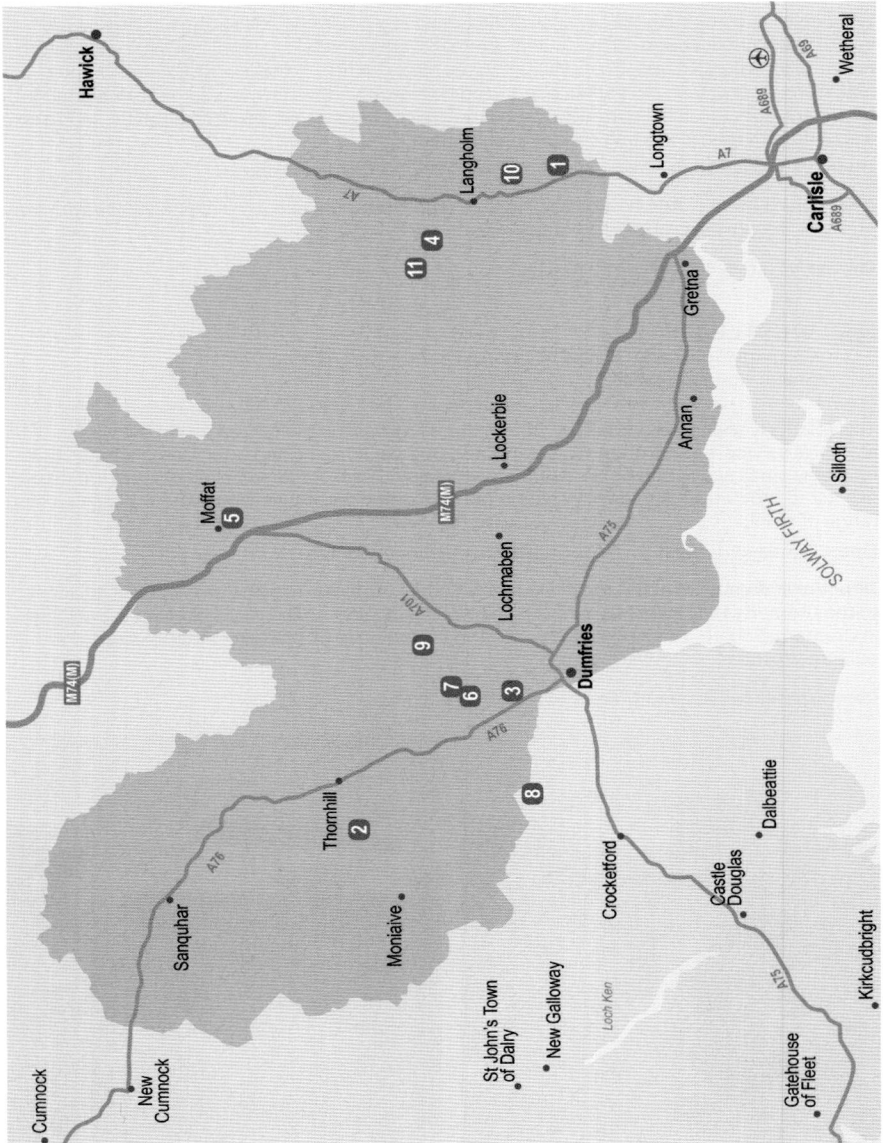

Dumfriesshire

OUR VOLUNTEER ORGANISERS

District Organiser:	Sarah Landale	Dalswinton House, Dalswinton, Dumfries DG2 0XZ info@scotlandsgardens.org
Area Organisers:	Fiona Bell-Irving Pamela Crosbie Liz Mitchell	Bankside, Kettleholm, Lockerbie DG11 1BY Dalswinton Mill, Dalswinton, Dumfries DG2 0XY Drumpark, Irongray DG2 9TX
District Photographer:	Stuart Littlewood	stu@f8.eclipse.co.uk
Treasurer:	Leslie Jack	Gledenholm House, Ae, Dumfries DG1 1RF

GARDENS OPEN ON A SPECIFIC DATE

Tinnisburn Plants, Upper Millsteads, Canonbie	Saturday/Sunday, 15/16 February
Craig, Langholm	Sunday, 16 February
Tinnisburn Plants, Upper Millsteads, Canonbie	Saturday/Sunday, 29/30 March
Dalswinton House, Dalswinton	Sunday, 11 May
Tinnisburn Plants, Upper Millsteads, Canonbie	Saturday/Sunday, 24/25 May
Westerhall, Bentpath, Langholm	Sunday, 25 May
Cowhill Tower, Holywood	Sunday, 1 June
Capenoch, Penpont, Thornhill	Sunday, 8 June
Byreburnfoot House, Byreburnfoot	Sunday, 3 August
Dalswinton Mill, Dalswinton	Sunday, 10 August

GARDENS OPEN REGULARLY

Tinnisburn Plants, Upper Millsteads, Canonbie	1 April - 31 August (Friday, Saturday & Sunday)
Craigieburn House, by Moffat	20 April - 31 October

GARDENS OPEN BY ARRANGEMENT

Gledenholm House, Ae Village, Dumfries	1 April - 31 July
Drumpark, Irongray	1 May - 31 August

Dumfriesshire

1 BYREBURNFOOT HOUSE

Byreburnfoot DG14 0XB
Paul and Julie Taylor
T: 01387 371967 E: julie@byreburnfoot.house
W: www.canonbieretreat.org.uk

When we moved here in the Autumn of 2020, we began redesigning and developing the garden. Today you'll find mostly young planting, plus areas of mature trees. Besides garden paths with arches, a rose crown and a pergola, the individual garden areas boast attractive mixed borders interspersed with conifers, shrubs and trees for interest in every season. You'll also see areas dedicated to fruit and vegetable production along with a small polytunnel. We've recently added some gravelled areas around the site with a variety of pots. All the garden areas have seating, some with tables and parasols.

Open: Sunday 3 August, 1pm - 5pm, admission £5.00, children free.

Directions: Do not follow SatNav! Byreburnfoot House can only be accessed via Canonbie. At the bridge over the River Esk in Canonbie, turn on to the *no through road* with 20mph sign. We are situated on the right, about a mile along this lane.

Opening for: Canonbie Primary School

Byreburnfoot House

Dumfriesshire

2 CAPENOCH
Penpont, Thornhill DG3 4LZ
Mr and Mrs John Gladstone
E: jbgladstone@gmail.com

There are rare trees throughout the grounds and the main garden is the remnant of that laid out in Victorian times. There is a pretty little raised knot garden called the Italian Garden and a lovely old Victorian conservatory. Parking is available in a field half way up the drive, but you may prefer to park in Penpont Village and walk the whole way to Capenoch. There are lovely wildflowers in the oak woods on either side of the drive.

Open: Sunday 8 June, 2pm - 5pm, admission £5.00, children free. Please note there is disabled parking at the House and picnics are allowed.

Directions: Take the A702 west from Thornhill, drive through Penpont and the entrance to the house is at the lodge on the left-hand side, just at the speed restriction sign.

Opening for: Ronald McDonald House Glasgow

3 COWHILL TOWER
Holywood DG2 0RL
Mr and Mrs P Weatherall
T: 01387 720304 E: clara@cowhill.co.uk

This is an interesting walled garden. There are topiary animals, birds and figures and beautiful woodland and river walks. Splendid views can be seen from the lawn right down the Nith Valley. There is also a variety of statues, including several from the Far East.

Open: Sunday 1 June, 2pm - 5pm, admission by donation. The South West Scotland Piping & Drumming Academy (www.swspda.co.uk), will be playing throughout the afternoon.

Directions: Holywood is one-and-a-half miles off the A76, five miles north of Dumfries.

Opening for: Maggie's

4 CRAIG
Langholm DG13 0NZ
Mr and Mrs Neil Ewart
T: 013873 70230 E: nmlewart@googlemail.com

Craig snowdrops have evolved over the last 40 or so years. Round the house and policies, a large variety has been planted with a varied flowering season stretching from the start of January until April and peaking mid-February. Large drifts of *Leucojum vernum* (winter snowflake) have started to naturalise here and along the riverbank, a variety of snowdrops swept down by the river have naturalised in the adjacent woodland, known as the Snowdrop Walk.

Open: Sunday 16 February, noon - 4pm for Snowdrops and Winter Walks, admission £5.00. Teas will be available at Bentpath Village Hall. Bentpath is one mile further on towards Eskdalemuir. Snowdrops for sale.

Directions: Craig is three miles from Langholm on the B709 towards Eskdalemuir.

Opening for: Kirkandrews Kirk Trust: The Friends of Kirkandrews Church

Dumfriesshire

5 CRAIGIEBURN HOUSE

by Moffat DG10 9LF
Janet and Peter McGowan
T: 07557 928648 E: bideshi2024@outlook.com

A beautiful and varied six-acre, plant-lovers' garden in a natural location in scenic Moffat Dale. Meconopsis, trilliums, rhododendrons, magnolias, arisaemas, bamboos, hoherias and many more types of plants flourish in the shelter of mature woodland. A Himalayan glen has been recreated with plants from the region where the Craigie Burn tumbles down a gorge with a series of waterfalls. Downstream is a fern garden with over 70 varieties. Candelabra primulas, rodgersias, cardiocrinum, orchids and other rare plants thrive in the bog garden and woodland glades. Double herbaceous borders come into their own later in the summer and keep the display going throughout the season. Other garden areas include a rose garden, formal pond and autumn garden. A nursery sells hardy plants propagated on site, many of them rare or unusual. The garden has been created over the past 30 years by Janet and Peter, with Dawa Sherpa, building on its old setting, and continues to evolve. Its links to Robert Burns – including his song 'Craigieburn Wood' – provide another layer of history.

Open: The garden is open to visitors from Sunday 20 April to Friday 31 October, 10.30am-6pm (every day except Mondays, but open on Bank Holidays). Many of the special plants in the garden may be purchased at the nursery area.

Directions: Three miles from the A74(M) (junction 15), two miles east of Moffat on the A708 Selkirk Road. Coming from Moffat, there are traffic lights straight ahead at the end of the bend. You can't miss the lodge and prayer flags.

Opening for: All proceeds to SGS Beneficiaries

6 DALSWINTON HOUSE

Dalswinton DG2 0XZ
Mr and Mrs Peter Landale
T: 01387 740220 E: sarahlandale@gmail.com

Late 18th-century house sits on top of a hill surrounded by herbaceous beds and well-established shrubs, including rhododendrons and azaleas, overlooking the loch. Attractive walks through woods and around the loch. It was here that the first steamboat in Britain made its maiden voyage in 1788 and there is a life-size model beside the water to commemorate this. Over the past years, there has been much clearing and development work around the loch, which has opened up the views considerably.

Open: Sunday 11 May, 2pm - 5pm, admission £5.00, children free. Homemade teas will be available from 2 - 5pm. Picnics are allowed in the Walled Garden, around the loch and on the lawns up by the House.

Directions: Take the A76 north from Dumfries to Thornhill. After seven miles, turn right to Dalswinton. Drive through Dalswinton village, past the red church on the right and follow estate wall on the right. Entrance is by either the single lodge or double lodge entrance set in the wall.

Opening for: Kirkmahoe Parish Church of Scotland

Dumfriesshire

Dalswinton House

7 DALSWINTON MILL
Dalswinton DG2 0XY
Colin and Pamela Crosbie
T: 01387 740070 E: colincrosbiehort@btinternet.com

A newly-created, plantsman's garden set around an 18th-century watermill with the Pennyland Burn running through it. The garden contains a wide range of perennials, trees and shrubs that favour the local climate and have been planted during the last few years. A variety of statuary can be found throughout the garden which sits in a hollow and can be only accessed by steps and there are slopes throughout the garden. Unfortunately, this makes the garden unsuitable for anyone with mobility requirements.

Open: Sunday 10 August, 11am - 5pm, admission £6.00, children free. Entrance includes access to the Garden, mini plant fair and talks and demonstrations throughout the day.

Directions: Garden lies in Dalswinton, halfway between the A76 and the A701 on the Auldgirth to Kirkton Road. From Auldgirth take the first left after the Dalswinton Village Hall. The Mill is on the corner before the bridge. We are unable to offer disabled parking.

Opening for: Loch Arthur

8 DRUMPARK
Irongray DG2 9TX
Mr and Mrs Iain Mitchell
T: 01387 820323 or 07743 895351 E: iain.liz.mitchell@gmail.com

Well-contoured woodland garden and extensive policies nurture mature azaleas, rhododendrons and rare shrubs among impressive specimen trees. Water garden with primulas and meconopsis. Victorian walled garden with fruit trees and garden produce. There is also a beautiful herbaceous border. All planting is set in a natural bowl providing attractive vistas. Champion Trees: *Abies cephalonica, Abies procera, Chamaecyparis lawsoniana, Cryptomeria japonica..*

Open: by arrangement 1 May - 31 August, admission by donation.

Directions: Dumfries bypass, head north on the A76 for a half mile, turn left at the signpost to *Lochside Industrial Estates* and immediately right onto Irongray Road; continue for five miles; the gates are next to a lodge looking like a gingerbread house and set in a sandstone wall on the left (half-mile after Routin' Brig).

Opening for: Loch Arthur

Dumfriesshire

9 GLEDENHOLM HOUSE

Ae Village , Dumfries DG1 1RF
Les Jack
T: 01387860278 E: les@gledenholm.co.uk

Developed over the past 35 years, this garden of two acres is set in countryside near Ae Village with some original planting of mature trees dating back to the 1870s. The garden is at its best from April to June, with spring bulbs flowering under species rhodedendrons, azaleas and Japanese maples. The beds feature cottage garden favourites, with clematis and a large rambling rose arch. The progress of the making of the garden can be seen on the SGS website at: scotlandsgardens.org/the-creation-of-a-garden/.

Open: by arrangement 1 April - 31 July, admission £5.00, children free.

Directions: The garden is ten miles north of Dumfries, near Ae Village. Take the A701 from Dumfries and after seven miles take a left turn to Ae Village. At the village take a sharp left at the four-way junction and travel for 0.7 miles. Gledenholm House is then the second on the right with black cast iron gates.

Opening for: All proceeds to SGS Beneficiaries

Gledenholm House

Dumfriesshire

10 **TINNISBURN PLANTS**
Upper Millsteads, Canonbie DG14 0RY
Helen Knowles
T: 07544 373815 E: helen@tinnisburn.co.uk
W: tinnisburn.co.uk

Developed over the last 36 years, this one-acre, plantsman's garden is home to an eclectic mix of truly hardy perennials, trees and shrubs. Planted for year-round colour and interest and to provide habitats for wildlife, there is something new to see each month. There is a woodland garden, rockery, bog garden, herbaceous borders and much more. Meconopsis grow well here and more are being planted out every year. In addition to the garden, there is a small orchard, wildlife ponds and mown paths through the wildflower meadows and, if you're lucky, you may spot red squirrels.
National Plant Collection: *Scilla (Chionodoxa).*

Open: Saturday/Sunday, 15/16 February, 10am - 3pm for Snowdrops and Winter Walks. Advance booking required. **Please visit Tinnisburn website to book.** Then open Saturday/Sunday, 29/30 March, 10am - 4pm for Scilla National Plant Collection. Open Saturday/Sunday, 24/25 May, 10am - 4pm for Meconopsis. Open regularly 1 April - 31 August (Friday, Saturday & Sunday), 10am - 4pm. Admission £5.00, children free.

Directions: Take the B6357 north from Canonbie. At Harelaw turn left onto the B6318 and after 1 mile turn right onto our track. It is 1.5 miles long and is untarmacked but suitable for all vehicles. Just drive slowly and carefully.

Opening for: *Macmillan Cancer Support & Fauna & Flora International*

11 **WESTERHALL**
Bentpath, Langholm DG13 0NQ
Mrs Peter Buckley
E: mary.buckley@hotmail.co.uk

An extensive collection of azaleas, rhododendrons, rare shrubs and mature trees set in a landscape of follies, sculpture and stunning vistas. The Walled Garden contains a glasshouse with some exotic plants collected from around the world.

Open: Sunday 25 May, 1pm - 5pm, admission £5.00, children free. Cream teas will be served in the village hall.

Directions: From Langholm take the B709 towards Eskdalemuir. After approximately five miles, in the village of Bentpath, turn right by white house. Go down through the village, over a bridge and turn right by the church. Continue on this road for approximately one mile. Parking at farm which will be signed.

Opening for: *Westerkirk Parish Trust*

Dunbartonshire

Sponsored by
❁ RATHBONES

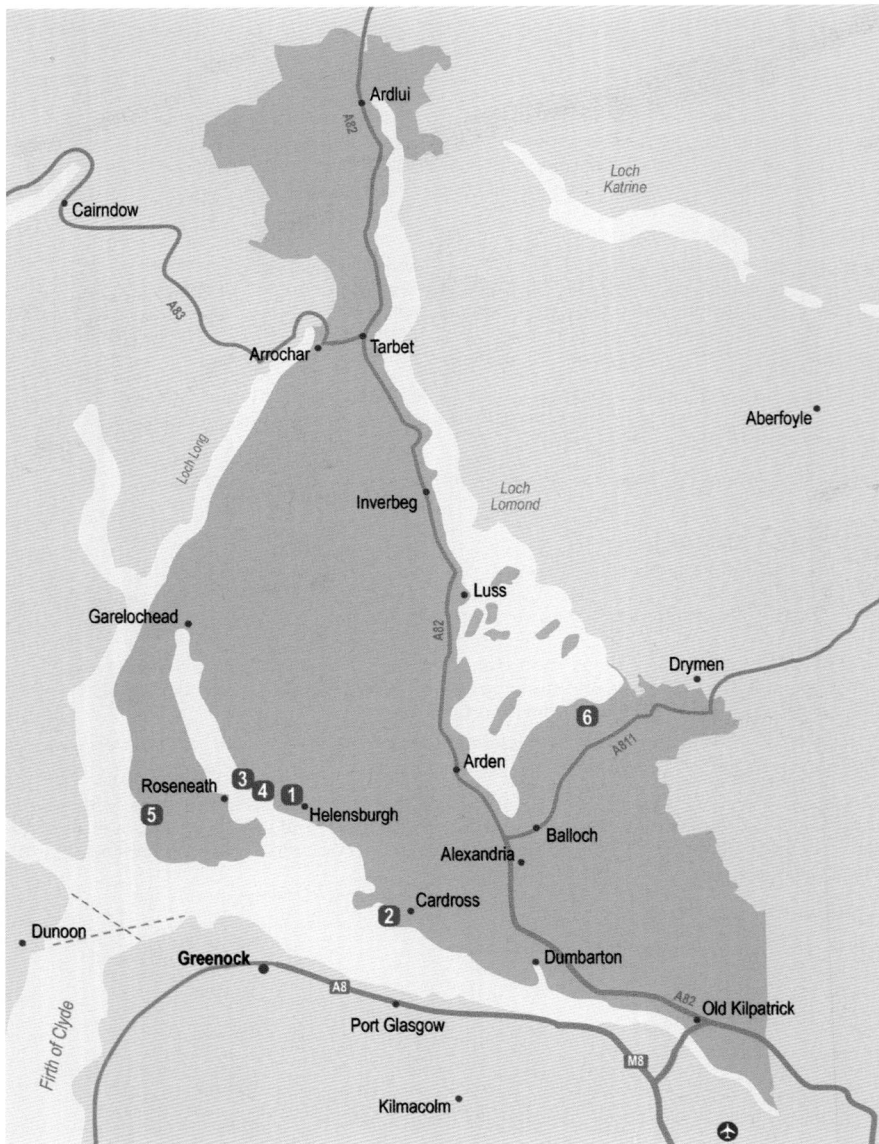

Ardlui

A82

Loch
Katrine

Cairndow

A83

Arrochar • Tarbet

Aberfoyle •

Loch Long

Inverbeg

Loch
Lomond

Luss

Garelochead •

Drymen •

A811

6

Roseneath • **3** **4** **1**
5 Helensburgh

Arden

Balloch

Alexandria

Cardross

2

Dunoon •

Greenock •

A8

Dumbarton •

A82 Old Kilpatrick •

Port Glasgow

M8

Firth of Clyde

Kilmacolm •

✈

Dunbartonshire

OUR VOLUNTEER ORGANISERS

District Organiser:	Tricia Stewart	High Glenan, 24a Queen Street, G84 9LG info@scotlandsgardens.org
Area Organisers:	Jim and Adrienne Kerr	Stonecroft, Ardenconnel Way, Rhu, G84 8RZ
	Kathleen Murray	4 Cairndhu Gardens, Helensburgh G84 8PG
	Lesley and Norman Quirk	Whistler's Burn, Garelochhead Road , Rhu, Helensburgh G84 8NH
	Gavin Smith	Flat 1/2, 4 Hanover Street, Helensburgh G84 7AL
Treasurer:	Claire Travis	54 Union Street, Alexandria G83 9AH

GARDENS OPEN ON A SPECIFIC DATE

18 Duchess Park with Westburn, Helensburgh	Sunday, 11 May
Ross Priory, Gartocharn	Sunday, 18 May
Geilston Garden, Main Road, Cardross	Sunday, 1 June
Glenarn Plant Sale, Glenarn Road, Rhu, Helensburgh	Sunday, 17 August

GARDENS OPEN REGULARLY

Glenarn, Glenarn Road, Rhu, Helensburgh	21 March - 21 September
Linn Botanic Gardens, Cove, By Helensburgh	18 June - 17 August (not Monday & Tuesday)

Linn Botanic Gardens

Dunbartonshire

1 **18 DUCHESS PARK WITH WESTBURN**
Helensburgh G84 9PY
Stewart and Sue Campbell (18 Duchess Park)
Sheila Baker, Cameron and Anne Foy (Westburn)

18 Duchess Park The garden is small, about 40 years old, and is still being developed. The garden backs on to Duchess Wood, which is our local nature reserve. The rear garden is sloping with steps on one side and a gravel path on the other side to get to the upper garden. It is a woodland garden with two large oak trees, over 50 species and hybrid rhododendrons, and many other interesting woodland trees and plants. Sycamore in the wood behind the garden have been felled in the last year, giving more light at the back, and they have been replaced by trial planting of lower-growing shrubs and trees, both native and hybrid. Mid-May should be a good time to enjoy many of the rhododendrons in full bloom. Almost all the plants are clearly named! Short guided wildflower walks in Duchess Wood will be offered during the afternoon by the Friends of Duchess Wood. The bluebells should be in bloom. If the weather is poor, 'stout' shoes are recommended.

Westburn A woodland garden of just over two acres. The Glennan Burn runs through a woodland of oak and beech trees with bluebells in the springtime. Some of the paths are steep, but there are bridges over the burn and handrails in places. There is also an air raid shelter, and the remains of a kiln where James Ballantyne Hannay manufactured artificial diamonds in the 1800s. A lawn is surrounded by rhododendrons and azaleas, and there is a vegetable garden. Areas of the garden are currently being pruned and replanted.

Open: Sunday 11 May, 2pm - 5pm, admission £6.00, children free. Homemade teas will be served at 18 Duchess Park and there will be a plant stall at Westburn.

Directions: From Sinclair Street, travel west along Queen Street until it becomes Duchess Park, a cul de sac. **Number 18** is at the far end on the right.

Proceed along West Montrose Street from Sinclair Street and take the fourth turn on the right. The entrance of **Westburn** is 100 yards up Campbell Street on the right-hand side.

Opening for: Scottish SPCA, Friends of Duchess Wood & St Michael & All Angels Church

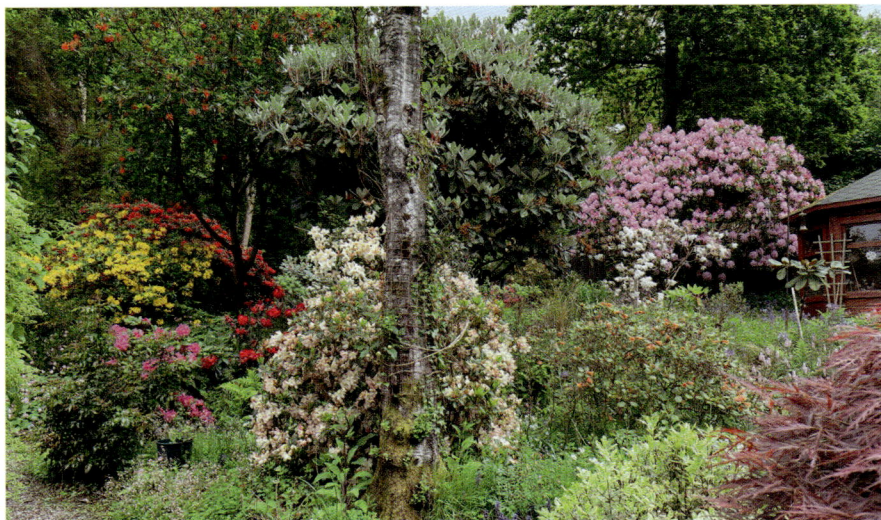

18 Duchess Park

Dunbartonshire

2 **GEILSTON GARDEN**
Main Road, Cardross G82 5HD
The National Trust for Scotland
T: 01389 849187 E: geilstongarden@nts.org.uk
W: www.nts.org.uk/visit/places/Geilston-Garden/

Geilston Garden has many attractive features including the walled garden with herbaceous border providing summer colour, tranquil woodland walks and a large working kitchen garden. This is the ideal season for viewing the Siberian iris in flower along the Geilston Burn and the Japanese azaleas.

Open: Sunday 1 June, 2pm - 5pm, admission details can be found on the garden's website. Last entry to the garden is at 4pm. Garden open until 5pm. Plant sale and homemade teas will be served.

Directions: On the A814, one mile from Cardross towards Helensburgh.

Opening for: Donation to SGS Beneficiaries

3 **GLENARN**
Glenarn Road, Rhu, Helensburgh G84 8LL
Michael and Sue Thornley
T: 01436 820493 E: masthome@btinternet.com
W: www.glenarn.com

Glenarn survives as a complete example of a ten-acre garden which spans from 1850 to the present day. There are winding paths through miniature glens under a canopy of oaks and limes, sunlit open spaces, a vegetable garden with beehives, and a rock garden full of surprise and season-long colour. The famous collections of rare and tender rhododendrons and magnolias give way in midsummer to roses rambling through the trees and climbing hydrangeas, followed by the starry white flowers of hoherias and eucryphias to the end of the season. There is a Silent Space at the top of the garden with views over the Gareloch. Champion Trees: Notably *Magnolia rostrata*.

Open: 21 March - 21 September, dawn - dusk, admission £6.00, children free. Season Ticket – £18.00. There may be local plants for sale.

Directions: On the A814, two miles north of Helensburgh, up Pier Road. Cars to be left at the gate unless passengers have limited mobility.

Opening for: Amma : Birth Companions (SCIO)

4 **GLENARN PLANT SALE**
Glenarn Road, Rhu, Helensburgh G84 8LL
Michael and Sue Thornley

Magnolias, rhododendrons, maples, meconopsis and other ericaceous plants raised by cuttings from Glenarn plants or from specialist seed exchanges plus lots of other interesting plants. Homemade scones and teas will be served.

Open: Sunday 17 August, 2pm - 5pm, admission £6.00, children free.

Directions: On the A814, two miles north of Helensburgh, up Pier Road. Cars to be left at the gate unless passengers have limited mobility.

Opening for: Rhu and Shandon Parish Church of Scotland: Tower Appeal

Dunbartonshire

Glenarn

5 LINN BOTANIC GARDENS
Cove, By Helensburgh G84 0NR
Matthew Young
W: www.thelinn.co.uk

The Linn Botanic Gardens used to be one of the only privately owned gardens to be accredited as a botanical garden, under the stewardship of its creators, Jim and Jamie Taggart. Sadly Jamie died on a plant-hunting expedition to Vietnam in 2013, and Jim's failing health and old age limited the care he could take of the place from that point onwards. He himself then passed away in 2019, at which point the garden was closed and was not maintained at all until 2021 when it was purchased by the current owners. Since then extensive work has been taking place to renovate and reopen the gardens, and to rebuild the disintegrating villa at their heart. It is still very much a work in progress, but large parts of the old plant collection remain intact. You are invited to explore what has been restored and to discuss the plans to complete the repair work and then further develop the garden in the future, but please do bear in mind that it is a long way from being the finished article just yet.

Open: 18 June - 17 August (not Monday & Tuesday), 10am - 5pm, admission £5.00, children free.

Directions: From Helensburgh, head North to Garelochhead. Go through Garelochhead and turn left on the B833, towards Rosneath and Kilcreggan. Drive around the whole peninsula, through both those villages until you reach Cove. Past Cove Country Store and Cove Burgh Hall you will see Cove picnic area by the shore on your left, which is the only public parking facility. From there, walk up the wee lane along the burn, between the two garden walls and we are 20 metres along on the left. Alternatively you can take the 316 bus to Coulport from Colquhoun Square in Helensburgh and ask the driver to let you off at Cove picnic area.

Opening for: Scottish Refugee Council

Dunbartonshire

6 | **ROSS PRIORY**
Gartocharn G83 8NL
University of Strathclyde

Mansion house with glorious views over Loch Lomond with adjoining garden. Wonderful rhododendrons and azaleas are the principal plants in the garden, with a varied selection of trees and shrubs throughout. Spectacular spring bulbs, border plantings of herbaceous perennials, shrubs and trees. Extensive walled garden with glasshouses, pergola and ornamental plantings. Children's play area near the House.

Open: Sunday 18 May, 2pm - 5pm, admission £6.00, children free.

Directions: Ross Priory is one and a half miles off the A811 at Gartocharn. Bus from Balloch to Gartocharn.

Opening for: Friends Of Loch Lomond & The Trossachs & Loch Lomond Rescue Boat

Ross Priory

East Lothian

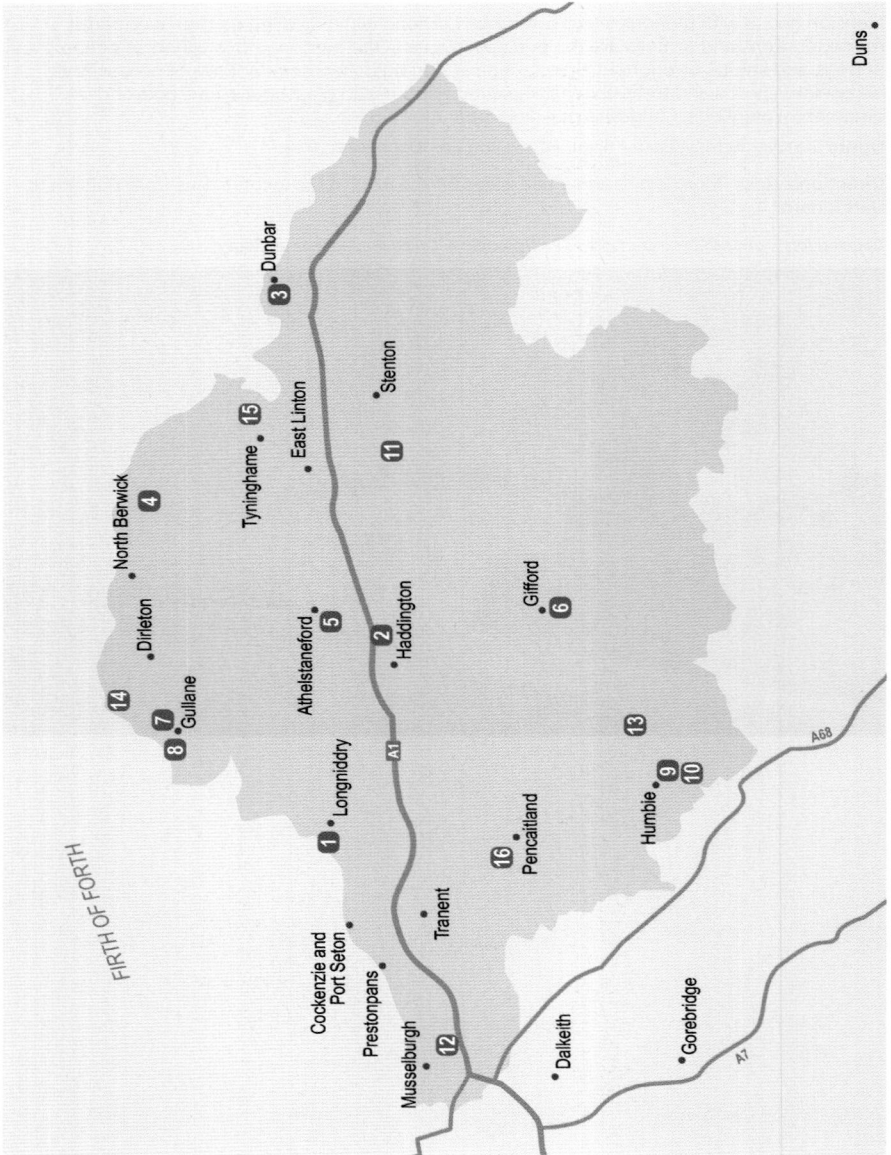

Duns

Dunbar
3

Stenton

Tyninghame   15
East Linton
11

North Berwick
4

Dirleton
Gifford
Haddington   6
Athelstaneford   5
2

14
7   Gullane
8

1   Longniddry
13

Humble   9
10

16   Pencaitland

Tranent

A1
A68

FIRTH OF FORTH

Cockenzie and
Port Seton
Prestonpans
12
Musselburgh

Dalkeith
Gorebridge
A7

East Lothian

OUR VOLUNTEER ORGANISERS

District Organiser:	Joan Johnson	eastlothian@scotlandsgardens.org
Area Organisers:	Jane Craiglee	
	Frank Kirwan	
	Claire Turnbull	
District Photographers:	Delia Ridley-Thomas	
	Malcolm Ross	
Treasurer:	Colin Wilson	

Follow our District on Instagram: @scotgardens_lothians

GARDENS OPEN ON A SPECIFIC DATE

Shepherd House, Inveresk, Musselburgh	Sunday, 16 February
Humbie Dean, Humbie	Wednesday, 19 March
Winton Castle, Pencaitland	Sunday, 30 March
Humbie Dean, Humbie	Wednesday, 2 April
A Blackbird Sings, 20 Kings Park, Longniddry	Saturday, 12 April
Humbie Dean, Humbie	Wednesday, 16 April
Longwood, Humbie	Wednesday, 16 April
Blackdykes Garden, Blackdykes Farmhouse, North Berwick	Friday, 18 April
Blackdykes Garden, Blackdykes Farmhouse, North Berwick	Friday, 25 April
A Blackbird Sings, 20 Kings Park, Longniddry	Saturday, 3 May
Tyninghame House and The Walled Garden, Dunbar	Sunday, 11 May
Humbie Dean, Humbie	Wednesday, 14 May
Longwood, Humbie	Wednesday, 14 May
Shepherd House, Inveresk, Musselburgh	Sunday, 18 May
A Blackbird Sings, 20 Kings Park, Longniddry	Saturday, 31 May
Belhaven House with Belhaven Hill School, Belhaven Road, Dunbar	Sunday, 8 June
Humbie Dean, Humbie	Wednesday, 11 June
Longwood, Humbie	Wednesday, 11 June
A Blackbird Sings, 20 Kings Park, Longniddry	Saturday, 14 June
Gullane House, Sandy Loan, Gullane	Saturday/Sunday, 14/15 June
Greywalls, Gullane	Saturday/Sunday, 14/15 June
Gifford Village with Gifford Bank and Broadwoodside, Gifford	Sunday, 22 June
Tyninghame House and The Walled Garden, Dunbar	Sunday, 29 June
Papple Steading, Papple, Haddington	Saturday/Sunday, 5/6 July
Humbie Dean, Humbie	Wednesday, 9 July
Amisfield Walled Garden, Haddington	Saturday/Sunday, 19/20 July
A Blackbird Sings, 20 Kings Park, Longniddry	Saturday, 19 July
The Gardens at Archerfield Walled Garden, Dirleton, North Berwick	Saturday, 9 August

East Lothian

GARDENS OPEN ON A SPECIFIC DATE – CONTINUED

A Blackbird Sings, 20 Kings Park, Longniddry	Saturday, 16 August
Humbie Dean, Humbie	Wednesday, 27 August
A Blackbird Sings, 20 Kings Park, Longniddry	Saturday, 6 September
Fairnielaw, Athelstaneford, North Berwick	Sunday, 7 September

GARDENS OPEN REGULARLY

Shepherd House, Inveresk, Musselburgh	4 - 27 February (Tues & Thurs) & 15 April - 31 July (Tues & Thurs)
Stobshiel House, Humbie	5 March - 24 September (Wed only)

GARDENS OPEN BY ARRANGEMENT

A Blackbird Sings, 20 Kings Park, Longniddry	1 April - 15 September

Fairnielaw © Malcolm Ross

East Lothian

1 **A BLACKBIRD SINGS**
20 Kings Park, Longniddry EH32 0QL
Graham and Maxine Pettigrew
T: 01875 853003

Situated in the Glassel Park Estate, the planting of this long garden reflects East Lothian habitats including moorland, grassland and woodland, as well as areas of related plant varieties such as rockery, roses, ferns, heucheras and peonies. Together they form a pattern of gardens within a garden accessed by boardwalks and woodland paths. A large water lily pond houses newts and a second pond within a rockery is fed by a waterfall, A cold conservatory contains cacti and insectivorous plants. Vertical structure is provided by a large number of specimen small trees such as Cornus, maples, magnolias, contorted Robinia, Chinese rowan, Davidia and Honey Locust. Animal and bird carvings in wood by Graham reflect local fauna.

Open: Saturday 12 April, Saturday 3 May, Saturday 31 May, Saturday 14 June, Saturday 19 July, Saturday 16 August & Saturday 6 September, 1pm - 5pm, admission £5, cash only, children free. Also open by arrangement 1 April - 15 September. T: 01875 853003.

Directions: By car: enter Dean Road from A198, right at Kings Avenue, right at Kings Park. House is at the end of the second cul-de-sac. By bus (124, X5): Cunningham Court stop, down Cunningham Court and Old Dean Road to turn right on Kings Avenue and then right at Kings Park.

Opening for: Scottish Wildlife Trust Ltd & Leuchie

2 **AMISFIELD WALLED GARDEN**
Haddington EH41 3TE
Amisfield Preservation Trust
W: www.amisfield.org.uk

A large, 18th-century walled garden, abandoned for many years until the early 2000s and since transformed by volunteers. The garden, which is eight acres in size, is completely enclosed by 16 foot-high walls of dressed stone. Each corner features an elegant stone pavilion. Over the years, herbaceous borders, vegetable plots and fruit trees have been planted. A hornbeam walk, maze, sensory gardens, potager and woodland area have been added. The mixed fruit orchards and apple espaliers are home to over 40 varieties of apples. Willow and Cornus beds surround the Winter Garden. A wildflower meadow and pond have been introduced as a further step in our biodiversity plan. This is a garden of interest and joy all year round.

Open: Saturday 10am - 3pm/Sunday 11am - 3pm, 19/20 July, admission £6.00, children free. Free children's activities. Guided tours of the garden. Garden posies and fresh produce. Tea, coffee and home baking available on both days.

Directions: Take the A199 from Haddington; turn south one mile east of Haddington at Stevenson/Hailes Castle junction – brown *Amisfield Walled Garden* sign. Turn right just after the bridge over River Tyne. Parking available.

Opening for: Amisfield Preservation Trust

East Lothian

3 BELHAVEN HOUSE WITH BELHAVEN HILL SCHOOL
Belhaven Road, Dunbar EH42 1NN
Mr and Mrs Jon Bruneau and Mr Olly Langton

Belhaven House has four acres of formal Georgian gardens. It comprises raised herbaceous borders with topiary features for structure, beautiful abundant rose archways and a walled vegetable and fruit garden with box-edged borders. There is also a woodland area with specimen trees dating from the early 20th century and in springtime this area is carpeted with daffodils and bluebells. The garden has been associated with a succession of people interested in plants since the 19th century, most notably Sir George Taylor, a former director of Kew Gardens.

Belhaven Hill School Originally called Winterfield House, the school has retained the garden in front of the walled garden which is accessed through an ornate gate and archway and is laid to lawn with box-edged borders, some containing wildflowers. A gate from the playing field leads to the Belhaven House garden.

Open: Sunday 8 June, 2pm - 5pm, admission £6.00, children free. Tickets and parking for both gardens will be in the school grounds through the school gates.

Directions: By car, approaching Dunbar from A1 on A1087, Belhaven House is opposite Brewery Lane on the junction with Duke Street and the school entrance is a further 300 yards past a high stone wall. Public transport — bus X7 to Dunbar from Edinburgh.

Opening for: Can Do

Greywalls © Delia Ridley-Thomas

East Lothian

4 BLACKDYKES GARDEN
Blackdykes Farmhouse, North Berwick, East Lothian EH39 5PQ
Sir Hew and Lady Dalrymple

Blackdykes Garden was created 30 years ago from open fields. The three-acre site has extensive views southwards towards the Lammermuirs. The formal heart of the garden consists of a series of rooms hemmed in by stone walls and clipped hedges of yew, beech and hornbeam. These are planted with roses, irises, climbers and perennials. Surrounding the formal garden is a network of mown grass paths and avenues, carpeted with fritillaries, narcissi, muscari and cowslips. The informal garden is planted with ornamental cherries, magnolias, species roses and topiary.

Open: Friday 18 April & Friday 25 April, 11am - 4:30pm, admission £6.00, children free.

Directions: Leave North Berwick on the A198 towards Dunbar. Half a mile after Tesco, turn right at Rhodes Holdings. After one mile you will arrive at Blackdykes.

Opening for: Leuchie

Blackdykes garden © Delia Ridley-Thomas

5 FAIRNIELAW
Athelstaneford, North Berwick EH39 5BE
Alison Johnston
T: 07747 862841 E: alison@fairnielawhouse.co.uk

Fairnielaw is a two-and-a-half-acre garden set on a rocky ridge where the wind blows frequently through the Garleton Hills and hits us side on. To provide shelter we planted a mixed-tree, mini forest and created a series of 'rooms' enclosed by beech hedges and dry-stone walls. The garden is on several levels and is a mixture of both formal and wild areas with beautiful views towards Traprain Law and the Garleton Hills at the highest point.

Open: Sunday 7 September, 11am - 4pm, admission £6.00, children free.

Directions: Fairnielaw House is in the village of Athelstaneford set back from the road behind tall trees opposite the church. It is served by a bus service that runs between Haddington and North Berwick several times a day.

Opening for: Trellis

East Lothian

6 GIFFORD VILLAGE WITH GIFFORD BANK AND BROADWOODSIDE

Gifford EH41 4QU

Gardeners of Gifford; Elaine and Richard Austin (Gifford Bank); Anna and Robert Dalrymple (Broadwoodside)

Gifford Village The gardens vary in size and type, from the compact and informal to the large and formal. Gifford was laid out in the early 18th century and has retained much of its original charm. The village includes a beautiful church built in 1708, the Lime Avenue of Yester House and a community woodland — all gardens are within walking distance of each other. In addition to several gardens within the village centre, entry is also included to the larger gardens of Gifford Bank and Broadwoodside, both within easy walking distance.

Broadwoodside (EH41 4JQ) 'is a remarkable achievement. It is a country house that is both memorable and noteworthy, without ever falling into the trap of architectural pretension. That is perhaps because the humble origins of the steading still shine through the transformation to lend texture and interest to the buildings. No less remarkable is the way that the house graduates into the garden and the garden into the landscape. This is a house that feels not merely at home in its setting, but born from it. Finally, there is the delight of the place, enlivened with colour, inscriptions and beautiful things.' *Country Life*, 2023.

Gifford Bank (EH41 4JE) is a Georgian house set in four acres on the edge of the village. Lawns to the front and side of the house are edged by woodland whilst a walled garden provides a more formal area; this includes a circular lawn, raised beds for soft fruit, a herb and rose garden and an orchard. There are large herbaceous borders and scented climbing roses. The garden to the rear of the house includes water features and a large, fire bowl planter.

Open: Sunday 22 June, 11am - 5pm, admission £10.00, children free. Tickets which include entry to all gardens are available at village hall and Broadwoodside. Homemade teas will be available in the village hall where Gifford Art Group is holding an art exhibition.

Directions: Gifford sits between the A1 and the A68 roads about five miles south of Haddington. The village is well signposted from Haddington, Pencaitland and Duns. When leaving Gifford on the B6355 Edinburgh Road, Gifford Bank is the last property on the right before the de-restriction signs. The drive into Broadwoodside is opposite the Golf Course.

Opening for: Gifford Horticultural Society

7 GREYWALLS

Gullane EH31 2EG

W: greywalls.co.uk

Six-acre formal garden attributed to Gertrude Jekyll, surrounding Greywalls Hotel with stunning views over East Lothian and the Forth. The garden was featured on *The Beechgrove Garden* in September 2015, in *The English Garden* in July 2019, *Scottish Field* in September 2019 and *Country Life* in September 2022. Highlights of the garden are straight and curved walls which create rooms and vistas, with radiating paths that link entrances and exits. Everywhere there are places to sit, in the sun and in the shade.

Open: Saturday/Sunday, 14/15 June, 2pm - 5pm, admission £6.00, children free.

Directions: Signposted on the A198 south east of Gullane. From Edinburgh take the A1 south, then the A198 to Gullane, then last turning on the left side. From the south take the A1 north to Haddington, *Gullane* is signposted. Further information is on our website.

Opening for: Leuchie

East Lothian

8 GULLANE HOUSE
Sandy Loan, Gullane EH31 2BH
William and Judy Thomson

A traditional walled garden of three acres. The front of the house looks onto rose-hedged twin herbaceous borders with successional planting, the south border having been refreshed for 2023. A small lily pond leads through to the rose and lavender garden planted in 2018. The next 'room' is reached through a beech hedge and houses soft fruits and vegetables and an informal barbecue area. The orchard boasts a selection of fruit trees and there are magnificent mature trees throughout the garden.
Champion Trees: Elm, Oak.

Open: Saturday/Sunday, 14/15 June, 1pm - 5pm, admission £6.00, children free.

Directions: Gullane House is situated on Sandy Loan about 30 yards from the main street in Gullane. Public transport: regular buses from Edinburgh stop in Gullane.

Opening for: The Ridge SCIO

9 HUMBIE DEAN
Humbie EH36 5PW
Frank Kirwan
E: frank.kirwan@gmail.com

A two-acre ornamental and wooded garden on a variety of levels, sandwiched between two burns at 600 feet, planted for year-round interest. The palette of plants includes hostas, hellebores, perennial geraniums, primula, meconopsis, martagon lilies, clematis, spring bulbs, ground cover, herbaceous and shrub planting, erythronium, daffodil and bluebell meadow, mature and recent azalea and rhododendron planting, and vegetable beds. The lower sections of the garden are only accessible by a series of steps.

Open: Wednesday 19 March, Wednesday 2 April, Wednesday 16 April, Wednesday 14 May, Wednesday 11 June, Wednesday 9 July & Wednesday 27 August, 10:30am - 4pm, admission £6.00, children free.

Directions: Enter Humbie from the A68, pass the school and the village hall on the left then immediately turn right just before the Humbie Hub. Take the second left and Humbie Dean is on the left between two small bridges. Limited parking. Find using what3words: shorthand. frog.limbs

Opening for: Mamie Martin Fund

East Lothian

10 LONGWOOD
Humbie EH36 5PN
Linda Flockhart and Sandra Gentle

An extensive, long-established country garden at 800 feet, undergoing renewal. There are ducks and hens, stream and ponds as well as areas of wild garden and borders including roses, vegetables, lawns and woodlands. Stunning views over the Forth.

Open: Wednesday 16 April, Wednesday 14 May & Wednesday 11 June, 10:30am - 4pm, admission £5.00, children free.

Directions: From the B6368 (Humbie to Haddington road) about one mile east of Humbie take the direction south to *Blegbie Farm* (signposted). Follow the road for circa two miles, passing Humbie Mains Farm as you go. You will find Blegbie Farm at a hard right-hand bend. The drive for Longwood will be straight in front of you, right beside Blegbie. Go straight up the drive and park at the bottom of the cottages. Do not turn right or left. What3words: mermaids.steepest.animals

Opening for: *Médecins Sans Frontières*

11 PAPPLE STEADING
Papple, Haddington EH41 4QD
George and Eri Mackintosh
T: 07941 157785 E: verity.sinclair@papple.com
W: www.papple.com

Papple Steading is a collection of rural farm buildings built in 1860 by AJ Balfour. The gardens (maintained using natural and environmentally friendly methods) have a developing herbaceous collection, lawns, a very productive organic fruit patch, large informal beds and a small herb area. The paddock has meandering paths cut through tall grasses and wildflowers. The adjoining Papple Wood is an ancient, largely deciduous woodland where a trail takes you past follies and sculptures set amongst native trees. A short walk from the Steading is Papana Wood and Wildflower Meadow, possibly the largest meadow of its kind in the county. The Papana Water flows alongside the meadow which was planted in 2020 with Scottish native wildflowers. In 2022 we planted a forest garden in the grounds; this is gradually becoming a wild foraging paradise!

Open: Saturday/Sunday, 5/6 July, 11am - 4pm, admission £6.00, children free.

Directions: From the A199 at East Linton, follow signs to Traprain and Whittingehame, signposted to Papple, 1.5 miles. What3words: formation:painted:honest

Opening for: *Leuchie*

East Lothian

12 SHEPHERD HOUSE
Inveresk, Musselburgh EH21 7TH
Sir Charles and Lady Fraser
T: 0131 665 2570 E: ann.shepherdhouse@gmail.com
W: www.shepherdhousegarden.co.uk

A constantly evolving artist's garden that never stands still, with lots of surprises including a shell house built in 2014, rose parterres, a rill and fountains. At its heart are the plants filling every border, spilling over arches and lining paths, which are the inspiration for Ann's paintings. The season starts with the snowdrop collection of over 70 cultivars, moves on through hellebores, tulips, irises and roses. One of the garden's features is a mirror steel diamond sculpture to commemorate the Frasers' diamond wedding anniversary and 60 years in this garden.

Open: Tuesdays and Thursday, 2 - 4pm from 4 - 27 February, and Sunday 16 February, 11am - 4pm for snowdrops. Then Tuesdays and Thursdays from 15 April - 31 July, 2 - 4pm and Sunday 18 May, 11am - 4pm.

Directions: The garden is near Musselburgh. From the A1 take the A6094 exit signposted Wallyford and Dalkeith and follow signs to Inveresk.

Opening for: Barrahormid Trust

13 STOBSHIEL HOUSE
Humbie EH36 5PD
Mr Maxwell and Lady Sarah Ward
T: 01875 833646 or 07876 350725 E: stobshiel@gmail.com

The garden at Stobshiel House is effectively split into four main parts viz., the walled garden, the shrubbery, the pond and lawns and the woodland areas. Each area is laid out and planted to provide the visitor with all year round interest from swathes of aconites, snowdrops and narcissi in spring to a vast array of perennials, roses, clematis and annuals throughout summer and autumn. The extensive collection of shrubs and mature trees offer a fantastic backdrop during all seasons.

Open: Wednesdays only from 5 March to 24 September, 9am - 3.30pm, admission £6.00, children free. Tea, coffees, lunch and home baking available at Humbie Hub.

Directions: Travelling from Humbie towards Haddington B6368. Take the **second** sign on the right opposite Gilchriston, having passed over a very narrow bridge. Go up hill until you see two stone pillars on a corner. If coming from Haddington to Humbie. Take the B6368 and turn uphill to the left at the **first** sign to *Stobshiel*. Continue uphill until you see the two stone pillars on your right at a sharp corner. What3words: acclaim.reform.breached

Opening for: Marie Curie

East Lothian

14 THE GARDENS AT ARCHERFIELD WALLED GARDEN

Archerfield Estate, Dirleton, North Berwick, East Lothian EH39 5HQ
Kerry Lyall, Head Gardener
W: www.archerfieldwalledgarden.com

Our gardens comprise a series of themed spaces designed for year-round interest. Explore our perennial meadow with swaying grasses and fruit trees. See incredible edibles in the potager; a productive polytunnel complete with grapevine; colourful cutting gardens and a wildlife area with willow tunnels, stumpery and pond. Our light and dark borders brim with monochrome and textural plants and our new water-saving garden features drought tolerant species in shades of blue, rust and orange. Visit the potting shed, where our artist-in-residence creates beautiful botanical casts and take wee ones on a minibeast trail. Come wander, sit and enjoy. There is so much to see!

Open: Saturday 9 August, 11am - 5pm, admission £6.00, children free. Children's activities: minibeast trail (free) and fairy garden workshop (drop-in £3). Garden tours 11.30 and 3pm. Homemade cakes and cordials on the lawn, freshly cut flowers, take-away cakes, produce and preserves. Botanical casting exhibition.

Directions: By bus East Coast Buses no 124 from Edinburgh. Bus stops (2nd stop) after Gullane, at entrance to Archerfield Estate then a 10 minute walk to Archerfield Walled Garden. By car via the A198 East Lothian coast road, turn in to Archerfield Estate, one minute drive to car park at Archerfield Walled Garden. Or refer to our website.

Opening for: Stepping Out Project

Gullane House

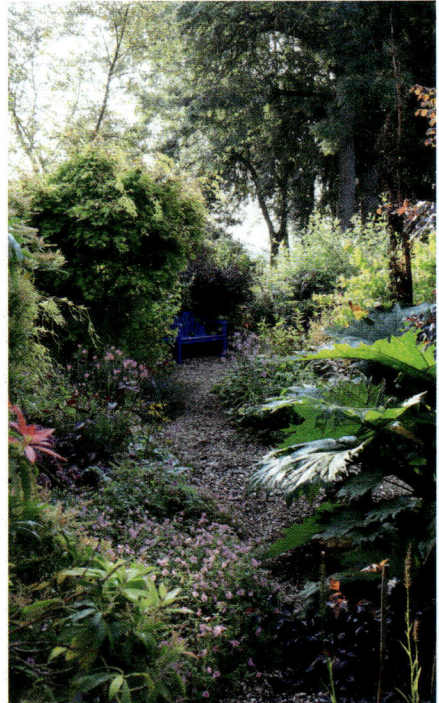

Humbie Dean © Delia Ridley-Thomas

East Lothian

15 TYNINGHAME HOUSE AND THE WALLED GARDEN
Tyninghame House, Dunbar EH42 1XW
Mrs C Gwyn, Tyninghame Gardens Ltd

The Walled Garden, Tyninghame Dunbar EH42 1XW (Mrs C Gwyn): The formal walled garden combines the lawn, sculpture and yew hedges, an Apple Walk, extensive herbaceous planting including roses and peonies with an informal arboretum. Splendid 17th century sandstone Scottish baronial house, remodelled in 1829 by William Burn.
Tyninghame House Dunbar EH42 1XW (Tyninghame Gardens Ltd): The gardens include herbaceous border, formal rose garden, Lady Haddington's Secret Garden with old fashioned roses and an extensive wilderness spring garden with rhododendrons, azalea, flowering trees and bulbs. Grounds include a one-mile beech avenue to the sea. The Romanesque ruin of St Baldred's Church commands views across the Tyne Estuary and Lammermuir Hills. Tyninghame has been awarded 'Outstanding' for every category in the Inventory of Gardens and Designed Landscapes of Scotland.
Champion Trees: Two British and seven Scottish.

Open: Sunday 11 May, 1pm - 5pm. Also open Sunday 29 June, 1pm - 5pm. Admission £6.00, children free.

Directions: Gates on the A198 at Tyninghame Village. Bus 120.

Opening for: Leuchie (Sunday 11 May) & Lynton Day Centre (Sunday 29 June)

16 WINTON CASTLE
Pencaitland EH34 5AT
Sir Francis Ogilvy, Winton Trust
T: 01875 340222
W: www.wintoncastle.co.uk

An historic Renaissance and neo Gothic Castle estate in East Lothian, just 30 minutes from Edinburgh, set in mature and seasonally colourful grounds. A glorious spring display of daffodils and cherry blossom surrounds the castle, whilst extensive mixed borders and a wisteria walkway provide interest in the Walled Garden. Take a walk around Sir David's Loch, the natural woodland area at The Dell and enjoy the beautiful borders of the castle terraces, accessed by gravelled sloping pathways and stone steps.

Open: Sunday 30 March, noon - 4:30pm, admission £6.00, children free. Guided Castle and Garden Tours available (pre-booking online advisable). Teas, home baking and light refreshments available at Cafe Winton, dogs are welcome within grounds.

Directions: Entrance off the B6355 Tranent/Pencaitland Road.

Opening for: East Lothian Foodbank

Edinburgh, Midlothian & West Lothian

Sponsored by

❀ RATHBONES

Edinburgh, Midlothian & West Lothian

OUR VOLUNTEER ORGANISERS

District Organisers:	Jerry & Christine Gregson	101 Greenbank Crescent, Edinburgh EH10 5TA
Area Organisers:	Kate Fearnley	23 Lasswade Road, Eskbank EH22 3EE
	Annette Henderson	5 Melville Terrace, Eskbank EH22 3AR
	Caroline Pearson	42 Pentland Avenue, Edinburgh EH13 0HY
	Gillian Polley	3 Swanston Road, Edinburgh EH10 7BB
Media Volunteer:	Fiona Taylor	
Treasurer:	Kevin Maginnis	69 Ferryfield, Edinburgh EH5 2PS

Follow our District on Instagram: @scotgardens_lothians and Facebook: @sgsedinburgh

GARDENS OPEN ON A SPECIFIC DATE

Preston Hall Walled Garden, Pathhead	Saturday/Sunday, 15/16 February
Eglinton and Glencairn Gardens, Eglinton Crescent, Edinburgh	Sunday, 27 April
Newliston, Kirkliston	Thursday - Sunday, 1-4 May
Dr Neil's Garden, Duddingston Village	Saturday/Sunday, 3/4 May
Greentree, 18 Greenhill Park, Edinburgh	Sunday, 4 May
Newliston, Kirkliston	Wednesday - Sunday, 7-11 May
Bridgend Farmhouse Community Allotments, 41 Old Dalkeith Road	Saturday, 10 May
Belgrave Crescent Gardens, Edinburgh	Sunday, 11 May
Newliston, Kirkliston	Wednesday - Sunday, 14-18 May
Regent, Royal and Carlton Terrace Gardens, Edinburgh	Saturday, 17 May
Temple Village Gardens, Temple	Sunday, 18 May
Moray Place and Bank Gardens, Edinburgh	Sunday, 18 May
Newliston, Kirkliston	Wednesday - Sunday, 21-25 May
Newliston, Kirkliston	Wednesday, 28 May - Sunday, 1 June
14 East Brighton Crescent, Portobello, Edinburgh	Sunday, 1 June
Newliston, Kirkliston	Wednesday, 4 June
Oatridge College Campus – SRUC, Ecclesmachan, Broxburn	Saturday, 7 June
Redcroft, 23 Murrayfield Road, Edinburgh	Saturday, 7 June
Maggie's Edinburgh, Western General Hospital, Crewe Rd, Edinburgh	Sunday, 8 June
Dean Gardens, Edinburgh	Sunday, 8 June
Rivaldsgreen House, 48 Friars Brae, Linlithgow	Saturday, 14 June
Learmonth Place Garden, 9 Learmonth Place	Sunday, 15 June
5 Greenbank Crescent, Edinburgh	Sunday, 15 June
Stockbridge Open Gardens, Edinburgh	Sunday, 22 June
Claremont, Redmill	Sunday, 22 June
Rosemount, 12 Hillhead, Bonnyrigg	Sunday, 22 June
Whitehouse & Grange Bowling Club, 18a Hope Terrace, Edinburgh	Sunday, 29 June
77 Kirk Brae, Edinburgh	Sunday, 6 July
Bridgend Farmhouse Community Allotments, 41 Old Dalkeith Road	Sunday, 20 July

Edinburgh, Midlothian & West Lothian

GARDENS OPEN ON A SPECIFIC DATE – CONTINUED

Claremont, Redmill	Sunday, 20 July
Craigentinny Telferton Allotments, Telferton Road, off Portobello Road	Sunday, 27 July
39 Nantwich Drive, Edinburgh	Saturday/Sunday, 2/3 August
Silverburn Village, 23 Biggar Road, Silverburn	Saturday, 2 August
Hunter's Tryst, 95 Oxgangs Road, Edinburgh	Sunday, 3 August
Whitburgh House Walled Garden, Pathhead, Midlothian	Sunday, 24 August
Whitburgh House Walled Garden, Pathhead, Midlothian	Tuesday, 26 August
Quinn Garden, 41 Morningside Drive, Edinburgh	Saturday, 30 August

GARDENS OPEN BY ARRANGEMENT

Kevock Garden, 16 Kevock Road, Lasswade	1 January - 29 December
Hunter's Tryst, 95 Oxgangs Road, Edinburgh	1 April - 30 September
101 Greenbank Crescent, Edinburgh	1 May - 31 August

Rivaldsgreen House

Edinburgh, Midlothian & West Lothian

1 | **101 GREENBANK CRESCENT**
Edinburgh EH10 5TA
Jerry and Christine Gregson
T: 0131 447 6492 E: jerry_gregson@yahoo.co.uk

The house is on a busy bus route, but it hides a fascinating garden on a sloping site. There are views over Braidburn Valley Park to the Pentland Hills. Paths wind down from the oval lawn, past a handsome magnolia tree, to a terrace which overlooks a water feature and flowering shrubs. Further steps lead past a scree bed of azalea and rhododendron to a productive area of vegetable beds and a neatly-concealed composting area. We aim to have colour, contrast and interest all year round.

Open: by arrangement 1 May - 31 August, admission £5.00, children free. Please note the garden is not suitable for anyone with limited mobility.

Directions: From the city centre take the A702 through Morningside. Continue uphill and turn right at Greenbank Church on to Greenbank Crescent. Buses 5 and 16; the stop is for Greenbank Row.

Opening for: St.Columba's Hospice Care

2 | **14 EAST BRIGHTON CRESCENT**
Portobello, Edinburgh EH15 1LR
Jim and Sue Hurford
E: sue.hurford@gmail.com

Roughly two thirds of an acre suburban garden, developed over 40 years. People have said the following about it: 'A little bit of countryside in the town', 'Booming with green', 'A bosky bower' and 'There is such a wide range of plant material and every little corner holds a new gem'.

Open: Sunday 1 June, 2pm - 5pm, admission £5.00, children free.

Directions: Buses 21, 12 and 49 to Brighton Place, and 15, 26, 40 and 45 to Portobello High Street. Brighton Place intersects Portobello High Street just east of the bus stops.

Opening for: The Trussell Trust

3 | **39 NANTWICH DRIVE**
Edinburgh EH7 6RA
Michael and Susan Burns

Large wildlife-friendly garden run on organic principles. Includes mini orchard, pond, mixed borders, greenhouse and a secret garden. There are mini woodland walks and an allotment for vegetables, plus a compost area, worm bin and rotary bin.

Open: Saturday/Sunday, 2/3 August, 2pm - 5pm, admission £5.00, children free. Please note there is no wheelchair access.

Directions: Bus 19 to Craigentinny Road or bus 26 to Kekewich Drive.

Opening for: Garden Organic

Edinburgh, Midlothian & West Lothian

4　5 GREENBANK CRESCENT
Edinburgh EH10 5TE
Sandy Corlett
T: 0131 4471119 E: sandycorlett@hotmail.co.uk

South-facing, newly designed, sloping terraced garden with views over Braidburn Valley Park to the Pentlands. Colourful chaos of herbaceous plants, shrubs, roses and small trees. Hard features include a gazebo, pergola, greenhouse and water feature.

Open: Sunday 15 June, 2pm - 5pm, admission £5.00, children free.

Directions: From the city centre take the A702 through Morningside, continue uphill on Comiston Road, turn right at Greenbank Church on to Greenbank Crescent. Buses 5, 16, 11.

Opening for: *NASS: Spinal Arthritis*

5　77 KIRK BRAE
Edinburgh EH16 6JN
Michael Brown and Angela Casey
E: mvbrown55@gmail.com

A south Edinburgh garden of roughly 1200 square metres surrounded by a stone wall. This family garden features a mix of mature and younger trees, herbaceous beds and borders, a vegetable patch, lawn, a 19th century cast iron vinery, an old monkey puzzle, pond and a patio. Since 2002 the garden has evolved from the traditional and formal to an informal, wildlife-friendly garden with a wide variety of plants, trees and shrubs. The planting aims for year-round colour and variety with fruit, vegetables and different areas for just sitting and enjoying. Still on its journey and a work in progress, the newest initiative is to turn some of the lawn into a small wildflower meadow. All inputs are peat-free and as organic as possible.

Open: Sunday 6 July, 2pm - 5pm, admission £5.00, children free.

Directions: 77 Kirk Brae is towards the top of the hill on the left hand side, the number 77 is clearly marked on the main and side gates. Parking is on Kirk Brae or in the quieter Wolrige Road nearby. The 31 bus stops close to the property in each direction at the *Kirk Park* stop.

Opening for: *SupportED – The Community Eating Disorder Charity*

6　BELGRAVE CRESCENT GARDENS
Edinburgh EH4 3AJ
The Residents of Belgrave Crescent

City centre private garden of seven acres beside the historic Dean Bridge. Shrubs, trees, herbaceous and mixed borders provide a haven of peace close to the city, with wild areas and magnificent views of the Dean Bridge and over the Water of Leith.

Open: Sunday 11 May, 2pm - 5pm, admission £6.00, children free. Children's play area for under 12s. Children must be supervised by parent or other responsible adult. Sorry no dogs.

Directions: The garden is a five-minute walk from the West End. Enter from the East Gate in Belgrave Crescent. Buses 19, 22, 36, 37, 41, 43, 47 and 113 (Dean Bridge stop).

Opening for: *Fresh Start*

Edinburgh, Midlothian & West Lothian

7 **BRIDGEND FARMHOUSE COMMUNITY ALLOTMENTS**
41 Old Dalkeith Road EH16 4TE
Bridgend Farmhouse Community Allotments
T: 07738 399185 E: jo@bridgendfarmhouse.org.uk
W: www.bridgendfarmhouse.org.uk

Discover a hidden gem in south Edinburgh, a peaceful community growing space where everyone is welcome. Under the backdrop of Arthur's Seat, we grow annual and perennial vegetables and fruit, and enjoy it with our community. We are an organic garden, with an emphasis on biodiversity and sustainable gardening practices. Why not take a moment to wander around the rest of the Bridgend Farmhouse site, explore our peace garden, café and workshop spaces.

Open: Saturday 10 May & Sunday 20 July, 11am - 3pm, admission £5.00, children free. Tours of the garden throughout the day. Bug hunt for kids and grown ups! Plants, herbal teas and items from the garden for sale. Café open to public.

Directions: There is only disabled parking at Bridgend Farmhouse, so we encourage visitors to come by bike, bus (24, 33, 38, 49), or park at Cameron Toll Shopping Centre, a 10 minute walk away.

Opening for: Bridgend Farmhouse

8 **CLAREMONT**
Redmill EH47 0JY
Trevor and Faye Yerbury
E: info@yerburystudio.com

'Claremont' is situated only two minutes from J4 of the M8 and yet is an idyllic oasis. It is an eclectic garden created over 20 years; before we moved in it was just grass with a few rhododendrons. The garden has three areas, to the front are various herbaceous borders, to the side we have our hosta collection. Our garden contains over 150 hostas. To the rear there are herbaceous borders, plus a stumpery/fernery created in 2022. We have three ponds, one very large, a rockery, a dovecot, newly created rose garden and interesting trees including a grand monkey puzzle. New for 2025: the stumpery has been extended over the winter.

Open: Sunday 22 June, 1pm - 4pm. Also open Sunday 20 July, 1pm - 4pm. Admission £5.00, children free. Home baking and refreshments, small plant stall and an exhibition of pottery by Carl Radford of Pisces Pottery in our gallery.

Directions: Take the M8 and leave at J4 heading for Whitburn. At the first set of traffic lights turn right for Whitburn. After 100 metres turn first right at the bollards and come straight down.

Opening for: Marie Curie

9 **CRAIGENTINNY TELFERTON ALLOTMENTS**
Telferton Road, off Portobello Road, Edinburgh EH7 6XG
The Gardeners of Craigentinny and Telferton
E: ctallotments@gmail.com

Established in 1923, this independent allotment site is a tranquil and charming place, hidden away in a built-up area, where the local community benefit from growing their own vegetables and fruit. Come and enjoy tea, home baking and a chat with our friendly plot-holders.

Open: Sunday 27 July, 2pm - 5pm, admission £4.00, children free.

Directions: Park on Telferton Road. Buses 15, 26, 45.

Opening for: Craigentinny Telferton Allotments

Edinburgh, Midlothian & West Lothian

10 DEAN GARDENS
Edinburgh EH4 1QE
Dean Gardens Management Committee

Nine acres of semi-woodland garden with spring bulbs on the steep banks of the Water of Leith in central Edinburgh. Founded in the 1860s by local residents, the Dean Gardens contain part of the great structure of the Dean Bridge, a Thomas Telford masterpiece of 1835. Lawns, paths, trees and shrubs with lovely views to the weir in the Dean Village and to St Bernard's Well. There is also a children's play area.

Open: Sunday 8 June, 2pm - 5pm, admission £5.00, children free.

Directions: Entrance at Ann Street or Eton Terrace.

Opening for: All proceeds to SGS Beneficiaries

11 DR NEIL'S GARDEN
Duddingston Village EH15 3PX
Dr Neil's Garden Trust
E: info@drneilsgarden.co.uk
W: www.drneilsgarden.co.uk

A wonderful, secluded landscaped garden on the lower slopes of Arthur's Seat including conifers, heathers, alpines, a physic garden, herbaceous borders and ponds.

Open: Saturday/Sunday, 3/4 May, 2pm - 5pm, admission £5.00, children free.

Directions: Park at the kirk car park on Duddingston Road West and then follow signposts through the manse garden.

Opening for: Dr Neil's Garden Trust

12 EGLINTON AND GLENCAIRN GARDENS
Eglinton Crescent, Edinburgh EH12 5DD
Eglinton and Glencairn Gardens Association
W: www.eglintonglencairngardens.co.uk

The Eglinton and Glencairn Gardens are an oasis of calm in Edinburgh's West End. Covering two acres, they consist of lawns, flower beds and a fine collection of trees including a Camperdown Elm. They are well used and enjoyed by the residents of the two crescents and include a small children's play area. The gardens are maintained on organic principles. Situated just off Palmerston Place, they are probably at their best in spring time with a profusion of blossom. Created at the end of the nineteenth century, the paths wander through the trees, shrubs and lawns, with plenty of places to sit and enjoy the peace of the gardens.

Open: Sunday 27 April, 2pm - 5pm, admission £5.00, children free. Children in the playground must be supervised by a responsible adult at all times.

Directions: The gardens lie off Palmerston Place, between Eglinton Crescent and Glencairn Crescent, 10 minutes walk from Haymarket station, which can be reached by tram and Lothian buses including numbers 26 and 31 stopping outside the station and 4 and 44 in Dalry Road

Opening for: The Trussell Trust

Edinburgh, Midlothian & West Lothian

13 GREENTREE
18 Greenhill Park, Edinburgh EH10 4DW
Alison Glen

A rare opportunity to appreciate a mature garden which, with the exception of one magnificent old copper beech tree, is completely planted and created by its owner Alison Glen. Designed with an artist's appreciation of form, this woodland garden shelters a large collection of rhododendrons. There are many beautiful specimen trees and shrubs including *Hoheria glabrata*, *Halesia carolina* and several magnolia species. The garden is fully wheelchair accessible and there are several ways to move through it; from the Japanese-inspired stream garden presided over by a mature *Pinus wallichiana* at one end, to the newly developed borders at the other.

Open: Sunday 4 May, 10am - 5pm, admission £5.00, children free.

Directions: Buses 11, 16, 15, 23, 5. By car: from the east – Chamberlain Road, Strathearn Road, from the north – Morningside Road, from the west – Colinton Road.

Opening for: Alzheimer Scotland

14 HUNTER'S TRYST
95 Oxgangs Road, Edinburgh EH10 7BA
Jean Knox
T: 07708 653584 E: jean.knox@blueyonder.co.uk

Well-stocked and beautifully designed, mature, medium-sized town garden comprising herbaceous and shrub beds, lawn, fruit and some vegetables, water features, seating areas, trees and an example of cloud pruning. This is a wildlife-friendly garden that has been transformed from a wilderness 40 years ago and continues to evolve. In 2017 two raised beds were added to the front garden. This hidden treasure of a garden was featured on *Beechgrove* in June 2015 and on *The Instant Gardener* in June 2016.

Open: Sunday 3 August, 2pm - 5pm. Also open by arrangement 1 April - 30 September. Admission £5.00, children free.

Directions: From Fairmilehead crossroads head down Oxgangs Road to Hunter's Tryst roundabout and it's the last house on the left. Buses 4, 5, 27, 400. The bus stop is at Hunter's Tryst and the garden is opposite.

Opening for: St. Columba's Hospice Care & Lothian Cat Rescue

15 KEVOCK GARDEN
16 Kevock Road, Lasswade EH18 1HT
David and Stella Rankin
E: stella@kevockgarden.co.uk W: www.kevockgarden.co.uk

This wonderful hillside garden has magnificent views over the North Esk Valley. Its steep slope creates a range of different habitats with a wide diversity of plants, ranging from those that love hot, sunny conditions to those that prefer the cool, damp places near the pond and woodland glades. Mature specimen trees, rhododendrons, azaleas and unusual shrubs are underplanted with many rare woodland plants. Lawns have been relaid, surrounding borders have been planted, and there is a new rock garden. Kevock Garden has featured in many magazine articles and gardening programmes.

Open: by arrangement 1 January - 29 December, admission £5.00, children free. Individuals and couples are welcome as well as groups. Please email to arrange.

Directions: Kevock Road lies to the south of the A678 Loanhead/Lasswade Road. 5 minutes from the city bypass Lasswade Junction and on the 31 Lothian Bus route to Polton/Bonnyrigg Road.

Opening for: Fischy Music

Edinburgh, Midlothian & West Lothian

16 **LEARMONTH PLACE GARDEN**
9 Learmonth Place EH4 1AX
Libby Webb
W: Instagram@docleaves

A unique reimagining of a city-centre, mid-terrace, walled garden. The garden is only 7 x 14 metres, but contains two ponds, a pergola and is accessed by garden paths through arches. The lawn has been lifted entirely and the space is tightly planted with trees and mainly perennial plants. The effect of the garden is of a city centre woodland/cottage garden, which gives the illusion of being bigger than it is by blurring the sandstone wall boundaries.

Open: Sunday 15 June, 1pm - 5pm, admission £6.00, children free. There are deep ponds in a small and potentially crowded space, children should therefore be closely supervised.

Directions: Buses 19, 22, 24, 29, 36, 37, 43, 113 stop nearby. Local on-street parking is likely to be available at weekends.

Opening for: CHAS & The Woodland Trust Scotland

17 **MAGGIE'S EDINBURGH**
Western General Hospital, Crewe Road, Edinburgh EH4 2XU
Maggie's Centre
W: www.maggies.org

At Maggie's we believe that gardens can have an amazing, positive effect on health and well-being. Each of our centres has a beautiful garden designed alongside the building to ensure a strong connection between the outside and inside. The garden was designed by Emma Keswick and has been adapted to grow and flourish alongside two new extensions. The walled garden and statue gardens create a connection with nature and the ever-changing seasons. Emma's planting design ensures the garden has year-round colour and creates a calming transition away from the hospital. The garden is fully accessible for all with enclosed spaces cleverly interspersed with more open areas with longer views.

Open: Sunday 8 June, 2pm - 5pm, admission £5.00, children free. Homemade teas and plants for sale. There will also be guided tours of the Maggie's Centre available.

Directions: Maggie's is located behind Ward 1 at the Western General Hospital. Enter the hospital at the Crewe Road entrance (Hospital Main drive), follow the path under the road bridge and take the first left into Maggie's. Lothian Buses: 19, 19A, 28, 28B, 29, 37, 37A, 38; First Bus: 129. For vehicle access enter the hospital via the Telford Road entrance, parking is free, follow parking signs on the day.

Opening for: Maggie's

Edinburgh, Midlothian & West Lothian

18 MORAY PLACE AND BANK GARDENS
Edinburgh EH3 6BX
The Residents of the Moray Feu

Bank Gardens Edinburgh EH3 6BX (The Residents of Bank Gardens): Join us to celebrate the gardens of the Moray Feu in their spring and summer colours. Nearly six acres of secluded wild gardens with lawns, trees and shrubs with banks of bulbs down to the Water of Leith and stunning views towards Dean Bridge.

Moray Place Edinburgh EH3 6BX (The Residents of Moray Place): Private garden of three-and-a-half acres in the Georgian New Town is framed by the polygon of Moray Place, and is laid out with shrubs, trees and flower beds offering an atmosphere of tranquillity in the city centre.

Open: Sunday 18 May, 2pm - 4:30pm, admission £5.00, children free. There will be tea, coffee and home baking.

Directions: Bank Gardens enter by the gate at the top of Doune Terrace.

Moray Place enter by the north gate in Moray Place.

Opening for: Euan Macdonald Centre for Motor Neurone Disease Research

19 NEWLISTON
Kirkliston EH29 9EB
Mr and Mrs R C Maclachlan
T: 0131 333 3231 E: newliston@gmail.com

A well preserved 18th-century parkland/designed landscape rather than a garden as such. Full of mature rhododendrons and azaleas, fine vistas and allées of trees. The walk around the woods and lake is a carpet of wild garlic and bluebells in the spring. The wood to the east of the house is in the pattern of the Union Jack, best appreciated by standing in the centre where all the radiating paths meet. The house, designed by Robert Adam, is also open.

Open: Thursday 1 May - Wednesday 4 June (not Mondays and Tuesdays) 2pm - 6pm, admission £5.00, children free.

Directions: Four miles south of the Forth Road Bridge, entrance off the B800.

Opening for: CHAS

Edinburgh, Midlothian & West Lothian

20 OATRIDGE COLLEGE CAMPUS – SRUC

Ecclesmachan, Broxburn, West Lothian EH52 6NH
Oatridge College Campus – SRUC
T: 01506 864800 E: gmcgillivray@sruc.ac.uk
W: www.sruc.ac.uk

SRUC Oatridge Campus situated within 700 acres of mixed grounds, is a land-based college comprised largely of agricultural with arable areas, but also hosts Horticulture and Landscaping, the Scottish National Equestrian Centre, Engineering and Animal Care departments. Benefitting from formal planted areas with named and labelled specimen plants, the campus presents an inviting and diverse mixture of planting styles to explore. From prairie planting, an alpine rockery, numerous specimen trees, productive allotment areas, a woodland walk and herbaceous borders, the visit is sure to have something for everyone. The student polytunnels and glasshouses offer an additional glimpse of some of the propagation techniques demonstrated by students. Visitors can explore the extensive woodland walks of the *National Paths For All* demonstration site. This project was developed to show several different materials, design and construction methods to use when creating walking paths.

Open: Saturday 7 June, noon - 5pm, admission £6.00, children free. Our students and staff will be delivering gardening workshops throughout the afternoon. Follow us on social media: SRUC Oatridge Campus

Directions: The college is well signposted. Turn into Ecclesmachan Village, then immediately left and up the main college drive. The car park is on the left at the top of the drive. Buses 31 and 32 from Linlithgow, Uphall Station and Livingston, then approximately a six-minute walk.

Opening for: SRUC: Student Hardship Fund

21 PRESTON HALL WALLED GARDEN

Pathhead EH37 5UG
William and Henrietta Callander
T: 07971 028697 E: henrietta@prestonhall.co.uk
W: www.prestonhall.co.uk

Preston Hall is a 3.5 acre walled garden based in Pathhead. Restoration of the 18th century walled garden started in 2011, and today Head Gardener Kate Danesh oversees the ever-evolving transformation. February will see the first glimpse of life again in the garden with the appearance of snowdrops. The Walled Garden and surrounding parkland are carpeted in the beautiful white flowers.

Open: Saturday/Sunday, 15/16 February, 10am - 4pm for Snowdrops and Winter Walks, admission £5.00, children free.

Directions: Twelve miles south of Edinburgh off the A68, one mile east of Pathhead Village.

Opening for: MY Name'5 Doddie Foundation

Edinburgh, Midlothian & West Lothian

22 QUINN GARDEN
41 Morningside Drive, Edinburgh EH10 5LZ
Mrs Elisabeth Quinn
W: oyfulgarden.co.uk

With its tranquil, oasis-like atmosphere, our family garden offers a peaceful escape from city life. In just two years, we've transformed this space from a concrete wasteland into a vibrant haven for both people and wildlife. Wander through areas alive with roses, dahlias, and *Verbena bonariensis*, or find a cozy spot under the pergola to enjoy the sights and sounds of bees, butterflies, and birds. A beautiful wildlife pond attracts newts and frogs, adding to the garden's natural charm. During your visit, enjoy homemade cakes and explore a plant sale to take a piece of the garden home with you. A perfect place to relax and unwind, this little sanctuary invites you to pause and enjoy nature's beauty.

Open: Saturday 30 August, 2pm - 5pm, admission £5.00, children free.

Directions: Buses 5, 11, 15, 16, 23, 36. There is some on street parking.

Opening for: *Craigmillar Literacy Trust*

23 REDCROFT
23 Murrayfield Road, Edinburgh EH12 6EP
James and Anna Buxton
T: 07989 977701 E: annabuxtonb@aol.com

Redcroft is a mature walled garden surrounding an attractive Arts and Crafts house. It is a hidden haven off a busy road with a variety of different features and habitats: old shrubberies and trees, an orchard, a rockery, a pond, and an extensive lawn with contrasting longer grass. It is well maintained with clipped shrubs and some cloud pruning. June is very colourful with many flowering shrubs and wall plants, and there should be a good display in the greenhouse. Children and buggies are very welcome, dogs on leads too. We hope older children will enjoy our treehouse.

Open: Saturday 7 June, 4pm - 7pm, admission £7.00, children free. This is a change from our usual two day afternoon openings in mid May, and is more of an early evening gathering with drinks and light refreshments. Plant sale, music in the garden: No Strings Attached Wind Band will play. Mostly wheelchair accessible.

Directions: Murrayfield Road runs north from Corstorphine Road to Ravelston Dykes. There is easy free parking. Buses 12, 26, and 31, get off at Murrayfield Stadium. Bus 38 goes along Murrayfield Road.

Opening for: *The Church of the Good Shepherd, Murrayfield*

Edinburgh, Midlothian & West Lothian

24 REGENT, ROYAL AND CARLTON TERRACE GARDENS
17a Royal Terrace Mews, Carlton Terrace Lane Entrance, Edinburgh EH7 5BZ
RRCT Gardens Association

The largest of Edinburgh's New Town gardens still in private ownership, it remains largely unchanged since its formation in 1830. The design consists of an upland lawn of seven acres planted with specimen trees. The flanking woodlands of five acres are planted with spring bulbs giving a carpet of colour. Sitting on the lower slope of Calton Hill, the garden has beautiful views of Edinburgh and the surrounding countryside.

Open: Saturday 17 May, noon - 4pm, admission £7.50, children free. Dogs welcome but they must be on short leads.

Directions: Trams: To Picardy Place then walk along Blenheim Place and Royal Terrace turning right onto Carlton Terrace Lane, where the green garden gate is straight ahead. Buses: to Elm Row or London Road and directions above.

Opening for: Flourish

25 RIVALDSGREEN HOUSE
48 Friars Brae, Linlithgow EH49 6BG
Dr Ian Wallace
T: 07801 855146 E: ianwjw1940@gmail.com

Mature two-acre garden with lovely mixed herbaceous, rose, and tree planting.

Open: Saturday 14 June, 2pm - 5pm, admission £5.00, children free.

Directions: From the west end of the High Street turn into Preston Road, after crossing the canal turn left into Priory Road and at the T junction turn left down Friars Brae. There is car parking available.

Opening for: St John of Jerusalem Eye Hospital Group

26 ROSEMOUNT
12 Hillhead, Bonnyrigg EH19 2AH
Brian and Yvonne Hillyard
E: yphillyard@gmail.com

Rosemount is a large cottage garden with lawns to the front and rear of the house and a wide range of shrubs and perennial plants, as well as some mature trees, including a *Parrotia persica*, a *Liriodendron tulipifera* and a *Eucryphia nymansensis*, and some recent additions such as a *Cryptomeria*, a *Davidia involucrata* (handkerchief tree) and a *Cornus controversa* (wedding cake tree). Other features include a greenhouse with a Black Hamburg vine, a wildlife pond, a small rockery, and a developing crevice garden. Beyond the ornamental part is a productive fruit and vegetable section. The present owners have been working since 2014 to restore and replant the garden; it is still under development.

Open: Sunday 22 June, 2pm - 5pm, admission £5.00, children free.

Directions: Hillhead is the main route through Bonnyrigg (B704) and is on the no 31 bus route (alight at Broomieknowe Gardens), Rosemount is situated on the crest of the hill 100 yards to the south of this.

Opening for: Scottish SPCA

Edinburgh, Midlothian & West Lothian

27 SILVERBURN VILLAGE
23 Biggar Road, Silverburn EH26 9LJ
The Gardeners of Silverburn Village

A variety of village gardens all surviving at 800 feet and the now well-established arboretum and wildflower trail. Enjoy the lovely Pentland Hill views and the *Beechgrove Garden* around the Hall. Visit the plant stall with specialist plants and lots for new gardeners and children.

Open: Saturday 2 August, 2pm - 5pm, admission £7.00, children free. Afternoon tea and our famous home baking available in the Village Hall: Adults £3.00, children £2.00, family ticket (more than four members) £10.00. Specialist plant, local craft and harvest stalls. Children's nature trail, messy cakes and an 'eco' treasure hunt.

Directions: Parking available. Disabled access. Buses: Houston 101/102 Edinburgh-Dumfries route. On the A702 ten miles from Edinburgh city centre, six miles from the city bypass and two miles from Penicuik via Hopelands Road.

Opening for: Mary's Meals

28 STOCKBRIDGE OPEN GARDENS
Garden trail runs between Logie Green Gardens EH7 4HE and
Royal Circus Gardens North EH3 6TN
Gardeners of Stockbridge
E: jw.homeoffice@gmail.com

Visit some of the surprising horticultural delights behind the discreet terraces of Stockbridge/New Town and relax in a classic Georgian leisure garden. Bringing fresh air and wildlife into the heart of the city, the collection provides lots of creative solutions to urban gardening with year-round interest through a mix of seasonal planting and structural evergreens which the gardeners will be on hand to talk about.

Open: Sunday 22 June, noon - 4:30pm, admission £8.50, children free. Tickets and route maps available at both trail ends. Plants for sale at Logie Green Gardens. **See Scotland's Gardens Scheme website for up-to-date details.**

Directions: Buses 23 and 27 to Dundas Street and Canonmills, 8 to Rodney Street and Canonmills, 36 to Hamilton Place and Broughton Road, 29 to Royal Circus.

Opening for: Shelter Scotland & Médecins Sans Frontières

Edinburgh, Midlothian & West Lothian

29 TEMPLE VILLAGE GARDENS
Temple EH23 4SQ
Temple Village Gardeners
T: 01875 830253 E: de.apsandy@gmail.com

Temple Village is situated on the east bank of the River South Esk, to the south west of Gorebridge and is one of Midlothian's most attractive and historic conservation villages. Between the 12th and 14th centuries Temple was the headquarters of the Knights Templar. More recently the village has been home to Sir William Gillies, the famous Scottish painter. A number of village gardens will be open, from the charming riverside garden of the Mill House, to the delightful front and rear gardens of some of the village houses on the Main Street. Planted in a variety of different styles, they display contrasting designs and plant combinations, reflecting the villagers' many distinctive horticultural interests.

Open: Sunday 18 May, 2pm - 5pm, admission £7.00, children free. This is a **cash only event**, thank you for your understanding. Tickets and maps will be available from the village hall and the Mill House only. Parking is only available on entrance and exit of the village, with limited parking near the Mill House for those who have difficulty walking on the hill. Temple Village is famous for its wonderful teas and home baking, which will be served in the village hall, a separate charge applies. The plant sale will be at the Mill House.

Directions: On the B6372, three miles off the A7 from Gorebridge.

Opening for: Temple Village Halls Association

30 WHITBURGH HOUSE WALLED GARDEN
Pathhead, Midlothian EH37 5SR
Mrs Elizabeth Salvesen
E: eesal39@gmail.com

This contemporary, stylish one-acre walled garden, over 700 feet above sea level, is a lively forward-looking and unexpected gem. The solidity and graphic quality of clipped foliage act as a foil for the many perennials, grasses, annuals, fruit and vegetables. A spiral path leads through an acre of white birches. There is also a variety of ponds and fine sculptures spread around 14 acres of policies. Whitburgh garden has featured recently in *Country Life* and *RHS 'The Garden'* as well as other publications.

Open: Sunday 24 August & Tuesday 26 August, 2:30pm - 5pm, admission £7.00, children free. **Please bring cash as local network connectivity is poor.**

Directions: From the north – a half mile south of Pathhead on the A68 turn left and follow the *SGS* signs. From the south – one mile north of Blackshiels on the A68 turn right at the sign to *Fala Dam* and follow *SGS* signs. Whitburgh House is about two miles from either turn off and south east of Pathhead.

Opening for: Horatio's Garden

Edinburgh, Midlothian & West Lothian

Whitburgh House Walled Garden © Delia Ridley-Thomas

31 WHITEHOUSE & GRANGE BOWLING CLUB
18a Hope Terrace, Edinburgh EH9 2AR
Whitehouse & Grange Bowling Club
E: wandgbc@icloud.com
W: www.wandgbc.com

The walled garden provides a backcloth for those bowling on the green or just sitting on the sidelines. The main feature is the Rose Garden, but we also plant trees to mark significant occasions such as the Club's 150th anniversary in 2022. Last year, during our Garden Open Day, the Lord Provost planted a tree to mark Edinburgh 900. On 11 July, we planted a rowan tree to mark the exact time 100 years earlier that Eric Liddell won his gold medal at the 1924 Paris Olympics.

Open: Sunday 29 June, 2pm - 5pm, admission £5.00, children free. Teas, coffees, scones and cakes, Luca's ice cream, licensed bar.

Directions: Heading south on Marchmont Road, cross over Strathearn Road onto Kilgraston Road, past the church on the left side and take the first turning on the right. Buses: 5, 9 and 24 to Beaufort Road stops.

Opening for: The Eric Liddell Community & St.Columba's Hospice Care

Fife

Sponsored by

❀ RATHBONES

Fife

OUR VOLUNTEER ORGANISERS

District Organisers:	David Buchanan-Cook (West Fife)	Helensbank House, 56 Toll Rd, Kincardine FK10 4QZ
	Catherine Erskine (East Fife)	Cambo Farmhouse, Kingsbarns KY16 8QD
Area Organisers:	Alison Aiton	Craigview Cottage, Blebo Craigs, Cupar KY15 5UQ
	Pauline Borthwick	96 Hepburn Gardens, St Andrews KY16 9LP
	Anna Morton	
	Fay Smith	37 Ninian Fields, Pittenweem, Anstruther KY10 2QU
	Julia Young	South Flisk, Blebo Craigs, Cupar KY15 5UQ
Treasurer:	Clare Ansell	Coul House, Maree Way, Glenrothes KY7 6NW

GARDENS OPEN ON A SPECIFIC DATE

Dunimarle Castle, Balgownie West, Culross	Saturday/Sunday, 8/9 February
Teasses Gardens, near Ceres	Friday, 21 February
Lindores House, by Newburgh	Saturday, 22 February
Edenhill, Kennedy Gardens, St Andrews	Friday/Saturday/Sunday, 2/3/4 May
The Gardens of Monimail Tower, Monimail Tower Project, by Letham	Sunday, 4 May
Craig Cottage, Blebo Craigs	Sunday, 18 May
South Flisk, Blebo Craigs, Cupar	Sunday, 18 May
The Garden with the Dragon, 2, Upper Wellheads, Limekilns	Saturday, 24 May
Kirklands, Saline	Sunday, 25 May
Earlshall Castle, Leuchars	Sunday, 25 May
Swallows Rest, Lindores	Sunday, 25 May
Lindores House, by Newburgh	Sunday, 25 May
The Garden with the Dragon, 2, Upper Wellheads, Limekilns	Saturday, 31 May
Coul House, Coul House, Maree Way, Glenrothes	Sunday, 8 June
Teasses Gardens, near Ceres	Wednesday, 18 June
Newburgh – Hidden Gardens, Newburgh	Sunday, 29 June
Earlshall Castle, Leuchars	Sunday, 29 June
Kirkbrae House, Culross	Sunday, 29 June
Crail: Gardens in the Burgh, Crail	Saturday/Sunday, 5/6 July
Blanerne, West Road, Charlestown	Saturday/Sunday, 12/13 July
Balcarres, Colinsburgh	Sunday, 13 July
Wester Craigfoodie, Dairsie	Sunday, 20 July
Kirkbrae House, Culross	Sunday, 20 July
Pitlochie House, Gateside	Sunday, 27 July
Blanerne, West Road, Charlestown	Saturday, 16 August
Coul House, Coul House, Maree Way, Glenrothes	Sunday, 17 August
Kirklands, Saline	Sunday, 17 August

Fife

GARDENS OPEN ON A SPECIFIC DATE – CONTINUED

Kirkbrae House, Culross	Sunday, 24 August
Greenhead Farmhouse, Greenhead of Arnot, Leslie	Friday, 5 September
Kirkbrae House, Culross	Sunday, 21 September
Fife Plant Sale at St Andrews Botanic Garden, St Andrews	Sunday, 28 September
Wormistoune House, Crail	Date to be confirmed
Fife Carol Concert	Date to be confirmed

GARDENS OPEN REGULARLY

Cambo Gardens, Kingsbarns	1 January - 31 December
Willowhill, Forgan, Newport-on-Tay	Saturday, Sunday and Monday 26/27/28 April, Mondays and Saturdays 7/9 and 14/16 June, Mondays and Saturdays from 1 July until 31 August

GARDENS OPEN BY ARRANGEMENT

Harthill, Reediehill Farm, Auchtermuchty	6 January - 31 October
Dawson's Garden, The Old Post Office, Kilmany	6 January - 21 December
Kirklands, Saline	1 April - 30 September
The Tower, 1 Northview Terrace, Wormit	1 April - 30 September
Rosewells, Baldinnie, Ceres	1 April - 31 August
South Flisk, Blebo Craigs, Cupar	1 April - 30 June
Glassmount House, by Kirkcaldy	1 April - 30 September
46 South Street, St Andrews	1 April - 31 July
Willowhill, Forgan, Newport-on-Tay	26 April - 31 August
48 Rumblingwell, 48 Rumblingwell, Dunfermline	1 May - 1 July
Kirkbrae House, Culross	1 June - 30 September
Helensbank House, Kincardine	16 June - 31 August

Fife

1 ## 46 SOUTH STREET
St Andrews KY16 9JT
Mrs June Baxter
T: 01334 474995 E: ejbaxter986@gmail.com

Renowned town garden in medieval long rig, with orchard underplanted with wildflowers and bulbs, and many unusual flowering shrubs. Roses and other climbers clothe the surrounding high walls. Shrub roses planted in a delightful central parterre fill the air with scent. An historic and unique feature in St Andrews, but also a wonderfully planted space where different styles of planting complement the range of plants used. Historic doocot.

Open: by arrangement 1 April - 31 July, admission £5.00, children free.

Directions: Access and parking information on request.

Opening for: Friends of Craigtoun

2 ## 48 RUMBLINGWELL
48 Rumblingwell, Dunfermline KY12 9AS
Rik Morley
T: 07733 855794 E: rik.morley@gmail.com

Welcome to our compact city garden! On entering you are welcomed by a small butterfly meadow, planted rockery and a newly-established fernery. A splash of colour from the early May alliums and rhododendrons leads through to an alpine-planted water feature and cascading ponds with a Japanese/cottage garden aesthetic. A key feature of the garden is the many bearded and species irises (over 100) adorning each garden bed. Uncommon ornamental trees and shrubs (many from Asia) add layers of height, shade and fruits in the summer. Come and join us for a cup of tea and take a moment to enjoy our tranquil space.

Open: by arrangement 1 May - 1 July, admission £5.00, children free.

Directions: The garden is approached via a short path which is opposite Stephens drive-through bakery and by the side of Simpson's Motors. The No.4 bus from Dunfermline bus station runs regularly to a stop very close to the house.

Opening for: Wader Quest

Blanerne

Fife

3 BALCARRES
Colinsburgh KY9 1HN
The Earl and Countess of Crawford and Balcarres
T: 01333 340205 (Estate Office)

Set on the south-facing slopes of Fife, with spectacular views over the Firth of Forth, Balcarres Garden is a summer haven welcoming visitors to explore its natural beauty. In July, the Rose Garden will be in full bloom, showcasing a mixture of David Austin shrub roses, hybrid tea, and floribunda varieties, offering a stunning display of colour and fragrance. Alongside the roses, the herbaceous borders will be alive with vibrant *phlox, geranium, alstromeria, veronicastrum, aconitum, astrantia, campanula, nepeta, eryngium, macleaya, thalictrum, telekia* and *lythrum*. The herbaceous borders, with their generous and informal planting style, offer a delightful contrast to the structure and formality of the lower terrace. Framed by magnificent 200-year-old yew hedges, the terrace provides a stunning architectural backdrop that enhances the natural beauty of the garden. Visitors will also enjoy the rich foliage along Mary's Walk and Chapel Walk, together with Jim's Grove, its woodland character a further must-see for plant enthusiasts. Balcarres Garden offers a perfect retreat for a summer's day.

Open: Sunday 13 July, 2pm - 5pm, admission £7.50, children free.

Directions: Half-a-mile north of Colinsburgh off A942. Bus to Colinsburgh.

Opening for: Children 1st: for a family holiday in East Neuk & Colinsburgh Community Trust Ltd: for Colinsburgh Community Gardens

4 BLANERNE
West Road, Charlestown KY11 3EW
Lesley and Geoff Fenlon
E: lesleyabloomer@gmail.com

South-facing hidden village garden with lots of paths to follow and many places to sit, both sunny and shaded. The centrepiece of the garden is a large oval pond with wildlife-friendly planting. Surrounding the pond are several mini-gardens including a rose courtyard garden with catmint, salvias, beech, false indigo and featuring a bubble fountain. There is also a vegetable patch, woodland, a shady courtyard and a summerhouse garden enclosed by a young purple beech/wild rose hedge.

Open: Saturday/Sunday, 12/13 July & Saturday 16 August, 11am - 4pm, admission £6.00, children free.

Directions: Driving: follow signs from the A985 into Charlestown. Follow the road until you see the village shop, The Sutlery, available for takeaway all day Saturday and Sunday mornings – these can be eaten in the garden. Parking is behind the Charlestown Workshop, next to the shop. **Cycling:** National Route76 passes about 20m from the house. **Public transport:** bus 6/6A from Dunfermline. Alight at The Green in Charlestown, walk towards the shop. Walk west about 20m along West Road. Turn left down the tarmac driveway opposite 10 West Road, the garden is on the right hand side at the end.

Opening for: Mary's Meals

Fife

5 CAMBO GARDENS
Kingsbarns KY16 8QD
Trustees of Cambo Heritage Trust
T: 01333 451040 E: hello@cambogardens.org.uk
W: www.cambogardens.org.uk/

Best known for snowdrops (mail order February), but exciting throughout the year, this Victorian walled garden features constantly evolving, magnificent herbaceous borders featuring rare and unusual plants, many of which are propagated for sale at Cambo. The garden is renowned too for its tulips and a stunning rose collection. Outside the main garden an inspiring Winter Garden and North American Prairie continue to be developed. Woodland walks to the sea.
National Plant Collection: *Galanthus*.
Champion Trees: Bundle Beech.

Open: Open year round, admission details can be found on the garden's website. Cafe, gift shop and plants for sale throughout the year. Check our website for events throughout the year.

Directions: A917 between Crail and St Andrews.

Opening for: Donation to SGS Beneficiaries

6 COUL HOUSE
Coul House, Maree Way, Glenrothes KY7 6NW
Dean and Clare Ansell
T: 07525 791277 E: Clareansell5@gmail.com

A hidden gem, Coul garden lies within the grounds of Coul House, an imposing B-listed Victorian farmhouse which dates back to circa 1875. A mix of hydrangeas, roses, rhododendron and wisteria are contained in this ever-evolving amateur garden. The garden has more recently been redesigned with hard landscaping and includes a small pond. Come and take a walk around and enjoy a cup of tea and home baking.

Open: Sunday 8 June & Sunday 17 August, 11am - 3pm, admission £6.00, children free.

Directions: From the A92, follow signs for Pitcairn.

Opening for: Breakthrough T1D & Glenrothes & District Foodbank

7 CRAIG COTTAGE
Blebo Craigs KY15 5UQ
David and Elizabeth Wallace

Situated a few hundred yards from South Flisk is the charming Craig Cottage – a total contrast to South Flisk but the two gardens complement each other perfectly. Most of the garden has been planted since the owners moved here in 2014, although the small area of shrubs close to the cottage is original. Half of the lawn is now 'meadow' with a recent planting of fritillaries. The rest of the garden has borders with interesting plants, a rose screen, rhododendrons, azaleas, specimen and fruit trees and a productive vegetable plot. A recently extended rockery leads to an area of paths between thymes, camomile and other ground cover plants broken up by hedges and trees to provide windbreaks. The garden has fine examples of dry stone walling, most of which is the restoration of the original. A half acre field adjacent to the existing gardens has recently been added. The intention is to have meadow grasses with a small number of trees.

Open: Sunday 18 May, 11am - 5pm, admission £8.00, children free. Opening in conjunction with South Flisk at which parking is available for visiting both gardens. The entry fee of £8 includes entry to both gardens.

Directions: A short walk from South Flisk – see separate listing.

Opening for: Médecins Sans Frontières

Fife

8 CRAIL: GARDENS IN THE BURGH
Crail KY10 3UT
Gardeners of Crail

Take an enjoyable stroll around this quintessential East Neuk village and explore its many beautiful gardens. These include gardens of various styles and planting schemes – cottage, historic, plantsman's and bedding. The stunning coastal location presents some challenges for planting but also allows for a great range of more tender species to flourish.

Open: Saturday/Sunday, 5/6 July, 2pm - 5pm, admission £7.50, children free. Tickets and maps are available on both days from Crail Museum (card payments) and participating gardens (cash only).

Directions: Approach the village from either St Andrews or Anstruther on the A927. Parking is available at Marketgate.

Opening for: Crail Community Partnership

9 DAWSON'S GARDEN
The Old Post Office, Kilmany KY15 4PT
Liz Murray
T: 07531 571045 E: kilmanyartist@gmail.com

A small cottage garden, full of surprises. Developed from a bare rectangle of grass by the late artist Dawson Murray, it was designed to please the senses all year round with colour, form and scent. Stone paths edged with box meander out of sight past 13 apple trees and a plum tree; two varieties of fig; both a red and a green grape vine and roses chosen for scent. There are plenty of areas to sit and relax: by the pond, in a small grassy area through a rose and clematis arch, outside the studio facing the kitchen garden or up on the patio. All are accessible by wheelchair.
Champion Trees: Red Hazel.

Open: by arrangement 6 January - 21 December, admission £6.00, children free.

Directions: The Old Post Office is in the centre of the small hamlet of Kilmany, just off the A92, eight miles from Dundee or 1½ miles after Rathillet coming from the opposite direction. It can also be reached from Cupar via Foodieash.

Opening for: Overcoming MS

Fife

10 DUNIMARLE CASTLE
Balgownie West, Culross KY12 8JN
George Fleming
T: 07713 629040 E: castledunimarle@gmail.com
W: www.dunimarlecastle.co.uk

Dunimarle Castle sits on the outskirts of the historic village of Culross, surrounded by 52 acres of formal gardens, meadows and woodlands. Entering the grounds from the rose arch on the main road, you will find the imposing Victorian gothic-style chapel, beautifully framed by the striking tulip tree and rhododendrons. Follow the path up towards the castle to the Italianate yew-lined terrace with its south-facing wall, home to a growing collection of grapes and other fruiting plants. The Bastion Garden provides a perfect backdrop to the original Georgian part of the castle with its colourful borders and trees. A stroll up the once grand 'North Drive' takes you past specimen monkey puzzle trees sandwiched between dramatic redwoods and rhododendrons.
Champion Trees: Tulip Tree, Cedar, Monkey Puzzle, Redwood.

Open: Saturday/Sunday, 8/9 February, 10am - 4pm for Snowdrops and Winter Walks, admission by donation.

Directions: Situated on the B9037 to the west of Culross, approximately 500 yards from the village. Parking is available in the village's west car park. From there, follow the coastal path west to the Rose Arch.

Opening for: WFW

11 EARLSHALL CASTLE
Leuchars KY16 0DP
Paul and Josine Veenhuijzen
T: 01334 839205

Extensive, historically important and Quixotic topiary gardens designed by Sir Robert Lorimer in the 1890s to complement the Castle. The grounds also include a rose garden, croquet lawn, vegetable garden, orchard, park and wooded area.

Open: Sunday 25 May, 2pm - 5pm. Also open Sunday 29 June, 2pm - 5pm. Admission £6.00, children free.

Directions: On Earlshall Road, three-quarters of a mile east of Leuchars Village (off A919).

Opening for: Leuchars St Athernase and Tayport Church of Scotland (Sunday 25 May) & The Royal Scots Dragoon Guards Charity: Leuchars (Sunday 29 June)

Fife

12 EDENHILL
Kennedy Gardens, St Andrews KY16 9DJ
Mr John Angus
T: 07710 369747 E: 1edenhill@gmail.com

Behind the imposing exterior of a handsome Victorian house in St Andrews lies a true hidden gem of a garden, Edenhill. This is a mature garden designed and planted some years ago with the help of Michael Innes and lovingly nurtured and developed by the owner, John Angus. The garden is enclosed by handsome old walls clothed in clematis and honeysuckle and there are several mature trees, including a monkey puzzle. Beneath some rather special species rhododendrons, there are carpets of colourful anemones, rare trilliums and some beautiful peonies. The sculptor, James Parker, has created some eye-catching sculptures for Edenhill and the most recent addition to this fascinating garden is a rill, the sound of which adds to the tranquillity of this very special garden.

Open: Friday/Saturday/Sunday, 2/3/4 May, 2pm - 5pm, admission £6.00, children free.

Directions: Kennedy Gardens is situated off Hepburn Gardens in residential St Andrews, only 5 minutes walk from St Andrews bus station (through Kinburn Park). The street sits above the University Science campus.

Opening for: Sightsavers

13 FIFE CAROL CONCERT
Mr David Buchanan-Cook for tickets
E: Helensbank@aol.com

This annual daytime Advent Carol Concert will be held once again on a Saturday afternoon in a fabulous Fife venue – to be confirmed closer to the event. Festive music and readings, performed by Bel Canto in an idyllic setting, will guarantee the perfect mood-setting for a memorable start to your festivities. Tickets are limited and must be booked in advance. Ticket price includes interval refreshments and mince pies. Please check the Scotland's Garden Scheme website from the beginning of November 2025 for details and how to obtain tickets.

Open: Tickets including refreshments (children free) must be booked in advance as numbers are restricted. The event quickly sold out last time so do book early to avoid disappointment. All proceeds raised will be split evenly between Scotland's Gardens Scheme and a local charity of significance to the venue. **Date to be confirmed.**

Directions: Directions will be provided once the venue has been confirmed.

Fife

14 FIFE PLANT SALE AT ST ANDREWS BOTANIC GARDEN
St Andrews KY16 8RT
St Andrews Botanic Garden

The famous Fife Autumn Plant Sale returns to St Andrews Botanic Garden. A fabulous selection of bare-root and potted plants, the vast majority grown locally in Fife and donated by our generous garden openers. This is a unique opportunity to give your established border a facelift at seriously knockdown prices or, if you are creating a newer garden, this is **the** place to find all the plants you need and which have been proven to flourish in local conditions. The 2025 sale will include a stall selling tulip bulbs.

Open: Sunday 28 September, 10:30am - 1pm, admission £3.00, children free. Admission gives you **free** entry to the Botanics (the usual fee will be waived).

Plant donations – large and small – will be extremely welcome on the Friday and Saturday preceding the sale. For delivery details please contact Julia Young at *southfliskgarden@gmail.com* or David Buchanan-Cook at *helensbank@aol.com.*

Directions: The garden is located on The Canongate, situated a 10 minute walk from the town centre. Follow the signs from the town down Viaduct Walk, which is a shared path for cyclists and pedestrians. The 99C bus route goes past the garden and takes 5 minutes from the town centre. Free parking at the Botanics and in nearby streets.

Opening for: St Andrews Botanic Garden Trust

15 GLASSMOUNT HOUSE
by Kirkcaldy KY2 5UT
Peter, James and Irene Thomson
T: 01592 890214 E: mcmoonter@yahoo.co.uk

Densely planted walled garden with surrounding woodland. An A-listed sundial, Mackenzie & Moncur greenhouse and historical doocot are complemented by a number of newer structures. Daffodils are followed by a mass of candelabra and cowslip primula, meconopsis and *Cardiocrinum giganteum*. Hedges and topiary form backdrops for an abundance of bulbs, clematis, rambling roses and perennials, creating interest through the summer into September. The garden is now extending beyond the walls, with new areas of naturalistic planting blending the boundary between the surrounding fields and the woodland.

Open: by arrangement 1 April - 30 September, admission £6.00, children free. Scottish finalist in Channel 4's *Garden of the Year* programme in 2022.

Directions: From Kirkcaldy, head west on the B9157. Turn left immediately after the railway bridge on the edge of town. Follow the single track road for one-and-a-half miles and cross the crossroads. Glassmount House is the first turning on your right.

Opening for: Parkinsons UK

16 GREENHEAD FARMHOUSE
Greenhead of Arnot, Leslie KY6 3JQ
Malcolm and Maggie Strang Steel
T: 01592 840459

Greenhead is a medium-sized garden with beautiful borders which have a backbone of perennial shrubs among herbaceous planting, plus a scattering of annuals which provide on-going interest. September is one of the best months to visit this garden.

Open: Friday 5 September, 2pm - 5pm, admission £6.00, children free.

Directions: A911 between Auchmuirbridge and Scotlandwell.

Opening for: SSAFA Forces Help: SSAFA Kinross Branch

Fife

17 HARTHILL
Reediehill Farm, Auchtermuchty KY14 7HS
Nichola and John Fletcher
T: 01337 828369 E: info@nicholafletcher.com
W: www.nicholafletcher.com

Harthill enjoys a tranquil setting in the hills just above Auchtermuchty with beautiful views and, if you are lucky, sightings of the stunning herd of white deer who also live there. The garden, of approximately one acre, offers a large varied flower garden with vegetable, fruit and nursery areas; two separate wild gardens planted with specimen trees, a lochan and a small woodland. In late May to early June our meconopsis and primula beds, with woodland plants, are at their best. Summer offers herbaceous interest including a pergola dripping with roses and a large mound with grasses, thalictrum and many large plants. Autumn colours are in the trees and shrubs, with grasses and cyclamen through to early winter.

Open: by arrangement 6 January - 31 October, admission by donation. By prior arrangement, teas, coffee and cake, or lunch can be provided for groups.

Directions: Find 'Reediehill Deer Farm' on Google maps. Go 50 metres up the concrete drive then turn left at *Harthill* sign. Continue over the cattle grid up the drive to reach Harthilll house. Directions can be emailed.

Opening for: TST: The Tim Stead Trust

18 HELENSBANK GARDEN CONCERT
Helensbank House FK10 4QZ
David Buchanan-Cook
T: 07739 312912 E: Helensbank@aol.com
W: www.helensbank.ccm

This popular summer event returns to Helensbank Garden for 2025. Bel Canto, conducted by David Buchanan-Cook, will perform a selection of unaccompanied music for a summer's day, interspersed with humorous and gardening-themed readings. Tickets – which **must** be booked in advance – will be available direct from the venue. Entry includes access to the gardens and interval refreshments, including the now famous selection of home-crafted canapes. The date will be either the last Saturday in June or first Saturday in July, when the 100+ roses should be at their peak. The confirmed date will be updated on the SGS website towards the end of May. National Plant Collection: Portland Roses.

Open: Date to be confirmed. Note – due to the unpredictable Scottish weather, please dress accordingly!

Directions: The garden is down a lane off the main Toll Road. *SGS* signs. Apart from disabled access, parking for the concert will be restricted to neighbouring streets.

Opening for: All proceeds to SGS Beneficiaries

Fife

19 HELENSBANK HOUSE
Kincardine FK10 4QZ
David Buchanan-Cook
T: 07739 312912 E: Helensbank@aol.com
W: www.helensbank.com

Hidden away from public view, this is an 18th-century walled garden, with main feature a Cedar of Lebanon, reputedly planted in 1750 by the sea captain who built the house. The tree is registered as a 'Notable Tree' and while it provides challenges for planting, in terms of shade and needle fall, the microclimate it provides has encouraged the owner's passion for pushing boundaries and growing unusual and exotic plants. Distinctive garden 'rooms' in part of the garden comprise a perennial blue and white cottage garden, a formal rose garden and an Italian double courtyard with citrus trees in pots. A 'hot' courtyard contains exotics including varieties of banana, *acacia, iochroma, impatiens, melianthus* and *brugmansia*. A shaded walk along the bottom of the garden leads to a Japanese themed area including a pagoda and dry river. A large glasshouse hosts various exotic and climbing plants. The garden has well over a hundred roses, including the National Collection of Portland roses.
National Plant Collection: Portland Roses.
Champion Trees: The garden has a 'notable' Cedar of Lebanon, the second largest in Fife.

Open: by arrangement 16 June - 31 August, admission £6.00, children free. See separate listing for the annual Helensbank Summer Garden concert.

Directions: The garden is down a lane off the main Toll Road. *SGS* signs.

Opening for: Perennial

20 KIRKBRAE HOUSE
Culross KY12 8JD
Sandra Bannister
E: Sandra.bannister18@gmail.com

An acre of walled garden sitting high in the village of Culross in the shadow of the Abbey. With meandering paths through perennial beds, bright annuals and shrubs and trees from as far as South America and Asia, the garden provides interest from late spring until autumn. The garden aims to provide an environment of joy, surprise and opportunity to sit and enjoy the spectacular garden views of the River Forth.

Open: Sunday 29 June, Sunday 20 July, Sunday 24 August & Sunday 21 September, 2pm - 5pm. Also open by arrangement 1 June - 30 September. Admission £6.00, children free.

Directions: The garden is located on Kirk Street. On leaving the lower village start to climb up to the Abbey, the garden gates open directly onto Kirk Street. Car parking is either below the garden or near the Abbey. Buses come into the village from Dunfermline and Kincardine.

Opening for: Perennial & Pancreatic Cancer Scotland

Fife

21 KIRKLANDS
Saline KY12 9TS
Peter and Gill Hart
T: 07787 115477 E: peter@kirklandsgarden.co.uk
W: www.kirklandsgarden.co.uk

Kirklands, built in 1832, has been the Hart family home for 48 years. Over the years we have created a garden. The walled garden was reinstated from a paddock to include terracing and raised beds. In 2023 we introduced two bee hives. The woodland garden comes into life in February with snowdrops followed, over the months, by bluebells, hellebores, trilliums, fritillaries, rhododendrons, meconopsis, candelabra primulas and irises. The rockery displays dwarf rhododendrons and azaleas. The herbaceous borders reach their peak in the summer, continuing into early autumn with a display of bright yellow rudbeckia, verbena and echinacea. Down by the Saline Burn there are 30 species of primula in all colours of the rainbow. Over the red or blue bridge there are 20 acres of naturally regenerating woodland with a pathway by the stream. To keep the grandchildren occupied, Peter built a tree house, climbing frame and rope swing, though we hope they will take an interest in gardening too!

Open: Sunday 25 May, 2pm - 5pm. Also open Sunday 17 August, 2pm - 5pm. And open by arrangement 1 April - 30 September. Admission £6.00, children free.

Directions: Junction 4, M90, then B914. Parking in the centre of the village, then a short walk to the garden. Limited disabled parking at Kirklands.

Opening for: Saline & Steelend Gardening Club (Sunday 17 August) & Saline & District Heritage Society (Sunday 25 May & 1 April - 30 September)

22 LINDORES HOUSE
by Newburgh KY14 6JD
Robert and Elizabeth Turcan & John and Eugenia Turcan
T: 01337 840369

Situated between Lindores House and Lindores Loch, and with stunning views over the loch, the garden has been developed by the current owners over the last 45 years. It now includes extensive lochside and woodland walks with banks of snowdrops, leucojum, hostas, gunnera manicata, primula, astilbes, crocuses, fritillaria, spring and autumn cyclamen, hellebores and a notably impressive collection of trilliums. As well as the much older established trees – and in particular the splendid 17th century yew (believed to be the largest in Fife which you can actually walk inside) there are more recent plantings of interesting specimen trees and shrubs. The herbaceous beds are mainly laid out formally around the old tennis court overlooking the loch. There is a one-acre walled garden, mainly used for growing fruit and vegetables, and a new garden in front of the recently converted stable building is under construction.

Open: Saturday 22 February, 11am - 2pm for Snowdrops and Winter Walks. Homemade bread and soup will be available. Also open Sunday 25 May, 2pm - 5pm with homemade teas and a plant sale with trilliums. Admission £6.00, children free. Opening in conjunction with Swallows Rest on 25 May – park at Lindores House and walk to Swallows Rest.

Directions: Off A913 two miles east of Newburgh. Bus from Cupar.

Opening for: Siobhan's Trust (Saturday 22 February) & RC Diocese Of Dunkeld: St Columba's RC Church, Cupar (Sunday 25 May)

Fife

23 NEWBURGH – HIDDEN GARDENS
Newburgh KY14 6AJ
Gardeners of Newburgh

Hidden behind the 18th-century facades of Newburgh High Street and surrounding streets lie a jumble of wonderful old gardens, some of them dating back centuries. Many have spectacular views of the Tay Estuary. We are opening for the fifth time and, as before, the gardens will include a mixture of those which have opened previously together with some gardens opening in 2025 for the first time. Those previously opened will have been developed considerably and, as before, there will be a wide mix of flowers, vegetables, herbaceous borders, orchards and a fair few hens and ducks!

Open: Sunday 29 June, noon - 5pm, admission £6.00, children free. Newburgh sits on a hill. In addition, access to some gardens is via narrow closes and vennels. As such, disabled access to some gardens may be restricted.

Directions: On the A913 between Perth and Cupar. There is a car park at each end of the town, with tickets and teas available nearby.

Opening for: Newburgh Community Trust: Community Choir & Memorial Garden

24 PITLOCHIE HOUSE
Gateside KY14 7SQ
George and Fay Orr
T: 07730 135953

This established garden has year-round interest. A restoration project with quirky features, characters and surprises! Comprising lots of different areas, the garden is carpeted in spring with snowdrops, daffodils, camassia and then bluebells. Following on there are over 140 varieties of hosta, plus heuchera, hellebores, roses, clematis, and lilies. There are formal herbaceous borders within two walled gardens, hedges, woodland, shaded planting, glass house, fruit trees, rhododendrons and azaleas. And pots of all description in every available corner.

Open: Sunday 27 July, 10am - 6pm, admission £6.00, children free.

Directions: On the A912 Gateside to Perth. The garden is on the right hand side, 200 metres from the village main street

Opening for: Gateside And District Community Association

Fife

25 ROSEWELLS
Baldinnie, Ceres KY15 5LE
Birgitta and Gordon MacDonald
E: g.macdonald54@hotmail.co.uk

Rosewells, designed by the garden owners, has developed over the last 30 years. It started as a one-and-a-half acre, overgrown paddock. The design is based on the texture and foliage of trees and shrubs to create year-round interest. In spring and summer, colour and scent become increasingly important. In spring, highlights are around 55 magnolias and numerous rhododendrons, many of which are chosen for their foliage. Other highlights include flowering cornus, trillium, fritillaries, erythroniums, peonies, roses, ferns and acers. There have been a number of developments in recent years. More winding paths have been developed creating wildlife friendly areas. There is a new lavender walk which leads to a covered seating area at the bottom of the garden.

Open: by arrangement 1 April - 31 August, admission £6.00, children free.

Directions: B940 between Pitscottie and Peat Inn, one mile from Pitscottie. Rosewells is the ochre-coloured house.

Opening for: Save the Children UK

26 SOUTH FLISK
Blebo Craigs, Cupar KY15 5UQ
Mr and Mrs George Young
T: 01334 850859 E: southfliskgarden@gmail.com
W: www.standrewspottery.co.uk

The spectacular views to Perthshire and Angus and large flooded quarry full of fish (and occasional otter) planted with impressive marginals, make this garden very special. Flights of old stone steps, cliffs, boulders, exotic ferns and mature trees form a backdrop for carpets of primroses, bluebells, spring bulbs and woodland plants like trilliums, camassia, meconopsis and colourful primulas, with rhododendrons in flower from March to July. In front of the house is a charming, mature walled garden with traditional cottage-garden planting. Next to the house is the St Andrews Pottery where George will demonstrate his pottery skills for those who need a break from the garden! A new water garden with a stream running through was created in 2023.

Open: Sunday 18 May, 11am - 5pm. Also open by arrangement 1 April - 30 June. Admission £8.00, children free (Sunday 18 May) and £6.00, children free (1 April - 30 June). On 18 May, South Flisk is opening in conjunction with Craig Cottage just down the road – see its separate listing.

Directions: Six miles west of St Andrews off B939 between Strathkinness and Pitscottie. There is a small stone bus shelter opposite the road into the village and sign *Blebo Craigs*. See map on our website – standrewspottery.co.uk. Bus to Blebo Craigs.

Opening for: Médecins Sans Frontières

Fife

27 SWALLOWS REST
Lindores KY14 6JD
Stuart & Elaine Ingram
T: 07703 435055 E: elaine.ingram@icloud.com

The current owners moved in at the beginning of 2011 to a garden of grass and weeds. Since then, beds have been hand-dug, a slope filled with dwarf conifers and heathers, a pond and small stream made, and step-over fruit trees planted. The garden also hosts many perennials, shrubs, trees and acid-loving plants. Over 50 varieties of narcissus prolong spring interest, along with many hellebores and rhododendrons.

Open: Sunday 25 May, 2pm - 5pm, admission £6.00, children free.

Directions: Two miles east of Newburgh on the A913 past Den of Lindores, on the left, house with a white door with a stained glass panel of a swallow scene. The garden is opening on 25 May in conjunction with Lindores House – see above listing. As there is limited parking at Swallows Rest, visitors are advised to park at, and walk from, Lindores House.

Opening for: All proceeds to SGS Beneficiaries

28 TEASSES GARDENS
near Ceres KY8 5PG
E: events@teasses.com
W: www.teasses.com

Two special events set in the wonderful gardens and grounds of Teasses.

21st February – a magical candlelit snowdrop walk. There will be two 'sittings', one starting at 4pm and the other at 7:30pm. The cost – including refreshments – will be £25 per car.

18th June – a Summer Solstice evening tour of the garden accompanied by the Estate Manager and former Head Gardener. Tickets are £15 per head (children free) including wine and nibbles.

Please note that tickets for both events are limited and **must** be booked in advance – please see the SGS website for details.

Open: Friday 21 February, two time slots at 4pm then 7.30pm for the candlelit snowdrop walk. Admission £25.00 per car including refreshments. Also open Wednesday 18 June, evening, times to be confirmed. Admission £15.00, children free, refreshments included.

Directions: Between Ceres and Largo. Access via farm entrance on Woodside Road.

Opening for: All proceeds to SGS Beneficiaries

29 THE GARDEN WITH THE DRAGON
2, Upper Wellheads, Limekilns KY11 3JQ
Mr and Mrs Duncan Philp
T: 01383 872047 E: df.philp@btinternet.com

A quirky coastal garden hidden behind a walled plot. Scatterings of California poppies, bluebells and a varied mix of annuals and perennials with a small clear pond. Different themes blend in the garden, all overseen by a majestic dragon sculpture perched on a tree.

Open: Saturday 24 May & Saturday 31 May, 2pm - 4pm, admission £5.00, children free.

Directions: Take the A985 from Rosyth or Kincardine and follow directions for Limekilns and Charlestown. The No.6 bus from Dunfermline bus station on the hour.

Opening for: PETA

Fife

30 THE GARDENS OF MONIMAIL TOWER
Monimail Tower Project, by Letham KY15 7RJ
The Gardeners of Morimail Tower Project
T: 07505 424905 E: monimailtower@posteo.uk
W: www.monimailtower.org

Monimail Tower gardens is situated in the Howe of Fife, a 19th century walled garden and orchard, built around a 15th century tower, the remains of Cardinal Beaton's summer palace. The garden has been an organic vegetable garden since 1985. We are now developing flower beds, but very much in a natural and wildlife friendly way. You will find peacefulness and tranquillity, but not the formality associated with walled gardens. It is a haven for invertebrates and birds. The garden hosts a site for allotments for local people and the woodlands and orchard are open to the general public all year round with a carpet of snowdrops, aconites, then followed by wild garlic in spring. The garden has a marvellous aspect sloping south, surrounded by ancient yew trees and an orchard. The tower is open to visitors and hosts a little museum. You can climb up to the roof and enjoy a beautiful view.

Open: Sunday 4 May, 10am - 4pm, admission by donation.

Directions: Monimail Tower Project is situated in Monimail, a hamlet on the road between Letham and Collessie

Opening for: Monimail Tower Project Ltd

The Gardens of Monimail Tower

Fife

31 **THE TOWER**
1 Northview Terrace, Wormit DD6 8PP
Peter and Angela Davey
T: 07768 406946 E: adavey541@btinternet.com

Situated four miles south of Dundee, this one-acre Edwardian landscaped garden has panoramic views over the River Tay. Set on a hill, a series of paths meander around ponds and a small stream, rockeries featuring hellebores and low-level planting, a curved lawn and larger borders. Original woodland paths lead to a granite grotto with a waterfall pool. At the rear of the house the vegetable garden features raised beds made from granite sets. The garden is colourful throughout the summer, with many architectural plants accentuating the clever hard landscape design.

Open: by arrangement 1 April - 30 September, admission £6.00, children free.

Directions: From B946 park on Naughton Road outside Spar shop. Walk up the unmade path outside and to the left of the shop. The garden enrance is the second gate on the right.

Opening for: Brain Tumour Research

The Tower

Fife

32 WESTER CRAIGFOODIE
Dairsie KY15 4RU
Mr & Mrs Robert Murray Brown and Mrs Joan Gilbert

Wester Craigfoodie shelters beneath Craiglug. Elevation gives the house and gardens their wonderful views, tranquillity and informal charm. The organic no dig walled garden, attached to the B listed house, is arranged in wind resistant 'rooms' planted with perennials, shrubs and fruit trees. Views to the sea, St Andrews and its Links await visitors at the top. To the front lie the curved rose wall and inscription stone. From here, under the giant Douglas Fir, views stretch across the Eden Valley towards Kemback Wood. To the west is the new (2023) prairie garden, views to the south, polytunnel and gate to Ruthven Cottage's new (2024) garden. Bees are abundant with a hive overlooking the pond. Beds of bee-friendly perennials, specimen trees and shrubs frame the views. A gate opens onto the hills beyond via the old drovers' track.

Open: Sunday 20 July, 2pm - 5pm, admission £5.00, children free. Home baking, jams and preserves for sale. There are two separate but linked gardens in the the one visit – separately owned and managed. The walk from the village is a tarmac track, partly uphill – approximately ten minutes. It is possible to walk back to the village from the gardens via the Fingask track which creates a very nice circular walk.

Directions: From Dairsie main street on A91, the Cupar end, turn down past the Primary School (opposite village hall). Pass the school and bear right past line of three cottages. Stay on tarmac (not to Fingask) and then bear left up hill to Craigfoodie House. Stay left at top and follow signs. W3W – ///playoffs.huddled.alike Ten minute walk from bus stop by the school.

Opening for: Guide Dogs

Willowhill

Fife

33 WILLOWHILL
Forgan, Newport-on-Tay DD6 8RA
Eric Wright and Sally Lorimore
T: 01382 542890 E: willowhillfife@btinternet.com
W: www.willowhillgarden.weebly.com

An evolving three-acre garden. The house is surrounded by a series of mixed borders designed with different vibrant colour combinations for effect in all seasons. Spectacular mix of roses, herbaceous perennials and annuals planted through the wide borders are a highlight in mid to late summer. A 'no dig' 160-foot border in shades of white, blue, purple and pale yellow was created in 2019/2020. The most recent addition to the garden is another 'no dig' border in shades of peach, burgundy, yellow, chocolate and acid yellow. Come and see! April and May for late spring bulbs and flowers; June and July for roses and high summer colour; August for late summer colour. The plant stall includes a lovely selection from the garden. Visitors are welcome to bring their own refreshments and picnic in the garden. A season ticket for all these dates, and by arrangement, is £25 plus p&p and admits the ticket holder plus guest. It comes with a limited edition of the Willowhill Garden Guide: 35 pages of beautiful photographs with descriptions of key garden features and plantings. A **season ticket** with booklet is a perfect gift for garden lovers for a birthday or at Christmas and do treat yourself too! Season tickets are available online at **tinyurl.com/yxcj2mzy** or by post (cheque for £27.76 payable to Scotland's Garden Scheme) from Scotland's Gardens Scheme, 23 Castle Street, Edinburgh EH2 3DN.

Open: by arrangement from 26 April to 31 August and open Saturday, Sunday and Monday 26/27/28 April. Then open Mondays and Saturdays 7/9 and 14/16 June. Then Mondays and Saturdays from 1 July until 31 August. The garden will be open from 1-5pm on all dates. Admission £6.00, children free. Teas available at cafes/bakeshops in Newport-on-Tay. Feel free to buy tickets in advance or simply drop in on the day.

Directions: 1.5 miles south of Tay Road Bridge. Take the B995 to Newport off the Forgan roundabout. Willowhill is the first house on the left-hand side next to West Friarton Farm Strawberry Shed.

Opening for: Rio Community Centre

34 WORMISTOUNE HOUSE
Crail KY10 3XH
Baron and Lady Wormiston
T: 07561262239 E: gemmawormiston@aol.com

The ongoing restoration and transformation of this 'pocket' estate's 17th-century Scot's tower house and gardens continues to evolve and delight. Within the walled garden, imaginatively clipped yew hedges enclose 'rooms' filled with luxuriantly planted herbaceous borders, a productive potager garden, wildflower meadows, an intricate box parterre, water features and a magical shade garden which is home to four of Scotland's largest *Griselinia littoralis* specimens. In recent years planting has extended into the wider woodland policies and highlights include a new Nuttery (inspired by Sissinghurst), extensive wildflower meadows and waterside plantings surrounding an impressively landscaped pond.

Open: Date to be confirmed, please check website for further details. Admission £6.00, children free.

Directions: One mile north of Crail on the A917 Crail to St Andrews road. Crail/St Andrews bus.

Opening for: Families First – St Andrews

Glasgow & District

Sponsored by

❀ RATHBONES

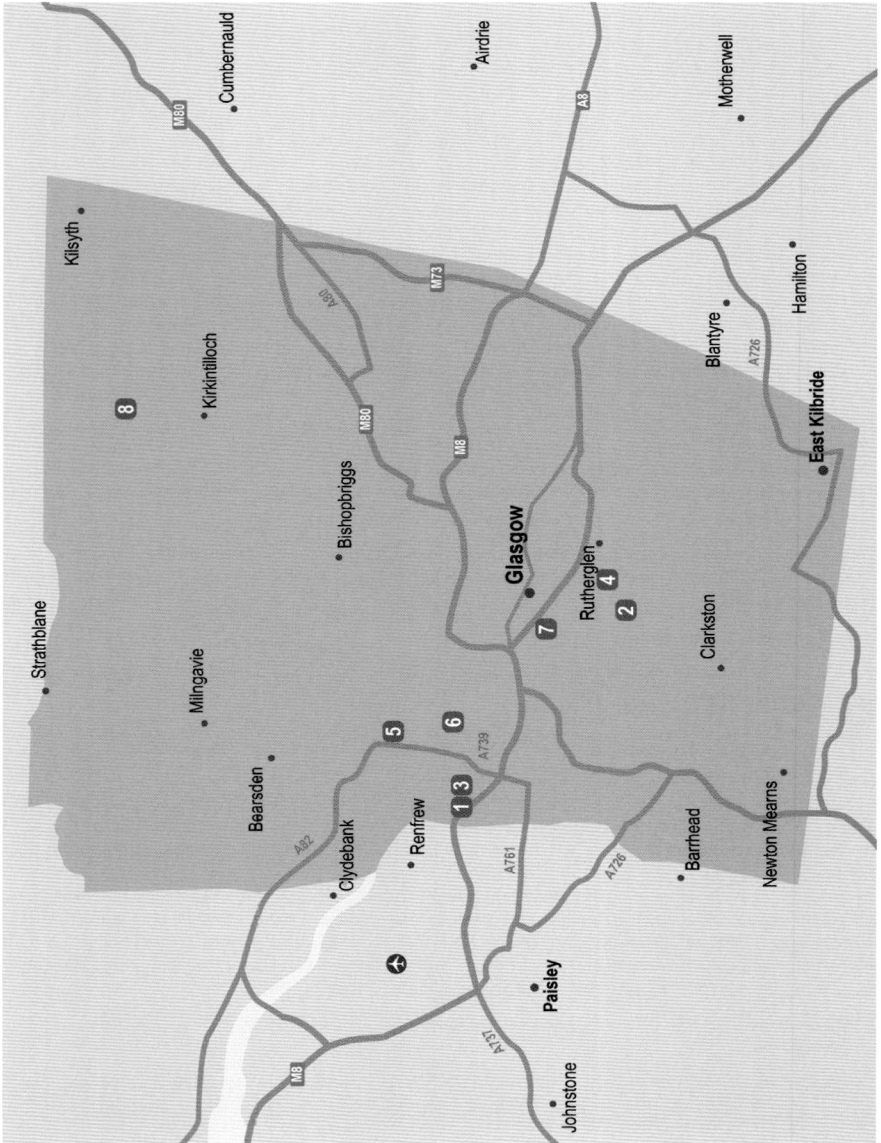

Glasgow & District

OUR VOLUNTEER ORGANISERS

District Organiser:	Heidi Stone	info@scotlandsgardens.org
Area Organisers:	Ian Angus	
	Mandy Bryan	
	Hilda Kelly	
District Photographer:	Alison Cummings	
Treasurer:	Vivien Pritchard	

GARDENS OPEN ON A SPECIFIC DATE

Elsewhere Garden, QEUH, Govan Road, Glasgow	Sunday, 8 June
Maggie's, Gartnavel Hospital 1053 Great Western Road Glasgow	Sunday, 15 June
SWG3 Community Garden, 100 Eastvale Place, Glasgow	Sunday, 13 July
The Milton of Campsie Community Garden, Antermony Road	Sunday, 10 August
Grow Cook Inspire, 125 Ormonde Avenue, Netherlee, Glasgow	Sunday, 17 August
Horatio's Garden, National Spinal Unit, QEUH, Govan Road, Glasgow	Sunday, 31 August

GARDENS OPEN REGULARLY

King's Park Walled Garden, 325 Carmunnock Road, Glasgow	1 January - 31 December
The Hidden Gardens, 25a Albert Drive, Glasgow	1 January - 31 December

Glasgow & District's year of children in the garden

We are delighted to share that Glasgow & District are celebrating the year 2025 for 'Children in the Garden' featuring children's activities, making for a perfect family day out. Look out for this symbol: 👥

Glasgow & District

1 **ELSEWHERE GARDEN**
Queen Elizabeth University Hospital, Govan Road, Glasgow G51 4TF
Shiona Blackie
W: www.teapot-trust.org/elsewhere-garden-glasgow

Tucked in a hidden nook of the grounds of Glasgow's Royal Hospital for Children, the Elsewhere Garden has transformed what was once a purposeless grassed landscape into a playful refuge for patients and staff. The garden was commissioned by Teapot Trust, a charity bringing play and art therapy to chronically sick children. It was designed by Semple Begg, who chose a palette of plants to inspire creativity and imagination, for which they won a gold medal at *RHS Chelsea* in 2023. The planting was adapted for the Glasgow location, and further enhanced by a donation of plants from Dior's Drummond Castle fashion show in June 2024. In the garden you'll meet an array of colourful perennials, and the characterful *Picea abies* 'Inversa'. The wide, snaking paths will take you by shady beds of ferns, sun-loving salvias, whimsical grasses, and candy-coloured blooms. Pause at one of the many seating spots and let your imagination roam – what do the plant forms conjure up for you?

Open: Sunday 8 June, 2pm - 5pm, admission £5.00, children free. There will be children's activities at this garden.

Directions: Follow the signs to *QEUH G51 4TF* and the *SGS yellow* signs.

Opening for: Teapot Trust: 30% to the Elsewhere Garden

Elsewhere Garden

2 **GROW COOK INSPIRE**
125 Ormonde Avenue, Netherlee, Glasgow G44 3SN
Helen Cross

Join Scottish presenter, school gardening champion and author Helen Cross in her own garden on the southside of Glasgow, which inspired her first book, *Grow Cook Inspire*. Helen's small but mighty garden, is a haven for wildlife and biodiversity and her garden illustrates that you don't have to have acres of land to be able to grow a wide range of fruit, vegetables, cut flowers and also have space to entertain friends and family. It is a garden jam packed with personality, colour and vibrancy and you'll leave feeling uplifted come rain or shine.

Open: Sunday 17 August, 2pm - 5pm. Helen will be on hand to sign copies of her book. There will be a chance to create your own flower crown and design your own tote bag, through the art of flower pounding. There will be children's activities at this garden. **Advance booking is essential so please visit the SGS website for further details.**

Directions: Park on Ormonde Avenue or Ormonde Drive. Enter through the back gate, via the back lane, opposite from *Netherlee* and *Stamperland Church*. Follow the *SGS* yellow road signs.

Opening for: Scottish Action for Mental Health

Glasgow & District

Grow Cook Inspire

3 HORATIO'S GARDEN

National Spinal Unit, Queen Elizabeth University Hospital, Govan Road, Glasgow G51 4TF
Horatio's Garden
E: chelsea.lowe@horatiosgarden.org.uk
W: horatiosgarden.org.uk

Carefully created by acclaimed garden designer and RHS Judge, James Alexander-Sinclair, Horatio's Garden Scotland opened in 2016 and nurtures the wellbeing of people affected by spinal injury from across the whole of Scotland, their loved ones and NHS staff. The gardens provide a peaceful horticultural haven. Horatio's Garden Scotland features a half acre woodland garden awash with striking seasonal blooms and framed by a beautiful collection of *Betula pendula* trees, as well as artfully planted borders, vibrant courtyard garden, gorgeous garden room, fragrant glasshouse and much more. There's plenty to explore in this thoughtful, therapeutic garden; one which rarely opens to the public and is unusually nestled right in the heart of a Greater Glasgow & Clyde NHS hospital.

Open: Sunday 31 August, 2pm - 5pm, admission £7.00, children free. Children's play area.

Directions: From the east or west of the city: on the M8 motorway to Junction 25, follow signs for the *Clyde Tunnel* (A739) for ¾ mile, then follow signs for the *Queen Elizabeth Hospital*. Turn left into Govan Road and the hospital is on the left. From north of the River Clyde: go through the Clyde Tunnel (A739) and follow signs for the hospital. Please look at our website for the hospital estate map for directions to the garden and available parking.

Opening for: Horatio's Garden

Glasgow & District

Horatio's Garden

4 **KING'S PARK WALLED GARDEN**
Kings Park, 325 Carmunnock Road, Glasgow G44 5HL
Friends of King's Park
E: contactus@friendsofkingsparkglasgow.co.uk
W: friendsofkingsparkglasgow.co.uk

The C-listed walled garden within King's Park would have served as a kitchen garden for the original James Hamilton estate in the 18th century, with colourful beds and borders and fruit trees. In recent years, Friends of King's Park have adopted the garden from Glasgow City Council with the aim of reinstating it to its former glory. The garden is split into quarters, two of which the Friends have planted with trees, shrubs, perennials and spring bulbs between 2022 and 2023. The east-facing bed has been planted with weeping cherry trees, underplanted with a selection of bulbs and a variety of perennials. The north-facing bed has a row of beautiful cherry trees. The south-facing wall will showcase cordons of a range of fruiting trees, which the Friends extended over winter 2023. We aim to further enrich the experience of visiting this garden and as a charitable organisation, will continue to raise funds to fully restore the walled garden.
Champion Trees: Yew trees (in main King's Park).

Open: 1 January - 31 December, 9am - 4:45pm, admission free but donations welcome.

Directions: Free on-street parking is available in all streets surrounding the park. King's Park is accessible by public transport: buses 5 and 31 for the Carmunnock Road entrances, 34 and 75 for the Menock Road entrance. King's Park train station is a two-minute walk from the Menock Road entrance.

Opening for: Donation to SGS Beneficiaries

Glasgow & District

5 MAGGIE'S, GLASGOW
Gartnavel Hospital, 1053 Great Western Road, Glasgow G12 0YN
Maggie's Centre
T: 0141 357 2269
W: www.maggies.org/our-centres/maggies-glasgow/

If you, or someone you love, has been diagnosed with cancer, Maggie's is here for you. Our centres are built in the grounds of hospitals, near to the NHS cancer centre. In every centre, you'll find a bright and welcoming space full of the kind of support that people facing cancer need and deserve. Our centre in Glasgow is a striking, single storey building, designed by Rem Koolhaas. It is formed as a ring shape around a landscaped internal courtyard and is nestled among the woodland in the grounds of Gartnavel Hospital. The centre is a space for being together or for a moment alone, for getting going again or for meeting people who just get it. Our Cancer Support Specialists have expert knowledge about cancer and treatment. No appointment or referral is necessary, just come in. As well as expert support and guidance we also run a programme of therapeutic classes, workshops and courses. All our support is free. Lily Jencks, daughter of Maggie's co-founders, Maggie Keswick Jencks and Charles Jencks, designed the internal courtyard plantings and the wooded glades areas surrounding the centre. *'Everything has been designed to show an enthusiasm for life and you need that when you're fighting cancer – you need something to give you a bit of life and power.'* Lily Jencks

Open: Sunday 15 June, 2pm - 5pm, admission £5.00, children free.

Directions: From Great Western Road (car, bus or foot): Enter Gartnavel Hospital site and turn right at the traffic lights onto Shelley Road. Follow the yellow *SGS* open signs.

Opening for: Maggie's: Glasgow

6 SWG3 COMMUNITY GARDEN
100 Eastvale Place, Glasgow G3 8QG
Jeremy Needham, Head Gardener

Situated behind the main SWG3 warehouse building, it's a surprise to walk up the steps leading to this space and be delighted by the sight of trees, grasses, shrubs and perennials making a beautiful garden where there was once only derelict land between two railway lines. The garden has wide paths curving through the beds and the various indigenous trees subtly define the shape of the garden. Apart from the interesting planting, this garden, which was designed by the horticulturist and garden designer Jeremy Needham, has beehives and two different heights of raised beds which are used by the local community as allotments. To celebrate Glasgow SGS 2025 *Year of Children in The Garden* there will be lots of children's events.

Open: Sunday 13 July, 2pm - 5pm, admission £8.00, children £2.00. Teas are included in the price. Children's activities include: a painting activity; plant propagation; seed sowing into small pots to take home. The plant sale will include a stand for herbaceous perennials and grasses, particularly those in the garden and a stand selling vegetable and salad plugs in the allotment area of the garden.
Directions: The nearest station to SWG3 in Glasgow is Kelvinhall SPT Subway Station, Partick, which is a 14 minute walk away. Free parking is available on Eastvale Place and Kelvinhaugh Street on Saturdays and Sundays.

Opening for: Studio Warehouse

Glasgow & District

SWG3 Community Garden

7 THE HIDDEN GARDENS
25a Albert Drive, Glasgow G41 2PE
The Hidden Gardens Trust
T: 0141 433 2722 E: info@thehiddengardens.org.uk
W: thehiddengardens.org.uk

The multi-award winning gardens have been designed to reflect the legacy of this historic site as well as the ever-changing character and needs of the local area. The north to south borders echo the layout of the site when it was a nursery in the 1800s, supplying trees and shrubs to major gardens in Scotland, whilst the retained tramlines and the chimney reflect its industrial past. A number of artworks are integrated into the overall design, for example Alec Finlay's Xylotheque, a library of wooden books detailing 17 native Scottish trees. The Hidden Gardens is an independent charity offering learning and social activities and opportunities for the whole community to participate in its development. It is a calm, green space where you can relax away from the busy city streets: take a meditative walk along the square route path around the formal lawn; brush past the aromatic herb border; admire the white wall border with its herbaceous plantings and espalier fruit trees; stroll through the wildlife area; connect with nature in the woodland glade; and enjoy the naturalistic planting of the grassy or wild flower meadows or buy some young plants propagated here. Volunteer-led guided tours are available to book during most of the year, for free.

Open: Please check the garden's website for up-to-date opening details and events. There will be children's activities at this garden.

Directions: Travel directions are available on the garden's website *thehiddengardens.org.uk/explore/visit/*

Opening for: *Donation to SGS Beneficiaries*

Glasgow & District

8 THE MILTON OF CAMPSIE COMMUNITY GARDEN
Antermony Road G66 8DB
T: 07958 760169

The community garden in Milton of Campsie is the creation of one man, covering roughly an acre of hillside beside the Glazert Water. A small beach area where otters and kingfishers can be spotted, is a great place for children to play at the water's edge or for water-loving dogs. The garden was conceived as a memorial garden and as you walk through the willow tunnel to the various sections you will come across memorandum and dedications. With no shortage of relaxing seating areas you can sit and enjoy the children's lawn (created for the local nursery) complete with a miniature gypsy caravan with inside fittings, or the ancient ruin with its chimney and barbecue. Children will enjoy running over the two bridges that cross the water lily pond (they may even spot a newt). The variety and ingenuity make this an unmissable garden.

Open: Sunday 10 August, 2pm - 5pm, admission by donation.

Directions: From Kilsyth and Kirkintilloch follow signs to Milton of Campsie and then follow the yellow *SGS* signs.

Opening for: *Cancer Research UK*

The Milton of Campsie Community Garden

Inverness, Ross, Cromarty & Skye

Sponsored by

❁ RATHBONES

Helmsdale
Brora
Golspie
Pittentrail
Lairg
Bonar Bridge
Dornoch Firth
Dornoch
Nigg Ferry
Cromarty
Tain
Forres
Kinloss
Burghead
Nairn
Fortrose
Dingwall
Inverness/Inbhir Nis
Grantown-on-Spey
Nethy Bridge
Aviemore
▲ Ben Macdui 1309m
Braemar
Tomatin
Carrbridge/Drochaid Chàrr
Kingussie
Dawhinnie
Strathpeffer
Conon Bridge
Beauly
Alness
Dores
Drumnadrochit
Newtonmore
Laggan
Kinloch Laggan
Achnasheen
Cannich
Foyers
Invermoriston
Fort Augustus
Invergarry
Spean Bridge
Loch Shin
Inverclassley
Loch Fannich
Inchnadamph
Lochinver
Elphin
Ledmore
Achiltibuie
Ullapool
Dundonnel
Kinlochewe
Craig
Torridon
Achintee
Stromeferry
Dornie
Shiel Bridge
Kinloch Lagan
Glenfinnan
Corpach
Fort William/An Gearasdan
Ben Nevis 1344m
Enard Bay
Laide
Aultbea
Poolewe
Gairloch
Shieldaig
Lochcarron
Kyle of Lochalsh/Caol Loch Aillse
Scalpay
Skulumus
Broadford
Ardvasar
Aird of Sleat
Mallaig
Lochailort
Acharacle
Butt of Lewis/Rubha Robhanais
Port of Ness/Port Nis
Stornoway/Steòrnabhagh
Tarbert/An Tairbeart
Leverburgh/An t-Ob
Carlabhagh
ISLE OF LEWIS/EILEAN LEODHAIS
Harris Na Hearadh
Scarp
Taransay/Tarasaigh
Scalpay/Scalpaigh
THE MINCH
NORTH MINCH
Kilmaluag
Staffin
Uig
Carbost
Bracadale
Dunvegan
Sligachan
Luib
Portree
Raasay
Rona
Inner Sound
Sound of Raasay
Loch Snizort
ISLE OF SKYE
Soay
Rum
Canna
Sound of Canna
Sound of Rum
Sound of Sleat
Eigg Arisaig
Muck
Loch Morar
Sound of Arisaig
Egg

1 Dundonnel
9
2
3
4
5
6
7
8
10
11
12
13
14 16
15
17 Carlabhagh
18
19
20 Portree
21

Inverness, Ross, Cromarty & Skye

OUR VOLUNTEER ORGANISERS

District Organiser:	Lucy Lister-Kaye	House of Aigas, Aigas, Beauly IV4 7AD lucy.listerkaye@gmail.com T: 01463 782443
Area Organiser:	Emma MacKenzie	Glenkyllachy, Tomatin IV13 7YA emmaglenkyllachy@gmail.com T: 01808 531204
Treasurer:	Sheila Kerr	11 Drumdevan Road, Inverness IV2 4BZ sheila.kerr@talk21.com T: 07730 148451

GARDENS OPEN ON A SPECIFIC DATE

Dunvegan Castle and Gardens, Isle of Skye	Thursday, 13 February
Dunvegan Castle and Gardens, Isle of Skye	Saturday, 15 February
Dunvegan Castle and Gardens, Isle of Skye	Tuesday, 18 February
Dundonnell House, Little Loch Broom, Wester Ross	Thursday, 10 April
Old Allangrange, Munlochy	Sunday, 25 May
Struanbridge, Essich Road, Inverness	Saturday, 31 May
Dundonnell House, Little Loch Broom, Wester Ross	Saturday, 31 May
Glenkyllachy, Tomatin	Sunday, 15 June
House of Aigas and Field Centre, by Beauly	Sunday, 22 June
Struanbridge, Essich Road, Inverness	Saturday, 28 June
7 Braes of Conon, Conon Bridge	Sunday, 29 June
Kiltarlity Gardens, Kiltarlity, Beauly	Sunday, 13 July
Struanbridge, Essich Road, Inverness	Saturday, 26 July
House of Aigas and Field Centre, by Beauly	Sunday, 27 July
2 Durnamuck, Little Loch Broom, Wester Ross	Sunday, 3 August
Old Allangrange, Munlochy	Sunday, 3 August
Dundonnell House, Little Loch Broom, Wester Ross	Thursday, 21 August
Struanbridge, Essich Road, Inverness	Saturday, 30 August
Struanbridge, Essich Road, Inverness	Saturday, 27 September

GARDENS OPEN REGULARLY

Oldtown of Leys Garden, Inverness	1 January - 31 December, except 1 May - 31 Oct. (not Thursday & Friday)
Highland Liliums, 10 Loaneckheim, Kiltarlity	1 January - 31 December
Raasay Walled Garden, Isle of Raasay	1 January - 31 December
Inverness Botanic Gardens, Bught Lane, Inverness	3 January - 21 December
Abriachan Garden Nursery, Loch Ness Side	1 February - 30 November
Attadale, Strathcarron	1 April - 31 October
Dunvegan Castle and Gardens, Isle of Skye	1 April - 15 October
Glenkyllachy, Tomatin	1 May - 31 October (Monday & Tuesday)
Leathad Ard, Upper Carloway, Isle of Lewis	1 May - 30 September (not Sunday)

Inverness, Ross, Cromarty & Skye

GARDENS OPEN REGULARLY – CONTINUED

Balmeanach House, Balmeanach, nr Struan, Isle of Skye	1 May - 4 October
Gorthleck House Garden, Stratherrick	24 May - 1 June
5 Knott, Clachamish, Portree, Isle of Skye	29 June - 30 September (Monday, Tuesday & Sunday)

GARDENS OPEN BY ARRANGEMENT

Berryfield House, Lentran, Inverness	1 April - 31 July
Leathad Ard, Upper Carloway, Isle of Lewis	1 April - 30 April
House of Aigas and Field Centre, by Beauly	1 April - 31 October
Dundonnell House, Little Loch Broom, Wester Ross	1 April - 31 October
Struanbridge, Essich Road, Inverness	1 May - 31 October
Glenkyllachy, Tomatin	1 May - 31 October
Old Allangrange, Munlochy	1 May - 31 October
2 Strathview, Alcaig, Conon Bridge	1 June - 30 September
5 Knott, Clachamish, Portree, Isle of Skye	1 June - 30 September
2 Durnamuck, Little Loch Broom, Wester Ross	1 July - 30 September

5 Knott

Inverness, Ross, Cromarty & Skye

1 **2 DURNAMUCK**
Little Loch Broom, Wester Ross IV23 2QZ
Will Soos and Susan Pomeroy
T: 07789 390028 E: sueandwill@icloud.com
W: 2Durnamuckgarden.com. You can also find us on Facebook.

Our garden is south-east facing on the edge of Little Loch Broom. It is a coastal plantsman's garden with a rich mix of herbaceous borders, trees and shrubs, vegetables, drystone wall planting. South African/Mediterranean plants, a wild meadow and stunning views. Many of the plants have been collected from all over the world, and growing them has provided obvious challenges but with a pleasing outcome. Featured in 2019 entries in *Gardens Illustrated, Homes & Gardens* and *Beechgrove.* Entry in the *English Garden* magazine in September 2020.

Open: Sunday 3 August, 11am - 4pm. Also open by arrangement 1 July - 30 September. Admission £5.00, children free. Teas by donation. A wood and stone accommodation, The Garden Bothy, is available for garden passionate people. It is small and compact but very beautiful in its own garden. Enquiries to sueandwill@icloud.com and 2Durnamuckgarden.com

Directions: On the A832, between Dundonnell and Ullapool, take the turning along the single-track road signed *Badcaul*, continue to the egg shack, turn right, go to the bottom of the hill and 2 Durnamuck is the house with the red roof. There is parking down by the house if needed.

Opening for: Sandpiper Trust

2 **2 STRATHVIEW**
Alcaig, Conon Bridge IV7 8HS
Mike and Babs Crocker
T: 01349 862799 Text 07817 042206 E: mpbecrock@gmail.com

A medium-sized garden with mature apple trees and a shady maze of paths through beds packed with perennials sloping down to sea level where there are plenty of birds on the estuary to view. Featuring a small greenhouse, steam model railway which works if weather allows. There are a couple of water features fed by rainwater, leading to a small deep pond. Stunning panoramic view across the Cromarty Firth seen from a 'food forest', with fruit trees growing on a set of home designed arches, runner beans, strawberries and apple trees. Achilty stone retaining walls and steps have been added over the last 14 years. Many plants have been chosen for their perfume. There are various seating areas.

Open: by arrangement 1 June - 30 September, admission £5.00, children free. We do not have contactless payments, so please bring cash. Pot-luck sales table with homemade jam, frozen fruit sauce, craft items and plants. Teas £5.00. Sorry, smoking is not permitted in the garden.

Directions: From Tore roundabout head north for Ullapool on the A835. Take the right turn for *Findon* onto the B9163. After about one mile, turn left along a tree-lined lane (just before the wooden sign for *Alcaig*). Parking is limited to two cars in one party.

Opening for: Friends of Alcaig Telephone Box (SCIO)

Inverness, Ross, Cromarty & Skye

2 Strathview

3 **5 KNOTT**
Clachamish, Portree, Isle of Skye IV51 9NZ
Brian and Joyce Heggie
T: 07495 442468 E: jbheggie@hotmail.co.uk
W: www.knottskye.co.uk

An informal, organic garden on a gently-sloping half-acre site. Perimeter hedging has enabled a sheltered and tranquil oasis to be created. Winding paths meander through the densely-planted borders filled with a diverse range of perennials, annuals and shrubs. There is also a vegetable area with raised beds and a large polytunnel. A developing wildflower meadow with sea loch views leads onto a sheltered bay and a shoreside walk to the headland. There are regular sightings of seals, otters, sea eagles and harbour porpoises. There is garden seating in several locations. The garden is situated in an easily-reached, particularly quiet and scenic area of Skye. The garden was featured on *Beechgrove* in 2023.

Open: 29 June - 30 September (Monday, Tuesday & Sunday), 2pm - 5pm. Also open by arrangement 1 June - 30 September. Admission £4.00, children free.

Directions: From Portree, take the A87 to Uig/Dunvegan. After approximately three miles, take the A850 towards Dunvegan. Six miles on, pass the *Treaslane* sign. Turn right on the bend at the signpost for *Knott*.

Opening for: *Crossroads Care Skye & Lochalsh & The Way Forward Group*

Inverness, Ross, Cromarty & Skye

4 **7 BRAES OF CONON**
Conon Bridge IV7 8AX
Mr Nigel Stanton

A beautifully-designed garden created by a professional nurseryman. Nigel Stanton moved to the Highlands in 2014. The garden needed imported local topsoil and a lot of manure. Now, with the help of raised beds and paved paths, the fruits of his endeavours are a delight. Specialities include magnificent delphiniums, rampant sweet peas and subtly blended roses.

Open: Sunday 29 June, 2pm - 5pm, admission £5.00, children free. Homemade teas by donation. Sorry no dogs.

Directions: Coming into Conon Bridge on the A862 from Muir of Ord, turn right into the Braes of Conon and follow the road signs to Number 7. From Dingwall, take the A835 towards Tore at the Maryburgh roundabout, then turn first right towards Conon Bridge, and follow the signs.

Opening for: Highland Hospice: Aird branch

5 **ABRIACHAN GARDEN NURSERY**
Loch Ness Side IV3 8LA
Mr and Mrs Davidson
T 01463 861232 E: info@lochnessgarden.com
W: www.lochnessgarden.com

This is an outstanding garden with over four acres of exciting plantings with winding paths through native woodlands. Seasonal highlights include snowdrops, hellebores, primulas, meconopsis, hardy geraniums and colour-themed summer beds. Views over Loch Ness.

Open: 1 February - 30 November, 9am - 7pm, admission £4.00, children free. Open for snowdrops and winter walks in the spring.

Directions: On the A82 Inverness/Drumnadrochit road, about nine miles south of Inverness.

Opening for: Highland Hospice

6 **ATTADALE**
Strathcarron IV54 8YX
Joanna Macpherson
T: 01520 722217 E: info@attadalegardens.com
W: www.attadalegardens.com

The Gulf Stream, surrounding hills and rocky cliffs create a microclimate for 20 acres of outstanding water gardens, old rhododendrons, unusual trees and a fern collection in a geodesic dome. There is also a sunken fern garden developed on the site of an early 19th-century drain, a waterfall into a pool with dwarf rhododendrons, sunken garden, peace garden and kitchen garden. Other features include a conservatory, Japanese garden, sculpture collection and giant sundial.

Open: 1 April - 31 October, 10am - 5pm, admission £10.00, children free.

Directions: On the A890 between Strathcarron and South Strome.

Opening for: Highland Hospice

Inverness, Ross, Cromarty & Skye

7
BALMEANACH HOUSE
Balmeanach, nr Struan, Isle of Skye IV56 8FH
Mrs Arlene Macphie
T: 01470 572320 E: info@skye-holiday.com
W: www.skye-holiday.com

Very much a plantsman's garden, begun in the early 1990s after a third-of-an-acre of croft land was fenced. A shelter belt now permits a plethora of diverse plants in exuberant herbaceous borders, which give nectar and pollen to keep the buzzing and fluttering going until autumn, plus rockeries and raised beds. Native trees rub shoulders with more exotic ornamental varieties, providing a canopy for shade-loving plants and nesting sites for the many birds who make the garden their home. A small pond in a sunken garden; a larger pond divided in two by a path over a culvert and a bog garden, give scope for marginal and moisture-loving plants. Meandering pathways lead through a small bluebell wood, an arbour garden, shrubbery and small birch wood, full of azaleas and rhododendrons. Plenty of seating throughout provides an invitation to sit, relax and enjoy the garden and stunning scenery beyond.

Open: 1 May - 4 October, 11am - 4pm, admission £4.00, children free. No teas on Saturdays and Sundays.

Directions: A87 to Sligachan, turn left and Balmeanach is five miles north of Struan and five miles south of Dunvegan.

Opening for: Scottish SPCA & Redwings

Balmeanach House

8
BERRYFIELD HOUSE
Lentran, Inverness IV3 8RJ
Lynda Perch-Nielsen
T: 01463 831346 M: 07547 960341 E: lyndazpn@gmail.com

An open garden of trees and bushes with views across the Beauly Firth to Ben Wyvis. There are large swathes of bulbs: crocus, dogtooth violets and heritage daffodils. A three-acre wildflower meadow with meandering paths adjoins the garden.

Open: by arrangement 1 April - 31 July, admission by donation.

Directions: Halfway between Inverness and Beauly on the A862. From Inverness, four-and-a-quarter miles on the left from crossing over the Clachnaharry railway bridge. From Beauly, one-and-a-quarter miles on the right from The Old North Inn.

Opening for: Action Medical Research

Inverness, Ross, Cromarty & Skye

9 DUNDONNELL HOUSE
Little Loch Broom, Wester Ross IV23 2QW
Dundonnell Estates
T: 07789 390028 E: sueandwill@icloud.com

Camellias, magnolias and bulbs in spring, rhododendrons and laburnum walk in this ancient walled garden. Exciting planting gives all year round interest, centred around one of the oldest yew trees in Scotland. A water sculpture, unique Victorian glass house, riverside walk, arboretum – all in the valley below the peaks of An Teallach.
Champion Trees: Yew and Holly.

Open: Thursday 10 April, Saturday 31 May, Thursday 21 August, 2pm - 5pm. And open by arrangement 1 April - 31 October. Admission £5.00, children free. Teas and plant sales only available on 31 May.

Directions: Turn off the A835 at Braemore on to the A832. After 11 miles take the Badralloch turn for a ½ mile.

Opening for: *Médecins Sans Frontières & Environmental Investigation Agency*

10 DUNVEGAN CASTLE AND GARDENS
Isle of Skye IV55 8WF
Hugh Macleod of Macleod
T: 01470 521206 E: info@dunvegancastle.com
W: www.dunvegancastle.com

Any visit to the Isle of Skye is incomplete without enjoying the wealth of history and horticultural delights at award-winning 5* Dunvegan Castle & Gardens, now an RHS partner garden. The five acres of formal gardens began life in the 18th century. In stark contrast to the barren moorland and mountains which dominate Skye's landscape, the Castle's Water Garden, Round Garden, Walled Garden and woodland walks provide an oasis for an eclectic mix of flowers, exotic plants, shrubs and specimen trees, framed by shimmering pools fed from waterfalls. After visiting the Water Garden with its ornate bridges and islands replete with colourful plants along the riverbanks, wander through the elegant formal Round Garden. The Walled Garden, formerly the Castle's vegetable garden, now has a diverse range of plants and flowers completing the attractive features, including a water lily pond, garden museum, 17th century lectern sundial, glass house and the 'Dunvegan Pebble', a rotating 2.7 ton Carrara marble sculpture. The informal areas of the garden are kept wild to encourage wildlife, creating a more natural aesthetic framed by the coastal scenery. The present Chief, Hugh MacLeod, and his dedicated team of gardeners, continue to build on this unique legacy for future generations to enjoy.

Open: Thursday 13 February, Saturday 15 February and Tuesday 18 February, 10am - 2pm for Snowdrops and Winter Walks. Also open 1 April - 15 October, 10am - 5:30pm (last entry 5pm) Admission details can be found on the garden's website. The castle, gardens and cafe are open from 1 April to 15 October. Catering available from the MacLeod Tables Cafe in the car park.

Directions: One mile from Dunvegan village, 23 miles west of Portree. Follow the signs for *Dunvegan Castle.*

Opening for: *Donation to SGS Beneficiaries*

Inverness, Ross, Cromarty & Skye

11 GLENKYLLACHY
Tomatin IV13 7YA
Mr and Mrs Philip Mackenzie
E: emmaglenkyllachy@gmail.com

In a magnificent Highland glen, 1200 feet above sea level, Glenkyllachy is a beautiful garden of shrubs, herbaceous plants, rhododendrons, trees, and spectacular views down the Findhorn River. There are some rare specimens and a recently planted arboretum. Rhododendrons and bulbs flower in May/June, herbaceous plants bloom through July/August with glorious autumn colours in September and October. There is a very productive vegetable garden, polytunnel, fruit cage and greenhouse as well as original sculptures and a Highgrove-inspired wall which provide year round interest. Featured on TV *Beechgrove*, in *The English Garden Magazine* and recently in *Scottish Field* (November 2023). The garden is constantly evolving with new areas being developed and planting schemes changed.

Open: Open every Monday & Tuesday 10.00am - 5.00pm from 1 May - 31 October, and for groups or individuals by arrangement any time during these months. Special Open Day Sunday 15 June 2.00pm - 5.00pm with plant sales, teas, stalls and live music. Admission £5.00 children free.

Directions: Turn off the A9 at Tomatin and take the Coignafearn/Garbole single-track road down the north-side of the River Findhorn, there is a cattle grid and gate on the right 500 yards **after** the humpback bridge and the sign to *Farr*.

Opening for: Marie Curie

12 GORTHLECK HOUSE GARDEN
Stratherrick IV2 6UJ
Steve and Katie Smith
T: 07710 325903 E: gorthleckgarden@gmail.com

Gorthleck is an unusual 20-acre woodland garden built in an unlikely place, on and around an exposed rocky ridge which offers long views of the surrounding countryside in the 'borrowed landscape' tradition of Japanese gardens. The layout of the garden works with the natural features of the landscape with numerous paths, hedges and shelter belts creating clearly defined areas where a large collection of trees and shrubs are thriving. The garden includes over 400 different varieties of rhododendrons, half of which are species, and a large variety of bamboos. It is a large garden so allow sufficient time to see it properly.

Open: 24 May - 1 June, 10am - 6pm, admission £5.00, children free.

Directions: From the A9, take the B851 towards Fort Augustus to join the B862. Go through the village of Errogie where there is a sharp left-hand bend on the road. After approximately one mile, there is a small church on the left. The Gorthleck drive is directly opposite the church and the house can be seen on the hill to the left as you follow the drive to the left of the new house. Visitors can park on the verges at the top of the drive.

Opening for: Maggie's

Inverness, Ross, Cromarty & Skye

13 HIGHLAND LILIUMS

10 Loaneckheim, Kiltarlity IV4 7JQ
Laura Evans
T: 01463 741698 E: shop@highlandliliums.co.uk
W: www.highlandliliums.co.uk

Highland Liliums is a working retail nursery with spectacular views over the Beauly valley and Strathfarrar hills. A wide selection of home-grown plants are available including alpines, ferns, grasses, herbaceous, herbs, liliums, primulas and shrubs.

Open: All year, 9am - 5pm. See website for seasonal changes, admission free. Also open as part of Kiltarlity Gardens on Sunday 13 July.

Directions: Signposted from Kiltarlity Village, which is just off the Beauly to Drumnadrochit road (A833), approximately 12 miles from Inverness.

Opening for: Donation to SGS Beneficiaries

14 HOUSE OF AIGAS AND FIELD CENTRE

by Beauly IV4 7AD
Sir John and Lady Lister-Kaye
T: 01463 782443 E: info@aigas.co.uk
W: www.aigas.co.uk

The House of Aigas has a small arboretum of named Victorian specimen trees and modern additions. The garden consists of extensive rockeries, herbaceous borders, ponds and shrubs. Aigas Field Centre rangers lead regular guided walks on nature trails through woodland, moorland and around a loch.
Champion Trees: Douglas fir, Atlas cedar and *Sequoiadendron giganteum.*

Open: Sunday 22 June and Sunday 27 July, 2pm - 5pm. And open by arrangement 1 April - 31 October. Admission £5.00, children free. Homemade Teas £5.00. Sorry no dogs.

Directions: Four-and-a-half miles from Beauly on the A831 Cannich/Glen Affric road.

Opening for: Highland Hospice: Aird branch

House of Aigas and Field Centre

Inverness, Ross, Cromarty & Skye

15 INVERNESS BOTANIC GARDENS

Bught Lane, Inverness IV3 5SS
Pamela Sutherland
T: 01463 701019 E: inverness.botanics@highlifehighland.com
W: highlifehighland.com/inverness-botanicgardens/

We are the most northerly botanic gardens in the UK and host a wide variety of plants, shrubs and trees with year-round interest. There is a large Tropical House and a Cactus House with plants from around the globe. In spring come to see our bulb displays, in summer our herbaceous borders and specimen trees, in autumn for late herbaceous and leaf colour and in winter for evergreens, specimen trees in flower and those with wonderful bark. The GROW Project is also housed within our gardens which is run by a special needs group, it has an allotment, herbaceous borders, wildflower areas, ponds, children's play areas and much, much more! There is a lovely cafe onsite serving soups, sandwiches and cakes alongside local artworks and plants. We are a charity and so the entry is free with donation boxes to be found inside the cafe.

Open: 3 January - 21 December, 9:30am - 4pm (open for Snowdrops and Winter Walks 25 January - 11 March), admission by donation. Please check website for more details.

Directions: From Inverness city centre follow signs to Drumnadrochit. Then follow the brown signs to the Leisure Centre (turn left at the Cemetery before the canal).

Opening for: Donation to SGS Beneficiaries

16 KILTARLITY GARDENS

Kiltarlity, Beauly IV4 7JH
Sheila Ross, Laura Evans, Dickon and Barbara Sandbach & Sue Marshall

Aird View 30a Camault Muir, Kiltarlity IV4 7JH (Sheila Ross): The garden at Aird View offers a mix of borders, a water feature, an arbour and a newly-added herbaceous border. There are also fruit trees and vegetable beds. Vintage tractors on display.
Buchollie House (NEW) Buchollie House, Boblainy, Kiltarlity IV4 7HX (Sue Marshall): Buchollie House has an informal but varied woodland garden of about one acre. It incorporates herbaceous borders, raised vegetable beds, and a shaded glade planted with rhododendrons and azaleas, as well as more natural areas and a wildflower patch. There is a large wildlife pond and the garden attracts a huge variety of woodland birds and animals. It is a good example of a large garden that is relatively easy to manage and maintain.
Highland Liliums 10 Loaneckheim, Kiltarlity IV4 7JQ (Laura Evans): Highland Liliums is a working retail nursery with spectacular views over the Beauly valley and Strathfarrar hills. A wide selection of home-grown plants are available including alpines, ferns, grasses, herbaceous, herbs, liliums, primulas and shrubs.
Monarda House Kiltarlity, Beauly IV4 7HX (Dickon and Barbara Sandbach): An evolving, productive garden with a mix of ornamental and native plantings over four acres. An easy circuit, in proximity to the house on even paths, displays a variety of conifers, shrubs and herbaceous plants, with a summer house. A wider circuit, for which stouter footwear is recommended, includes raised vegetable beds, polytunnel, chicken run, a young orchard, nuttery and mature woodland, with a pine-lined avenue up to the fledgling arboretum. Beyond is a rough-pathed area of regenerative wood, wildflower meadow, mature trees and willow coppice, to the old stable apiary, returning along a track sided with ornamental cherries.

Open: Sunday 13 July, 2pm - 5pm, admission £8.00, children free. Homemade teas and discounted plants for sale at Highland Liliums. Entrance fee covers all four gardens.

Inverness, Ross, Cromarty & Skye

Directions: Aird View: Take the A833 Beauly to Drumnadrochit Road, pass Brockies Lodge. Turn right at the bus shelter and follow the single track road to the junction at the school. Turn left and go up the hill to the top, at the junction Aird View is on the right.

Buchollie House and Monarda House: From the A833 Beauly to Drumnadrochit road, turn into Kiltarlity. Drive through the village, over a small bridge, then take the first left to Clunevackie. Continue for approx one mile where you will see Buchollie House on the left side of road. Disabled parking is available at the house, but main parking approx 200 metres further up the hill at Monarda House which is on the right hand side of the road after it bears left ahead of a forestry track. What3words: valuables.teaches.brave.

Highland Liliums is signposted from Kiltarlity Village.

Opening for: Highland Hospice: Aird branch

Monarda House

17 **LEATHAD ARD**
Upper Carloway, Isle of Lewis HS2 9AQ
Rowena and Stuart Oakley
T: 01851 643204 E: leathad.ard@gmail.com
W: www.leathadard.org.uk

A one-acre sloping garden with stunning views over East Loch Roag. It has evolved along with the shelter hedges that divide the garden into a number of areas giving a new view at every corner. With shelter and raised beds, the different conditions created permit a wide variety of plants to be grown. Features include herbaceous borders, cutting borders, bog gardens, grass garden, exposed beds, patios, a pond and vegetables and fruit grown both in the open ground and the Keder greenhouse. Some of the vegetables are grown to show standards.

Open: 1 May - 30 September (not Sunday), 10am - 6pm. Also open by arrangement 1 April - 30 April. Admission £5.00, children free.

Directions: On the A858 Shawbost-Carloway take the first right after the Carloway football pitch, and it is the first house on the right. By bus take the Westside circular bus, exit Stornoway and head for Carloway football pitch.

Opening for: British Red Cross

Inverness, Ross, Cromarty & Skye

18 **OLD ALLANGRANGE**
Munlochy IV8 8NZ
J J Gladwin
T: 01463 811304 E: office@blackislegardendesign.com

We have an ornamental garden surrounding the house (new information discovered dates it from the 17th rather than 18th Century), and a three acre productive garden with two Keder greenhouses, designed using agroforestry and permaculture principles and gardened bio-dynamically using no-dig technique. The ornamental garden has different areas with distinctive characters. There is a parterre in front of the house with informal planting, a lower garden, an ornamental propagation garden, a mound and orchard. Hedges, (pleached lime, yew, beech, box, holly and mixed species field hedges) clipped in various styles connect the different areas of the garden. We have started to remove perimeter wire fences replacing them with log hedges and brash bunds. With a keen interest in gardening for biodiversity from the soil upwards, no chemicals have been used since our arrival in 1995. The development and improvement of the garden is ongoing.
Champion Trees: Yew and sweet chestnut.

Open: Sunday 25 May and Sunday 3 August, 2pm - 5pm. Also open by arrangement 1 May - 31 October. Admission £7.50, children free. There will be no teas, but there will be a baking stall, and visitors are welcome to bring a picnic. Guided tours given on the hour from 2pm - 4pm on open days. Tickets for self guided tours at other times can be bought from the Brewery Shop at a cost of £6.00 per head. Open by arrangement bookings for guided groups (minimum 10 people).

Directions: From Inverness head four miles north on the A9, and follow the directions for *Black Isle Brewery*. Park up at the Brewery and walk down to the garden. Directions will be given in the shop.

Opening for: Flourish

19 **OLDTOWN OF LEYS GARDEN**
Inverness IV2 6AE
David and Anne Sutherland
T: 01463 238238 E: ams@oldtownofleys.com

Established in 2003, on the outskirts of Inverness, with views over the town, this large garden of three acres has year-round interest. Spring rhododendrons and azaleas, summer herbaceous plantings, autumn trees and shrubs and winter appeal from the conifers, evergreens and structures. Features include a rockery, ponds, musical instruments, a stumpery and a new area of late summer colour.

Open: 1 January - 31 December (closed Thursday and Friday 1 April - 31 October), 8am - 8pm, admission by donation.

Directions: Turn off Southern Distributor road (B8082) at Leys roundabout towards Inverarnie (B861). At the T-junction turn right. After 50 metres turn right into Oldtown of Leys.

Opening for: Highland Hospice & Alzheimer Scotland

Inverness, Ross, Cromarty & Skye

20 RAASAY WALLED GARDEN
Isle of Raasay IV40 8PB
Raasay Community
T: 07939 106426 E: raasaywalledgarden@gmail.com.
You can also find us on Facebook and Instagram
W: Raasay.com/the-walled-garden-raasay

Accessed from the road behind Raasay House, just a 10 minute walk from the Ferry Terminal, is the Category A listed community owned walled garden. Visited by Boswell and Johnson in 1773, the garden suffered neglect before coming into community ownership. Ongoing restoration began in 2013 and the 1.43 acre garden now supplies vegetables, fruit, salad, herbs and cut flowers to the community and visitors. Features an orchard, rose beds, polytunnels, a fruit cage, wildflowers for pollinators and insects, and plenty of seats. We have a composting toilet for visitors' use. June to August provide the most colourful time and our main produce harvests take place from May to September. We run events during the year – please check our Facebook page for details. The garden isn't always staffed, so please contact us for further details.

Open: 1 January - 31 December, 9am - 7pm, admission by donation. Plants for sale occasionally, vegetables for sale once/twice weekly during the season.

Directions: Take the Calmac Ferry to Raasay (20 minute journey) from Sconser, between Broadford and Portree on the Isle of Skye. The garden is an easy walk from the terminal and there is plenty to do and see on Raasay on foot, although cars can also cross.

Opening for: *Donation to SGS Beneficiaries*

21 STRUANBRIDGE
Essich Road, Inverness IV2 6AH
Marcus and Catriona Jenks
E: mjenks@greenx.co.uk

A small, well-stocked garden approximately three miles from Inverness city centre, set on three levels each with its own distinct character. The entrance to the garden includes a decking area with a small fruit garden and raised beds. The small mid-tier area consists of mainly hydrangeas and rhododendrons and the very informal, hidden lower garden includes a wildlife pond, raised beds, and shaded garden area with a greenhouse, all framed by an old stone bridge and a small burn. Due to its layout, the garden is not suitable for wheelchairs and requires the ability to climb a number of steps to view.

Open: Saturdays 31 May, 28 June, 26 July, 30 August and 27 September, noon - 5pm. Also open by arrangement 1 May - 31 October. Admission £4.00, children free. Admission to the garden along with homemade teas £7.00 (special dietary requirements can be catered for).

Directions: From the Inverness Southern Distributor road (A8082) exit the Essich roundabout onto Essich Road. Struanbridge is located exactly a ½ mile from the roundabout, on the left. Parking is restricted.

Opening for: *Mikeysline*

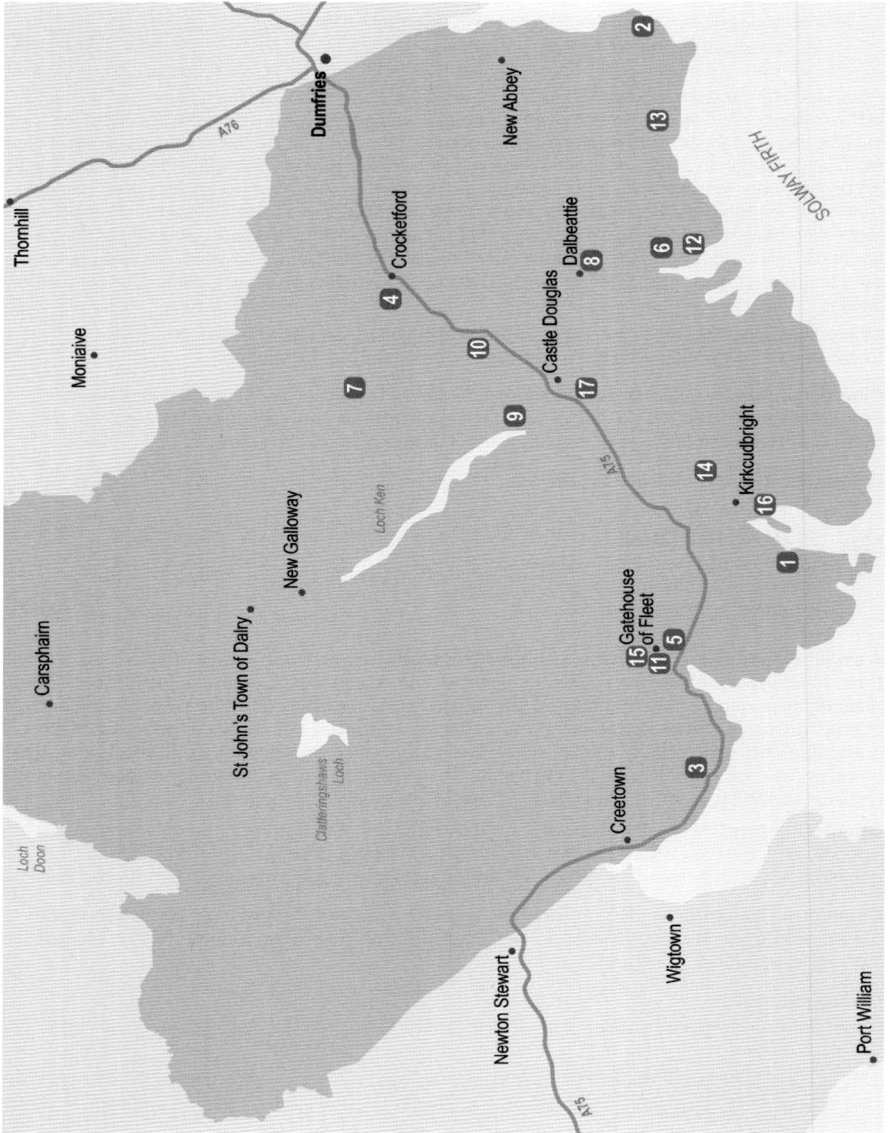

Kirkcudbrightshire

Sponsored by

✿ RATHBONES

Dumfries

New Abbey

Thornhill

A76

Moniaive

Crocketford

Castle Douglas

Dalbeattie

SOLWAY FIRTH

Kirkcudbright

Loch Ken

New Galloway

Carsphairn

St John's Town of Dalry

Clatteringshaws Loch

Loch Doon

Gatehouse of Fleet

Creetown

Newton Stewart

Wigtown

Port William

A75

Kirkcudbrightshire

OUR VOLUNTEER ORGANISERS

District Organisers:	Theodora Stanning	Seabank, Merse Road, Rockcliffe DG5 4QH
	Julian Stanning	Seabank, Merse Road, Rockcliffe DG5 4QH
Assistant District Organiser:	Alison Kinsella	The Park, Dundrennan DG6 4QH
Area Organisers:	May Lockhart	25 Victoria Park, Kirkcudbright DG6 4EN
	Norman McClure	142 Cotton Street, Castle Douglas DG7 1DG
	Lesley Pepper	Anwoth Old Schoolhouse DG7 2EF
	George Thomas	Savat, Meikle Richorn, Dalbeattie DG5 4QT
Media Volunteer:	Alison Forrest	Conifers, Rockcliffe, Dalbeattie DG5 4QF
District Photographer:	Stuart Littlewood	stu@f8.eclipse.co.uk
Treasurer:	Russell Allan	Braeburn, 6 Barcloy Mill, Rockcliffe DG5 4QL

GARDENS OPEN ON A SPECIFIC DATE

Danevale Park, Crossmichael	Sunday, 16 February
The Limes, Kirkcudbright	Sunday, 23 March
3 Millhall, Shore Road, Kirkcudbright	Sunday, 13 April
The Limes, Kirkcudbright	Sunday, 27 April
Threave Garden, Castle Douglas	Monday, 5 May
Cally Biodiversity Gardens, Cally Avenue, Gatehouse of Fleet	Sunday, 11 May
Arbigland House, Kirkbean, Dumfries	Sunday, 18 May
Corsock House, Corsock, Castle Douglas	Sunday, 25 May
Brooklands, Crocketford	Sunday, 1 June
The Limes, Kirkcudbright	Sunday, 8 June
Southwick House, Southwick	Sunday, 29 June
Dalbeattie Community Allotments Association, Port Road, Dalbeattie	Sunday, 13 July
Kings Grange House, Castle Douglas	Sunday, 20 July
3 Millhall, Shore Road, Kirkcudbright	Sunday, 31 August
Cally Biodiversity Gardens, Cally Avenue, Gatehouse of Fleet	Sunday, 28 September
Seabank, The Merse, Rockcliffe	Date to be confirmed

Kirkcudbrightshire

GARDENS OPEN BY ARRANGEMENT

Stockarton, Kirkcudbright	1 January - 31 December
The Limes, Kirkcudbright	1 January - 31 December
Barholm Castle, Gatehouse of Fleet	1 January - 31 December
Kings Grange House, Castle Douglas	1 February - 31 August
Brooklands, Crocketford	1 February - 28 February and 1 May - 30 September
Danevale Park, Crossmichael	10 February - 22 February
Luckie Harg's, Anwoth, Gatehouse of Fleet, Castle Douglas	1 March - 30 September
3 Millhall, Shore Road, Kirkcudbright	1 March - 31 October
Tal-y-Fan, Laurieston Road, Gatehouse of Fleet, Kirkcudbrightshire	1 March - 30 September
Corsock House, Corsock, Castle Douglas	1 April - 31 May
Clonyard Farm, Colvend, Dalbeattie	15 June - 30 June

Kirkcudbrightshire

1 **3 MILLHALL**
Shore Road, Kirkcudbright DG6 4TQ
Mr Alan Shamash
T: 01557 870352 E: shamash@freeuk.com

Impressive five-acre garden with a large collection of mature shrubs, including over 200 rhododendron species, many camellias, magnolias including *campbellii*, embothriums, telopeas, perennials, over 200 hydrangeas and many other rare Southern Hemisphere plants. The garden has several interesting paths and is on a hillside running along the rocky shore of the Dee Estuary in Kirkcudbright Bay.

Open: Open: Sunday 13 April & Sunday 31 August, 2pm - 5pm. Also open by arrangement 1 March - 31 October. Admission £5.00, children free.

Directions: On the B727 between Kirkcudbright and Borgue on the west shore of the Dee Estuary. Parking at Dhoon Beach public car park, about three miles south of Kirkcudbright. There is a five-minute walk to the house. Please note there will be no vehicular access to 3 Millhall and all visitors should park at Dhoon Beach and walk up to the property.

Opening for: Alzheimer's Research UK

3 Millhall

Kirkcudbrightshire

2 ARBIGLAND HOUSE
Kirkbean, Dumfries DG2 8BQ
Alistair Alcock and Wayne Whittaker
T: 01387 880764 E: alcockalistair@gmail.com
W: www.arbiglandhouseandgardens.co.uk

Arbigland House is an Adam-style 18th-century mansion surrounded by 24 acres of woodland gardens running down to a beach on the Solway Firth. The gardens date from the 18th century but the more formal areas were developed in the late 19th and early 20th centuries and are currently undergoing a programme of restoration and development by the current owners Wayne Whittaker and Alistair Alcock. There are 200 year-old trees lining the Broad Walk which runs down to the Solway and a huge variety of rhododendrons and azaleas. Within the woodland are a range of features including a stream-fed lake and a Japanese garden, with a more formal sundial garden and sunken rose garden, all in the process of renewal. Amongst these are a diverse collection of mature trees and shrubs.

Open: Sunday 18 May, 2pm - 5pm, admission £5.00, children free. Short tours available of the principal rooms of the House.

Directions: Take the A710 to Kirkbean. In the village turn off towards Carsethorn and, after 200 yards, turn right and follow signs to *John Paul Jones Cottage.* After a mile or so, turn left at the T junction through white gates and down the drive through ornamental gates to Arbigland House.

Opening for: Absolute Classics & The Arts Society, Dumfries and Galloway

3 BARHOLM CASTLE
Gatehouse of Fleet DG7 2EZ
Drs John and Janet Brennan
T: 01557 840327 E: barholmcastle@gmail.com

Barholm Castle, a 16th-century tower, was restored from a ruin in 2005. The gardens surrounding the tower have been mostly developed from scratch and are now mature. There is a recently-extended walled garden, with a gate designed by the artist blacksmith Adam Booth; a courtyard garden; a wooded ravine with huge hybrid rhododendrons from Benmore; a pond and a large fernery with over 100 varieties of fern, including very large tree ferns; a large Victorian-style greenhouse filled with succulents and tender perennials; and a large open garden with island beds of shrubs and perennials and a pond. Directly around the castle are rockeries and shrub borders. Views over Wigtown Bay are magnificent. The garden is planted for year-round colour, from February, when the castle ravine is a river of snowdrops, to October, when autumn colour is splendid.

Open: by arrangement 1 January - 31 December, admission £5.00, children free.

Directions: Off the A75 at the Cairn Holy turn off, fork right three times and drive up a steep narrow road for half-a-mile.

Opening for: Home-Start Wigtownshire

Kirkcudbrightshire

4 BROOKLANDS
Crocketford DG2 8QH
Mr and Mrs Robert Herries
T: Gardener, Matthew Grieve: 07765 491902

Large old walled garden with a wide selection of plants, including some interesting shrubs and climbers and a kitchen garden. Mature woodland with many established rhododendrons and azaleas, and carpeted with snowdrops in February.

Open: Open: Sunday 1 June, 2pm - 5pm (Teas will be weather dependent). Also open by arrangement 1 February - 28 February for snowdrops and 1 May - 30 September. A minimum of four adults for by arrangement openings. Admission £5.00, children free.

Directions: Turn off the A712 Crocketford to New Galloway Road one mile outside Crocketford at the Gothic gatehouse (on the right travelling north).

Opening for: All proceeds to SGS Beneficiaries

Brooklands

5 CALLY BIODIVERSITY GARDENS
Cally Avenue, Gatehouse of Fleet DG7 2DJ
Kevin Hughes
T: 01557 815228 E: info@callygardens.co.uk
W: www.callygardens.co.uk

A one hectare walled garden containing an outstanding collection of rare and common plants from around the world assembled to create naturalistic habitat for our native fauna. Some plants can be found in no other Scottish garden whilst many are first introductions to gardens in the UK. This is an example of gardening harmoniously with nature where declining birds such as Garden warbler can be seen nesting amongst Himalayan poppies and American Prairie plants whilst lucky people might glimpse harvest mice in our unique Grassland Ecology Garden. We use no artificial fertiliser or pesticide and this is also true of the plants we grow for our plant sale area which has a wide range of less common plants.

Open: Sunday 11 May & Sunday 28 September, 10am - 5pm, admission £5.00, children free.

Directions: From Dumfries take the Gatehouse of Fleet turning off the A75, follow the B727 and turn left through the Cally Palace Hotel gateway from where the gardens are well signposted. A regular bus service will stop at the end of Cally Drive if requested.

Opening for: WWF-UK

Kirkcudbrightshire

6 **CLONYARD FARM**
Colvend, Dalbeattie DG5 4QW
Matthew and Pam Pumphrey
E: clonyard@btinternet.com

Open by arrangement for wildflowers. Informal garden around traditional stone buildings with views over pasture, wetland and a loch to mature mixed forest. The garden joins a wildflower meadow dominated by black knapweed and established yellow rattle. It features three species of native orchids and a former mill pond, a notable damselfly site. Both are maintained specifically to allow native wildlife and plants to thrive. There is an ornamental vegetable garden and around the house mixed plantings merge from sun to shade and woodland planting to provide all-year-round interest. There are meadow, wetland and woodland walks to two lochs and a crannog. Refreshments available on request.

Open: by arrangement 15 June - 30 June, admission £5.00, children free.

Directions: On the north side of the A710 approximately four miles from the crossroads with the A711 in Dalbeattie, adjacent to Clonyard House Hotel and one mile from Colvend village. Parking at the Farm. Bus service from Dalbeattie but current timetables should be checked. Clonyard Farm is a request stop.

Opening for: Marie Curie: DG5 Group

Clonyard Farm

Kirkcudbrightshire

7 CORSOCK HOUSE

Corsock, Castle Douglas DG7 3DJ
The Ingall family
T: 01644 440250 E: jingall@hotmail.com

Corsock House garden, renowned for its substantial collection of rhododendrons, includes an amazing variety of designed landscape, from a strictly formal walled garden, through richly planted woodlands full of different vistas, artfully designed water features and surprises to extensive lawns showing off the Bryce baronial mansion. This is an Arcadian garden with pools and temples, described by Ken Cox as 'perhaps my favourite of Scotland's many woodland gardens'.

Open: Sunday 25 May, 2pm - 5pm. Also open by arrangement 1 April - 31 May. Admission £5.00, children free.

Directions: Off the A75, Dumfries is 14 miles, Castle Douglas is 10 miles, Corsock Village is half a mile on the A712.

Opening for: Corsock & Kirkpatrick Durham Church Of Scotland

8 DALBEATTIE COMMUNITY ALLOTMENTS ASSOCIATION

Port Road, Dalbeattie DG5 4AZ
Dalbeattie Community Allotments Association
E: dcaa74@hotmail.com

Dalbeattie Community Allotments Association was formed in 2008 and the site was officially opened in August 2010. A local landowner has leased the land for 25 years at £1 per year, initially providing for 47 plots. The initial results were so successful that the area is now increased to provide for 81 productive plots where local residents can grow their own fruit, vegetables and flowers. Come and enjoy a stroll around the site, chat to members or relax in one of the community areas with a cup of tea. Information will be available and photos of the development of the site will be on display.

Open: Sunday 13 July, 2pm - 5pm, admission £5.00, children free.

Directions: The allotment site can be found on the Dalbeattie bypass (A710) next to Craignair Health Centre. what3words: cloud.eased.reward

Opening for: Dalbeattie Community Initiative

9 DANEVALE PARK

Crossmichael DG7 2LP
Lucy and Charlie Simpson
T: 01556 670223 E: lucysimpson078@gmail.com

First opening for snowdrops in 1951, these mature grounds have a wonderful display of snowdrops as well as aconites and many other wildflowers. Walks through the woods and alongside the River Dee make this a memorable afternoon. We will have snowdrops for sale and homemade teas in the house.

Open: Sunday 16 February, noon - 4pm for Snowdrops and Winter Walks. Also open by arrangement 10 February - 22 February. Admission £5.00, children free. By arrangement opening for a minimum of four adults.

Directions: On the A713 two miles from Castle Douglas and one mile short of Crossmichael.

Opening for: Crossmichael Community Trust SCIO

Kirkcudbrightshire

KINGS GRANGE HOUSE
10

Castle Douglas DG7 3EU
Christine and Peter Hickman
T: 07787 535889

An extensive garden surrounded by mature trees and shrubberies, with views to the south west over the surrounding countryside. Originally Victorian, the garden is being restored by the present owners with a colourful variety of herbaceous mixed borders, beds and rockeries. There are snowdrops in February and banks of daffodils and a carpet of white narcissus in the lawns and around the pergola in springtime.

Open: Sunday 20 July, 2pm - 5pm. Also open by arrangement 1 February - 31 August. Admission £5.00, children free. Jazz ensemble featuring Dave McCullough and friends on Sunday 20th July.

Directions: Take the B794 north off the A75, two miles east of Castle Douglas. Kings Grange House is approximately one mile on the left.

Opening for: RNLI & Marie Curie

Kings Grange House

Kirkcudbrightshire

11 LUCKIE HARG'S

Anwoth, Gatehouse of Fleet, Castle Douglas DG7 2EF
Drs Carole and Ian Bainbridge
T: 01557 814141 E: luckiehargs@btinternet.com

A new and developing garden on the outskirts of Gatehouse of Fleet. A rock and spring herbaceous garden of around an acre, with a wide range of alpines, Himalayan and New Zealand plants, shrubs and small trees. There is a rock garden, modern crevice gardens, troughs, a large alpine house and bulb frame. New boulder, scree and stumpery beds, a pond and a woodland area are being developed. Small productive vegetable and fruit garden, plus a bluebell bank in May.

Open: by arrangement 1 March - 30 September, admission £5.00, children free.

Directions: From Gatehouse High Street, turn north onto Station Road, immediately west at the Fleet Bridge by The Ship Inn. After almost one mile turn left signed to *Anwoth Old Church*. Luckie Harg's is the first on the right after 400 yards. The nearest bus stop is on Gatehouse High Street, walk about 15 minutes to Luckie Harg's.

Opening for: *Scottish Rock Garden Club*

12 SEABANK

The Merse, Rockcliffe DG5 4QH
Julian and Theodora Stanning
T: 01556 630244

This one-and-a-half-acre garden extends to the high water mark with westerly views across a wildflower meadow to the Urr Estuary, Rough Island and beyond. The house is flanked by raised beds, and overlooks a cottage-style garden; peripheral plantings of mixed shrubs and perennials are interspersed with spring bulbs and summer annuals for all-year-round interest. There is a greenhouse with a range of succulents and tender plants. To the rear of the property is a new walled garden stocked with top and soft fruit, perennial vegetables (sea kale, asparagus and globe artichokes), a range of annual vegetables and flower borders. A further greenhouse is used for tomatoes and cucumbers, and has peaches growing against the back wall. A plantswoman's garden with a range of interesting and unusual plants.

Open: Date to be confirmed

Directions: Park in the public car park at Rockcliffe. Walk down the road about 50 yards towards the sea and turn left along The Merse, a private road. Seabank is the sixth house on the left.

Opening for: *Marie Curie: DG5 Group*

Kirkcudbrightshire

13 SOUTHWICK HOUSE
Southwick DG2 8AH
Mr and Mrs R H L Thomas

The extensive gardens at Southwick House comprise three main areas. The first is a traditional formal walled garden with potager and large glasshouse producing a range of fruit, vegetables and cutting flowers. Adjacent to this is a hedged formal garden with herbaceous, shrub and rose beds centred around a lily pond, with roses being a notable feature. Outwith the formal gardens there is a large water garden with two connected ponds with trees, shrubs and lawns running alongside the Southwick Burn.

Open: Sunday 29 June, 2pm - 5pm, admission £5.00, children free.

Directions: On the A710 near Caulkerbush. Dalbeattie 7 miles, Dumfries 17 miles.

Opening for: Loch Arthur

14 STOCKARTON
Kirkcudbright DG6 4XS
Lt Col and Mrs Richard Cliff
T: 01557 330430

This garden was started in 1995 by Carola Cliff, a keen and knowledgeable plantswoman, and contains a collection of unusual shrubs and small trees, which are growing well. Her aim has been to create different informal gardens around a Galloway farm house, leading down to a lochan. Above the lochan there is a sweet cottage, used for holiday retreats, with its own interesting garden. In 1996 a three-acre arboretum was planted as a shelter belt and it now contains some rare oak trees.

Open: by arrangement 1 January - 31 December, admission £5.00, children free.

Directions: On the B727 Kirkcudbright to Gelston Road. Kirkcudbright three miles, Castle Douglas seven miles.

Opening for: Loch Arthur

15 TAL-Y-FAN
Laurieston Road, Gatehouse of Fleet, Kirkcudbrightshire DG7 2BE
Janet and Sarah Wood
T: 01557 815287 E: woodhill2uk@yahoo.co.uk

An over mature one acre plot is being developed into a many faceted garden with a varied mix of interesting plants. The Secret Path leads to Acer Valley and the Won-Kei Parterre, overlooked by the Loch Corbie Monster. A narrow log-lined way leads to West Wood, from where you follow the Burnside Path by the Flame Tree Forest and through the bamboo arch to Dry Wood to find Wood's Henge. Then up through Bluebell Wood to the top of The Rock, where Big Red, the giant squirrel resides, with views across the Fleet Valley. Back down and cross the lawns below the pond before heading up the granite path to the greenhouse, polytunnel, compost bins and the car park, with its collection of pots and troughs. Visit the front lawn and its well-stocked beds on your way out. Light refreshments may be available by arrangement.

Open: by arrangement 1 March - 30 September, admission £5.00, children free.

Directions: Take the Laurieston Road north from Gatehouse of Fleet. After one mile fork right and then right at postcode sign. Turn left at top of slope. Tal-y-Fan (red roof) is at the very end.

Opening for: All proceeds to SGS Beneficiaries

Kirkcudbrightshire

16 THE LIMES

Kirkcudbright DG6 4XD
David and Carolyn McHale
E: carolyn.mchale@btinternet.com

This one-and-a-quarter acre plantswoman's garden has a variety of different plant habitats: woodland, dry sunny gravel beds, rock garden, crevice garden and mixed perennial and shrub borders. There is also a large productive vegetable garden. The McHales like to grow most of their plants from seed obtained through various international seed exchanges. You can expect to see a large number of unusual and exciting plants. The garden is full of colour with an abundance of spring flowers in March, and in late May and early June the meconopsis should be at their best. The gravel garden comes into its own in July and continues through until winter. Hardy cyclamen are a big favourite and one species or another is in flower in almost every month of the year. Winter is a good time to admire their varied leaf forms.

Open: Sunday 23 March, Sunday 27 April and Sunday 8 June, 2pm - 5pm. Also open by arrangement 1 January - 31 December. Admission £5.00, children free.

Directions: In Kirkcudbright go straight along St Mary Street towards Dundrennan. The Limes is on the right, about half a mile from the town centre crossroads, on the edge of the town.

Opening for: Friends Of Kirkcudbright Swimming Pool

17 THREAVE GARDEN

Castle Douglas DG7 1RX
The National Trust for Scotland
T: 01556 502 575 E: threave@nts.org.uk
W: www.nts.org.uk/visit/places/threave-garden

Threave Garden and Nature Reserve SGS Open Day is a one-day event at the home of the National Trust for Scotland's School of Heritage Gardening in Dumfries and Galloway, celebrating all aspects of horticulture. There will be plant nurseries, a craft fair, local producers, and plant-related talks from Threave's Garden Instructors. In addition to this there will be children's activities including a storyteller, face painting and bug hunting. Threave Garden Café, gift shop and plants sales will be open as normal on the day.
Champion Trees: *Acer platanoides* 'Princeton Gold'; *Carpinus caroliniana; X Cuprocyparis leylandii* 'Picturesque' and a further 25 Scottish Champion Trees.

Open: Monday 5 May, 10am - 4pm, admission £6.00, children free.

Directions: Off the A75, one mile west of Castle Douglas.

Opening for: The National Trust for Scotland: School of Gardening Heritage

Lanarkshire

Sponsored by

RATHBONES

Lanarkshire

OUR VOLUNTEER ORGANISERS

District Organiser:	Vanessa Rogers	8 Springdale Drive, Biggar, Lanarkshire ML12 6AZ info@scotlandsgardens.org
Area Organiser:	Nicky Eliott Lockhart	Stable House, Cleghorn Farm, Lanark ML11 7RW
District Photographer:	Calum Steen	
Treasurer:	Sheila Munro Tulloch	Castlegait House, Castlegait, Strathaven ML10 6FF

GARDENS OPEN ON A SPECIFIC DATE

Cleghorn, Stable House, Cleghorn Farm, Lanark	Sunday, 2 March
Old Farm Cottage, The Ladywell, Nemphlar, Lanark	Sunday, 4 May
Lanark Town Gardens, Waterloo Road. Lanark	Sunday, 13 July
Covington Mill Farmhouse, Covington Road, Thankerton, Biggar	Sunday, 27 July
New Lanark Roof Garden, Mill 2, New Lanark World Heritage Site, Lanark	Saturday/Sunday, 9/10 August
Stobwood Cottage Garden, Stobwood Cottage, Stobwood, Forth,	Saturday/Sunday, 16/17 August
Little Sparta, Stonypath, Dunsyre	Tuesday, 26 August
Little Sparta, Stonypath, Dunsyre	Tuesday, 2 September

GARDENS OPEN BY ARRANGEMENT

Old Farm Cottage, The Ladywell, Nemphlar, Lanark	18 April - 30 September
Hawk House Gardens, Hawk House, Covington Road, Thankerton, Biggar	1 June - 31 August

Lanarkshire

1 CLEGHORN
Stable House, Cleghorn Farm, Lanark ML11 7RN
Mr and Mrs R Eliott Lockhart
T: 01555 663792 E: eliottlockhart.nicky@gmail.com
W: www.cleghornestategardens.com

Eighteenth-century garden gradually being returned to its former layout. Lawns with mature trees, shrubs, abundant snowdrops and a woodland walk along the valley, formed by 12th-century dams that were originally built to form fish ponds. The valley has been totally cleared in the last couple of years and the burn and snowdrops are now visible from both sides of the valley. Visitors are welcome to return when the daffodils are in flower.

Open: Sunday 2 March, 2pm - 4pm for Snowdrops and Winter Walks, admission by donation.

Directions: Cleghorn Farm is situated two-miles north of Lanark off the A706.

Opening for: Hope and Homes for Children

2 COVINGTON MILL FARMHOUSE
Covington Road, Thankerton, Biggar ML12 6NE
Sharon Pearson
T: 07827 236771 E: sharon.pearson69@outlook.com

Set amongst eight acres, the gardens have been transformed since 2019 from pastureland to a landscape of woodlands, wildlife habitats, formal gardens and recently, a prairie-inspired garden. A restored watermill building and lade runs through the whole area, creating a meditative backdrop to the matrix and drift planting schemes surrounding them.

Open: Sunday 27 July, 1pm - 5pm, admission £5.00, children free.

Directions: From the A73 turn off at Tinto Hill into the village of Thankerton and follow the *SGS* signs. Buses 31 and 91 run to Thankerton village.

Opening for: The Linda Norgrove Foundation

3 HAWK HOUSE GARDENS
Hawk House, Covington Road, Thankerton, Biggar ML12 6NE
Mr and Mrs A Milner-Brown
T: 07831645527 E: angela@therathouse.com

NEW

We invite you to explore our formal and wild gardens at Hawk House, hidden inside protective mixed hedges, with formal gardens, a wildflower meadow, woodland and far-reaching views to the Scottish Borders and Tinto Hills. Since moving here in 2022, bringing many plants from our extensive collections from the nearby manse, we have developed new garden features. These include herbaceous borders, an alpine garden, and hosta beds; there is also a pond, vegetables and fruit, leading to the established wildflower meadow (80 species in 2024) and a hilltop pavilion nestled into the woodland. The garden has a strong environmental ethic, whilst, we hope, adding touches of humour and colour to this two-plus acre plot.

Open: by arrangement 1 June - 31 August, admission £5.00, children free.

Directions: Please contact owner for full directions: location: w3w.co/stun.scorched.footsteps

Opening for: Buglife – The Invertebrate Conservation Trust

Lanarkshire

4 LANARK TOWN GARDENS
Waterloo Road. Lanark ML11 7QH
The Gardeners of Lanark Town

Opening this year are six gardens in the Waterloo Road area of Lanark town. The easily-walked route provides an eclectic mix of gardens. Some of the highlights on offer include a miniature orchard, topiary including Knotwilg trees which are traditional in the Netherlands, an extensive rock garden with a collection of alpines, a colourful, partially-walled garden with a focus on wildlife, a remodelled garden full of interest and surprise and a carnivorous plant collection. Homemade teas can be enjoyed in the colourful surrounds of Lanark Bowling Club, where there will also be the opportunity for all visitors to enjoy a game.

Open: Sunday 13 July, 1pm - 5pm, admission £6.00, children free. Tickets and teas available at Lanark Bowling Club.

Directions: Waterloo Road is a ten-minute walk from Lanark railway station and a five-minute bus ride from the adjacent bus interchange.

Opening for: Maggie's

5 LITTLE SPARTA
Stonypath, Dunsyre ML11 8NG
Pantea Cameron
T: 01899 810711 E: contact@littlesparta.org.uk
W: www.littlesparta.org.uk

Little Sparta is Ian Hamilton Finlay's greatest work of art. Ian and Sue Finlay moved to the farm of Stonypath in 1966 and began to create what would become an internationally acclaimed garden across seven acres of a wild and exposed moorland site. Collaborating with stone carvers, letterers and other artists and poets, the numerous sculptures and artworks created by Finlay explore themes as diverse as the sea and its fishing fleets, our relationship to nature, classical antiquity, the French Revolution and the Second World War. Individual poetic and sculptural elements, in wood, stone and metal, are sited in relation to carefully structured landscaping and planting. Please note that there is a 700m uphill walk from the car park and livestock grazing in the fields. For visitors with limited mobility, it may be possible to book a space near the house; call the garden for details.

Open: Tuesday 26 August & Tuesday 2 September, 1pm - 4pm, admission details can be found on the garden's website. Last entry 3pm. Pre-booking of tickets is required.

Directions: Check www.littlesparta.org.uk/visit/ for directions.

Opening for: Little Sparta Trust

Lanarkshire

6 NEW LANARK ROOF GARDEN

Mill 2, New Lanark World Heritage Site, Lanark, S Lanarkshire ML11 9DB
New Lanark World Heritage Site
T: 01555 661345 E: trust@newlanark.org
W: www.newlanark.org

Created on the 9,000 square feet of roof on one of our mill buildings, our amazing Roof Garden is the largest of its kind in Scotland and is one of the highlights of our Visitor Centre. The garden is open to visitors all year round and is the perfect location to enjoy a spectacular bird's-eye view of the surrounding natural scenery and the historic village. The garden is maintained with the generous support of our volunteers. Designed by Douglas Coltart of Viridarium, the garden and viewing platform offer splendid and seasonally changing views. The Roof Garden is part of the New Lanark World Heritage Site, and will be accessible via the Hotel on the specific open days.

Open: Saturday/Sunday, 9/10 August, noon - 4pm, admission £5.00, children free. Additionally, refreshments will be available from the Visitor Attraction cafe. Admission to the Roof Garden is also available all year round as part of our Visitor Attraction admission: newlanark.digitickets.co.uk/tickets There is parking (£3) and a shuttle bus available from the car park to the village.

Directions: New Lanark is one mile south of Lanark and around an hour from Glasgow (M74/A72) and Edinburgh (A70). From the south, the village is 30 minutes from M74 Junction 13/Abington – main trunk road to Edinburgh.

Opening for: COVEY

Old Farm Cottage

New Lanark Roof Garden

Lanarkshire

7 OLD FARM COTTAGE

The Ladywell, Nemphlar, Lanark ML11 9GX
Ian and Anne Sinclair
T: 01555 663345 M: 07833 204180 E: anniesinclair58@gmail.com

Ian and Anne have been developing this delightful one-acre garden for twenty five years and it now has something to interest visitors from springtime through until autumn. In April and May daffodils, narcissi, camassias, hellebores, trilliums, spring-flowering shrubs and trees light up the garden. A large array of colourful trees, shrubs and herbaceous plantings, many of them scented, can be enjoyed throughout the rest of the year. *Prunus Amanogawa, Amelanchiers, Katsura* trees and the spectacular fruit of *Cornus kousas* are just a few of the plants that you can expect to see. The garden will be of interest not only for gardeners but bird watchers, walkers and photographers.

Open: Sunday 4 May, 11am - 4pm. Also open by arrangement 18 April - 30 September. Admission £4.00, children free. Groups are welcome by arrangement. There is limited parking in the yard but there is parking at the village hall.

Directions: Leave the A73 at Cartland Bridge (Lanark to Carluke Road) or the A72 (Clyde Valley Road) at Crossford. Both routes are well signposted. The garden is on the Nemphlar spur of the Clyde Walkway, just off the West Nemphlar Road on Ladywell Lane. One mile walk from Cartland Bridge bus stop.

Opening for: Dogs Trust

8 STOBWOOD COTTAGE GARDEN

Stobwood Cottage, Stobwood, Forth, South Lanarkshire ML11 8ET
Jamie and Kayleigh Robertson
T: 07885 701642 E: jamierobertson04@hotmail.co.uk

A four-times winner of West Lothian Gardener of the year, Jamie invites you to Stobwood Cottage. In just four years he has established a hugely impressive garden in the South Lanarkshire countryside. Just shy of half an acre, colour dominates this garden. Wide herbaceous borders surround a velvet lawn. Stunning hanging baskets and tubs clothe the front of the cottage and are dotted around elsewhere. There is also a feature pond with a bridge, a cacti house, a polytunnel growing corn, pumpkins and squashes plus there is a productive vegetable plot to explore. A must for those less-experienced gardeners, and a delight for those who have a little more knowledge.

Open: Saturday/Sunday, 16/17 August, 1pm - 5pm, admission £5.00, children free.

Directions: Travelling from the South, 1.5 miles north of Braehead on the B7016. From the North, turn off the A706 onto the B7016 at Wilsontown.

Opening for: Braehead Village Trust

Moray & Nairn

Sponsored by

❀ RATHBONES

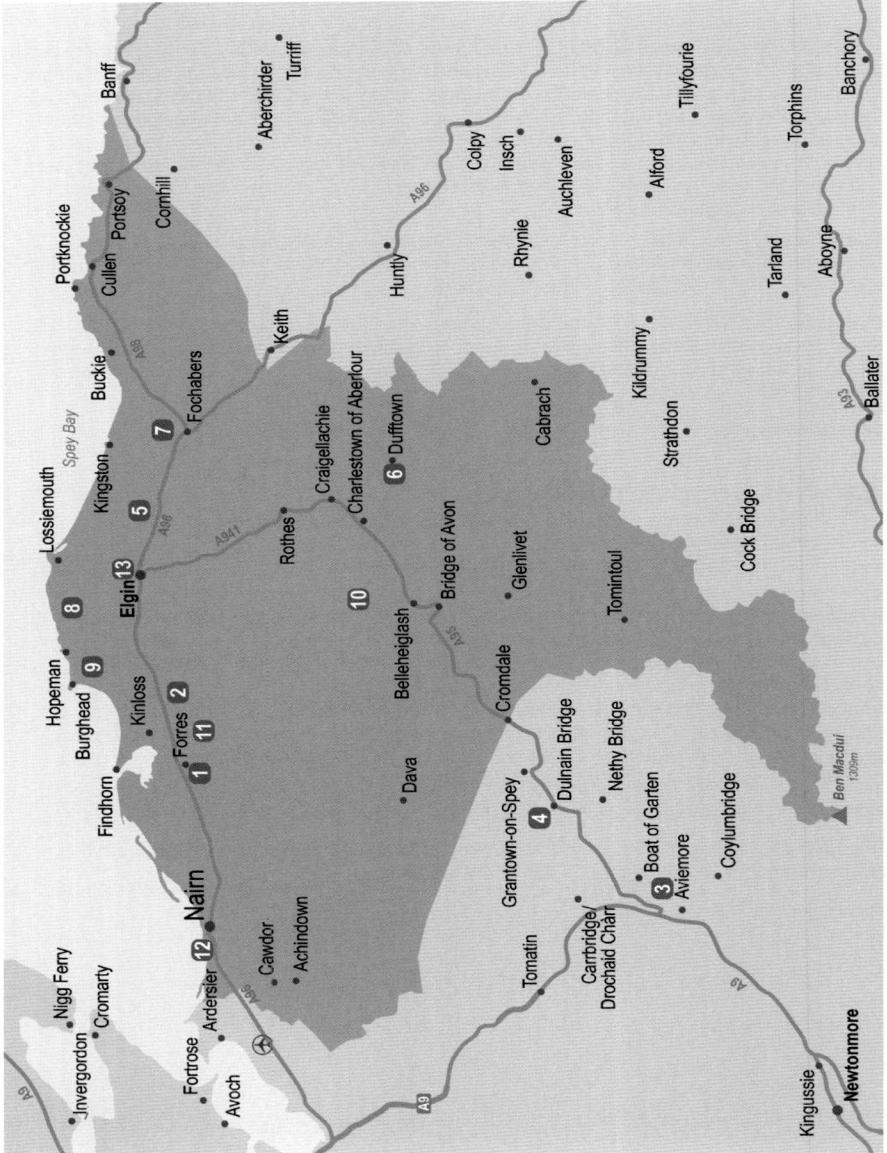

Moray & Nairn

OUR VOLUNTEER ORGANISERS

District Organiser:	James Byatt	info@scotlandsgardens.org
Area Organisers:	Ed Bollom	
	Lorraine Dingwall	
	David Hetherington	
	Gwynne Hetherington	
	Jo Mackenzie	
	Annie Stewart	
Treasurer:	David Barnett	

Follow our District on Facebook: @SGSmoraynairn

GARDENS OPEN ON A SPECIFIC DATE

The Biblical Garden, King Street, Elgin, Moray	Saturday, 3 May
Easter Laggan, Dulnain Bridge, Grantown-on-Spey	Saturday, 7 June
Lindisfarne, Knockando	Saturday, 28 June
Haugh Garden, College of Roseisle	Saturday/Sunday, 5/6 July
Glebe House, Main Street, Urquhart	Sunday, 6 July
Earth House Apothecary Gardens, Pityoulish House, Pityoulish	Saturday, 26 July
Naturally Useful, Marcassie Farm, Rafford, Forres	Sunday, 3 August
Gordonstoun, Duffus, near Elgin	Date to be confirmed

GARDENS OPEN REGULARLY

Burgie Arboretum, Between Forres and Elgin	1 January - 31 December
Gordon Castle Walled Garden, Fochabers, Moray	3 January - 31 December

GARDENS OPEN BY ARRANGEMENT

10 Pilmuir Road West, Forres	25 January - 11 March
Ruthven Cottage Hardy Plant Nursery, Delnies, Nairn	1 April - 30 September
10 Pilmuir Road West, Forres	1 June - 1 September
Glenrinnes Lodge, Dufftown, Keith, Banffshire	2 June - 30 September (not Saturday & Sunday)

Moray & Nairn

1 10 PILMUIR ROAD WEST
Forres IV36 2HL
Mrs Lorraine Dingwall
T: 01309 674634 E: fixandig@aol.com

Plantswoman's small town garden with over 300 cultivars of hostas, an extensive collection of hardy geraniums together with many other unusual plants. Managed entirely without the use of artificial fertilisers or chemicals, the owner encourages hedgehogs, toads and wild birds to control slugs. In early spring there are approximately 150 named snowdrops to be seen, some of which are very rare.

Open: by arrangement 25 January - 11 March for Snowdrops and Winter Walks. Also open by arrangement 1 June - 1 September. Admission £5.00, children free. There is a well-stocked plant sales area.

Directions: From Tesco roundabout at Forres continue along Nairn Road. Take the first left onto Ramflat Road, then go right at the bottom and first left onto Pilmuir Road West.

Opening for: Macmillan Cancer Support

2 BURGIE ARBORETUM
Between Forres and Elgin IV36 2QU
Hamish Lochore
T: 01343 850231 E: hamish@burgie.org

A rare opportunity to see a sizeable woodland garden/arboretum in its infancy. It has a good collection of rhododendrons, *Sorbus*, alder, birch and *Tilia* but also includes many unusual trees from around the world. The arboretum is zoned into geographic areas and species type. It includes a Japanese Garden, bog garden, bog wood, loch and quarry garden. First created in 2005 and is ongoing. Most plants are grown from hand-collected seed and propagated in the Georgian greenhouse.

Open: 1 January - 31 December, 8am - 5pm, admission by donation. Also open for snowdrops during the Scottish Snowdrop Festival, 28 February - 11 March.

Directions: A96 between Forres and Elgin. Four miles east of Forres. Six miles west of Elgin. Sign to *Burgie Mains* along the A96 is set in wrought iron decorated with horses and cattle. South off the main road and one mile to the Woodland Garden car park.

Opening for: Sandpiper Trust & World Horse Welfare

Ruthven Cottage Hardy Plant Nursery © Mari Reid

Moray & Nairn

3 **EARTH HOUSE APOTHECARY GARDENS**
Pityoulish House, Pityoulish PH22 1RD
Dianne Dain and Salem Avan
E: contact@ph-22.com
W: earthhousescotland.com/Instagram @earth_house_scotland

Beautiful wildflowers and trees surround an ancient site with a restored fishing lodge looking over the Spey. The garden consists of a beautiful, mixed woodland with standing stones, Labyrinth and a beech hedge tunnel. Recent developments include wildflower meadows, heritage fruit orchard and a courtyard herb garden including culinary and medicinal herbs. Apothecary will also be open for viewing. Plans designed by Jo Mackenzie.

Open: Saturday 26 July, 10am - 7pm, admission £6.00, children free.

Directions: Turn into Pityoulish estate drive and head up the middle drive. Limited parking available in front of the house, additional parking lot across the street from entrance drive.

Opening for: Maggie's

4 **EASTER LAGGAN**
Dulnain Bridge, Grantown-on-Spey PH26 3NU
Rob and Julie Forrest

A garden under development, designed by Jens Nielsen. It has stunning views of the River Spey and the Cairngorm mountains and is a haven for wildlife, including red squirrels. Five acres in size, the garden consists of some formal lawns with herbaceous borders, newly-created rockeries and drystone walls and the beginnings of a Japanese garden. A stream enters the garden and flows into a newly restored pond. The stream then winds its way through the garden back in to the surrounding fields. Gravel driveways allow some wheelchair access with assistance.

Open: Saturday 7 June, 1pm - 5pm, admission £5.00, children free.

Directions: From Grantown-on-Spey take the A95 towards Aviemore. Take the first turn signed to Dulnain Bridge, then turn immediately right on to the old road. Turn immediately left up the track signed to *Easter Laggan*. Parking is available in a paddock by the house.

Opening for: The Rotherham Hospice Trust

5 **GLEBE HOUSE**
Main Street, Urquhart IV30 8LG
Melanie Collett
E: mel.collett2015@outlook.com

Early 19th-century formal walled garden of the former manse by Alexander Forteath, also incorporating a unique doocot in its construction of clay dab. The garden consists of colourful herbaceous borders within the walled garden and box hedge symmetry. A wide variety of roses together with an orchard and kitchen garden area to the south.

Open: Sunday 6 July, noon - 3pm, admission £6.00, children free.

Directions: Off the main street in Urquhart, find the walled entrance at the end of the street. Follow parking signs.

Opening for: The Royal Air Force Benevolent Fund

Moray & Nairn

Glebe House © James Byatt

6 GLENRINNES LODGE

Dufftown, Keith, Banffshire AB55 4BS
Mrs Kathleen Locke (please contact Glenrinnes Farms Ltd Estate Office)
T: 01340 820384/073939 28049
W: www.glenrinnes.com

The garden and policies surrounding Glenrinnes Lodge are typical of a Victorian lodge. They are full of exciting colourful borders. Newly-developed areas are now beginning to establish and give year-round seasonal interest in the kitchen garden and glasshouse, the secret garden, labyrinth and bog garden. There are also woodland walks and a flight pond and meadow. If you are lucky, you may spot our red squirrel, otter and pine marten, all caught on our woodland trail camera.

Open: by arrangement 2 June - 30 September (not Saturday & Sunday), admission £10.00, children free. Guided tours Monday - Friday, £10 per person. Please phone to arrange a visit.

Directions: In the centre of Dufftown at the Clock Tower take the B9009 road to Tomintoul for about one mile. After passing Dufftown Golf Club on your right there is a lane to the left, which leads to two stone pillars to Glenrinnes Lodge.

Opening for: Alzheimer's Research UK

Moray & Nairn

7 **GORDON CASTLE WALLED GARDEN**
Fochabers, Moray IV32 7PQ
Angus and Zara Gordon Lennox
T: 01343 612317 E: info@gordoncastlescotland.com
W: www.gordoncastle.co.uk

At almost eight acres in size, Gordon Castle has one of the oldest and largest walled gardens in Britain. Lovingly restored to its former glory with a modern design by award-winning designer Arne Maynard, this beautiful garden is overflowing with vegetables, fruit, herbs, and cut flowers. The onsite cafe has a 'Plant, Pick, Plate' ethos using wonderful fresh produce grown in the garden. There is a children's natural play area and shop.

Open: 3 January - 31 December, seasonal admission details can be found on the garden's website. Café open Wednesday to Sunday.

Directions: The main entrance is at the western end of the village of Fochabers, just off the A96, nine miles east of Elgin and 12 miles west of Keith.

Opening for: *Donation to SGS Beneficiaries*

8 **GORDONSTOUN**
Duffus, near Elgin IV30 5RF
The Principal
E: principalpa@gordonstoun.org.uk
W: www.gordonstoun.org.uk

Gordonstoun is famous for educating the Royal family, but its history dates much further back and was the 18th century Georgian home of the first Marquis of Huntly. The school gardens consist of formal herbaceous borders, an ornamental lake and an apple orchard. Visitors can take a self-guided tour of the extensive school grounds including the unique 'Round Square' former farm building (now boarding house) which has an unusual echo and can stroll down the 'silent walk' to the 17th century kirk where former students including members of the Royal Family would have worshipped.

Open: Date to be confirmed.

Directions: Entrance off B9012, four miles from Elgin at Duffus village.

Opening for: *All proceeds to SGS Beneficiaries*

Lindisfarne © James Byatt   Haugh Garden

Moray & Nairn

9 HAUGH GARDEN

College of Roseisle IV30 5YE
Gwynne and David Hetherington
T: 01343 835790 E: davidhetherington26@gmail.com

A lovely two-acre garden to relax in with continuing developments to enjoy. Wander through woodlands and meadows, and in and around eye-catching perennial borders with unusual plants and shrubs, a pond and an orchard, all attracting a diversity of insects and birds. Our organic vegetable garden and polytunnel keep us well supplied and using the no-dig method, without need for artificial fertiliser or chemicals. Our garden delights us with year-round interest starting with various spring bulbs and flowering shrubs and continuing through to late autumn colours.

Open: Saturday/Sunday, 5/6 July, 2pm - 5pm, admission £6.00, children free. Homemade teas, plants, leaf sculptures and plant bowls for sale.

Directions: From Elgin take the A96 west, then the B9013 Burghead Road to the crossroads at the centre of College of Roseisle. The garden is on the right, enter from the Duffus Road. Car parking at the village hall off Kinloss road. Drop off and disabled parking is available at the house.

Opening for: *Alzheimer Scotland & WWF-UK*

10 LINDISFARNE

Knockando AB38 7RY
Sally Mackenzie

Sally started transforming her wildlife-friendly garden in 2008 with a native-species hedge. She has since added a pond and rain garden system fed by roof run-off; it's brilliant to see birds coming down to drink and the variety of invertebrates and amphibians living in it. A self-sustaining wildflower meadow grows in size every year, left to set seed, providing seeds for the large flock of house and tree sparrows. The latest addition is a green roof on the woodshed, which should be bursting with colour in July. Fruit trees, bushes and a variety of veggies are dotted throughout the garden, the architectural kale plants providing a fantastic contrast with purple poppies and evening primrose.

Open: Saturday 28 June, noon - 4pm, admission £5.00, children free. Donation for teas.

Directions: Follow signs for Cardhu Distillery but continue on the single track road past the distillery and round to the left following signs towards Knockando Church and Primary School. We are the last bungalow before the school and there is parking close by.

Opening for: *Beaver Trust*

Moray & Nairn

11 NATURALLY USEFUL, MARCASSIE FARM

Rafford, Forres IV36 2RH
Karen Collins
T: 01309 675052 E: karen@naturallyuseful.co.uk
W: naturallyuseful.co.uk/

We grow willow, grasses for fibre, plants for dyeing and flowers for printing. We harvest and, by hand, transform these raw materials into something beautiful and useful.

Open: Sunday 3 August, 1pm - 5pm, admission £5.00, children free.

Directions: If using SatNav, only use the address Marcassie Farm (the postcode sends you to the castle). The willow field is on the right of the track just over the bridge.

Opening for: Quarriers: Willow Field Health and Wellbeing Project

12 RUTHVEN COTTAGE HARDY PLANT NURSERY

Delnies, Nairn IV12 5NT
Mari and Kevin Reid
T: 07874 779705 E: kevin.mari@gmail.com

The garden has exciting interest all year round. It features several large colourful herbaceous borders and many of the plants are sold at the nursery. The naturalistic style of planting with grasses and perennials looks good from late spring to late summer. There is also a pond, greenhouse and chickens.

Open: by arrangement 1 April - 30 September, admission by donation.

Directions: From Inverness take the A96 to Nairn, Ruthven Cottage is on your left just before the *Sandown Road Crossroads*. From Nairn the entrance is on your right off the A96. Ruthven Cottage is at the end of the lane.

Opening for: All proceeds to SGS Beneficiaries

13 THE BIBLICAL GARDEN

King Street, Elgin, Moray IV30 1HU
The Friends of the Biblical Garden
W: biblicalgardenelgin.co.uk

The Biblical Garden opened to the public in June 1996. The success of the garden since its opening relies on a good working partnership among the Friends of the Biblical Garden, Moray Council and UHI Moray. The Garden, cared for by horticulture students studying at UHI Moray, has grown and developed over the years and is now host to a broad range of garden features, interesting plants and mature trees. The main central area is paved and, together with the surrounding borders, reflects a Celtic cross. A large rose arbour represents the neighbouring cathedral. The gardens also host a rock garden, woodland garden, winter border, herbaceous border and an oriental-themed garden. Visitors will also be able to visit the teaching and growing areas behind the scenes.

Open: Saturday 3 May, 11am - 3pm, admission by donation. Refreshments available.

Directions: The gardens are on King Street, off North College Street and are adjacent to Elgin Cathedral. Parking along King Street is limited. All main bus routes stop along the A96 and the garden is in easy walking distance from these.

Opening for: All proceeds to SGS Beneficiaries

Peeblesshire & Tweeddale

Sponsored by

✻ RATHBONES

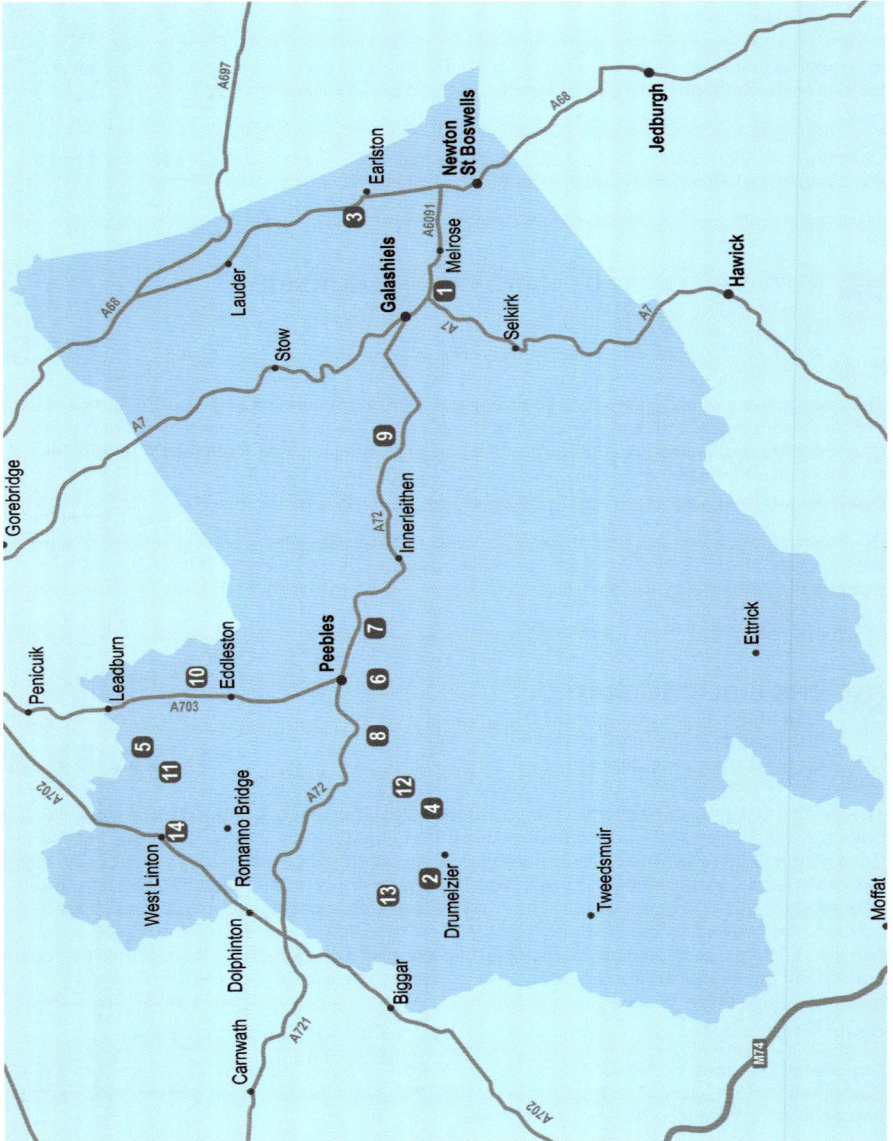

Peeblesshire & Tweeddale

OUR VOLUNTEER ORGANISERS

District Organiser:	Lesley McDavid	Braedon, Medwyn Road, West Linton EH46 7HA info@scotlandsgardens.org
Deputy District Organiser:	John Bracken	Gowan Lea, Croft Road, West Linton EH46 7DZ
Area Organisers:	Jennifer Barr	Allerly, Gattonside, Melrose TD6 9LT
	Jenny Litherland	Laidlawstiel House, Clovenfords, Galashiels TD1 1TJ
Treasurer:	Marie Gilmour	Primrose Cottage, Portmore, Peebles EH45 8QU

GARDENS OPEN ON A SPECIFIC DATE

Kailzie Gardens, Peebles	Sunday, 23 February
Laidlawstiel House, Clovenfords, Galashiels	Wednesday/Thursday, 28/29 May
Beechwood, Broughton, Peeblesshire	Saturday 31 May - 1 June
Quercus Garden Plants, Whitmuir Farm, West Linton	Sunday, 1 June
Stobo Japanese Water Garden, Stobo Farm, Stobo	Sunday, 1 June
Beechwood, Broughton, Peeblesshire	Saturday/Sunday, 21/22 June
Portmore, Eddleston	Saturday, 28 June
Carolside, Earlston	Sunday, 13 July
Kailzie Gardens, Peebles	Sunday, 20 July
West Linton Village Gardens, West Linton	Sunday, 27 July
Quercus Garden Plants, Whitmuir Farm, West Linton	Sunday, 24 August
Diadan, Madrissa Farm, Lamancha	Sunday, 24 August
Dawyck Botanic Garden, Stobo	Sunday, 5 October

GARDENS OPEN REGULARLY

Abbotsford, Melrose	1 March - 31 December
Haystoun, Peebles	1 - 31 May (Wednesday only)
The Potting Shed, Broughton Place, Broughton, Biggar	4 June - 2 July (Wednesday only, not 18 June)
Kirkton Manor House, Peebles	12 February - 16 July (Wednesday only)
Portmore, Eddleston	2 July - 27 August (Wednesday only)

GARDENS OPEN BY ARRANGEMENT

Kirkton Manor House, Peebles	12 February - 16 July
Beechwood, Broughton, Peeblesshire	1 May - 30 September
The Potting Shed, Broughton Place, Broughton, Biggar	1 May - 31 October
Portmore, Eddleston	1 June - 31 August

Peeblesshire & Tweeddale

1 ABBOTSFORD
Melrose TD6 9BQ
The Abbotsford Trust
T: 01896 752043 E: enquiries@scottsabbotsford.co.uk
W: www.scottsabbotsford.com

The garden was designed by Sir Walter Scott with advice from artists, architects and friends. It is a rare surviving example of a Regency garden layout and completely different from the English landscape garden style of Capability Brown. Scott's garden aims to provide a harmonious transition between the luxury and comfort of the interiors of the house with wonders of nature in the wider estate through a series of secluded, richly detailed and sheltered 'rooms'. In its day it would have showcased the latest plants discovered from around the globe, both in its borders and 'stove houses'. Regular tours are held exploring Scott's vision for the garden and the hidden meanings of its design. Check the Abbotsford website for details.

Open: 1 March - 31 December; March, November, December 10am - 4pm, 1 April - 31 October 10am - 5pm. Admission details can be found on the garden's website.

Directions: Off the A6091 near Melrose. Buses X62 and 72 from Edinburgh and Peebles. Train from Waverley to Tweedbank. Minibus or one-mile walk from train station.

Opening for: Donation to SGS Beneficiaries

2 BEECHWOOD
Broughton, Peeblesshire ML12 6HH
Susheila and James Gordon
T: 07810 837068 or 01899 830443 E: susheilarachan@gmail.com
W: www.rachan.co.uk

A sculptor's informal garden adjacent to a mature woodland and pond. A well-planted stream runs through the garden. There are varied perennial meadows to encourage wildlife and provide forage for the resident bees. It also features many examples of the owners' artworks which are inspired by the natural world.

Open: Saturday 31 May & Sunday 1 June, 11am - 5pm. Also open Saturday/Sunday, 21/22 June, 11am - 5pm. And open by arrangement 1 May - 30 September. Admission £5.00, children free.

Directions: Approximately one mile south of Broughton take the B712 off the A701. Then first left turn onto unmade road.

Opening for: MND Scotland

Peeblesshire & Tweeddale

3 ## CAROLSIDE
Earlston TD4 6AL
Mr and Mrs Anthony Foyle
T: 01896 849272 E: info@carolside.com
W: www.carolside.com

A traditional and romantic garden set in a beautiful 18th-century landscape. This garden is best known for its historically-important collection of roses, with a national collection of pre-19th century Gallica roses and for its design of garden rooms with soft, delicate herbaceous planting. Visit the oval walled garden, spilling with roses and billowing herbaceous borders, the herb garden with yellow and white roses set against acid green herbs or sit in the secret garden, planted in silver and pale pink. Walk to the apple orchard of historic apple trees and wildflowers or through the rose gates to the 18th century bridge and into the park and sit by the river. Carolside is said to be 'one of Scotlands finest private gardens'.
National Plant Collection: Pre-19th century *Rosa* Gallica.

Open: Sunday 13 July, 11am - 5pm, admission £8.00, children free. Dogs on leads in the park only.

Directions: One mile north of Earlston on the A68. Entrance faces south. Garden accessible by Borders Bus 51, ask to get off at Carolside gate.

Opening for: Marie Curie

4 ## DAWYCK BOTANIC GARDEN
Stobo EH45 9JU
A Regional Garden of the Royal Botanic Garden Edinburgh
T: 01721 760254
W: www.rbge.org.uk/dawyck

Dawyck is a regional garden of the Royal Botanic Garden Edinburgh which had its 350th anniversary in 2020. Stunning collection of rare trees and shrubs. With over 300 years of tree planting, Dawyck is a world-famous arboretum with mature specimens of Chinese conifers, Japanese maples, Brewer's spruce, the unique Dawyck beech and sequoiadendrons from North America which are over 150 feet tall. Bold herbaceous plantings run along the burn. Range of trails and walks. Fabulous autumn colours.
National Plant Collection: *Larix* spp. and *Tsuga* spp.
Champion Trees: Numerous.

Open: Sunday 5 October, 10am - 5pm, admission details can be found on the garden's website.

Directions: Eight miles south-west of Peebles on the B712.

Opening for: Donation to SGS Beneficiaries

Peeblesshire & Tweeddale

5 DIADAN
Madrissa Farm, Lamancha EH46 7BD
Vicki Masters

Nestled in the corner of a sheep farm, this three-quarter acre garden has been steadily evolving since 2020. Formerly a derelict plot, it now features beautiful hard landscaping built from local stone, bounded by a new high stone wall with portholes which complement the wall of the old barn next door. The wide herbaceous border and long rockery at the front are planted for seasonal interest and provide a colourful entrance, whilst the rear has a more natural design with two large adjoining ponds, some tree planting, a willow tunnel and winding paths through a meadow and for those with keen eyes, the occasional piece of sculpture awaits discovery.

Open: Sunday 24 August, 2pm - 5pm, admission £6.00, children free.

Directions: On the A701 on left hand side coming from Edinburgh, about half a mile before Lamancha Hub.

Opening for: Omaleshe Projects Trust

6 HAYSTOUN
Peebles EH45 9JG
Mrs Mary Coltman
T: 01721 720645

This seventeenth-century house (not open) has a charming walled garden with an ancient yew tree, herbaceous beds and vegetable garden. There is a wonderful burnside walk created since 1980, with azaleas and rhododendrons leading to a small ornamental loch (cleared in 1990) with stunning views up Glensax Valley.

Open: 1 - 31 May (Wednesday only) 1:30pm - 5pm, admission £7.00, children free.

Directions: Cross the River Tweed in Peebles to the south bank and follow *Scotland's Gardens Scheme* sign for approximately one mile.

Opening for: St. Columba's Hospice Care

Haystoun © Kathy Henry

Peeblesshire & Tweeddale

7 KAILZIE GARDENS
Peebles EH45 9HT
Susan and Steve Plag
T: 01721 720682
W: kailziegardens.com

Kailzie Gardens sits at the heart of the Tweed Valley just a mile east of Peebles occupying a beautiful position on the River Tweed. At its heart lies the stunning walled garden with plantings of many unusual shrubs, laburnum arches, an enchanting rose garden and spectacular herbaceous borders and one of the best examples of a Mackenzie and Moncur glasshouse still in existence, filled with fuchsias, pelargoniums and exotics. The garden also features prize winning show vegetables. The surrounding woodlands have one of the best laid arboretums in Scotland, with champion trees and specimens (including the oldest larch), providing acres of captivating woodland and burnside walks and spectacular vistas. Champion Trees: Larch planted 1725.

Open: Sunday 23 February, 10am - 4pm for Snowdrops and Winter Walks. Also open Sunday 20 July, 10am - 4pm. Admission details can be found on the garden's website. See website for other opening times.

Directions: A mile east of Peebles on the B7062.

Opening for: Tweed Togs SCIO

8 KIRKTON MANOR HOUSE
Peebles EH45 9JH
Mrs Rosemary Thorburn
T: 01721 740220 E: rpthorburn@icloud.com

Kirkton Manor House has a delightful, three-acre, informal country garden set in the beautiful Manor Valley. It enjoys spectacular open views and calling curlews from its riverside position. Bluebells flank the impressive entrance leading to a new shrub border. Stone steps continue through to terraced slopes filled with bulbs, roses and hellebores providing height, interest and fragrance. Grass paths meander along the burn where snowdrops, blue and white camassia, meconopsis, and ligularia thrive in this sunny meadow environment. Later, in June, sisyrinchiums, irises, orchids and many flowering shrubs and roses are abundant. The natural woodland includes many interesting trees.

Open: 12 February - 16 July (Wednesday only), 1pm - 4pm. Snowdrops and Winter Walks mid-February to mid-March. Visits can be made by arrangement on other dates between mid-February and mid-July. Individuals and small groups are welcome. Admission £5.00, children free.

Directions: Turn off the A72 west of Neidpath Castle, signposted to *Kirkton Manor*. After crossing the River Tweed, enter a garden gate which is a mile downhill, opposite a *Beware Horses* sign.

Opening for: All proceeds to SGS Beneficiaries

Peeblesshire & Tweeddale

9 **LAIDLAWSTIEL HOUSE**
Clovenfords, Galashiels TD1 1TJ
Mr and Mrs P Litherland

Walled garden containing herbaceous border, fruit and vegetables in raised beds. There are colourful rhododendrons and azaleas as well as splendid views down to the River Tweed.

Open: Wednesday/Thursday, 28/29 May, 1pm - 5pm, admission £5.00, children free.

Directions: On the A72 between Clovenfords and Walkerburn turn up the hill signposted for *Thornielee*. The house is on the right at the top of the hill.

Opening for: *Horse Time SCIO*

Laidlawstiel House © Kathy Henry

10 **PORTMORE**
Eddleston EH45 8QU
Mr and Mrs David Reid
T: 07905 776894
W: www.portmoregardens.co.uk

Lovingly created by the current owners over the past 30 years; the gardens surrounding the David Bryce-designed mansion house contain mature trees and offer fine views of the surrounding countryside. Large walled garden with box-edged herbaceous borders is planted in stunning colour harmonies, potager, rose garden, pleached lime walk and ornamental fruit cages. The Victorian glasshouses contain fruit trees, roses, geraniums, pelargoniums and a wide variety of tender plants. There is also an Italianate grotto and water garden with shrubs and *meconopsis*. The woodland walks are lined with rhododendrons, azaleas and shrub roses. Starred in *Good Gardens Guide* and featured in Kenneth Cox's book *Scotland for Gardeners* and on *Beechgrove*.

Open: Saturday 28 June, 1pm - 5pm, Also open 2 July - 27 August (Wednesdays only), 1pm - 5pm. And open by arrangement 1 June - 31 August. Admission £7.00, children free (28 June and all Wednesday openings) and details can be found on the garden's website (1 June - 31 August). Self-service refreshments for 28th June and Wednesday openings. Homemade cream teas for groups over 15 people by prior arrangement. Please consult the garden's website.

Directions: Off the A703 one mile north of Eddleston. Bus 62.

Opening for: *Abundant Borders (SCIO)*

Peeblesshire & Tweeddale

Portmore © Kathy Henry

11 **QUERCUS GARDEN PLANTS**
Whitmuir Farm, West Linton EH46 7BB
Rona Dodds
T: 01968 660708 E: quercusgardenplants@gmail.com
W: www.quercusgardenplants.co.uk

We are a small, independent nursery growing and selling a wide range of happy, healthy plants propagated from our nursery gardens. At just under two acres, these gardens were started in 2015 to show visitors and customers what can be grown in our conditions here on a north-west-facing hill at 850 feet above sea level. Explore our herb garden, scented garden, wildlife garden, prairie-style garden, winter garden and all the other inspirational smaller borders. Our new woodland garden opened in Spring 2023. Many of the plants seen in the gardens are available to buy in the nursery.

Open: Sunday 1 June, 10am - 5pm. Also open Sunday 24 August, 10am - 5pm. Admission by donation. A percentage of plant sales on these dates will be donated to Scotland's Garden Scheme and Breast Cancer Now. The 16mm narrow gauge garden railway will be running from 2pm. Garden books and succulents will be available for a donation.

Directions: On the A701, four miles south of the Leadburn junction or two miles north of West Linton.

Opening for: *Breast Cancer Now*

Peeblesshire & Tweeddale

Stobo Japanese Water Garden © Kathy Henry

12 STOBO JAPANESE WATER GARDEN
Stobo Farm, Stobo EH45 8NX
E: enquiries@stobofarmestate.com

This is a mature, secluded woodland garden created in the early 1900s. Its most prominent feature is the constant presence of water that adds to the tranquillity of the garden, beginning with the drama of a waterfall at its head through a cascade of ponds, punctuated along the way by stepping stones and bridges. The garden was brought to life when Japanese style was the height of fashion – hence its cherry trees, maples, and iconic Japanese lanterns, 'tea house' and humpback bridge. The azaleas and rhododendrons provide a spectacular display in the spring. Limited disabled access due to gravel paths and steps. Visitors are advised to wear appropriate footwear.

Open: Sunday 1 June, 2pm - 5pm, admission £5.00, children free.

Directions: Off the B712 (Peebles/Broughton road) via *Stobo Castle* entrance. Bus 91

Opening for: Stobo and Drumelzier Church of Scotland, Firefly & Scotland's Charity Air Ambulance

13 THE POTTING SHED
Broughton Place, Broughton, Biggar ML12 6HJ
Jane and Graham Buchanan-Dunlop
T: 01899 830574 E: buchanandunlop@btinternet.com

A one-acre garden begun from scratch in 2008, on an exposed hillside at 900 feet. It contains herbaceous plants, climbers, shrubs and trees – all selected for wind resistance and ability to cope with the poor, stony soil. There are usually fine views to the Southern Uplands.

Open: Wednesday 4 June, Wednesday 11 June, Wednesday 25 June & Wednesday 2 July, 11am - 5pm. Also open by arrangement 1 May - 31 October. Admission £5.00, children free.

Directions: Signposted from the main A701 Edinburgh – Moffat Road, immediately north of Broughton village.

Opening for: Nomad Beat: Peebles Community Music School

Peeblesshire & Tweeddale

14 **WEST LINTON VILLAGE GARDENS**
West Linton EH46 7EW
West Linton Village Gardeners
T: 01968 660669 E: j.bracken101@gmail.com

A varied and interesting selection of gardens around the centre of the village. Bank House is an unusual and structured garden designed over 30 years by a non-gardener (he was however a 'spade monitor' at primary school). Also included are a walled manse garden in a beautiful riverside setting and two horticultural enthusiasts' gardens in sheltered positions.

Open: Sunday 27 July, 1pm - 5pm, admission £6.00, children free. Teas, tickets and plant sale at the New Church Hall in the centre of the village, which will be signposted.

Directions: About 15 miles south-west of Edinburgh, take the A701 or A702 and follow signs. Bus 101 or 102 to Gordon Arms Hotel.

Opening for: Ben Walton Trust & Perennial

Gowan Lea, West Linton Village Gardens © Kathy Henry

Perth & Kinross

Sponsored by

🌸 RATHBONES

Perth & Kinross

OUR VOLUNTEER ORGANISERS

District Organiser:	Fiona Stewart	7 Craigend Cottages, Craigend, Perth PH2 8PX info@scotlandsgardens.org
Area Organisers:	Gill Boardman	16 Acremoar Drive, Kinross KY13 8RE
	Jane Gallier	The Old Farmhouse, Dunning Road, Auchterarder PH3 1DU
	Henrietta Harland	Easter Carmichael Cottage, Forgandenny Road, Bridge of Earn PH2 9EZ
	Ruth Howell	Tomandroighne, Edradynate, Aberfeldy PH15 2JS
	Alex Lindsay	19 St Serfs Place, Auchterarder PH3 1QS
	Judy Norwell	Dura Den, 20 Pitcullen Terrace, Perth PH2 7EQ
	Mary Jane Thompson	Mosspark House, Rumbling Bridge KY13 0QE
	Heather Wood	Mill of Forneth, Forneth, Blairgowrie PH10 6SP
Treasurer:	Michael Tinson	Parkhead House, Parkhead Gardens, Burghmuir Road, Perth PH1 1JF

GARDENS OPEN ON A SPECIFIC DATE

Cloan, by Auchterarder	Sunday, 16 February
Scone Palace Garden, Perth	Saturday, 22 February
Princeland House, Blairgowrie Road, Coupar Angus, Blairgowrie	Saturday/Sunday, 22/23 February
Princeland House, Blairgowrie Road, Coupar Angus, Blairgowrie	Saturday/Sunday, 1/2 & 8/9 March
Mill of Forneth, Forneth, Blairgowrie	Sunday, 30 March
Fingask Castle, Rait	Sunday, 6 April
Megginch Castle, Errol	Sunday, 27 April
The Steading at Clunie, The Steading	Sunday, 4 May
Cloan, by Auchterarder	Sunday, 11 May
Overdale, Kirk Wynd, Blairgowrie	Saturday, 17 May
Torwood House, St Mary's Road, Birnam	Sunday, 18 May
Tigh-na-Beithe, Birnam Glen, Birnam, Dunkeld	Sunday, 25 May
Bonhard House, Perth	Saturday/Sunday, 31 May - 1 June
Muckhart Open Gardens, Coronation Hall, Pool of Muckhart, Dollar	Saturday/Sunday, 31 May - 1 June
Mouse Cottage, Strathtay, Pitlochry	Friday/Saturday, 6/7 June
Cloan, by Auchterarder	Saturday/Sunday, 7/8 June
36 Muirfield, Perth	Sunday, 8 June
Mill of Forneth, Forneth, Blairgowrie	Sunday, 8 June
Blair Castle Gardens, Blair Atholl	Saturday, 14 June
An Caorann, Abernethy, Perthshire	Sunday, 15 June
Tarmangie, Glendevon, Dollar	Saturday/Sunday, 28/29 June
Bonhard House, Perth	Saturday/Sunday, 5/6 July
17 Strathallan Bank, Forgandenny, Perth	Saturday, 5 & 12 July
The Bield at Blackruthven, Blackruthven House, Tibbermore	Saturday, 12 July

Perth & Kinross

GARDENS OPEN ON A SPECIFIC DATE – CONTINUED

Tomandroighne, Edradynate, Aberfeldy	Tuesday, 29 July
Drummond Castle Gardens, Muthill, Crieff	Sunday, 3 August
Cloan, by Auchterarder	Sunday, 10 August

GARDENS OPEN REGULARLY

Fingask Castle, Rait	20 January - 6 March, Mondays/Tuesdays/Wednesdays/Thursdays only
Braco Castle, Braco	1 February - 31 October
Blair Castle Gardens, Blair Atholl	28 March - 31 October
Glendoick, Glencarse, Perthshire	1 April - 31 May
Ardvorlich, Lochearnhead	19 April - 31 May
Dowhill, Cleish	May & June (Wednesday only)
Bradystone House, Murthly	5 June to 11 September (Thursdays only)

GARDENS OPEN BY ARRANGEMENT

Mouse Cottage, Strathtay, Pitlochry	1 January - 29 November
Delvine, Murthly	1 February - 1 December
The Pond Garden, The Pond, Milnathort	1 February - 31 December
Pitcurran House, Abernethy	1 April - 31 August
Bonhard House, Perth	1 April - 31 October
Craigowan, Ballinluig	6 April - 30 June
Beech Cottage, The Wynd, Muthill	1 May - 1 September
The Old Farmhouse, Dunning Road, Auchterarder	1 May - 30 June
Carig Dhubh, Bonskeid, Pitlochry	1 May - 30 September
Craigowan, Ballinluig	20 September - 20 October

17 Strathallan Bank

Perth & Kinross

1 17 STRATHALLAN BANK

Forgandenny, Perth PH2 9FE
Iain Mahon
T: 01738 813344 E: ijcmahon@gmail.com

About half an acre, the garden has been developed from scratch over 17 years. Plants include astilbes, scabious, astrantia, agapanthus, phlox, hydrangeas and primulas with an emphasis on flowers for cutting. A range of trees include a large Douglas fir, cornus, acers, jacquemontii silver birch and fruit trees.

Open: Saturday 5 July & Saturday 12 July, 1pm - 5pm, admission £5.00, children free. Parking is on the grass verge with access to the garden by the roadside gate and limited disabled access by the house.

Directions: From Bridge of Earn, follow signs to Forgandenny and go right through Forgandenny taking a turn to the left signposted Ardargie, Path of Condie etc. After 150 yards turn right into Strathallan Bank. There is an irregular bus service – number 17.

Opening for: Maggie's

2 36 MUIRFIELD

Perth PH1 1JJ
Rob Mackay and Amanda Brown
T: 07704 978348 E: mackaybrownjoint@gmail.com

A small, suburban garden with a Japanese theme. The garden was designed and planted in 2019 with the aim of being low maintenance and offering a fun and safe environment for children. The Japanese features include a stone lantern, a water bowl, the placing of rocks, raked gravel and a timber building. The planting includes prunus, acer, bamboo, hostas, ferns and flowering plants. Foliage and texture are important elements. Views of the distant hills are seen as an extension of the garden in the Japanese tradition.

Open: Sunday 8 June, 2pm - 5pm, admission £5.00, children free. Entrance includes tea/coffee.

Directions: Muirfield connects Muirend Road with Burghmuir Road. 36 Muirfield is the white bungalow near the junction with Muirend Road on the left-hand side as you travel up the hill. The number 8 bus from Mill Street in the centre runs every hour, alight at Fairies Road just before the junction with Viewlands Road West. Go straight over the mini roundabout continuing along Fairies Road. At the next mini roundabout turn left into Muirend Road. Muirfield is the first turning on the right with number 36 the second house on the right. If coming by car please park on Muirend Road to avoid blocking neighbours' access.

Opening for: Amnesty International UK Section Charitable Trust

Perth & Kinross

3 AN CAORANN
Abernethy, Perthshire PH2 9LG
Paul Lacey
E: laceyp2@btinternet.com

A young garden under development designed by my late wife, Moira Lacey, with stunning views over the rivers Tay and Earn. Her talent as an artist is reflected in the plant choices and design. A haven for wildlife including woodpeckers, red squirrels and birds of prey. The garden includes herbaceous borders, alpines, conifers, a small vegetable garden and a pond full of water lilies.

Open: Sunday 15 June, noon - 4pm, admission £5.00, children free.

Directions: From the centre of Abernethy turn into Kirk Wynd and the garden is second on the right after the Williamson Hall car park. Parking is at the Williamson Hall with limited parking on the garden driveway. Accessible by public transport with a 10 minute walk.

Opening for: NHS Tayside Charitable Foundation: Cornhill Macmillan Centre

4 ARDVORLICH
Lochearnhead FK19 8QE
Mr and Mrs Sandy Stewart
T: 01567 830335

Beautiful hill garden featuring over 170 different species of rhododendrons and many hybrids, grown in a glorious setting of oaks and birches on either side of the Ardvorlich Burn. The paths are quite steep and rough in places and boots are advisable, especially when wet.

Open: 19 April - 31 May, 9am - dusk, admission £5.00, children free.

Directions: On South Loch Earn Road three miles from Lochearnhead, five miles from St Fillans.

Opening for: The Ghurka Welfare Trust

5 BEECH COTTAGE
The Wynd, Muthill PH5 2AP
Rosalyn Serex
T: 07590 813509 E: rosalyn@serex.me

Nestled at the foot of The Wynd in the conservation village of Muthill, the garden is surrounded by the ancient trees of Lindores. The main attraction of the garden is the collection of 200 roses interspersed with companion perennials. A well planted Koi pond provides a relaxing area to be seated.

Open: by arrangement 1 May - 1 September, admission by donation. Open from 11am - 5pm

Directions: The Wynd is a street perpendicular to Drummond Street. The street name is clearly displayed on the corner house. The cottage is at the bottom of The Wynd approx 80 metres slightly downhill. Please note The Wynd is very narrow and is not suitable for large vehicles and is extremely difficult to turn around. Recommend using Drummond Street to park where there are usually sufficient spaces. **Bus routes in Muthill:** 18 – Auchterarder/Crieff; 45 – Town Service/Crieff; 15A – Perth/ St Fillans or Stirling; 615 – Perth/ St Fillans or Stirling. Bus stops are on Drummond Street – from here, head east towards the church/old church monuments.

Opening for: The Dystonia Society

Perth & Kinross

6 BLAIR CASTLE GARDENS

Blair Atholl PH18 5TL
Blair Charitable Trust
T: 01796 481207 E: office@blair-castle.co.uk
W: www.blair-castle.co.uk

Blair Castle stands as the focal point in a designed landscape of some 2,500 acres within a Highland estate. Hercules Garden is a walled enclosure of about nine acres recently restored to its original 18th-century design with landscaped ponds, a Chinese bridge, contemporary plantings, and an orchard of more than 100 fruit trees. The glory of this garden in summer is the herbaceous border, which runs along the 275 yard south-facing wall. A delightful sculpture trail incorporates contemporary and 18th-century sculpture as well as eight new works, letter-carving on stone from the *Memorial and Commemorative Arts* charity's 'Art and Memory Collection'. Diana's Grove is a magnificent stand of tall trees including grand fir, Douglas fir, larch and wellingtonia running along the Banvie Burn, with the 12th-century ruins of St Bride's Church on the far bank.

Open: Saturday 14 June, 9:30am - 5pm, admission details can be found on the garden's website. Also open 28 March - 31 October, 9.30 am - 5pm (7 days a week). Last entry at 4pm for all dates.

Directions: Off A9, follow signs to *Blair Castle, Blair Atholl*.

Opening for: Donation to SGS Beneficiaries

7 BONHARD HOUSE

Perth PH2 7PQ
Stephen and Charlotte Hay
T: 07990 574570 E: stephenjohnhay@me.com

Traditional 19th-century garden of five acres approached through an avenue of magnificent oaks. Mature trees, six classified by the National Tree Register as 'remarkable', including a monkey puzzle (1852, one of the first 12 brought to Scotland), sequoias, Douglas fir and a variety of hollies. Reinstated and new herbaceous borders. Rhododendron and azalea beds. Recently planted spring and summer flowering meadow areas with a variety of fruit and nut trees. Beehive and a productive vegetable garden. A new larch arbour with climbing roses and clematis. Grass paths meander through a pond area with shrubs and mature trees. A pinetum with 25 different varieties. Garden emphasis on wildlife habitat as well as aesthetics. Resident red squirrels. Plentiful and varied birdlife.

Open: By arrangement 1 April – 31 October. Admission £5, children free. Groups welcome to enquire. Also open on the weekends of 31 May-1 June and 5-6 July, 10am – 4pm. Homemade teas on these weekends, otherwise please ask when arranging your visit.

Directions: On the A94 just under a mile north of Perth take the right turn, signed *Murrayshall Country Estate*. After approximately one mile take the entrance right marked *Bonhard House*, at a sharp left turn. From Balbeggie turn left, signposted for *Bonhard*, one mile north of Scone. Turn right in a half-a-mile, pass any sign for *Bonhard Nursery*, and enter the drive at sharp right turn.

Opening for: Freedom from Fistula Foundation

Perth & Kinross

8 BRACO CASTLE

Braco FK15 9LA
Mr and Mrs M van Bal.egooijen
T: 01786 880437

A 19th-century landscaped garden with a plethora of wonderful and interesting trees, shrubs, bulbs and plants. An old garden for all seasons that has been extensively expanded over the last 36 years. The partly-walled garden is approached on a rhododendron and tree-lined path featuring an ornamental pond. Spectacular spring bulbs, exuberant shrub and herbaceous borders and many ornamental trees are all enhanced by the spectacular views across the park to the Ochils. From snowdrops through to vibrant autumn colour, this garden is a gem. Look out for the embothrium in June, hoheria in August, eucryphia in September and an interesting collection of rhododendrons and azaleas with long flowering season.

Open: 1 February - 31 October, 10am - 5pm. February to early March for Snowdrops and Winter Walks, admission £5.00, children free. No dogs please.

Directions: Drive for 1 ½ miles from the gates at the north end of Braco Village, just west of the bridge on the A822. Parking at the castle is welcome.

Opening for: The Woodland Trust Scotland

Braco Castle

Perth & Kinross

9 **BRADYSTONE HOUSE**
Murthly PH1 4EW
Mrs James Lumsden
T: 01738 710308 E: pclumsden@me.com

A sophisticated cottage garden converted from a derelict farm steading. Imaginative and abundant planting with unusual and special perennials, clematis, roses, abutilons and shrubs. There is an interesting and bountiful plant stall. Small vegetable garden and orchard, meandering woodland walks and a duck pond. A tranquil setting with elegant planting. Garden groups welcome by arrangement. Dogs on leads please.

Open: Thursdays only from 5 June to 11 September, 11am - 4pm, admission £5, children free.

Directions: From south/north follow the A9 to Bankfoot, then signs to *Murthly*. At the crossroads in Murthly take the private road to Bradystone.

Opening for: Scotland's Charity Air Ambulance

10 **CARIG DHUBH**
Bonskeid, Pitlochry PH16 5NP
Jane and Niall Graham-Campbell
T: 01796 473469 E: niallgc@btinternet.com

'I don't know how Niall and Jane manage to grow their splendid meconopsis on the sand and rock of their garden but they do, most successfully.' In this stunning situation, when not admiring the views, you will find wonderful primulas, cardiocrinum and meconopsis, all interspersed between beautiful shrubs and other herbaceous plants. Look up and in July you will see roses flowering 40 feet up in the tree. This is a gem of a garden and you will be welcomed by Niall and Jane Graham-Campbell with all their expert knowledge.

Open: by arrangement 1 May - 30 September, admission £5.00, children free.

Directions: Take the old A9 between Pitlochry and Killiecrankie, turn west on the Tummel Bridge Road B8019, Carig Dhubh is three-quarters of a mile on the north side of the road.

Opening for: Earl Haig Fund Poppy Scotland

11 **CLOAN**
by Auchterarder PH3 1PP
Neil Mitchison
T: 07958 155831 E: niall@fastmail.co.uk

Two acres of wild garden, with a wide variety of rhododendrons and azaleas, and an impressive collection of trees, including metasequoia, cryptomeria, *Acer cappadocicum*, *Sequoia sempervirens*, *Quercus robur* 'Filicifolia', liriodendron, several Japanese maples, magnificent beech and Scots pine trees, and extensive yew topiary; also an acre of walled garden with embothriums, *Acer griseum*, several sorbus varieties, parrotia and a large herbaceous border. Fine views of Strathearn from the front of the house.

Open: Sunday 16 February, 11am - 3pm for Snowdrops and Winter Walks. Also open Sunday 11 May, Saturday/Sunday, 7/8 June and Sunday 10 August, 10am - 5pm, with teas and home baking available courtesy of Auchterarder Parish Church Ladies' Guild. Admission £4.00, children free.

Directions: From the A823, just south of the A9, follow the small road heading north east, signposted *Duchally*. Continue for approximately 2 ½ miles, turn right at the sign *Coulshill*. Continue for just under ½ mile. Follow the signs for *car parking*.

Opening for: Tiphereth: Camphill Scotland

Perth & Kinross

12 **CRAIGOWAN**
Ballinluig PH9 0NE
Simon Jones
T: 07856 859219 E: simonqjones@mail.com

We welcome you to view our five-acre, family-developed showpiece garden, maturing over the last 35 years. The extensive range of around a thousand species and hybrid rhododendrons flower from January to their peak in April and May depending on frost damage due to our location at 500 feet above sea level. These are backed up by ornamental trees, perennials and an extensive herbaceous border in a diverse mix of woodland, prepared beds and specialist rhododendron planting areas. We are on a hillside but have tried to make the garden as accessible as possible to all. Most visitors require at least an hour for a basic viewing.

Open: by arrangement only from 6 April - 30 June, then for autumn colour from 20 September - 20 October, admission £5.00, children free. Call Simon on number above to arrange a tour.

Directions: From north or southbound of the A9 to Ballinluig junction. Pass the Ballinluig filling station and motor grill on your right. Turn right at the primary school following the Tulliemet/Dalcapon sign; this is a single track road with passing places. About half-a-mile up the road take a left turning to Dalcapon, a further mile up the road is Craigowan garden. It is surrounded by a deer fence on the left. Please park on paviours adjoining the house.

Opening for: LUPUS UK

Overdale

Perth & Kinross

13 **DELVINE**
Murthly PH1 4LD
Mr David Gemmell
T: 07748 207647 E: gemmell.david@googlemail.com

The arboretum at Delvine covers more than 10 acres. The arboretum is situated on a flood plain, flanked by oxbow lakes on each side. This is the place to visit for those who seek a remote and peaceful setting. As one proceeds in a westerly direction, one enters an area of great drifts of chimonobambusa and miscanthus grasses with water and wildlife in abundance. The walking is easy, but not suitable for wheelchair users. This garden will appeal to those seeking the unusual.

Open: by arrangement 1 February - 1 December, admission £5.00, children free. Surfaces are mowed level grass, some uneven ground and damp areas away from paths. Dogs on leads, please.

Directions: On the A984, seven miles east of Dunkeld, four miles south-west of Blairgowrie. Turn through gateway and follow drive to wooden gates with *Arboretum* sign.

Opening for: Army Benevolent Fund

14 **DOWHILL**
Cleish KY4 0HZ
Mrs Colin Maitland Dougall
T: 01577 850207 E: pippamd@icloud.com

We're delighted that this garden is opening again after a break of five years. Please come along and see the garden's magnificent trees, woodland walks, ponds, blue poppies and swathes of primulas. There are lovely herbaceous borders near the house with perennials, shrubs and climbers, and below the house, one can walk around the linked ponds which are popular with wildfowl. Behind the house, there are woodland walks through rhododendrons and mature trees, leading up to Benarty Hill to the ruins of Dowhill Castle, with fine views over Loch Leven. Featured in *Scotland for Gardeners* by Kenneth Cox.

Open: Wednesdays only in May and June, 10am - 4pm. Admission £6.00, children free.

Directions: Three-quarters of a mile from M90, exit 5. Follow B9097 towards Crook of Devon, the entrance is between the trees on left.

Opening for: MND Scotland

15 **DRUMMOND CASTLE GARDENS**
Muthill, Crieff PH7 4HN
Grimsthorpe & Drummond Castle Trust Ltd
T: 01764 681433
W: www.drummondcastlegardens.co.uk

Activities and events for a great family day out. The gardens of Drummond Castle were originally laid out in 1630 by John Drummond, second Earl of Perth. In 1830 the parterre was changed to an Italian style. One of the most interesting features is the multi-faceted sundial designed by John Mylne, Master Mason to Charles I. The formal garden is said to be one of the finest in Europe and is the largest of its type in Scotland.

Open: Sunday 3 August, 1pm - 5pm, admission details can be found on the garden's website.

Directions: Entrance two miles south of Crieff on Muthill road (A822).

Opening for: BLESMA

Perth & Kinross

16 **FINGASK CASTLE**
Rait PH2 7SA
Mr and Mrs Andrew Murray Threipland
T: 01821 670777 ext 4 & 6 E: andrew@fingaskcastle.com
W: www.fingaskcastle.co.uk

Scotland's only surrealist garden: spectacular topiary staggers across the garden bumping into stone globes, marble balls, statues and a figure of Alice (in Wonderland). Other literary and historical characters are scattered among the 17th-century pleasure gardens. Bonnie Prince Charlie and his father are said to have approached the castle up the long yew avenue known as 'The King's Walk'. A 15-minute walk takes you down to the dell beneath the castle and St Peter's Well – a stopping place for medieval pilgrims on their way to the bones of the saintly Queen Margaret at Dunkeld Cathedral. Return via a Chinese bridge, Gabriel's bridge, an iron age fort, along a stream, past Sir Stuart's House and back to the castle via the Old Orchard. There are large drifts of snowdrops, daffodils and flowering shrubs in season. A wollemi pine has recently been planted. Giant 120 year old Redwoods: both Sempervirens and Giganteum Champion Trees: *Pinus wallichiana* (Bhutan Pine) Metasequoia glyptostroboides and the handsome remnants of what was the largest walnut in Scotland.

Open: 20 January - 6 March, Mondays/Tuesdays/Wednesdays/Thursdays only, 10am - 4pm for Snowdrops and Winter Walks. Also open Sunday 6 April, 1pm - 4:30pm. Admission for all dates £6.00, children free. Homemade teas on 6 April only.

Directions: Half way between Perth and Dundee. From the A90 follow signs to *Rait* until small crossroad, turn right and follow signs to *Fingask*.

Opening for: All Saints Episcopal Church & Fingask Follies

17 **GLENDOICK**
Glencarse, Perthshire PH2 7NS
Cox Family
T: 01738 860260 E: gardencentre@glendoick.com
W: www.glendoick.com

Glendoick's gardens and garden centre with its award-winning café is the ideal spring day out in April and May. Glendoick boasts a unique collection of plants from three generations of Cox plant-hunting expeditions in China and the Himalaya. Enjoy one of the finest collections of rhododendrons and azaleas, magnolias and other acid-loving plants in the woodland garden and the gardens surrounding the house. Many of the rhododendron and azalea species and hybrids have been introduced from the wild or bred by the Cox family. There are fine waterfall views in the woodland gardens. The award-winning Glendoick Garden Centre has one of Scotland's best selections of plants including their world-famous rhododendrons and azaleas as well as a gift shop and café.

Open: 1 April - 31 May, 10am - 4pm, admission £5.00, children free. For garden visit group bookings email gardencentre@glendoick.com. Café bookings (run separately) E: manager@garden-cafe.co.uk. Please note the woodland garden is not easily accessible to wheelchairs but some of the gardens by the house are. Toilets and refreshments are at the garden centre only. No dogs.

Directions: Follow the *brown* signs to Glendoick Garden Centre off the A90 Perth – Dundee road. The gardens are a half-mile behind the Garden Centre. After buying tickets at the Garden Centre, please drive up and park at the gardens (free parking).

Opening for: Donation to SGS Beneficiaries

Perth & Kinross

18 **MEGGINCH CASTLE**
Errol PH2 7SW
Giles Herdman and Catherine Drummond-Herdman
E: info@megginch.com
W: megginchcastle.com

We welcome you to come and enjoy the peace and beauty of Megginch. Wander through the golden daffodils and the cascades of pear and apple blossom in the ancient orchard. Finish up in the warm conservatory with the castle as your backdrop, overlooking the 19th century formal gardens. Have a (several – free refills included!) hot cup of tea in fine china cups and sample the delicious home baked creations from the castle kitchens! We love having your dogs on leads and your children running free! *Please note that Megginch is a family home and so not open to the public apart from the SGS day on Sunday 27th April.*
National Plant Collection: Scottish cider apples, Scottish Heritage apples and pears.
Champion Trees: *Acer palmatum.*

Open: Sunday 27 April, 2pm - 5pm, admission £6.00, children free.

Directions: Ten miles from Perth and Dundee directly off the A90, Perth-bound carriageway, 600 yards after the Errol/Rait flyover, on the left hand side, 300 yards after *Beware Pedestrians Crossing* sign.

Opening for: *All proceeds to SGS Beneficiaries*

19 **MILL OF FORNETH**
Forneth, Blairgowrie PH10 6SP
Mr and Mrs Graham Wood
E: gaw@forneth-mill.co.uk

Built on the site of a former watermill on the Lunan Burn, originally laid out in the 1970s by James Aitken, the Scottish landscape designer and naturalist. The sheltered four-acre garden has a range of mature trees, including a Himalayan blue cedar, large rhododendrons, azaleas and a wide range of shrubs. The former mill lade feeds rocky waterfalls and a lily pond. Planting includes established perennials with seasonal colours, many bulbs, primulas and heathers, plus a vegetable garden on the site of an old tennis court and a new wildflower meadow.

Open: Sunday 30 March & Sunday 8 June, 2pm - 4pm, admission £5.00, children free.

Directions: Take the A923 Dunkeld to Blairgowrie road. Six miles east of Dunkeld turn south onto a minor road signposted *Snaigow and Clunie*. Mill of Forneth is the first gate on the left-hand side. PLEASE NOTE due to wet weather conditions there may be limited safe meadow parking on site (exceptions will be made for people with mobility problems).

Opening for: *Perthshire Women's Aid*

Perth & Kinross

20 **MOUSE COTTAGE**
Strathtay, Pitlochry PH9 OPG
Penny Kennedy
T: 07799 678067 E: mymousecottage@outlook.com
W: www.mymousecottage.co.uk

Mouse Cottage sits on a south-facing hill overlooking Strathtay. Small but packed with interesting features, it is a semi-wild haven of secret places where self-seeders mix with annuals and more formal planting. The owner is an artist who adores her garden space and collects quirky planting containers such as dustbins and dolly tubs. Her Pear Parasol and Holly Brolly are amongst her favourite features. Gravel paths wind through shady places full of joyous surprises such as *Crambe cordifolia*. Self catering and B & B accommodation is available at: www.mymousecottage.co.uk

Open: Friday/Saturday, 6/7 June, 10am - 4pm. Also open by arrangement 1 January - 29 November. Admission £5.00, children free. (Ice cream, home-made lemonade and homebaking available on 6/7 June only.) Studio also open. No dogs and no disabled access.

Directions: From the A9 take the exit at Ballinluig signposted *Aberfeldy*. Go through Logierait, after about four miles turn right at T junction. At Grandtully turn right, over the bridge, up the hill to Strathtay Post Office. Turn right passing the golf course up to the red telephone box. Mouse Cottage is next opening on the left, signposted. Please beware of flying golf balls! NB: No parking at Mouse Cottage. On street parking possible at Strathtay. Bus 23 (Aberfeldy to Perth) stops at Grandtully Bridge.

Opening for: Donation to SGS Beneficiaries

Mouse Cottage © Penny Kennedy

Perth & Kinross

21 **MUCKHART OPEN GARDENS**
Coronation Hall, Pool of Muckhart, Dollar FK14 7JF
The Gardeners of Muckhart Village

A collection of gardens in and around the Pool o'Muckhart and Yetts o'Muckhart, some of which have not opened previously. For a small village Muckhart boasts an enchanting variety of cottage and informal gardens displaying some of the best and most thoughtfully considered aspects of amateur gardening in this part of Scotland. From wildlife-friendly gardens and magnificent trees, to beautiful and constantly-evolving gardens where paths meander through terraced beds and ponds, and pocket-sized cottage gardens. Visitors cannot fail to be inspired by the variety of gardens, and the commitment of our gardeners.

Open: Saturday 31 May & Sunday 1 June, 1pm - 5pm, admission £7.00, children free. (£10 for both days). Tickets, garden details and map are available at Muckhart Coronation Hall. Teas available from Coronation Hall between 2pm - 5pm for a small donation.

Directions: On the A91, four miles east of Dollar. Parking at Muckhart Coronation Hall, Pool of Muckhart FK14 7JF.

Opening for: Muckhart Kirk Session, Coronation Hall, Muckhart & Muckhart Primary School

22 **OVERDALE**
Kirk Wynd, Blairgowrie PH10 6HN
Samantha Peck
T: 07817822190 E: peckies4@gmail.com

A unique town garden and arboretum with magnificent views over Rattray, Blairgowrie and the Strathmore valley. Spread over 1.3 acres of southeast-facing slope, this garden has a wonderful collection of rhododendrons, acers, shrubs and collection of established trees. A series of paths winding down the steep slope takes you past the herbaceous borders, past a pond and through the tree collection. Species include *Magnolia acuminata, Cornus kousa, Acer rubrum, Eucalyptus globulus, Metasequoia glyptostroboides, Sambucus nigra f. porphyrophylla, Callicarpa bodinieri* and *Cercidiphyllum japonicum.*

Open: Saturday 17 May, 11am - 4pm, admission £5.00, children free. Homemade teas will be available. Access for visitors with disabilities is limited by the lack of on-site parking and the steep hill. Within the garden there is a broad level terrace with gravel surface and fine views, but otherwise there are steep paths and steps.

Directions: Parking on Kirk Wynd is not possible due to the steep narrow road. Free street parking is available in Blairgowrie for two hours and car parks are available. Buses 57, 58 & 58A stop at the High Street or Wellmeadow bus station. From the High Street take Upper Allan Street uphill turning right into Kirk Wynd. Overdale is on the right. Disabled visitors should arrange drop off and pick up at gates.

Opening for: RNLI

Perth & Kinross

23 PITCURRAN HOUSE
Abernethy PH2 9LH
The Hon Ranald and Mrs Noel-Paton
T: 01738 850933 / 07760 420485 E: patricianp@pitcurran.com

This end-of-village garden was created 21 years ago. It includes an interesting combination of trees, rare shrubs and herbaceous plants including azaleas, rhododendrons, tree peonies, trillium and veratrum. Also a rose pergola, eucryphias and a large west-facing hydrangea border for the later summer. Above the pond there is a good collection of pink and white-barked birch and a young arboretum, from which there are fine views over the Earn and Tay valleys.

Open: by arrangement 1 April - 31 August, admission £6.00, children free. Groups welcome.

Directions: South-east of Perth. From the M90 (exit nine) take the A912 towards Glenfarg, go left at the roundabout onto the A913 to Abernethy. Pitcurran House is at the far eastern end of the village. Buses run through Abernethy from Perth and the surrounding districts.

Opening for: Breakthrough T1D: (formerly Juvenile Diabetes RF)

24 PRINCELAND HOUSE
Blairgowrie Road, Coupar Angus, Blairgowrie PH13 9AU
Helen and Alastair Carmichael
T: 07864778170 E: carmichaelhf@hotmail.com

Sited on the edge of Coupar Angus, the wider grounds of Princeland House garden are currently under active renovation and replanting by Mrs Carmichael. There is a wooded area around the drive and entrance with an extended area of beautiful and different snowdrops planted in drifts among mature trees. Accommodation can be booked on princelandcottages.co.uk
Champion Trees: Wellington tree.

Open: Saturday/Sunday, 22/23 February, Saturday/Sunday, 1/2 March & Saturday/Sunday, 8/9 March, 10am - 3pm for Snowdrops and Winter Walks, admission £5.00, children free. There will be no refreshments. Dogs on a lead only. **Please call or email to book a time slot.**

Directions: From the outskirts of Coupar Angus, take the A94 Blairgowrie Road from the mini-roundabout junction with the A923, to the junction with School Road. Parking on the street is available for visitors, those with disabilities and mobility difficulties can park by the house. Entry to Princeland House is on the corner of School Road, past a lodge cottage on the left of the entrance.

Opening for: MND Scotland

Craigowan

Perth & Kinross

25 SCONE PALACE GARDEN

Perth PH2 6BD
The Earl and Countess of Mansfield
W: www.scone-palace.co.uk

Scone Palace will be hosting a day to celebrate the snowdrop display that grows in the gardens and grounds of this historic site. A waymarked 'Snowdrop Walk' will guide you through the Friars Den, Victorian Pinetum and down the old drive lined with an avenue of lime trees. Join the Palace gardens team as they plant up a wooded area of the grounds for a new snowdrop display. Here you will learn to increase your own snowdrop display at home where lifting, splitting and transplanting will be demonstrated. As a thank you, a gift of a few snowdrops will be given to improve or start your own collection.

Open: Saturday 22 February, 10am - 3pm for Snowdrops and Winter Walks, free access but an entry donation of £5 is requested. A small selection of specialised snowdrops will be for sale from our gift shop with our coffee shop open for a selection of refreshments.

Directions: Two miles from Perth on the A93 Perth/Braemar road. Well signposted.

Opening for: All proceeds to SGS Beneficiaries

26 TARMANGIE

Glendevon, Dollar FK14 7JY
Sandy Fraser and Susan Whyte
T: 07736 800356

A synthesis of cultivated land and the natural landscape. Informal 2.5 acre garden framed by the Ochil Hills and set in mature woodland and pasture. Features include approximately 70 juvenile species rhododendrons, an eclectic mix of unusual perennials, shrubs and ferns; bamboos, climbing and shrub roses, floral courtyard garden, large pond with feature water lilies and irises. An eco-friendly bug and wildlife haven, herbicide and pesticide-free, minimal dig philosophy, free-range hens, **everything** recycled, a garden for the free spirit.

Open: Saturday/Sunday, 28/29 June, 10am - 6pm, admission £6.00, children free. Donkey and miniature pony petting. No dogs please.

Directions: On the A823 between Muckhart and Auchterarder, the white house next to Glendevon Parish Church, on the left hand side of the road heading north.

Opening for: Ronald McDonald House Glasgow

Dowhill

Perth & Kinross

27 **THE BIELD AT BLACKRUTHVEN**
Blackruthven House, Tibbermore PH1 1PY
The Bield Christian Cc Ltd
T: 01738 583238 E: info@bieldatblackruthven.org.uk

The Bield is set in extensive grounds with well-maintained lawns, hedges, flower meadow and specimen trees. A labyrinth is cut into the grass of the old orchard and there is a wheelchair-friendly labyrinth. Traditional walled garden with richly-stocked borders and lawns, cut-flower garden, healing garden, glasshouse, trained fruit trees and organic veg plot. Walk through extensive woodland and visit the old curling pond. New in the grounds this year is a little Japanese Garden. Southton Smallholding is a social enterprise ten minutes walk away, featuring veg plots, polytunnels and a number of animals (not staffed on the day).

Open: Saturday 12 July, 2pm - 5pm, admission £5.00, children free. Homemade Teas £2.00.

Directions: From Dundee or Edinburgh, follow signs for *Glasgow, Stirling* and *Crianlarich* which lead onto the Perth bypass. Head west on the A85 signed to *Crieff/Crianlarich* to West Huntingtower. Turn left at crossroads to *Madderty/Tibbermore.* Entrance on left after ½ mile passing the gate lodge on your right. Parking signed to right at the steading.

Opening for: Ripple Effect

28 **THE OLD FARMHOUSE**
Dunning Road, Auchterarder PH3 1DU
Jane and Nigel Gallier
T: 01764 662471 E: thegalliers@msn.com

A garden of approximately one acre with herbaceous borders, a gravel garden, vegetable garden, trained fruit trees in half-wine barrels, wild areas under-planted with bulbs, and woodland areas, with other areas still being developed. As you approach the house, look out for our kamikaze hens. The garden is not always immaculate; a well-ordered winter garden and a floriferous summer garden.

Open: by arrangement 1 May - 30 June, admission £5.00, children free.

Directions: From the A9 take the A824 and halfway between Auchterarder and Aberuthven take the B8062 at Grand Eagles and head towards Dunning. We are on the left just before the A9 bridge.

Opening for: SSAFA Forces Help

The Pond Garden

Perth & Kinross

29 THE POND GARDEN

The Pond, Milnathort KY13 0SD
Fay Young and Ray Perman
T: 07767 407396 E: fay@fayyoung.org
W fayyoung.org/category/pond-cottage/

A wild woodland and wetland garden adapting to climate change. We learn from resilient plants and wildlife. There are flowers, fruits, seeds, and nuts to support birds, bats, bees, butterflies, red squirrels and tiny unknowns! Woodland paths lead through snowdrops, daffodils, bluebells, foxgloves, and ferns. Mature beeches and oaks mark boundaries of former Victorian estate. Mosses and mushrooms grow among log piles, stone shapes, and a stumpery. Since mid 1990s we have rebuilt and retrofitted the derelict farm cottage with external insulation and renewable energy. Now we plan Himalayan and native Scottish plantings overlooking the streams.

Open: by arrangement 1 February - 31 December, admission £5.50, children free (or donation). Open for seasonal highlights.

Directions: From Milnathort village. At the mini roundabout in the centre of the village take the north exit (signed for *Path of Condie*) up Wester Loan, then North Street. At the top of the hill, past the church on your left, you will cross the motorway again. Carry straight on for ½ mile, the gate to Pond Cottage is on the right after a field opening.

Opening for: CHAS: Children's Hospices Across Scotland

30 THE STEADING AT CLUNIE

The Steading PH10 6SG
Jean and Dave Trudgill
T: 01250 884263 E: davetrudgill@googlemail.com

'A little bit of paradise' a visitor once commented on a spring day when our wildflower meadow was covered with cowslips and cuckoo flower, and the banks of the Lunan Burn with primroses and wood anemones. The Steading at Newmill is on the north bank of the Lunan Burn midway between Lochs Clunie and Marlee. The grounds extend to about six acres with ponds, woodland, and bridges. There is an old mill building and mill lade and there are eight hundred metres of riverside walks. The Steading has a small cottage garden and a pond where children can feed the fish. A video of Newmill lasting eight minutes can be seen by going to Youtube and searching for 'Newmill: creating and managing an orchid meadow'. Narrow paths, bridges and flowing water. One dog on lead only. Holiday accommodation: the Bothy sleeps five and is available for weekly lets.

Open: Sunday 4 May, 2pm - 4pm, admission £5.00, children free.

Directions: Three miles west of Blairgowrie on the A923. About 600 metres west of the Kinloch Hotel take the track on the left, just after a mobile phone mast and a breeze-block wall.

Opening for: Save the Children UK

Perth & Kinross

31 TIGH-NA-BEITHE
Birnam Glen, Birnam, Dunkeld PH8 0BW
The Robbs
E: ericarobb555@gmail.com

An informal, shady woodland garden of 1.5 acres with a fine collection of mature shrubs and trees including copper beeches, an enormous flowering prunus and a beautiful Scots pine. Rhododendrons and azaleas are a beautiful sight in spring. The garden is a haven for wildlife with red squirrels and a wide variety of birds. Other features include a rockery, a perimeter pathway, a bluebell walk and seating areas. The ground is hilly, uneven and damp underfoot and sensible footwear is essential.

Open: Sunday 25 May, 11am - 5pm, admission £5.00, children free.

Directions: There is limited parking at the house. Please park at Birnam Village or Birnam and Dunkeld train station and walk to the garden up Birnam Glen footpath which is a five minute walk.

Opening for: The Salvation Army & Guide Dogs

32 TOMANDROIGHNE
Edradynate, Aberfeldy PH15 2JS
Ruth Howell

Tomandroighne is a garden of just under two acres located on a steep bank overlooking the River Tay. Quirky sculptures, stonework and salvaged items add interest as this challenging site is gradually improved. The garden hosts a collection of rhododendrons and azaleas, flowering in sequence late spring and early summer. A spring-fed water garden is home to many bog-loving plants including gunnera, rodgersia, candelabra primulas and ligularia. Herbaceous planting and flowering trees and shrubs give colour and texture all summer and autumn. There are many quiet areas for peaceful contemplation.

Open: Tuesday 29 July, 1pm - 5pm, admission £5.00, children free. Unfortunately not suitable for wheelchairs or those with mobility issues. Parking is limited and not suitable for large vehicles.

Directions: Coming from the A9, take the Ballinluig exit heading for Aberfeldy. At Grandtully turn right, crossing the River Tay via the metal bridge to Strathtay. From there turn left, following the signs to Cluny House Gardens for about three miles alongside the river. At the turning to Cluny House Gardens, turn right and then immediately left up a short steep drive. Tomandroighne is the white house at the top of the steep bank. Please note the SatNav map location is not correct, we are about ¼ mile east of the location given, at the bottom of the road up to Cluny House Gardens.

Opening for: The Aberfeldy Dementia-Friendly Collaborative

Perth & Kinross

33 **TORWOOD HOUSE**
St Mary's Road, Birnam PH8 OBJ
Jan Silburn

An eight-acre woodland garden developed over the last 40 years in a setting of great natural beauty. You will find a range of interesting shrubs such as enkianthus, cercidiphyllum, crinodendron, eucryphia, magnolias, cornus, amelanchier and abutilon, well-stocked herbaceous borders, beautiful rhododendrons and azaleas and some fine trees. This is an enchanting, quirky garden full of vibrant colours especially in the spring.

Open: Sunday 18 May, noon - 5pm, admission £5.00, children free.

Directions: On the hill above the Birnam Hotel, go up St Mary's Road and take first left turning over left cattle-grid. Bus stops at Birnam Hotel. Approx 200 metres.

Opening for: Scotland's Charity Air Ambulance

Torwood House

Tomandroighne

Renfrewshire

Sponsored by

❀ RATHBONES

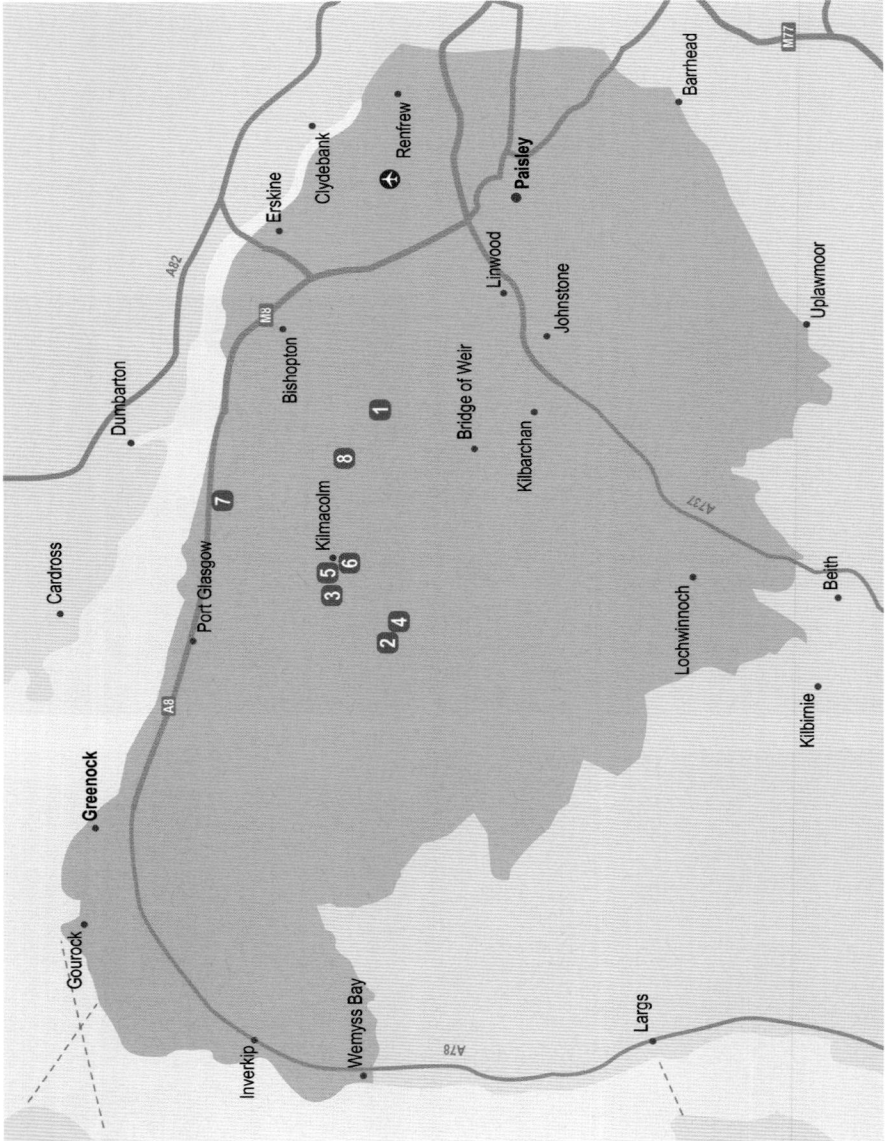

Renfrewshire

OUR VOLUNTEER ORGANISERS

District Organiser:	Alexandra MacMillan	Langside Farm, Kilmacolm, PA13 4SA
		info@scotlandsgardens.org
Area Organisers:	Helen Hunter	2 Bay Street, Fairlie, North Ayrshire KA29 0AL
	Barbara McLean	49 Middlepenny Road, Langbank, PA14 6XE
	Catriona Scriven	14 Taylor Avenue, Kilbarchan PA10 2LS
Treasurer:	Jean Gillan	Bogriggs Cottage, West Kilbride, North Ayrshire KA23 9PS

GARDENS OPEN ON A SPECIFIC DATE

SGS Kilmacolm Plant Sale, Outside Kilmacolm Library, Kilmacolm	Saturday, 19 April
Highwood, off Lochwinnoch Road, Kilmacolm	Sunday, 11 May
Gardens House, Houston Renfrewshire	Sunday, 25 May
The Bishop's House, Glencairn Road, Kilmacolm	Sunday, 8 June
Wraes, Corseliehill Road, nr Houston	Sunday, 29 June
SGS Kilmacolm Plant Sale, Outside Kilmacolm Library, Kilmacolm	Saturday, 12 July
Lochwinnoch Road Gardens, Kilmacolm	Sunday, 20 July
North Newton Farm, Kilmacolm	Sunday, 10 August

GARDENS OPEN BY ARRANGEMENT

The Croft, Houston Road Langbank	1 April - 31 October

Renfrewshire

1 GARDENS HOUSE
Houston Renfrewshire PA6 7AU
Mark and Melanie Crichton Maitland

This new garden covers ten acres including a Victorian arboretum. Work began in 2013 with the conversion of a spruce plantation, once the Houston House kitchen garden, into a structured landscape now showing impressive displays. A former banana house has been repurposed as a fernery. Beech hedging forms areas containing a collection of rhododendrons – 240 plants, 67 varieties – alongside magnolias, sorbus, acers, and bamboos on either side of an avenue of Dawn Redwoods. The old garden gates lead to a secret garden, home to a magnificent *katsura*, ancient azaleas and *enkianthus*, ten newly planted species of fir and a partially restored lily pond. The tree canopy has been selectively opened up and planted with large-leaved rhododendrons. South of the house, the landscape opens up into an informal park where a pond, created in 2018, adds a peaceful water element.

Open: Sunday 25 May, 2pm - 5pm, admission £5.00, children free. Parking will be in a field.

Directions: Satnav with postcode PA6 7AU takes you to the house. Signed off the B789 to *Langbank* 300 yards north of the end of Houston.

Opening for: Macmillan Cancer Support

2 HIGHWOOD
off Lochwinnoch Road, Kilmacolm PA13 4TF
Dr Jill Morgan

A beautiful woodland walk around 50 acres of native bluebells and primroses in a delightful setting bordering the Green Water river with tumbling waterfalls. Great outdoor space for children to run and explore and splash in the burn (under supervision). A haven of tranquillity only three miles from the centre of Kilmacolm. This opening is raising funds for Buildher (buildher.org) a social enterprise owned by Orkidstudio.

Open: Sunday 11 May, 2pm - 5pm, admission £5.00, children free. Stout footwear is recommended as the footpath is uneven and can be muddy in inclement weather. Dogs are welcome on a lead. A fantastic opportunity for lovers of wildflowers and photography.

Directions: Take the B786 Lochwinnoch road out of Kilmacolm and continue for approximately two miles. From Lochwinnoch take the B786 Kilmacolm road for approximately six miles. Turn up the road signposted for Killochries. Then follow the yellow *SGS* signs.

Opening for: Orkidstudio: Buildher

Renfrewshire

3 **LOCHWINNOCH ROAD GARDENS, KILMACOLM**
Kilmacolm PA13 4DY
Cameron Nicol, Rosemary Nott and Rachel Horne

Three residents of the beautiful village of Kilmacolm join to showcase a variety of planting ideas including perennial herbaceous borders, structural evergreens, topiary and colourful annuals.
Garden 1 – (Cameron Nicol) at the entrance stands a magnificent Copper Beech tree, this established garden has other mature trees and shrubs, mixed herbaceous borders and collection of beautiful roses and clematis.
Garden 2 – (Rosemary Nott) traditional villa with delightful cottage style border planted with mixed shrubs and perennials interspersed with bulbs and summer annuals for all year round interest.
Garden 3 – (Rachel Horne) 70s house planted at the front and side with a variety of structural evergreens. The garden to the rear of the house is planted in a different style with borders filled with colourful perennials and annuals and many different hydrangeas as well as a *Cytisus battandieri*.

Open: Sunday 20 July, 2pm - 5pm, admission £6.00, children free. Teas at Garden 3 and plant sale at Garden 2.

Directions: Lochwinnoch Road is in the centre of Kilmacolm and the gardens will be signed on the day with yellow *SGS* signs

Opening for: Ardgowan Hospice & Médecins Sans Frontières

4 **NORTH NEWTON FARM**
Kilmacolm PA13 4TE
Carole Cameron
E: carole.cameron100@btinternet.com

In six years, the new owners have transformed North Newton Farm garden. 'No straight lines' and 'any colour so long as it is pink, purple, blue or white' are the guidelines. Many 'finds' abandoned by the previous owners in and around the barns have been repurposed under the 'let's use what we have' philosophy. To suit the topography, the garden now has cultivated and wilder parts with stunning views. Many climbing plants and herbaceous borders surround the wildlife pond below a rockery. A small wooded area provides a lovely view. A Victorian style greenhouse and cold frames flank stone-built raised beds in a fruit and vegetable garden. The resident goats, chickens and donkeys provide ample fertiliser.

Open: Sunday 10 August, 1pm - 5pm, admission £5.00, children free. Parking will be in a field.

Directions: Take the B786 Lochwinnoch road out of Kilmacolm and continue for approximately two miles. From Lochwinnoch take the B786 Kilmacolm road for approximately six miles. Turn up the road signposted to *Killochries* at this point following the yellow *SGS* signs.

Opening for: Pancreatic Cancer Action

Renfrewshire

5 SGS KILMACOLM PLANT SALE
Outside Kilmacolm Library, Kilmacolm PA13 4LE
Scotland's Gardens Scheme

Spring and summer plant sales in the middle of Kilmacolm.

Open: Saturday 19 April & Saturday 12 July, 10am - noon, donations welcome.

Directions: The plant sales are held at the Cross outside the Library and Cargill centre in the middle of Kilmacolm. Accessible by McGill's buses.

Opening for: Pancreatic Cancer Action

6 THE BISHOP'S HOUSE
Glencairn Road, Kilmacolm PA13 4PD
The Yacoubian family

The Bishop's House is one of six villas in Kilmacolm designed by James Salmon in 1905. It was originally named Miyanoshta but renamed when it became the official residence of the Catholic Bishops of Paisley (1948-1993). The house is now a family home and much care has been taken in preserving the house and garden, both in landscaping and planting, which remain mostly as designed by Salmon. The house sits at the top of the garden and is framed by mature beech trees. There is a burn running down the side of the property (children should be supervised).

Open: Sunday 8 June, 2pm - 5pm, admission £5.00, children free. Please note there are gravel paths. Depending on the weather, there may be 'entertainment' at the garden opening. Please check website nearer the time.

Directions: Please access the garden from the Glencairn Road entrance. Turn off the A761 in the centre of Kilmacolm onto Houston Road or Porterfield Road for access to the garden on Glencairn Road. Follow *SGS* signage. Parking on-road. McGill's buses run through Kilmacolm on the A761.

Opening for: Glasgow Samaritans

The Croft

Renfrewshire

7 THE CROFT

Houston Road Langbank PA14 6XT
Oliver Miller
E: edburd@btinternet.com

This special one-acre garden is on a steep rocky site facing north overlooking the Clyde just opposite Dumbarton Rock. There were mature elms when we arrived in 1981 which have been replaced with several varieties of birch and rowan, a flowering *Davidia* also *Liriodendron* (tulip tree) and a *Metasequoia* (Dawn Redwood). There are some magnolias and a good collection of acers together with rhododendrons, azaleas and camellias. Around the waterfall, tree ferns are happy ferns in general enjoying the shady, damp conditions. The *Trachycarpus* palms from the mountains of China also grow well. Some of the newly-introduced bamboos with blue, black, golden and green culms (canes) are now over 25ft tall. In summer the hydrangeas take over; there is a wide selection including the *Aspera* section with their huge flowers and fuzzy leaves. Autumn brings the reds, oranges and yellows on acers, rowan, *Parrotia and Cercidiphyllum*. There is a rushing stream (usually) four springs and several ponds. The garden is steep, there are steps/paved paths and it can be wet. Stout footwear and care is essential.

Open: by arrangement 1 April - 31 October, admission £7.50, children free. **Important** – this garden is on a steep slope, some paths have hand rails but can be slippery. Good footwear is essential to get round the whole garden.

Directions: From Langbank, take the Houston Road out of the village, under railway bridge and The Croft is 100 yards on the left (look out for conical yews).

Opening for: Hessilhead Wildlife Rescue

8 WRAES

Corseliehill Road, nr Houston PA6 7HU
Tim and Jo Mack

A varied seven acre rural garden with far reaching views and a variety of planting areas, designed to take advantage of the natural terrain and be actively wildlife friendly. Raised formal herbaceous beds, several wildlife ponds, burnside walks, grass maze, spring garden, woodland with rhododendron collection (100 species). For those interested in growing their own food, there is a large no-dig productive area, with vegetables, fruit cage, orchard and wildflower meadow. There are lots of seating places to relax and enjoy the tranquillity while the kids tackle the maze or just have a good run around!

Open: Sunday 29 June, 2pm - 5pm, admission £5.00, children free.

Directions: From Houston follow Barochan Road towards Langbank B789 for about a mile, turn left down Corseliehill Road. From Kilmacolm leave the village on Houston Road, past the golf course, turn left down Corseliehill Road for about a mile.

Opening for: Breast Cancer Now

Stirlingshire

Map locations:

- A9
- Methven
- Auchterarder
- Powmill
- Pool of Muckhart
- **1**
- **11**
- Dollar
- Tillicoultry
- Clackmannan
- Kincardine
- A985
- Grangemouth
- Linlithgow
- Crieff
- A85
- Muthill
- Greenloaning
- A9
- Alva
- A91
- Alloa
- M9
- Falkirk
- M876
- Comrie
- Dunblane
- Bridge of Allan
- **7**
- **10**
- **3** Stirling
- **2**
- M80
- Denny
- Tay
- Loch
- St Fillans
- L Earn
- Callander
- A84
- Doune
- **8** Thornhill
- Kippen
- **5**
- Kilsyth
- Killin
- Lochearnhead
- Strathyre
- **9**
- A811
- **12**
- Buchlyvie
- Balfron
- **4**
- Strathblane
- LLyon
- A85
- Crianlarich
- Loch Katrine
- Aberfoyle
- **6** Gartmore
- Balmaha
- Drymen
- Gartocharn
- A811
- Balloch
- Alexandria
- Tyndrum
- Ardlui
- A82
- Loch Lomond
- Arrochar
- Tarbet
- A83
- Lochgoilhead
- Garelochhead
- Faslane
- Rhu
- Helensburgh
- Cardross
- Cairndow
- Loch Long
- Dunoon

Stirlingshire

OUR VOLUNTEER ORGANISERS

District Organiser:	Willie Campbell	13 Fir Road, Doune FK16 6HU
		info@scotlandsgardens.org
District Administrator:	Jo Dormer	info@scotlandsgardens.org
Area Organisers:	Sylvia Broomfield	
	Rosemary Leckie	
	Rachel Nunn	
Media Officer:	Fiona Campbell	13 Fir Road, Doune FK16 6HU
Treasurer:	Carol Freireich	18 Netherblane, Blanefield, Glasgow G63 9JW

Follow our District on Facebook: @sgsstirlingshire

GARDENS OPEN ON A SPECIFIC DATE

Oakmore, Blairhoyle, Port of Menteith, Stirling	Sunday, 11 May
Shrubhill, Dunblane	Sunday, 18 May
Kilbryde Castle, Dunblane	Sunday, 25 May
Thorntree, Arnprior	Sunday, 1 June
Gartmore Village, Main Street, Gartmore	Sunday, 15 June
Oakmore, Blairhoyle, Port of Menteith, Stirling	Sunday, 13 July
Mollan, Thornhill, Stirling	Sunday, 27 July
Braehead Community Garden, Broom Road, Braehead	Sunday, 10 August
Bannockburn House Gardens, Stirling	Sunday, 17 August

GARDENS OPEN REGULARLY

The Japanese Garden at Cowden, Dollar, Clackmannanshire	1 January - 31 December

GARDENS OPEN BY ARRANGEMENT

Gargunnock House Garden, Gargunnnock	1 February - 1 June
Kilbryde Castle, Dunblane	1 February - 30 September
Thorntree, Arnprior	1 May - 1 September
Arndean, by Dollar	6 May - 7 June
Gardener's Cottage Walled Garden, Ballochruin Road, Killearn	15 June - 15 October
Bannockburn House Gardens, Stirling	1 July - 30 September

Stirlingshire

1 **ARNDEAN**
by Dollar FK14 7NH
Johnny and Katie Stewart
T: 07940 530499 E: johnny@arndean.co.uk

Opening for more than 40 years, this is a beautiful mature garden extending to 15 acres including the woodland walk. There is a formal herbaceous part, a small vegetable garden and an orchard. In addition, there are flowering shrubs, abundant and striking rhododendrons and azaleas as well as many fine specimen trees. There is a tree house for children.

Open: by arrangement 6 May - 7 June, admission £5.00, children free.

Directions: Arndean is well signposted off the A977.

Opening for: Marie Curie

2 **BANNOCKBURN HOUSE GARDENS**
Stirling FK7 8EY
Bannockburn House Trust
T: 07980 284027 E: gardens@bannockburnhouse.scot
W: www.bannockburnhouse.scot

Bannockburn House, an A-listed mansion built in 1675 by Sir Hugh Paterson, now sits in 26 acres of woodland and gardens. Bonnie Prince Charlie visited in 1746 where he met Clementina Walkinshaw who would become his mistress. Local boy, John McLaren, creator of The Golden Gate Park in San Francisco, began his gardening career here in 1860. The house and gardens suffered from 50 years of neglect before coming into community ownership in 2017 with restoration ongoing. Features include an enclosed kitchen garden supplying fruit and vegetables to two local food banks; herb gardens, an orchard, fruit cages, pollinator garden, wisteria border, labyrinth, polytunnels and raised beds. A short woodland walk passes 'The Five Sisters' - our fabulous giant redwood trees; the Fountain Walk passes our veteran lime trees, a cast-iron fountain (built by Steven in 1888), and our award-winning apiary. On 17th August, short tours of the house will also be available - they must be booked online in advance through the Bannockburn House website. The gardens can be viewed by arrangement through July to end September.

Open: Sunday 17 August, 10am - 4pm. Also open by arrangement 1 July - 30 September. Admission £5.00, children free.

Directions: The house entrance is 0.2 miles from the Bannockburn Interchange (M9/Junction 9 roundabout) off the A91.

Opening for: Bannockburn House Trust

Stirlingshire

3

BRAEHEAD COMMUNITY GARDEN
Broom Road, Braehead FK7 7GU
Nikki Thomas, Development Officer
E: garden@braehead.org

Braehead Community Garden is an 11,000 square metre outdoor space, enjoying a direct view of Stirling Castle. Dedicated to fostering a vibrant, connected community that thrives with healthy and happy residents, we encourage people to grow their own produce and we sell our own home grown crops back to the community at an affordable price. At the heart of our mission is the belief that physical and mental well-being are intricately tied to the environment and socio-economic circumstances we live in and how better than to combine locally-grown food with the fun and exercise that comes with being a member of a garden! Our garden is an essential local hub for social interaction, exercise, and a sense of pride and belonging within our diverse membership. We offer an array of activities and facilities, including 126 micro allotments for hire, a communal toolshed, an apiary producing local honey, a large polytunnel for social events, a maintenance workshop, a clubhouse, and free-range eggs from our resident chickens. Volunteering opportunities abound, including composting, maintenance, growing team (market garden) and looking after our hens and bees. From gardening to crafts, we offer advice, support and produce sales. Garden members can also benefit from peer mentoring and external training to enhance skills, knowledge, and confidence.
We have a multitude of nectar beds and wild spaces, ensuring we are giving back to our environment and supporting and encouraging local wildlife. Our extensive rain water harvesting system keeps the garden running whilst reducing our carbon footprint. Come along and experience our special place in the centre of historic Stirling - we have amazing views, lovely plants, flowers and wonderful cakes and chat!

Open: Sunday 10 August, 11am - 4pm, admission £5.00, children free.

Directions: From north on the A9 towards Bannockburn, take the first exit on Linden Avenue leading to Broom Road, turn right and the gardens are on the left. From south, on the A91 turn left on Pike Road leading to Broom Road.

Opening for: Braehead, Broomridge & District Community Development Trust

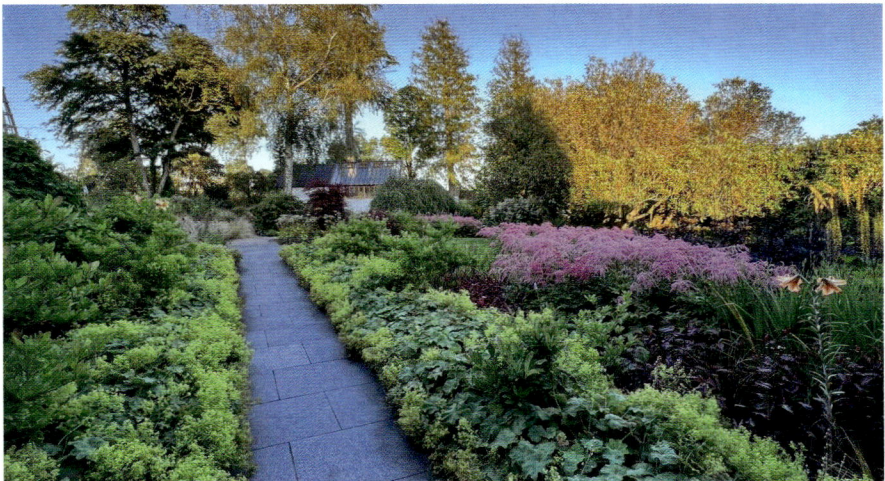

Mollan © Ruth Howieson

Stirlingshire

4 GARDENER'S COTTAGE WALLED GARDEN
Ballochruin Road, Killearn G63 9QB
Derek and Morna Knottenbelt
T: 01360 551682 E: mornaknottenbelt@hotmail.com

The walled garden, acquired in 2013 by the present owners, has been planted with extensive herbaceous borders, box hedging, roses and many unusual plants. There is a White Garden, a long shrub border with primulas and gentians and a former fernery with a collection of salvias, argyranthemums and peach and pear trees. June is a good time to visit when the roses are in bloom and borders with lupins, peonies, campanulas and other perennials are in flower. In July/August there is a fine collection of phlox in all of the borders, followed by dahlias, Michaelmas daisies, rudbeckias and blue aconitums from August to October. The Celtic Cross Garden was planted in May 2021 with a range of new plants including echinaceas, cardoons, lobelias, anthemis and lavender for mid to late summer colour. There are fine views of the Campsie Hills and the garden is surrounded by the conifers of the Designed Landscape of Carbeth.

Open: by arrangement 15 June - 15 October, admission £5.00, children free. The Garden Owners welcome visitors at short notice (the day before planned visits). Small numbers and individuals are welcome.

Directions: Follow SatNav to G63 0LF, which is Carbeth Home Farm on Ballochruin Road, halfway between Balfron and Killearn. We are the next entrance below the farm. Turn left on to the gravel road opposite the yellow Council salt bin and follow yellow *SGS* signs.

Opening for: The British Horse Society: Scotland

5 GARGUNNOCK HOUSE GARDEN
Gargunnnock FK8 3AZ
The Gargunnock Trustees
T: Garden contact: William Campbell 01786 842538
E: william.campbellwj@btinternet.com

Large mature garden five miles from Stirling, with a walled garden, well-established house garden, woodland walks with species and hybrid rhododendrons, massed plantings of azaleas and wonderful specimen trees. Snowdrops in February/March are followed by over 40 varieties of daffodils and the glorious displays of azaleas and rhododendrons in May. The three-acre walled garden contains perennial borders, cut-flower beds, greenhouses, fruit orchard and newly planted arboretum of specimen trees. The Walled Garden is now used by the charity Green Routes to give gardening education to adults with learning difficulties. Guided tours are available for groups.

Open: by arrangement 1 February - 1 June. Snowdrops and Winter Walks through February and March. Admission £5.00, children free.

Directions: Five miles west of Stirling on the A811. Car parking is at the entrance by the lodge.

Opening for: Rhododendron Species Conservation Group

Stirlingshire

6 GARTMORE VILLAGE
Main Street, Gartmore FK8 3RW
The Gardeners of Gartmore
E: ant@vinbay.co.uk

Several attractive and interesting medium and small gardens will be open in and around this beautiful peaceful village with splendid views. They will showcase a wide variety of planting with shrubs, roses and herbaceous borders, water features, also some vegetable gardens and fruit trees.

Open: Sunday 15 June, 1pm - 5pm, admission £6.00, children free. Maps and tickets will be available from the Village Hall, where there will also be a plant sale. Homemade teas will be available from the Black Bull. Please check the website for more information. Given relatively limited parking place availability, please park with consideration for the houses in the village.

Directions: Gartmore Village is on a small loop road off the A81 Glasgow - Aberfoyle road, and is well signposted. It is about 4 miles from Aberfoyle.

Opening for: Strathcarron Hospice

7 KILBRYDE CASTLE
Dunblane FK15 9NF
Sir James and Lady Campbell
T: 01786 824897 E: carolaandjames@googlemail.com
W: www.kilbrydecastle.com

Kilbryde Castle gardens cover some 12 acres and are situated above the Ardoch Burn and below the castle. The gardens are split into three parts: informal, woodland and wild. Natural planting (azaleas, rhododendrons, camellias and magnolias) is found in the woodland garden. There are glorious snowdrops, spring bulbs, and autumn colour provided by clematis and acers.

Open: by arrangement 1 February - 15 March for Snowdrops and Winter Walks. Also open Sunday 25 May, 11am - 5pm. And open by arrangement 16 March - 30 September. Admission £5.00, children free. On the 25th May opening there will be refreshments and a plant sale on offer.

Directions: Three miles from Dunblane and Doune, off the A820 between Dunblane and Doune. On Scotland's Gardens Scheme open days the garden is signposted from the A820.

Opening for: Leighton Library Trust

Stirlingshire

8 MOLLAN
Thornhill, Stirling FK8 3QJ
Iain and Ruth Howieson

Mollan is a large, three-acre garden in rural Stirlingshire set in softly rolling farmland. The garden is designed as a series of smaller interlocking gardens, each with a distinct character, packed with rich, colourful planting and meandering paths. There is a formal lawn, a wildflower meadow, two ponds and a productive kitchen garden.

Open: Sunday 27 July, noon - 4pm, admission £5.00, children free. There is artwork in the garden to be enjoyed too.

Directions: Leaving Thornhill on the A873 towards Aberfoyle, Mollan is on the left-hand side a mile outside the village. There are stone pillars and a knee-height sign saying *Mollan House* at the entrance which leads to a tree-lined drive.

Opening for: Thornhill Playgroup & Toddlers

9 OAKMORE
Blairhoyle, Port of Menteith, Stirling FK8 3LF
Rachel Nunn
T: 07872 068080

In 2014 this garden was a three-and-a-half acre field with a small wood and lots of rushes. Under the hands of a gardening fanatic and her willing husband, you will see a maturing garden with raised herbaceous borders, young orchards, a developing shrubbery, a rose garden, a bog garden and a variety of species trees. This is a garden for real plant enthusiasts and to enjoy it to the full, good footwear is recommended, particularly if it has been raining.

Open: Sunday 11 May & Sunday 13 July, 2pm - 5pm, admission £5.00, children free.

Directions: Blairhoyle is on the Thornhill to Port of Monteith road.

Opening for: Strathcarron Hospice & Macmillan Cancer Support

10 SHRUBHILL
Dunblane FK15 9PA
Tiff and Michaela Wright
T: 07821 693997 E: wrightrascals@gmail.com

Two acres of mixed, informal planting of some unusual rhododendrons, azaleas, specimen trees and other shrubs. Beautiful all-round views particularly over the Carse of Stirling and towards Ben Ledi and Ben Lomond. Herbaceous borders, meconopsis, late spring bulbs, water feature with a wide variety of primulas. Small walled garden predominantly for fruit and a greenhouse with a well-established vine. As well as homemade teas being on offer, there will be a plant sale.

Open: Sunday 18 May, 11am - 5pm, admission £5.00, children free. Parking is in a field.

Directions: Two miles from Keir roundabout on the B824 on the left, just after the *David Stirling Memorial,* follow the signs and parking advice. One mile from the A820 and on the right.

Opening for: Millimetres 2 Mountains Foundation CIO

Stirlingshire

11 THE JAPANESE GARDEN AT COWDEN
Dollar, Clackmannanshire FK14 7PL
Cowden SCIO
E: sales@cowdengarden.com
W: www.cowdengarden.com

Created in 1908, The Japanese Garden at Cowden is listed as an important example of its type in Western Europe. Nestled beneath the Ochil Hills the seven-acre garden wraps around a large pond. Enjoy the meandering walk by the water, taking in the changing scenes created by sculpted landforms, carefully placed stones, clipped shrubs and original stone lanterns. Picnic area, woodland, shop and cafe. Please check the garden's website for all admission information.

Open: Open 10.30am until 5pm during the spring and summer (closed Tuesdays) and until 4pm over winter (closed Mondays and Tuesdays). Please check the garden website for admission details, winter closures and changes to opening times.

Directions: The entrance to the garden is from the Upper Hillfoots Road, about half a mile west from the junction with the A91.

Opening for: Donation to SGS Beneficiaries

The Japanese Garden at Cowden

12 THORNTREE
Arnprior FK8 3EY
Mark and Carol Seymour
T: 01786 870710 E: carolseymour666@gmail.com
W: www.thorntreebarn.co.uk

See the amazing views from Aberfoyle and the hills beyond to Doune. Thorntree is a cottage garden that has evolved from growing dried flowers into triangle beds to meander through with more and more plants filling in gaps! This year's task was pruning trees to make sure the sun gets through. The garden is kept with the aid of WRAGS trainees, now our sixth - they come for a year to be trained two days a week. I am so grateful to them all. I kept the garden as much as possible as the farmer's wife who lived here before had it - 33 years ago! Every year is different. In 2024 the hydrangeas all flowered so well, and roses were still in full bloom in October. We are also usually here so come and see: just email to make sure we are not out.

Open: Sunday 1 June, 2pm - 5pm. Also open by arrangement 1 May - 1 September. Admission £5.00, children free. There will be a huge plant stall as plants are always available for sale as part of the trainee experience under the WRAGS scheme.

Directions: On the A811, to Arnprior, then take the Fintry Road; Thorntree is second on the right.

Opening for: Forth Driving Group RDA SCIO

Wigtownshire

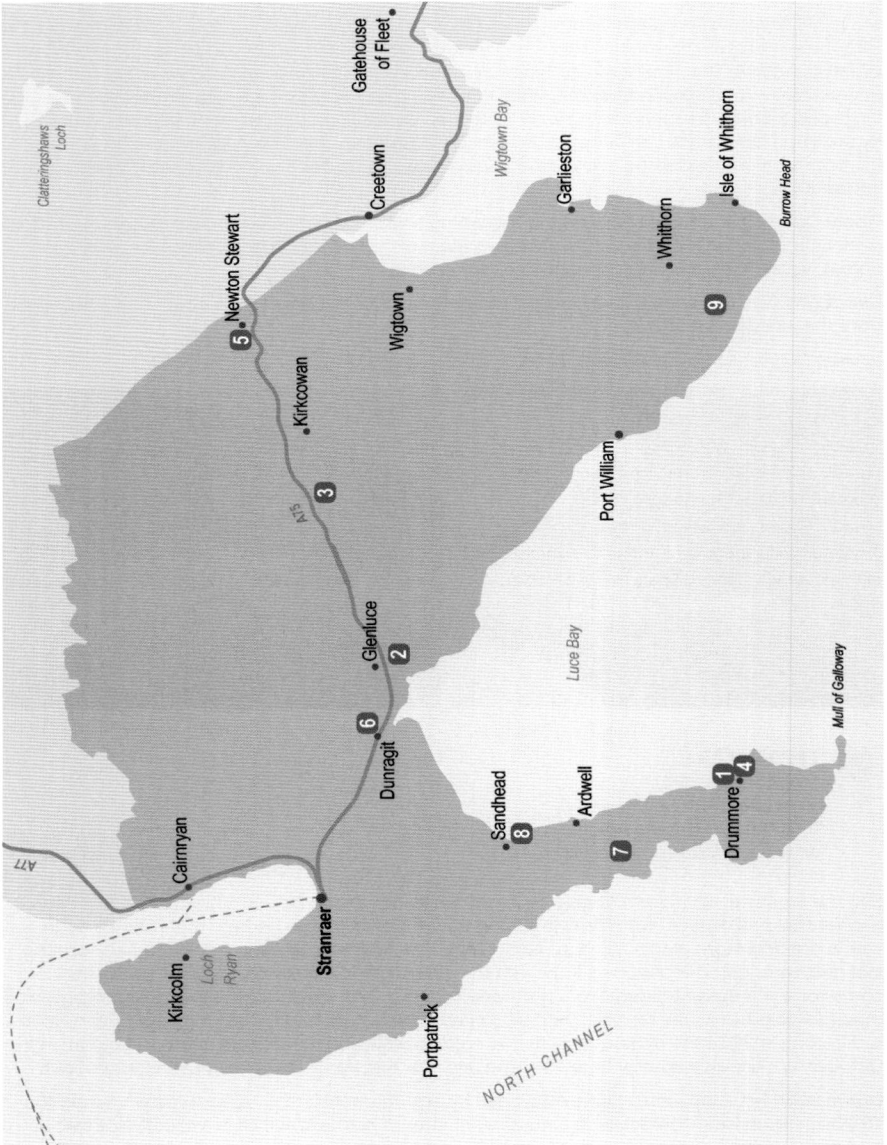

Clatteringshaws Loch

Gatehouse of Fleet

Wigtown Bay

Creetown

Garlieston

Isle of Whithorm

Burrow Head

Newton Stewart

5

Kirkcowan

Wigtown

Whithorm

9

3

A75

Port William

Glenluce

2

Luce Bay

6

Dunragit

Sandhead

Ardwell

Drummore

1 **4**

8

7

Cairnryan

A77

Stranraer

Kirkcolm

Loch Ryan

Portpatrick

Mull of Galloway

NORTH CHANNEL

Wigtownshire

OUR VOLUNTEER ORGANISERS

District Organiser:	Teri Birch	The Old Manse, Gruisey House, Sandhead DG9 9JT
		info@scotlandsgardens.org
Area Organisers:	Colin Belton	Amulree, 8 Mill Street, Drummore DG9 9PS
	Eileen Davie	Whitehills House, Minnigaff DG8 6SL
	Mary Gladstone	Craichlaw, Kirkcowan DG8 0DQ
	Annmaree Mitchell	Cottage 2, Little Float, Sandhead DG9 9LD
District Photographer:	Stuart Littlewood	Tayvallich, West Port, New Galloway DG7 3SB
Treasurer:	Neil Harper	

GARDENS OPEN ON A SPECIFIC DATE

Logan Botanic Garden, Port Logan, by Stranraer	Sunday, 18 May
Woodfall Gardens, Glasserton	Sunday, 18 May
Damnaglaur House, Drummore, Stranraer	Sunday, 1 June
Woodfall Gardens, Glasserton	Sunday, 15 June
Woodfall Gardens, Glasserton	Sunday, 20 July
Amulree, 8 Mill Street, Drummore, Stranraer	Saturday/Sunday, 2/3 August
Fernlea Garden, Corvisel Road, Newton Stewart	Sunday, 10 August

GARDENS OPEN REGULARLY

Glenwhan Gardens & Arboretum, Dunragit, by Stranraer	1 January - 31 December
Logan Botanic Garden, Port Logan, by Stranraer	1 February - 28 February
Logan Botanic Garden, Port Logan, by Stranraer	1 March - 15 November

GARDENS OPEN BY ARRANGEMENT

Craichlaw, Kirkcowan, Newton Stewart	1 January - 31 December
Fernlea Garden, Corvisel Road, Newton Stewart	1 April - 30 September
Barlockhart Lodge, Glenluce	1 May - 30 September
Damnaglaur House, Drummore, Stranraer	1 May - 30 September
The Old Manse, Sandhead, Stranraer	1 June - 30 September

Wigtownshire

1 AMULREE
8 Mill Street, Drummore, Stranraer DG9 9PS
Colin Belton and Gabrielle Reynolds
T: 07899 092070 E: gabygardeners@btinternet.com

Amulree is home to two complete plantaholics who probably should start taking their own advice and stop collecting quite so many plants! Starting from a blank canvas in 2017 the garden now consists of a sunny terrace with displays of half-hardy and tender plants, exuberantly planted borders separated by serpentine grass patches, a small vegetable patch, a glasshouse and a 'wild' bit. Amulree contains many unusual plants including a National Plant Collection.
National Plant Collection: *Nicotiana* species.

Open: Saturday/Sunday, 2/3 August, 10am - 4pm, admission £5.00, children free. Groups also welcome at other times by prior arrangement.

Directions: Follow the A716 signposted *Drummore and Mull of Galloway*. At the T-junction in Drummore turn right. Amulree is on the left, a few doors up from the shop. Bus route 407 from Stranraer.

Opening for: Kirkmaiden Old Kirk

2 BARLOCKHART LODGE
Glenluce DG8 0JG
Barlockhart Gardeners
T: 07821 776226 E: neilharper1962@btinternet.com

A newly-created garden, on a domestic scale, which is very much a work in progress. The main part is a reclaimed riding manege, which has been transformed with meandering paths around borders planted with perennials and grasses to reflect the local undulating landscape. A rockery border and greenhouse are to one side of the house and traditional cottage-style borders are to the front and other side. A small vegetable plot with raised beds and a polycarbonate greenhouse is to the rear. The garden is situated about a mile from Luce Bay and has the benefits of the Gulf Stream, but the disadvantages of an exposed, shadeless position.

Open: by arrangement 1 May - 30 September, admission £5.00, children free. There is plenty of off-road parking. Please do not park on the lane.

Directions: Take the A75 to Glenluce. On the hill which links the two Glenluce turnoffs, take the single-track unmarked lane, signposted for *Whithorn Way*. Property is roughly one mile along the lane, on the left.

Opening for: PIRSAC

Wigtownshire

3 ## CRAICHLAW
Kirkcowan, Newton Stewart DG8 0DQ
Mr and Mrs Andrew Gladstone
T: 01671 830208 E: craichlaw@aol.com

Formal garden with herbaceous borders around the house. Set in extensive grounds with lawns, lochs and woodland. A path around the main loch leads to a water garden returning past a recently planted arboretum in the old walled garden. The best times to visit the garden are early February for snowdrops, May to mid-June for the water garden and rhododendrons, and mid-June to August for herbaceous borders.

Open: by arrangement 1 January - 31 December. Snowdrops and Winter Walks February - mid March. Admission £5.00, children free.

Directions: Take the B733 for Kirkcowan, off the A75 at the Halfway House eight miles west of Newton Stewart and Craichlaw House is the first turning on the right.

Opening for: All proceeds to SGS Beneficiaries

4 ## DAMNAGLAUR HOUSE
Drummore, Stranraer DG9 9QN
Frances Collins
T: 01776 840636/ 07884 435353 E: chunky.collins@btinternet.com

Since moving into Damnaglaur House in 1991, its owners have totally transformed the garden, putting in a series of 'semi-terraces' and, following the planting of wind-defeating shrubs, they were able to introduce many special herbaceous plants and trees. Just short of half-an-acre, the garden has slowly evolved into one which feels substantially larger because of its design; the gravel paths weave their way through many hidden corners to come upon countless gems. The views from the garden are stunning, down to Drummore, across Luce Bay and in the far distance, to the Galloway Hills. An archway, arbour and pergola give extra height for the planting. Seating around the garden gives visitors a chance to sit and enjoy their surroundings, especially close to the pond with its numerous fish and trickling waterfall. The inevitable removal of a huge and very old but beloved ash tree with 'die back' was accomplished in 2023 but the disruption was amazingly short-lived. The young trees and shrubs planted nearby will take many years to compensate for its loss but the wider area now accommodates more rhododendrons and azaleas, surrounded by a surge of foxgloves. Various areas have been replanted over the past few years, with a small 'seaside' garden being introduced.

Open: Sunday 1 June, 1pm - 5pm. Also open by arrangement 1 May - 30 September. Admission £5.00, children free. Homemade teas will be available additionally on 1 June.

Directions: From Drummore, follow signs to the *Mull of Galloway* for a mile on the B7041 to junction with B7065; Damnaglaur is on the right.

Opening for: British Red Cross: Yemen appeal

Wigtownshire

5 FERNLEA GARDEN
Corvisel Road, Newton Stewart DG8 6LW
Mrs Jenny Gustafson
T: 07909 951885/ 01671 638273 E: floralbasket@proton.me

A secluded town garden of a third-of-an-acre, it was created in 2006 to complement a new house. There are many rare and unusual trees and shrubs. Two herbaceous borders, one with hot colours and the other pastels. A Chinese-inspired corner, small pond, fruit trees including a Galloway pippin apple and soft fruit. The upper part of the garden is hidden behind a tall beech hedge, where there is a summer house and adjacent woodland planting.

Open: Sunday 10 August, 2pm - 5pm. Also open by arrangement 1 April - 30 September. Admission £6.00, children free. Homemade teas available on 10 August. Teas can be provided for 'by arrangement' visitors by prior arrangement. We welcome enquiries from individuals and small groups for our openings by arrangement.

Directions: Turn right at the roundabout on the A75 if coming from Dumfries direction. Go left at the cattle market (opposite the Crown Hotel) and it is the first through road on the right.

Opening for: GDI: red squirrels, East Wigtownshire

Damnaglaur House

Wigtownshire

6 GLENWHAN GARDENS & ARBORETUM

Dunragit, by Stranraer DG9 8PH
Tessa and Ian Knott Sinclair
T: 07787 990702
W: www.glenwhangardens.co.uk

Described as one of the most beautiful gardens in Scotland, Glenwhan Gardens is situated at 300 feet and overlooks Luce Bay and the Mull of Galloway, with clear views to the Isle of Man. Forty-five years ago there was wild moorland, but now, following considerable dedication and vision, you can see glorious collections of plants from around the world. There is colour in all seasons and the winding paths, well-placed seats and varied sculptures, set around small lochans, add to the tranquil atmosphere. There is a 17-acre moorland wildflower walk, the chance to see red squirrels and well-marked garden and tree trails. Glenwhan has now been added to the Inventory of Gardens and Designed Landscapes, a record of nationally important gardens and designed landscapes and a major resource for enhancing appreciation and understanding of these sites, as well as promoting education and stimulating further research. Dara Parsons, Head of Designations at HES, said: 'Glenwhan Gardens is an excellent addition to, the inventory.'

Open: 1 January - 31 December, 2pm - 5pm , Snowdrops and Winter Walks 25 January - 11 March. Admission details can be found on the garden's website. Admission to gardens at the entrance. Tearoom and locally grown plants for sale.

Directions: Seven miles east of Stranraer, one mile off the A75 at Dunragit (follow brown *VisitScotland* and *yellow SGS arrows*).

Opening for: *Donation to SGS Beneficiaries*

7 LOGAN BOTANIC GARDEN

Port Logan, by Stranraer DG9 9ND
A Regional Garden of the Royal Botanic Garden Edinburgh
T: 01776 860231 E: logan@rbge.org.uk
W: www.rbge.org.uk/logan

Logan Botanic Garden lies at the south-western tip of Scotland, unrivalled as 'Scotland's Most Exotic Garden'. Warmed by the Gulf Stream, a remarkable collection of southern hemisphere plants flourish, making this a plantsman's paradise. Logan enjoys an almost subtropical climate where the garden's avenues and borders feature a spectacular and colourful array of half-hardy perennials. The garden is warmed by the Gulf Stream which enables plants from Australia, New Zealand, South and Central America and Southern Africa to thrive. Voted 'Best Garden in the UK' 2021, Logan promises a delightful day out for all.
National Plant Collection: *Gunnera, Leptospermum, Griselinia, Clianthus* and *Sutherlandia.*
Champion Trees: *Polylepis* and *Eucalyptus.*

Open: Open weekends in February, 10am - 4pm for Snowdrops and Winter Walks. Also open Sunday 18 May, 10am - 5pm. And open daily 1 March - 15 November, 10am - 5pm (4pm in November). Admission details can be found on the garden's website.

Directions: Ten miles south of Stranraer on the A716 then 2½ miles from Ardwell Village.

Opening for: *Board Of Trustees Of The Royal Botanic Garden Edinburgh*

Wigtownshire

Logan Botanic Garden

8 THE OLD MANSE
Sandhead, Stranraer DG9 9JT
Geoff and Teri Birch
T: 01776 830455 E: birchteri@gmail.com

A garden for plant lovers recently designed, landscaped and planted by the current owners. Comprising about half an acre, the garden is surrounded by stone walls and features a natural burn, two bridges, a Japanese inspired slope border, a formal parterre, a rose garden, rockeries and a shady woodland area. The Old Manse is close to Logan Botanic Gardens and enjoys the same temperate climate making a range of unusual and interesting plantings possible. The colour themed borders include herbaceous perennials, shrubs, young trees, alpines, roses, grasses and bulbs which ensure continuity of interest throughout the seasons.

Open: by arrangement 1 June - 30 September, admission £5.00, children free.

Directions: From Stranraer take the A716 south following signs for *Drummore*; past Sandhead, look for a tourist sign for *Kirkmadrine Stones and Clachanmore* and turn immediately right. The Old Manse is on the corner on the right (known locally as *Doctors' Corner*. A bus service is available from Stranraer and stops at Doctors' Corner.

Opening for: Board Of Trustees Of The Royal Botanic Garden Edinburgh

Wigtownshire

9 WOODFALL GARDENS
Glasserton DG8 8LY
Ross and Liz Muir
E: woodfallgardens@btinternet.com
W: www.woodfall-gardens.co.uk

This lovely three acre triple walled garden has been thoughtfully restored to provide year round interest and a wonderful environment for birds, bees, butterflies and even red squirrels. The Gulf Stream keeps the climate mild and enables many tender southern hemisphere plants to thrive. Some of the seasonal highlights are the exotic bulb beds, the candelabra primula walkway, hundreds of blue poppies and a huge variety of hydrangeas, rhododendrons and acers. There are many mature trees and shrubs, including many less common species, and extensive beds of fruit and vegetables that are interspersed with flowers. This well stocked garden, that still has traces of 18th century grandeur, is definitely worth a visit. We are very grateful to the people who visit annually – there is no better recommendation.

Open: Sunday 18 May, Sunday 15 June & Sunday 20 July, 10:30am - 4:30pm, admission £5.00, children free. Please check the garden's website for details of further openings.

Directions: Two miles south-west of Whithorn at junction off A746 and A747 (directly behind Glasserton Church).

Opening for: Whithorn Primary School

Woodfall Gardens

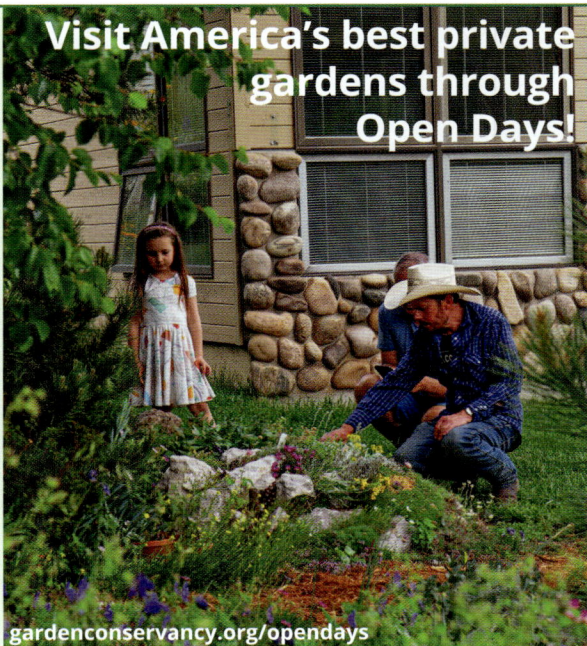

OAK

The Long Walk

MAPLE

Cherry
Lawn

Fountain

LIME

MAPLE

Lovers Walk

OAK

HOLM
OAK

MAPLE

CHESTNUT

Luccombe
Oak

Cork
Lawn

Holm
Oak

BIRCH

New
Lawn

James Byatt
Garden & Estate Cartography

www.jamesbyatt.com

Would you like your garden or garden business professionally photographed?

Delia Ridley-Thomas Garden Photography

Call Delia on **07909993298** or email **dridleythomas@icloud.com** with your project requests.

⟳ **@lothian_garden**

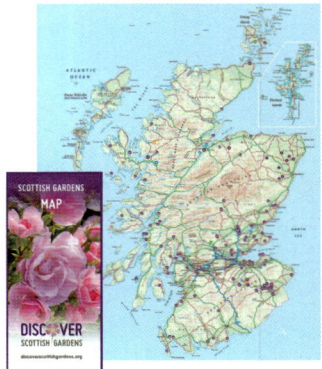

Plant Heritage

Do you love plants?

Especially growing a wide range of plants, and more unusual varieties?

Plant Heritage is a charity, founded in 1978 with a unique mission to protect the diversity of garden plants across the UK. With our members, we are safeguarding 95,000 different plants, from tiny Cacti to stunning Salvias or giant Beech trees. Why not join us?

Whether you are interested in starting your own National Plant Collection®, looking after a rare plant through our Plant Guardian® scheme, want to take part in our plant exchange, to talk plants with people who share your passion, there is something for everyone.

You can also support our conservation work by opening your garden with the SGS and donating the money you raise to Plant Heritage, or visiting the National Collections in gardens across Scotland. Look out for the symbol: NPC

Bruckhills Croft, National Plant Collection: *Galanthus*

Amulree, National Plant Collection: *Nicotiana* species
Photo credit: Ruth Belton

Find out more at **www.plantheritage.org.uk** or call **01483 447540**

Registered charity No. SC041785/1004009. Reg Company No. 2222953

Gardens open on a specific date

JANUARY
....

Monday - Thursday 20 - 30 January
Perth & Kinross   Fingask Castle, Rait

FEBRUARY
....

Monday & Tuesday 3/4 February
Perth & Kinross   Fingask Castle, Rait

Tuesday 4 February
East Lothian   Shepherd House, Inveresk, Musselburgh

Wednesday & Thursday 5/6 February
Perth & Kinross   Fingask Castle, Rait

Thursday 6 February
East Lothian   Shepherd House, Inveresk, Musselburgh

Saturday 8 February
Fife   Dunimarle Castle, Balgownie West, Culross

Sunday 9 February
Argyll & Lochaber   **NEW** Ardchattan Manse, Ardchattan, Oban, Argyll
Fife   Dunimarle Castle, Balgownie West, Culross

Monday & Tuesday 10/11 February
Perth & Kinross   Fingask Castle, Rait

Tuesday 11 February
East Lothian   Shepherd House, Inveresk, Musselburgh

Wednesday 12 February
Peeblesshire & Tweeddale   Kirkton Manor House, Peebles
Perth & Kinross   Fingask Castle, Rait

Thursday 13 February
East Lothian   Shepherd House, Inveresk, Musselburgh
Inverness, Ross, Cromarty & Skye   Dunvegan Castle and Gardens, Isle of Skye
Perth & Kinross   Fingask Castle, Rait

Saturday 15 February
Dumfriesshire   Tinnisburn Plants, Upper Millsteads, Canonbie
Edinburgh, Midlothian & West Lothian   Preston Hall Walled Garden, Pathhead
Inverness, Ross, Cromarty & Skye   Dunvegan Castle and Gardens, Isle of Skye

Sunday 16 February
Dumfriesshire   Craig, Langholm
Dumfriesshire   Tinnisburn Plants, Upper Millsteads, Canonbie
East Lothian   Shepherd House, Inveresk, Musselburgh
Edinburgh, Midlothian & West Lothian   Preston Hall Walled Garden, Pathhead
Kirkcudbrightshire   Danevale Park, Crossmichael
Perth & Kinross   Cloan, by Auchterarder

Monday & Tuesday 17/18 February
Perth & Kinross   Fingask Castle, Rait

Tuesday 18 February
East Lothian   Shepherd House, Inveresk, Musselburgh
Inverness, Ross, Cromarty & Skye   Dunvegan Castle and Gardens, Isle of Skye

Wednesday 19 February

Peeblesshire & Tweeddale   Kirkton Manor House, Peebles

Perth & Kinross   Fingask Castle, Rait

Thursday 20 February

East Lothian   Shepherd House, Inveresk, Musselburgh

Perth & Kinross   Fingask Castle, Rait

Friday 21 February

Fife   Teasses Gardens, near Ceres

Saturday 22 February

Angus, Dundee & Kincardineshire South   Kinblethmont House, by Arbroath, Angus

Berwickshire & Roxburghshire   Mellerstain, Mellerstain House and Gardens, Gordon

Fife   Lindores House, by Newburgh

Perth & Kinross   Princeland House, Blairgowrie Road, Coupar Angus, Blairgowrie

Perth & Kinross   Scone Palace Garden, Perth

Sunday 23 February

Angus, Dundee & Kincardineshire South   Kinblethmont House, by Arbroath, Angus

Peeblesshire & Tweeddale   Kailzie Gardens, Peebles

Perth & Kinross   Princeland House, Blairgowrie Road, Coupar Angus, Blairgowrie

Monday & Tuesday 24/25 February

Perth & Kinross   Fingask Castle, Rait

Tuesday 25 February

East Lothian   Shepherd House, Inveresk, Musselburgh

Wednesday 26 February

Peeblesshire & Tweeddale   Kirkton Manor House, Peebles

Perth & Kinross   Fingask Castle, Rait

Thursday 27 February

East Lothian   Shepherd House, Inveresk, Musselburgh

Perth & Kinross   Fingask Castle, Rait

MARCH

Saturday 1 March

Perth & Kinross   Princeland House, Blairgowrie Road, Coupar Angus, Blairgowrie

Sunday 2 March

Angus, Dundee & Kincardineshire South   Ecclesgreig Castle, St Cyrus

Lanarkshire   Cleghorn, Stable House, Cleghorn Farm, Lanark

Perth & Kinross   Princeland House, Blairgowrie Road, Coupar Angus, Blairgowrie

Monday - Wednesday 3 - 5 March

Perth & Kinross   Fingask Castle, Rait

Wednesday 5 March

East Lothian   Stobshiel House, Humbie

Peeblesshire & Tweeddale   Kirkton Manor House, Peebles

Thursday 6 March

Angus, Dundee & Kincardineshire South   Lawton House, Inverkeilor, by Arbroath

Perth & Kinross   Fingask Castle, Rait

Friday 7 March

Angus, Dundee & Kincardineshire South   Lawton House, Inverkeilor, by Arbroath

Saturday 8 March

Angus, Dundee & Kincardineshire South   Lawton House, Inverkeilor, by Arbroath

Perth & Kinross   Princeland House, Blairgowrie Road, Coupar Angus, Blairgowrie

Sunday 9 March

Angus, Dundee & Kincardineshire South   Lawton House, Inverkeilor, by Arbroath

Perth & Kinross   Princeland House, Blairgowrie Road, Coupar Angus, Blairgowrie

Wednesday 12 March
East Lothian   Stobshiel House, Humbie
Peeblesshire & Tweeddale   Kirkton Manor House, Peebles

Wednesday 19 March
East Lothian   Humbie Dean, Humbie
East Lothian   Stobshiel House, Humbie
Peeblesshire & Tweeddale   Kirkton Manor House, Peebles

Sunday 23 March
Kirkcudbrightshire   The Limes, Kirkcudbright

Wednesday 26 March
East Lothian   Stobshiel House, Humbie
Peeblesshire & Tweeddale   Kirkton Manor House, Peebles

Saturday 29 March
Dumfriesshire   Tinnisburn Plants, Upper Millsteads, Canonbie

Sunday 30 March
Dumfriesshire   Tinnisburn Plants, Upper Millsteads, Canonbie
East Lothian   Winton Castle, Pencaitland
Perth & Kinross   Mill of Forneth, Forneth, Blairgowrie

APRIL

Open throughout April
Perth & Kinross   Glendoick, Glencarse, Perthshire

Wednesday 2 April
Argyll & Lochaber   Ardchattan Priory, North Connel
East Lothian   Humbie Dean, Humbie
East Lothian   Stobshiel House, Humbie
Peeblesshire & Tweeddale   Kirkton Manor House, Peebles

Saturday 5 April
Ayrshire & Arran   **NEW** Caprington Castle, Kilmarnock

Sunday 6 April
Aberdeenshire   Auchmacoy, Ellon
Ayrshire & Arran   **NEW** Caprington Castle, Kilmarnock
Perth & Kinross   Fingask Castle, Rait

Wednesday 9 April
Argyll & Lochaber   Ardchattan Priory, North Connel
East Lothian   Stobshiel House, Humbie
Peeblesshire & Tweeddale   Kirkton Manor House, Peebles

Thursday 10 April
Inverness, Ross, Cromarty & Skye   Dundonnell House, Little Loch Broom, Wester Ross

Saturday 12 April
East Lothian   A Blackbird Sings, 20 Kings Park, Longniddry

Sunday 13 April
Berwickshire & Roxburghshire   Harlaw Farmhouse, Eccles near Kelso, Berwickshire
Kirkcudbrightshire   3 Millhall, Shore Road, Kirkcudbright

Tuesday 15 April
East Lothian   Shepherd House, Inveresk, Musselburgh

Wednesday 16 April
Argyll & Lochaber   Ardchattan Priory, North Connel
East Lothian   Humbie Dean, Humbie
East Lothian   Longwood, Humbie
East Lothian   Stobshiel House, Humbie
Peeblesshire & Tweeddale   Kirkton Manor House, Peebles

Thursday 17 April
East Lothian   Shepherd House, Inveresk, Musselburgh

Friday 18 April
East Lothian   Blackdykes Garden, Blackdykes Farmhouse, North Berwick

Saturday 19 April
Angus, Dundee & Kincardineshire South   17a Menzieshill Road, Dundee
Perth & Kinross   Ardvorlich, Lochearnhead
Renfrewshire   SGS Kilmacolm Plant Sale, Outside Kilmacolm Library,
                                                  Kilmacolm

Sunday 20 April
Aberdeenshire   Westhall Castle, Oyne, Inverurie
Angus, Dundee & Kincardineshire South   17a Menzieshill Road, Dundee
Perth & Kinross   Ardvorlich, Lochearnhead

Monday 21 April
Angus, Dundee & Kincardineshire South   Inchmill Cottage, Glenprosen, near Kirriemuir
Perth & Kinross   Ardvorlich, Lochearnhead

Tuesday 22 April
East Lothian   Shepherd House, Inveresk, Musselburgh
Perth & Kinross   Ardvorlich, Lochearnhead

Wednesday 23 April
Argyll & Lochaber   Ardchattan Priory, North Connel
East Lothian   Stobshiel House, Humbie
Peeblesshire & Tweeddale   Kirkton Manor House, Peebles
Perth & Kinross   Ardvorlich, Lochearnhead

Thursday 24 April
East Lothian   Shepherd House, Inveresk, Musselburgh
Perth & Kinross   Ardvorlich, Lochearnhead

Friday 25 April
East Lothian   Blackdykes Garden, Blackdykes Farmhouse, North Berwick
Perth & Kinross   Ardvorlich, Lochearnhead

Saturday 26 April
Fife   Willowhill, Forgan, Newport-on-Tay
Perth & Kinross   Ardvorlich, Lochearnhead

Sunday 27 April
Edinburgh, Midlothian & West Lothian   **NEW** Eglinton and Glencairn Gardens,
                                                  Eglinton Crescent, Edinburgh
Fife   Willowhill, Forgan, Newport-on-Tay
Kirkcudbrightshire   The Limes, Kirkcudbright
Perth & Kinross   Ardvorlich, Lochearnhead
Perth & Kinross   Megginch Castle, Errol

Monday 28 April
Fife   Willowhill, Forgan, Newport-on-Tay
Perth & Kinross   Ardvorlich, Lochearnhead

Tuesday 29 April
East Lothian   Shepherd House, Inveresk, Musselburgh
Perth & Kinross   Ardvorlich, Lochearnhead

Wednesday 30 April
Argyll & Lochaber   Ardchattan Priory, North Connel
East Lothian   Stobshiel House, Humbie
Peeblesshire & Tweeddale   Kirkton Manor House, Peebles
Perth & Kinross   Ardvorlich, Lochearnhead

MAY

Open throughout May

Perth & Kinross	Glendoick, Glencarse, Perthshire

Thursday 1 May

East Lothian	Shepherd House, Inveresk, Musselburgh
Edinburgh, Midlothian & West Lothian	Newliston, Kirkliston
Perth & Kinross	Ardvorlich, Lochearnhead

Friday 2 May

Edinburgh, Midlothian & West Lothian	Newliston, Kirkliston
Fife	Edenhill, Kennedy Gardens, St Andrews
Perth & Kinross	Ardvorlich, Lochearnhead

Saturday 3 May

Angus, Dundee & Kincardineshire South	17a Menzieshill Road, Dundee
Angus, Dundee & Kincardineshire South	2 Panmure Terrace, Dundee
Argyll & Lochaber	NEW 4 Port Ann, Lochgilphead, Argyll
Argyll & Lochaber	Kames Bay, Kilmelford
East Lothian	A Blackbird Sings, 20 Kings Park, Longniddry
Edinburgh, Midlothian & West Lothian	Dr Neil's Garden, Duddingston Village
Edinburgh, Midlothian & West Lothian	Newliston, Kirkliston
Fife	Edenhill, Kennedy Gardens, St Andrews
Moray & Nairn	The Biblical Garden, King Street, Elgin, Moray
Perth & Kinross	Ardvorlich, Lochearnhead

Sunday 4 May

Angus, Dundee & Kincardineshire South	17a Menzieshill Road, Dundee
Argyll & Lochaber	NEW 4 Port Ann, Lochgilphead, Argyll
Argyll & Lochaber	Kames Bay, Kilmelford
Ayrshire & Arran	Blair Castle & Estate, Dalry, Ayrshire
Edinburgh, Midlothian & West Lothian	Dr Neil's Garden, Duddingston Village
Edinburgh, Midlothian & West Lothian	Greentree, 18 Greenhill Park, Edinburgh
Edinburgh, Midlothian & West Lothian	Newliston, Kirkliston
Fife	Edenhill, Kennedy Gardens, St Andrews
Fife	The Gardens of Monimail Tower, Monimail Tower Project, by Letham
Lanarkshire	Old Farm Cottage, The Ladywell, Nemphlar, Lanark
Perth & Kinross	Ardvorlich, Lochearnhead
Perth & Kinross	The Steading at Clunie, The Steading

Monday 5 May

Argyll & Lochaber	NEW 4 Port Ann, Lochgilphead, Argyll
Kirkcudbrightshire	Threave Garden, Castle Douglas
Perth & Kinross	Ardvorlich, Lochearnhead

Tuesday 6 May

East Lothian	Shepherd House, Inveresk, Musselburgh
Perth & Kinross	Ardvorlich, Lochearnhead

Wednesday 7 May

Argyll & Lochaber	Ardchattan Priory, North Connel
East Lothian	Stobshiel House, Humbie
Edinburgh, Midlothian & West Lothian	Newliston, Kirkliston
Peeblesshire & Tweeddale	Haystoun, Peebles
Peeblesshire & Tweeddale	Kirkton Manor House, Peebles
Perth & Kinross	Ardvorlich, Lochearnhead
Perth & Kinross	Dowhill, Cleish

Thursday 8 May

Angus, Dundee & Kincardineshire South	Inchmill Cottage, Glenprosen, near Kirriemuir
Argyll & Lochaber	Baravalla Garden, by West Loch Tarbert, Argyll
East Lothian	Shepherd House, Inveresk, Musselburgh
Edinburgh, Midlothian & West Lothian	Newliston, Kirkliston
Perth & Kinross	Ardvorlich, Lochearnhead

Friday 9 May

Edinburgh, Midlothian & West Lothian	Newliston, Kirkliston
Perth & Kinross	Ardvorlich, Lochearnhead

Saturday 10 May

Caithness, Sutherland, Orkney & Shetland	16 Mulla, Voe, Shetland
Edinburgh, Midlothian & West Lothian	NEW Bridgend Farmhouse Community Allotments, 41 Old Dalkeith Road
Edinburgh, Midlothian & West Lothian	Newliston, Kirkliston
Perth & Kinross	Ardvorlich, Lochearnhead

Sunday 11 May

Angus, Dundee & Kincardineshire South	Dalfruin, Kirktonhill Road, Kirriemuir
Caithness, Sutherland, Orkney & Shetland	16 Mulla, Voe, Shetland
Dumfriesshire	Dalswinton House, Dalswinton
Dunbartonshire	18 Duchess Park with Westburn, Helensburgh
East Lothian	Tyninghame House and The Walled Garden, Tyninghame House, Dunbar
Edinburgh, Midlothian & West Lothian	NEW Belgrave Crescent Gardens, Edinburgh
Edinburgh, Midlothian & West Lothian	Newliston, Kirkliston
Kirkcudbrightshire	Cally Biodiversity Gardens, Cally Avenue, Gatehouse of Fleet
Perth & Kinross	Ardvorlich, Lochearnhead
Perth & Kinross	Cloan, by Auchterarder
Renfrewshire	Highwood, off Lochwinnoch Road, Kilmacolm
Stirlingshire	Oakmore, Blairhoyle, Port of Menteith, Stirling

Monday 12 May

Perth & Kinross	Ardvorlich, Lochearnhead

Tuesday 13 May

East Lothian	Shepherd House, Inveresk, Musselburgh
Perth & Kinross	Ardvorlich, Lochearnhead

Wednesday 14 May

Argyll & Lochaber	Ardchattan Priory, North Connel
East Lothian	Humbie Dean, Humbie
East Lothian	Longwood, Humbie
East Lothian	Stobshiel House, Humbie
Edinburgh, Midlothian & West Lothian	Newliston, Kirkliston
Peeblesshire & Tweeddale	Haystoun, Peebles
Peeblesshire & Tweeddale	Kirkton Manor House, Peebles
Perth & Kinross	Ardvorlich, Lochearnhead
Perth & Kinross	Dowhill, Cleish

Thursday 15 May

East Lothian	Shepherd House, Inveresk, Musselburgh
Edinburgh, Midlothian & West Lothian	Newliston, Kirkliston
Perth & Kinross	Ardvorlich, Lochearnhead

Friday 16 May

Edinburgh, Midlothian & West Lothian	Newliston, Kirkliston
Perth & Kinross	Ardvorlich, Lochearnhead

Saturday 17 May

Angus, Dundee & Kincardineshire South	Balhary Walled Garden, Balhary, Alyth, Blairgowrie
Angus, Dundee & Kincardineshire South	Milton of Finavon House, Forfar
Argyll & Lochaber	NEW Cruachan Lodge, North Connel, Oban
Argyll & Lochaber	NEW Kilchoan Gardens, Kilmelford
Edinburgh, Midlothian & West Lothian	Newliston, Kirkliston
Edinburgh, Midlothian & West Lothian	Regent, Royal and Carlton Terrace Gardens, 17a Royal Terrace Mews, Carlton Terrace Lane Entrance, Edinburgh
Perth & Kinross	NEW Overdale, Kirk Wynd, Blairgowrie
Perth & Kinross	Ardvorlich, Lochearnhead

Sunday 18 May

Aberdeenshire	Inchmarlo Retirement Village Garden, Inchmarlo, Banchory
Angus, Dundee & Kincardineshire South	Brechin Castle, Brechin
Argyll & Lochaber	NEW Cruachan Lodge, North Connel, Oban
Argyll & Lochaber	NEW Kilchoan Gardens, Kilmelford
Dunbartonshire	Ross Priory, Gartocharn
East Lothian	Shepherd House, Inveresk, Musselburgh
Edinburgh, Midlothian & West Lothian	Moray Place and Bank Gardens, Edinburgh
Edinburgh, Midlothian & West Lothian	Newliston, Kirkliston
Edinburgh, Midlothian & West Lothian	Temple Village Gardens, Temple
Fife	Craig Cottage, Blebo Craigs
Fife	South Flisk, Blebo Craigs, Cupar
Kirkcudbrightshire	Arbigland House, Kirkbean, Dumfries
Perth & Kinross	NEW Torwood House, St Mary's Road, Birnam
Perth & Kinross	Ardvorlich, Lochearnhead
Stirlingshire	Shrubhill, Dunblane
Wigtownshire	Logan Botanic Garden, Port Logan, by Stranraer
Wigtownshire	Woodfall Gardens, Glasserton

Monday 19 May

Perth & Kinross	Ardvorlich, Lochearnhead

Tuesday 20 May

East Lothian	Shepherd House, Inveresk, Musselburgh
Perth & Kinross	Ardvorlich, Lochearnhead

Wednesday 21 May

Argyll & Lochaber	Ardchattan Priory, North Connel
East Lothian	Stobshiel House, Humbie
Edinburgh, Midlothian & West Lothian	Newliston, Kirkliston
Peeblesshire & Tweeddale	Haystoun, Peebles
Peeblesshire & Tweeddale	Kirkton Manor House, Peebles
Perth & Kinross	Ardvorlich, Lochearnhead
Perth & Kinross	Dowhill, Cleish

Thursday 22 May

Angus, Dundee & Kincardineshire South	Inchmill Cottage, Glenprosen, near Kirriemuir
East Lothian	Shepherd House, Inveresk, Musselburgh
Edinburgh, Midlothian & West Lothian	Newliston, Kirkliston
Perth & Kinross	Ardvorlich, Lochearnhead

Friday 23 May

Aberdeenshire	Glenkindie House, Glenkindie, Alford
Edinburgh, Midlothian & West Lothian	Newliston, Kirkliston
Perth & Kinross	Ardvorlich, Lochearnhead

Saturday 24 May

Angus, Dundee & Kincardineshire South	Angus Plant Sale, Pitmuies Gardens, Guthrie, by Forfar
Argyll & Lochaber	Inveryne Woodland Garden, Kilfinan, Tighnabruaich
Dumfriesshire	Tinnisburn Plants, Upper Millsteads, Canonbie
Edinburgh, Midlothian & West Lothian	Newliston, Kirkliston
Fife	The Garden with the Dragon, 2, Upper Wellheads, Limekilns
Perth & Kinross	Ardvorlich, Lochearnhead

Sunday 25 May

Angus, Dundee & Kincardineshire South	NEW Craigellie House Gardens, Alyth
Argyll & Lochaber	Inveryne Woodland Garden, Kilfinan, Tighnabruaich
Dumfriesshire	Tinnisburn Plants, Upper Millsteads, Canonbie
Dumfriesshire	Westerhall, Bentpath, Langholm
Edinburgh, Midlothian & West Lothian	Newliston, Kirkliston
Fife	Earlshall Castle, Leuchars
Fife	Kirklands, Saline
Fife	Lindores House, by Newburgh
Fife	Swallows Rest, Lindores
Inverness, Ross, Cromarty & Skye	Old Allangrange, Munlochy
Kirkcudbrightshire	Corsock House, Corsock, Castle Douglas

Sunday 25 May *continued*

Perth & Kinross	NEW Tigh-na-Beithe, Birnam Glen, Birnam, Dunkeld
Perth & Kinross	Ardvorlich, Lochearnhead
Renfrewshire	NEW Gardens House, Houston Renfrewshire
Stirlingshire	Kilbryde Castle, Dunblane

Monday 26 May

Argyll & Lochaber	NEW 4 Port Ann, Lochgilphead, Argyll
Perth & Kinross	Ardvorlich, Lochearnhead

Tuesday 27 May

Argyll & Lochaber	NEW 4 Port Ann, Lochgilphead, Argyll
East Lothian	Shepherd House, Inveresk, Musselburgh
Perth & Kinross	Ardvorlich, Lochearnhead

Wednesday 28 May

Argyll & Lochaber	Ardchattan Priory, North Connel
East Lothian	Stobshiel House, Humbie
Edinburgh, Midlothian & West Lothian	Newliston, Kirkliston
Peeblesshire & Tweeddale	Haystoun, Peebles
Peeblesshire & Tweeddale	Kirkton Manor House, Peebles
Peeblesshire & Tweeddale	Laidlawstiel House, Clovenfords, Galashiels
Perth & Kinross	Ardvorlich, Lochearnhead
Perth & Kinross	Dowhill, Cleish

Thursday 29 May

East Lothian	Shepherd House, Inveresk, Musselburgh
Edinburgh, Midlothian & West Lothian	Newliston, Kirkliston
Peeblesshire & Tweeddale	Laidlawstiel House, Clovenfords, Galashiels
Perth & Kinross	Ardvorlich, Lochearnhead

Friday 30 May

Edinburgh, Midlothian & West Lothian	Newliston, Kirkliston
Perth & Kinross	Ardvorlich, Lochearnhead

Saturday 31 May

Aberdeenshire	NEW Elvanrock, Watson Street, Banchory
Angus, Dundee & Kincardineshire South	Hospitalfield Gardens, Hospitalfield House, Westway, Arbroath
Angus, Dundee & Kincardineshire South	Westgate, 12 Glamis Drive, Dundee
Ayrshire & Arran	River Garden, The Restoration of Auchincruive, The Bothy Office
Berwickshire & Roxburghshire	Mellerstain, Mellerstain House and Gardens, Gordon
East Lothian	A Blackbird Sings, 20 Kings Park, Longniddry
Edinburgh, Midlothian & West Lothian	Newliston, Kirkliston
Fife	The Garden with the Dragon, 2, Upper Wellheads, Limekilns
Inverness, Ross, Cromarty & Skye	Dundonnell House, Little Loch Broom, Wester Ross
Inverness, Ross, Cromarty & Skye	Struanbridge, Essich Road, Inverness
Peeblesshire & Tweeddale	Beechwood, Broughton, Peeblesshire
Perth & Kinross	Ardvorlich, Lochearnhead
Perth & Kinross	Bonhard House, Perth
Perth & Kinross	Muckhart Open Gardens, Coronation Hall, Pool of Muckhart, Dollar

JUNE

Sunday 1 June

Aberdeenshire	NEW Elvanrock, Watson Street, Banchory
Angus, Dundee & Kincardineshire South	Westgate, 12 Glamis Drive, Dundee
Argyll & Lochaber	Ardverikie with Aberarder, Kinloch Laggan, Newtonmore
Ayrshire & Arran	River Garden, The Restoration of Auchincruive, The Bothy Office
Berwickshire & Roxburghshire	West Leas, near Bonchester Bridge
Dumfriesshire	Cowhill Tower, Holywood
Dunbartonshire	Geilston Garden, Main Road, Cardross
Edinburgh, Midlothian & West Lothian	14 East Brighton Crescent, Portobello, Edinburgh
Edinburgh, Midlothian & West Lothian	Newliston, Kirkliston
Kirkcudbrightshire	Brooklands, Crocketford

Peeblesshire & Tweeddale	Beechwood, Broughton, Peeblesshire
Peeblesshire & Tweeddale	Quercus Garden Plants, Whitmuir Farm, West Linton
Peeblesshire & Tweeddale	Stobo Japanese Water Garden, Stobo Farm, Stobo
Perth & Kinross	Bonhard House, Perth
Perth & Kinross	Muckhart Open Gardens, Coronation Hall, Pool of Muckhart, Dollar
Stirlingshire	Thorntree, Arnprior
Wigtownshire	Damnaglaur House, Drummore, Stranraer

Tuesday 3 June

East Lothian	Shepherd House, Inveresk, Musselburgh

Wednesday 4 June

Argyll & Lochaber	Ardchattan Priory, North Connel
East Lothian	Stobshiel House, Humbie
Edinburgh, Midlothian & West Lothian	Newliston, Kirkliston
Peeblesshire & Tweeddale	Kirkton Manor House, Peebles
Peeblesshire & Tweeddale	The Potting Shed, Broughton Place, Broughton, Biggar
Perth & Kinross	Dowhill, Cleish

Thursday 5 June

East Lothian	Shepherd House, Inveresk, Musselburgh
Perth & Kinross	Bradystone House, Murthly

Friday 6 June

Perth & Kinross	Mouse Cottage, Strathtay, Pitlochry

Saturday 7 June

Ayrshire & Arran	River Garden, The Restoration of Auchincruive, The Bothy Office
Edinburgh, Midlothian & West Lothian	NEW Oatridge College Campus - SRUC, Ecclesmachan, Broxburn
Edinburgh, Midlothian & West Lothian	Redcroft, 23 Murrayfield Road, Edinburgh
Fife	Willowhill, Forgan, Newport-on-Tay
Moray & Nairn	Easter Laggan, Dulnain Bridge, Grantown-on-Spey
Perth & Kinross	Cloan, by Auchterarder
Perth & Kinross	Mouse Cottage, Strathtay, Pitlochry

Sunday 8 June

Aberdeenshire	Norton House, 1 North Deeside Road, Kincardine O'Neil, Aboyne
Angus, Dundee & Kincardineshire South	Arbuthnott House Gardens, Arbuthnott House, Laurencekirk
Argyll & Lochaber	NEW Ilha de Deus, Tiroran, Isle of Mull
Argyll & Lochaber	Ardchattan Priory, North Connel
Ayrshire & Arran	River Garden, The Restoration of Auchincruive, The Bothy Office
Caithness, Sutherland, Orkney & Shetland	NEW Laura's Wood, Hools, St. Margaret's Hope, Orkney
Caithness, Sutherland, Orkney & Shetland	Westlea, Cromarty Square, St. Margaret's Hope, Orkney
Dumfriesshire	Capenoch, Penpont, Thornhill
East Lothian	Belhaven House with Belhaven Hill School, Belhaven Road, Dunbar
Edinburgh, Midlothian & West Lothian	Dean Gardens, Edinburgh
Edinburgh, Midlothian & West Lothian	Maggie's Edinburgh, Western General Hospital, Crewe Road, Edinburgh
Fife	Coul House, Coul House, Maree Way, Glenrothes
Glasgow & District	NEW Elsewhere Garden, QEUH, Govan Road, Glasgow
Kirkcudbrightshire	The Limes, Kirkcudbright
Perth & Kinross	36 Muirfield, Perth
Perth & Kinross	Cloan, by Auchterarder
Perth & Kinross	Mill of Forneth, Forneth, Blairgowrie
Renfrewshire	The Bishop's House, Glencairn Road, Kilmacolm

Monday 9 June

Fife	Willowhill, Forgan, Newport-on-Tay

Tuesday 10 June

East Lothian	Shepherd House, Inveresk, Musselburgh

Wednesday 11 June

Argyll & Lochaber	Ardchattan Priory, North Connel
East Lothian	Humbie Dean, Humbie
East Lothian	Longwood, Humbie
East Lothian	Stobshiel House, Humbie
Peeblesshire & Tweeddale	Kirkton Manor House, Peebles
Peeblesshire & Tweeddale	The Potting Shed, Broughton Place, Broughton, Biggar
Perth & Kinross	Dowhill, Cleish

Thursday 12 June

Angus, Dundee & Kincardineshire South	Inchmill Cottage, Glenprosen, near Kirriemuir
East Lothian	Shepherd House, Inveresk, Musselburgh
Perth & Kinross	Bradystone House, Murthly

Saturday 14 June

Aberdeenshire	Two Gardens in Banchory Devenick, Banchory Devenick
Ayrshire & Arran	Barrmill Community Garden, Barrmill Park and Gardens
East Lothian	A Blackbird Sings, 20 Kings Park, Longniddry
East Lothian	Greywalls, Gullane
East Lothian	Gullane House, Sandy Loan, Gullane
Edinburgh, Midlothian & West Lothian	Rivaldsgreen House, 48 Friars Brae, Linlithgow
Fife	Willowhill, Forgan, Newport-on-Tay
Perth & Kinross	Blair Castle Gardens, Blair Atholl

Sunday 15 June

Aberdeenshire	Two Gardens in Banchory Devenick, Banchory Devenick
Angus, Dundee & Kincardineshire South	Edzell Village Gardens, Edzell
East Lothian	Greywalls, Gullane
East Lothian	Gullane House, Sandy Loan, Gullane
Edinburgh, Midlothian & West Lothian	5 Greenbank Crescent, Edinburgh
Edinburgh, Midlothian & West Lothian	NEW Learmonth Place Garden, 9 Learmonth Place
Glasgow & District	NEW Maggie's, Gartnavel Hospital 1053 Great Western Road Glasgow
Inverness, Ross, Cromarty & Skye	Glenkyllachy, Tomatin
Perth & Kinross	NEW An Caorann, Abernethy, Perthshire
Stirlingshire	Gartmore Village, Main Street, Gartmore
Wigtownshire	Woodfall Gardens, Glasserton

Monday 16 June

Fife	Willowhill, Forgan, Newport-on-Tay

Tuesday 17 June

East Lothian	Shepherd House, Inveresk, Musselburgh

Wednesday 18 June

Argyll & Lochaber	Ardchattan Priory, North Connel
East Lothian	Stobshiel House, Humbie
Fife	Teasses Gardens, near Ceres
Peeblesshire & Tweeddale	Kirkton Manor House, Peebles
Perth & Kinross	Dowhill, Cleish

Thursday 19 June

East Lothian	Shepherd House, Inveresk, Musselburgh
Perth & Kinross	Bradystone House, Murthly

Saturday 21 June

Angus, Dundee & Kincardineshire South	Gardyne Castle, by Forfar
Caithness, Sutherland, Orkney & Shetland	NEW Waulkmill Garden, Sandygill, Waulkmill, Orkney
Peeblesshire & Tweeddale	Beechwood, Broughton, Peeblesshire

Sunday 22 June

Aberdeenshire	Altries, Maryculter, Aberdeenshire
Angus, Dundee & Kincardineshire South	Brechin Gardens in June, Locations across Brechin
Angus, Dundee & Kincardineshire South	Estir Bogside, Alyth
East Lothian	Gifford Village with Gifford Bank and Broadwoodside, Gifford

Edinburgh, Midlothian & West Lothian	NEW Rosemount, 12 Hillhead, Bonnyrigg
Edinburgh, Midlothian & West Lothian	Claremont, Redmill
Edinburgh, Midlothian & West Lothian	Stockbridge Open Gardens, Garden trail runs between
	Logie Green Gardens and Royal Circus Gardens North
Inverness, Ross, Cromarty & Skye	House of Aigas and Field Centre, by Beauly
Peeblesshire & Tweeddale	Beechwood, Broughton, Peeblesshire

Tuesday 24 June

East Lothian	Shepherd House, Inveresk, Musselburgh

Wednesday 25 June

Argyll & Lochaber	Ardchattan Priory, North Connel
East Lothian	Stobshiel House, Humbie
Peeblesshire & Tweeddale	Kirkton Manor House, Peebles
Peeblesshire & Tweeddale	The Potting Shed, Broughton Place, Broughton, Biggar
Perth & Kinross	Dowhill, Cleish

Thursday 26 June

East Lothian	Shepherd House, Inveresk, Musselburgh
Perth & Kinross	Bradystone House, Murthly

Saturday 28 June

Berwickshire & Roxburghshire	NEW Morebattle Mains, Morebattle, Kelso
Caithness, Sutherland, Orkney & Shetland	NEW Mill House, Lyness, Hoy, Orkney
Inverness, Ross, Cromarty & Skye	Struanbridge, Essich Road, Inverness
Moray & Nairn	Lindisfarne, Knockando
Peeblesshire & Tweeddale	Portmore, Eddleston
Perth & Kinross	NEW Tarmangie, Glendevon, Dollar

Sunday 29 June

Aberdeenshire	Finzean House, Finzean, Banchory
Angus, Dundee & Kincardineshire South	NEW Dorward House, 24 Dorward Road, Montrose
Angus, Dundee & Kincardineshire South	The Doocot, Kinloch, Meigle, Blairgowrie
Berwickshire & Roxburghshire	NEW Morebattle Mains, Morebattle, Kelso
East Lothian	Tyninghame House and The Walled Garden,
	Tyninghame House, Dunbar
Edinburgh, Midlothian & West Lothian	Whitehouse & Grange Bowling Club,
	18a Hope Terrace, Edinburgh
Fife	Earlshall Castle, Leuchars
Fife	Kirkbrae House, Culross
Fife	Newburgh - Hidden Gardens, Newburgh
Inverness, Ross, Cromarty & Skye	7 Braes of Conon, Conon Bridge
Kirkcudbrightshire	Southwick House, Southwick
Perth & Kinross	NEW Tarmangie, Glendevon, Dollar
Renfrewshire	Wraes, Corseliehill Road, nr Houston

JULY

Tuesday 1 July

Ayrshire & Arran	Dougarie, Isle of Arran
East Lothian	Shepherd House, Inveresk, Musselburgh

Wednesday 2 July

Argyll & Lochaber	Ardchattan Priory, North Connel
East Lothian	Stobshiel House, Humbie
Peeblesshire & Tweeddale	Kirkton Manor House, Peebles
Peeblesshire & Tweeddale	Portmore, Eddleston
Peeblesshire & Tweeddale	The Potting Shed, Broughton Place, Broughton, Biggar

Thursday 3 July

East Lothian	Shepherd House, Inveresk, Musselburgh
Perth & Kinross	Bradystone House, Murthly

Friday 4 July

Berwickshire & Roxburghshire	NEW The Walled Garden at the Hugo Burge Foundation, Duns

Saturday 5 July

Angus, Dundee & Kincardineshire South   NEW Ashbrook Nursery and Garden Centre, Forfar Road, Arbroath

Angus, Dundee & Kincardineshire South   NEW St Bedes and Ashludie Wildflower Garden, Monifieth
Caithness, Sutherland, Orkney & Shetland   Round House, Berstane Road, Kirkwall, Orkney
East Lothian   Papple Steading, Papple, Haddington
Fife   Crail: Gardens in the Burgh, Crail
Fife   Willowhill, Forgan, Newport-on-Tay
Moray & Nairn   Haugh Garden, College of Roseisle
Perth & Kinross   NEW 17 Strathallan Bank, Forgandenny, Perth
Perth & Kinross   Bonhard House, Perth

Sunday 6 July

Aberdeenshire   Bruckhills Croft, Rothienorman, Inverurie
Angus, Dundee & Kincardineshire South   NEW St Bedes and Ashludie Wildflower Garden, Monifieth
Argyll & Lochaber   NEW Ilha de Deus, Tiroran, Isle of Mull
Caithness, Sutherland, Orkney & Shetland   Hattamoa, Rendall, Orkney
Caithness, Sutherland, Orkney & Shetland   Kierfiold House, Sandwick, Orkney
East Lothian   Papple Steading, Papple, Haddington
Edinburgh, Midlothian & West Loth an   77 Kirk Brae, Edinburgh
Fife   Crail: Gardens in the Burgh, Crail
Moray & Nairn   Glebe House, Main Street, Urquhart
Moray & Nairn   Haugh Garden, College of Roseisle
Perth & Kinross   Bonhard House, Perth

Monday 7 July

Fife   Willowhill, Forgan, Newport-on-Tay

Tuesday 8 July

East Lothian   Shepherd House, Inveresk, Musselburgh

Wednesday 9 July

Argyll & Lochaber   Ardchattan Priory, North Connel
East Lothian   Humbie Dean, Humbie
East Lothian   Stobshiel House, Humbie
Peeblesshire & Tweeddale   Kirkton Manor House, Peebles
Peeblesshire & Tweeddale   Portmore, Eddleston

Thursday 10 July

Angus, Dundee & Kincardineshire South   Inchmill Cottage, Glenprosen, near Kirriemuir
East Lothian   Shepherd House, Inveresk, Musselburgh
Perth & Kinross   Bradystone House, Murthly

Friday 11 July

Berwickshire & Roxburghshire   NEW The Walled Garden at the Hugo Burge Foundation, Duns

Saturday 12 July

Aberdeenshire   Parkvilla, 47 Schoolhill, Ellon
Angus, Dundee & Kincardineshire South   Balhary Walled Garden, Balhary, Alyth, Blairgowrie
Argyll & Lochaber   NEW Kilchoan Gardens, Kilmelford
Caithness, Sutherland, Orkney & Shetland   Amat, Amat Lodge, Ardgay
Fife   Blanerne, West Road, Charlestown
Fife   Willowhill, Forgan, Newport-on-Tay
Perth & Kinross   NEW 17 Strathallan Bank, Forgandenny, Perth
Perth & Kinross   The Bield at Blackruthven, Blackruthven House, Tibbermore
Renfrewshire   SGS Kilmacolm Plant Sale, Outside Kilmacolm Library, Kilmacolm

Sunday 13 July

Aberdeenshire   Douneside House, Tarland
Angus, Dundee & Kincardineshire South   Gallery, Gallery House, Montrose
Argyll & Lochaber   NEW Kilchoan Gardens, Kilmelford
Caithness, Sutherland, Orkney & Shetland   Amat, Amat Lodge, Ardgay
Fife   Balcarres, Colinsburgh
Fife   Blanerne, West Road, Charlestown
Glasgow & District   SWG3 Community Garden, 100 Eastvale Place, Glasgow
Inverness, Ross, Cromarty & Skye   Kiltarlity Gardens, Kiltarlity, Beauly

Kirkcudbrightshire	Dalbeattie Community Allotments Association, Port Road, Dalbeattie
Lanarkshire	NEW Lanark Town Gardens, Waterloo Road. Lanark
Peeblesshire & Tweeddale	Carolside, Earlston
Stirlingshire	Oakmore, Blairhoyle, Port of Menteith, Stirling

Monday 14 July

| Fife | Willowhill, Forgan, Newport-on-Tay |

Tuesday 15 July

| East Lothian | Shepherd House, Inveresk, Musselburgh |

Wednesday 16 July

Argyll & Lochaber	Ardchattan Priory, North Connel
East Lothian	Stobshiel House, Humbie
Peeblesshire & Tweeddale	Kirkton Manor House, Peebles
Peeblesshire & Tweeddale	Portmore, Eddleston

Thursday 17 July

| East Lothian | Shepherd House, Inveresk, Musselburgh |
| Perth & Kinross | Bradystone House, Murthly |

Friday 18 July

| Berwickshire & Roxburghshire | NEW The Walled Garden at the Hugo Burge Foundation, Duns |

Saturday 19 July

Angus, Dundee & Kincardineshire South	NEW Kinnordy Walled Garden, Kinnordy House, Kirriemuir, Angus
Ayrshire & Arran	NEW Beith Community Gardens, Beith Community Centre, Kings Road
East Lothian	A Blackbird Sings, 20 Kings Park, Longniddry
East Lothian	Amisfield Walled Garden, Haddington
Fife	Willowhill, Forgan, Newport-on-Tay

Sunday 20 July

Aberdeenshire	Tarland Community Garden, Tarland, Aboyne
Angus, Dundee & Kincardineshire South	NEW Airlie Castle Gardens, Airlie Castle, Airlie, By Kirriemuir, Angus
Berwickshire & Roxburghshire	Duns Open Gardens , Volunteer Hall, Langtongate, Duns
Caithness, Sutherland, Orkney & Shetland	Kierfiold House, Kierfiold House, Sandwick, Orkney
East Lothian	Amisfield Walled Garden, Haddington
Edinburgh, Midlothian & West Lothian	NEW Bridgend Farmhouse Comm. Allotments, 41 Old Dalkeith Road
Edinburgh, Midlothian & West Lothian	Claremont, Redmill
Fife	NEW Wester Craigfoodie, Dairsie
Fife	Kirkbrae House, Culross
Kirkcudbrightshire	Kings Grange House, Castle Douglas
Peeblesshire & Tweeddale	Kailzie Gardens, Peebles
Renfrewshire	NEW Lochwinnoch Road Gardens, Kilmacolm, Kilmacolm
Wigtownshire	Woodfall Gardens, Glasserton

Monday 21 July

| Fife | Willowhill, Forgan, Newport-on-Tay |

Tuesday 22 July

| East Lothian | Shepherd House, Inveresk, Musselburgh |

Wednesday 23 July

Argyll & Lochaber	Ardchattan Priory, North Connel
East Lothian	Stobshiel House, Humbie
Peeblesshire & Tweeddale	Portmore, Eddleston

Thursday 24 July

| East Lothian | Shepherd House, Inveresk, Musselburgh |
| Perth & Kinross | Bradystone House, Murthly |

Friday 25 July

| Berwickshire & Roxburghshire | NEW The Walled Garden at the Hugo Burge Foundation, Duns |

Saturday 26 July

Angus, Dundee & Kincardineshire South	Milton of Finavon House, Forfar
Ayrshire & Arran	The Pines, Southwood Road, Troon
Caithness, Sutherland, Orkney & Shetland	16 Mulla, Voe, Shetland
Caithness, Sutherland, Orkney & Shetland	Skelbo House, Skelbo, Dornoch
Fife	Willowhill, Forgan, Newport-on-Tay
Inverness, Ross, Cromarty & Skye	Struanbridge, Essich Road, Inverness
Moray & Nairn	NEW Earth House Apothecary Gardens, Pityoulish House, Pityoulish

Sunday 27 July

Angus, Dundee & Kincardineshire South	NEW 15 Fairfield Road, Broughty Ferry, Dundee
Ayrshire & Arran	The Pines, Southwood Road, Troon
Caithness, Sutherland, Orkney & Shetland	16 Mulla, Voe, Shetland
Caithness, Sutherland, Orkney & Shetland	Langwell, Berriedale
Caithness, Sutherland, Orkney & Shetland	Skelbo House, Skelbo, Dornoch
Caithness, Sutherland, Orkney & Shetland	The Quoy of Houton, Orphir, Orkney
Edinburgh, Midlothian & West Lothian	Craigentinny Telferton Allotments, Telferton Road, off Portobello Road
Fife	Pitlochie House, Gateside
Inverness, Ross, Cromarty & Skye	House of Aigas and Field Centre, by Beauly
Lanarkshire	Covington Mill Farmhouse, Covington Road, Thankerton, Biggar
Peeblesshire & Tweeddale	West Linton Village Gardens, West Linton
Stirlingshire	Mollan, Thornhill, Stirling

Monday 28 July

Fife	Willowhill, Forgan, Newport-on-Tay

Tuesday 29 July

East Lothian	Shepherd House, Inveresk, Musselburgh
Perth & Kinross	Tomandroighne, Edradynate, Aberfeldy

Wednesday 30 July

Argyll & Lochaber	Ardchattan Priory, North Connel
East Lothian	Stobshiel House, Humbie
Peeblesshire & Tweeddale	Portmore, Eddleston

Thursday 31 July

East Lothian	Shepherd House, Inveresk, Musselburgh
Perth & Kinross	Bradystone House, Murthly

AUGUST

Friday 1 August

Berwickshire & Roxburghshire	NEW The Walled Garden at the Hugo Burge Foundation, Duns

Saturday 2 August

Argyll & Lochaber	NEW 4 Port Ann, Lochgilphead, Argyll
Edinburgh, Midlothian & West Lothian	39 Nantwich Drive, Edinburgh
Edinburgh, Midlothian & West Lothian	Silverburn Village, 23 Biggar Road, Silverburn
Fife	Willowhill, Forgan, Newport-on-Tay
Wigtownshire	Amulree, 8 Mill Street, Drummore, Stranraer

Sunday 3 August

Angus, Dundee & Kincardineshire South	Glenbervie House, Drumlithie, Stonehaven
Argyll & Lochaber	NEW 4 Port Ann, Lochgilphead, Argyll
Argyll & Lochaber	NEW Ilha de Deus, Tiroran, Isle of Mull
Berwickshire & Roxburghshire	West Leas, near Bonchester Bridge
Caithness, Sutherland, Orkney & Shetland	Hattamoa, Rendall, Orkney
Dumfriesshire	NEW Byreburnfoot House, Byreburnfoot
Edinburgh, Midlothian & West Lothian	39 Nantwich Drive, Edinburgh
Edinburgh, Midlothian & West Lothian	Hunter's Tryst, 95 Oxgangs Road, Edinburgh
Inverness, Ross, Cromarty & Skye	2 Durnamuck, Little Loch Broom, Wester Ross
Inverness, Ross, Cromarty & Skye	Old Allangrange, Munlochy
Moray & Nairn	Naturally Useful, Marcassie Farm, Rafford, Forres
Perth & Kinross	Drummond Castle Gardens, Muthill, Crieff
Wigtownshire	Amulree, 8 Mill Street, Drummore, Stranraer

Monday 4 August

Argyll & Lochaber	NEW 4 Port Ann, Lochgilphead, Argyll
Fife	Willowhill, Forgan, Newport-on-Tay

Wednesday 6 August

Argyll & Lochaber	Ardchattan Priory, North Connel
Berwickshire & Roxburghshire	Larch House, Clerklands, Near Lilliesleaf
East Lothian	Stobshiel House, Humbie
Peeblesshire & Tweeddale	Portmore, Eddleston

Thursday 7 August

Perth & Kinross	Bradystone House, Murthly

Friday 8 August

Berwickshire & Roxburghshire	NEW The Walled Garden at the Hugo Burge Foundation, Duns

Saturday 9 August

Angus, Dundee & Kincardineshire South	Cotton of Craig, Kilry, Blairgowrie
East Lothian	The Gardens at Archerfield Walled Garden, Archerfield Estate, Dirleton
Fife	Willowhill, Forgan, Newport-on-Tay
Lanarkshire	NEW New Lanark Roof Garden, Mill 2, New Lanark World Heritage Site

Sunday 10 August

Aberdeenshire	Heatherwick Farm, Kintore, Inverurie
Angus, Dundee & Kincardineshire South	Cotton of Craig, Kilry, Blairgowrie
Dumfriesshire	Dalswinton Mill, Dalswinton
Glasgow & District	NEW The Milton of Campsie Community Garden, Antermony Road
Lanarkshire	NEW New Lanark Roof Garden, Mill 2, New Lanark World Heritage Site
Perth & Kinross	Cloan, by Auchterarder
Renfrewshire	North Newton Farm, Kilmacolm
Stirlingshire	Braehead Community Garden, Broom Road, Braehead
Wigtownshire	Fernlea Garden, Corvisel Road, Newton Stewart

Monday 11 August

Fife	Willowhill, Forgan, Newport-on-Tay

Wednesday 13 August

Argyll & Lochaber	Ardchattan Priory, North Connel
Berwickshire & Roxburghshire	Larch House, Clerklands, Near Lilliesleaf
East Lothian	Stobshiel House, Humbie
Peeblesshire & Tweeddale	Portmore, Eddleston

Thursday 14 August

Angus, Dundee & Kincardineshire South	Inchmill Cottage, Glenprosen, near Kirriemuir
Perth & Kinross	Bradystone House, Murthly

Friday 15 August

Berwickshire & Roxburghshire	NEW The Walled Garden at the Hugo Burge Foundation, Duns

Saturday 16 August

East Lothian	A Blackbird Sings, 20 Kings Park, Longniddry
Fife	Blanerne, West Road, Charlestown
Fife	Willowhill, Forgan, Newport-on-Tay
Lanarkshire	Stobwood Cottage Garden, Stobwood, Forth, South Lanarkshire

Sunday 17 August

Angus, Dundee & Kincardineshire South	Glensaugh, Glensaugh Lodge, Fettercairn, Laurencekirk
Dunbartonshire	Glenarn Plant Sale, Glenarn Road, Rhu, Helensburgh
Fife	Coul House, Coul House, Maree Way, Glenrothes
Fife	Kirklands, Saline
Glasgow & District	NEW Grow Cook Inspire, 125 Ormonde Avenue, Netherlee, Glasgow
Lanarkshire	Stobwood Cottage Garden, Stobwood, Forth, South Lanarkshire
Stirlingshire	Bannockburn House Gardens, Stirling

Monday 18 August
Fife   Willowhill, Forgan, Newport-on-Tay

Wednesday 20 August
Argyll & Lochaber   Ardchattan Priory, North Connel
Berwickshire & Roxburghshire   Larch House, Clerklands, Near Lilliesleaf
East Lothian   Stobshiel House, Humbie
Peeblesshire & Tweeddale   Portmore, Eddleston

Thursday 21 August
Inverness, Ross, Cromarty & Skye   Dundonnell House, Little Loch Broom, Wester Ross
Perth & Kinross   Bradystone House, Murthly

Friday 22 August
Berwickshire & Roxburghshire   NEW The Walled Garden at the Hugo Burge Foundation, Duns

Saturday 23 August
Angus, Dundee & Kincardineshire South   Balhary Walled Garden, Balhary, Alyth, Blairgowrie
Fife   Willowhill, Forgan, Newport-on-Tay

Sunday 24 August
Berwickshire & Roxburghshire   NEW Old Melrose, near Melrose
Edinburgh, Midlothian & West Lothian   Whitburgh House Walled Garden, Pathhead, Midlothian
Fife   Kirkbrae House, Culross
Peeblesshire & Tweeddale   NEW Diadan, Madrissa Farm, Lamancha
Peeblesshire & Tweeddale   Quercus Garden Plants, Whitmuir Farm, West Linton

Monday 25 August
Fife   Willowhill, Forgan, Newport-on-Tay

Tuesday 26 August
Edinburgh, Midlothian & West Lothian   Whitburgh House Walled Garden, Pathhead, Midlothian
Lanarkshire   Little Sparta, Stonypath, Dunsyre

Wednesday 27 August
Argyll & Lochaber   Ardchattan Priory, North Connel
Berwickshire & Roxburghshire   Larch House, Clerklands, Near Lilliesleaf
East Lothian   Humbie Dean, Humbie
East Lothian   Stobshiel House, Humbie
Peeblesshire & Tweeddale   Portmore, Eddleston

Thursday 28 August
Perth & Kinross   Bradystone House, Murthly

Friday 29 August
Aberdeenshire   Glenkindie House, Glenkindie, Alford
Berwickshire & Roxburghshire   NEW The Walled Garden at the Hugo Burge Foundation, Duns

Saturday 30 August
Angus, Dundee & Kincardineshire South   Carnoustie's Tropical Garden, 28 Prosen Bank, Carnoustie
Edinburgh, Midlothian & West Lothian   NEW Quinn Garden, 41 Morningside Drive, Edinburgh
Fife   Willowhill, Forgan, Newport-on-Tay
Inverness, Ross, Cromarty & Skye   Struanbridge, Essich Road, Inverness

Sunday 31 August
Glasgow & District   Horatio's Garden, National Spinal Unit, QEUH Hospital, Govan Road

Kirkcudbrightshire   3 Millhall, Shore Road, Kirkcudbright

SEPTEMBER

Tuesday 2 September
Lanarkshire   Little Sparta, Stonypath, Dunsyre

Wednesday 3 September
Argyll & Lochaber   Ardchattan Priory, North Connel
East Lothian   Stobshiel House, Humbie

Thursday 4 September

Angus, Dundee & Kincardineshire South   Inchmill Cottage, Glenprosen, near Kirriemuir
Perth & Kinross   Bradystone House, Murthly

Friday 5 September

Fife   Greenhead Farmhouse, Greenhead of Arnot, Leslie

Saturday 6 September

Berwickshire & Roxburghshire   Corbet Tower, Morebattle, near Kelso
East Lothian   A Blackbird Sings, 20 Kings Park, Longniddry

Sunday 7 September

East Lothian   Fairnielaw, Athelstaneford, North Berwick

Wednesday 10 September

Argyll & Lochaber   Ardchattan Priory, North Connel
East Lothian   Stobshiel House, Humbie

Thursday 11 September

Perth & Kinross   Bradystone House, Murthly

Wednesday 17 September

Argyll & Lochaber   Ardchattan Priory, North Connel
East Lothian   Stobshiel House, Humbie

Saturday 20 September

Argyll & Lochaber   NEW Cruachan Lodge, North Connel, Oban

Sunday 21 September

Argyll & Lochaber   NEW Cruachan Lodge, North Connel, Oban
Fife   Kirkbrae House, Culross

Wednesday 24 September

Argyll & Lochaber   Ardchattan Priory, North Connel
East Lothian   Stobshiel House, Humbie

Saturday 27 September

Inverness, Ross, Cromarty & Skye   Struanbridge, Essich Road, Inverness

Sunday 28 September

Argyll & Lochaber   Benmore Botanic Garden, Benmore, Dunoon
Fife   Fife Plant Sale at St Andrews Botanic Garden, St Andrews
Kirkcudbrightshire   Cally Biodiversity Gardens, Cally Avenue, Gatehouse of Fleet

OCTOBER

Wednesday 1 October

Argyll & Lochaber   Ardchattan Priory, North Connel

Sunday 5 October

Peeblesshire & Tweeddale   Dawyck Botanic Garden, Stobo

Wednesday 8 October

Argyll & Lochaber   Ardchattan Priory, North Connel

Saturday & Sunday 11/12 October

Angus, Dundee & Kincardineshire South   Westgate, 12 Glamis Drive, Dundee

Wednesday 15 October

Argyll & Lochaber   Ardchattan Priory, North Connel

Wednesday 22 October

Argyll & Lochaber   Ardchattan Priory, North Connel

Saturday 25 October

Berwickshire & Roxburghshire   Mellerstain, Mellerstain House and Gardens, Gordon

Wednesday 29 October

Argyll & Lochaber   Ardchattan Priory, North Connel

Index of Gardens

1 Burnton Road   86
2 Durnamuck   187
2 Panmure Terrace   48
2 Strathview   187
3 Millhall   201
4 Port Ann   69
5 Greenbank Crescent   144
5 Knott   188
7 Braes of Conon   189
10 Pilmuir Road West   218
14 East Brighton Crescent   143
15 Fairfield Road   47
16 Mulla   106
17a Menzieshill Road   47
17 Strathallan Bank   237
18 Duchess Park with Westburn   124
36 Muirfield   237
39 Nantwich Drive   143
46 South Street   159
48 Rumblingwell   159
77 Kirk Brae   144
101 Greenbank Crescent   143

A

Abbotsford   226
A Blackbird Sings   131
Abriachan Garden Nursery   189
Achnacloich   69
Airlie Castle Gardens   48
Altries   35
Amat   106
Amisfield Walled Garden   131
Amulree   270
An Cala   70
An Caorann   238
Angus Plant Sale   49
Angus's Garden, Barguillean   71
Arbigland House   202
Arbuthnott House Gardens   49
Ardchattan Manse   71
Ardchattan Priory   72
Ardkinglas Woodland Garden   72
Ardmaddy Castle   73
Ardno   74
Ardtornish   74
Ardverikie with Aberarder   75

Ardvorlich   238
Arndean   262
Ascog Hall Garden and Fernery   75
Ashbrook Nursery and Garden Centre   50
Attadale   189
Auchmacoy   35
Auldbyres Farm Garden   87

B

Balcarres   160
Balhary Walled Garden   50
Balmeanach House   190
Bannockburn House Gardens   262
Baravalla Garden   76
Barholm Castle   202
Barlockhart Lodge   270
Barochreal   76
Barrmill Community Garden   87
Beech Cottage   238
Beechwood   226
Beith Community Gardens   88
Belgrave Crescent Gardens   144
Belhaven House with   132
Belhaven Hill School
Benmore Botanic Garden   77
Berandhu   77
Berryfield House   190
Blackdykes Garden   133
Blair Castle & Estate   88
Blair Castle Gardens   239
Blanerne   160
Bonhard House   239
Braco Castle   240
Bradystone House   241
Braehead Community Garden   263
Brechin Castle   51
Brechin Gardens in June   52
Bridgend Farmhouse   145
Community Allotments
Brooklands   203
Broomhill Villa   96
Bruckhills Croft   36
Bughtrig   96
Burgie Arboretum   218
Burnside   89
Byreburnfoot House   116

C

Cally Biodiversity Gardens 203
Cambo Gardens 161
Capenoch 117
Caprington Castle 89
Carig Dhubh 241
Carnoustie's Tropical Garden 53
Carolside 227
Chaplains' Court 36
Charleston Forest Garden 53
Claremont 145
Cleghorn 212
Cloan 241
Clonyard Farm 204
Corbet Tower 96
Corsock House 205
Cotton of Craig 54
Coul House 161
Covington Mill Farmhouse 212
Cowhill Tower 117
Craichlaw 271
Craig 117
Craig Cottage 161
Craigellie House Gardens 54
Craigentinny Telferton Allotments 145
Craigieburn House 118
Craigowan 242
Crail: Gardens in the Burgh 162
Crinan Hotel Garden 78
Cruachan Lodge 78

D

Dal an Eas 78
Dalbeattie Community 205
Allotments Association
Dalfruin 55
Dalswinton House 118
Dalswinton Mill 119
Damnaglaur House 271
Danevale Park 205
Dawson's Garden 162
Dawyck Botanic Garden 227
Dean Gardens 146
Delvine 243
Diadan 228
Dorward House 55
Dougarie 90
Douneside House 37
Dowhill 243
Dr Neil's Garden 146
Drummond Castle Gardens 243
Drumpark 119
Dundonnell House 191

Dunimarle Castle 163
Dunninald Castle 56
Duns Open Gardens 97
Dunvegan Castle and Gardens 191

E

Earlshall Castle 163
Earth House Apothecary Gardens 219
Eas Mhor 79
Easter Laggan 219
Ecclesgreig Castle 56
Edenhill 164
Edzell Village Gardens 57
Eglinton and Glencairn Gardens 146
Elsewhere Garden 178
Elvanrock 37
Estir Bogside 57

F

Fairnielaw 133
Fernlea Garden 272
Fife Carol Concert 164
Fife Plant Sale at St Andrews 165
Botanic Garden
Fingask Castle 244
Finzean House 37
Floors Castle 97

G

Gallery 58
Gardener's Cottage Walled Garden 264
Gardens House 256
Gardyne Castle 58
Gargunnock House Garden 264
Gartmore Village 265
Geilston Garden 125
Gifford Village with Gifford Bank 134
and Broadwoodside
Glassmount House 165
Glebe House 219
Gledenholm House 120
Glenapp Castle 90
Glenarn 125
Glenarn Plant Sale 125
Glenbervie House 59
Glendoick 244
Glenkindie House 38
Glenkyllachy 192
Glenrinnes Lodge 220
Glensaugh 60
Glenwhan Gardens & Arboretum 273
Gordon Castle Walled Garden 221
Gordonstoun 221
Gorthleck House Garden 192
Grandhome 39
Greenhead Farmhouse 165

Greentree 147
Greywalls 134
Grow Cook Inspire 178
Gullane House 135

H

Harlaw Farmhouse 98
Harthill 166
Hattamoa 107
Haugh Garden 222
Hawk House Gardens 212
Haystoun 228
Heatherwick Farm 39
Helensbank Garden Concert 166
Helensbank House 167
Highland Liliums 193
Highlands Garden 107
Highwood 256
Horatio's Garden 179
Hospitalfield Gardens 60
House of Aigas and Field Centre 193
Humbie Dean 135
Hunter's Tryst 147

I

Ilha de Deus 79
Inchmarlo Retirement Village Garden 40
Inchmill Cottage 61
Inveraray Castle Gardens 80
Inverness Botanic Gardens 194
Inveryne Woodland Garden 80

K

Kailzie Gardens 229
Kames Bay 81
Keldaberg 108
Kevock Garden 147
Kierfiold House 108
Kilbryde Castle 265
Kilchoan Gardens 81
Kildalloig 82
Kiltarlity Gardens 194
Kinblethmont House 61
Kings Grange House 206
King's Park Walled Garden 180
Kinlochlaich Walled Garden 82
Kinnordy Walled Garden 62
Kirkbrae House 167
Kirklands 168
Kirkmuir Cottage 91
Kirkton Manor House 229
Knock Newhouse 83

L

Laidlawstiel House 230
Lanark Town Gardens 213
Langwell 108
Larch House 98
Laundry Cottage 40
Laura's Wood 109
Lawton House 62
Learmonth Place Garden 148
Leathad Ard 195
Lennel Bank 99
Lindisfarne 222
Lindores House 168
Linn Botanic Gardens 126
Little Sparta 213
Lochwinnoch Road Gardens, Kilmacolm 257
Logan Botanic Garden 273
Longwood 136
Luckie Harg's 207

M

Maggie's Edinburgh 148
Maggie's, Glasgow 181
Megginch Castle 245
Mellerstain 99
Mill House 109
Mill of Forneth 245
Milton of Finavon House 63
Mollan 266
Monteviot 100
Moray Place and Bank Gardens 149
Morebattle Mains 100
Mouse Cottage 246
Muckhart Open Gardens 247

N

Naturally Useful, Marcassie Farm 223
Netherbyres 100
Newburgh – Hidden Gardens 169
New Lanark Roof Garden 214
Newliston 149
Nonavaar 110
Norby 110
North Newton Farm 257
Norton House 41

O

Oakmore 266
Oatridge College Campus – SRUC 150
Old Allangrange 196
Old Farm Cottage 215
Old Melrose 101
Oldtown of Leys Garden 196
Orchard Cottage 63
Overdale 247

P

Papple Steading 136
Parkvilla 42
Pitcurran House 248
Pitlochie House 169
Pitmuies Gardens 64
Portmore 230
Preston Hall Walled Garden 150
Princeland House 248

Q

Quercus Garden Plants 231
Quinn Garden 151

R

Raasay Walled Garden 197
Redcroft 151
Regent, Royal & Carlton Terrace Gardens 152
Rivaldsgreen House 152
River Garden, Auchincruive 91
Rosemount 152
Rosewells 170
Ross Priory 127
Round House 110
Ruthven Cottage Hardy Plant Nursery 223
Ruthven House 102

S

Scone Palace Garden 249
Seabank 207
SGS Kilmacolm Plant Sale 258
Shepherd House 137
Shrubhill 266
Silverburn Village 153
Skelbo House 111
South Flisk 170
Southwick House 208
St Bedes and Ashludie Wildflower Garden 64
Stobo Japanese Water Garden 232
Stobshiel House 137
Stobwood Cottage Garden 215
Stockarton 208
Stockbridge Open Gardens 153
Struanbridge 197
Swallows Rest 171
SWG3 Community Garden 181

T

Tal-y-Fan 208
Tarland Community Garden 42
Tarmangie 249
Teasses Gardens 171
Temple Village Gardens 154
The Biblical Garden 223

The Bield at Blackruthven 250
The Bishop's House 258
The Carriage House 92
The Castle and Gardens of Mey 112
The Croft 259
The Doocot 65
The Gardens at Archerfield Walled Garden 138
The Gardens of Monimail Tower 172
The Garden with the Dragon 171
The Hidden Gardens 182
The Japanese Garden at Cowden 267
The Limes 209
The Milton of Campsie Community Garden 183
The Old Farmhouse 250
The Old Manse 274
The Pines 93
The Pond Garden 251
The Potting Shed 232
The Quoy of Houton 112
The Secret Garden 83
The Steading at Clunie 251
The Tower 173
The Walled Garden at the Hugo Burge Foundation 102
Thirlestane 103
Thorntree 267
Threave Garden 209
Tigh-na-Beithe 252
Tinnisburn Plants 121
Tomandroighne 252
Torwood House 253
Two Gardens in Banchory Devenick 43
Tyninghame House and The Walled Garden 139

W

Waulkmill Garden 113
Wester Craigfoodie 174
Westerhall 121
Westgate 65
Westhall Castle 43
Westlea 113
West Leas 103
West Linton Village Gardens 233
Whitburgh House Walled Garden 154
Whitehouse & Grange Bowling Club 155
Willowhill 175
Winton Castle 139
Woodfall Gardens 275
Wormistoune House 175
Wraes 259

Support our charity and make a £5.00 donation today

By donating to Scotland's Gardens Scheme you will make an instant difference as it will help us to continue and improve our volunteer support and develop our garden opening programme for all to enjoy.

Please donate on our website:
scotlandsgardens.org/donate/

or scan the QR code: